W9-BRM-773

Advanced Assembly Language

ALLEN L. WYATT, SR.

PROGRAMMING
SERIES

que

Advanced Assembly Language

©1992 by Que® Corporation

Library of Congress Catalog No.: 92-61692

ISBN: 1-56529-037-2

95 94 93 92   8 7 6 5 4 3 2 1

Interpretation of the printing code: the rightmost double-digit number is the year of the book's printing; the rightmost single-digit number, the number of the book's printing. For example, a printing code of 92-1 shows that the first printing of the book occurred in 1992.

Trademarks

To my kids, Lee, Eric, and Andrew, who sometimes forget what it is like to have a present-tense father.

CREDITS

Publisher
Lloyd J. Short

Associate Publisher
Rick Ranucci

Publishing Manager
Joseph Wikert

Acquisitions Editor
Sarah Browning

Editors
Jodi Jensen
Rebecca Whitney
Bryan Gambrel

Technical Editor
Greg Guntle

Editorial Assistant
Elizabeth D. Brown

Director of Production and Manufacturing
Jeff Valler

Production Manager
Corinne Walls

Proofreading/Indexing Coordinator
Joelynn Gifford

Production Analyst
Mary Beth Wakefield

Book Designer
Scott Cook

Cover Designer
Tim Amrhein

Graphic Image Specialists
Dennis Sheehan
Jerry Ellis
Susan VandeWalle

Indexer
Tina Trettin

Production
Claudia Bell, Julie Brown, Jodie Cantwell,
Paula Carroll, Bob LaRoche, Laurie Lee,
Caroline Roop, Linda Seifert, Sandra Shay,
Lisa Wilson, Phil Worthington

Composed in Cheltenham and MCPdigital by Prentice Hall Computer Publishing

Allen L. Wyatt, Sr.

Allen Wyatt has been working with small computers for more than a dozen years, and has worked in virtually all facets of programming and computer publishing. He has written more than 15 books related to computing, programming, and programming languages. He is the president of Discovery Computing, Inc., a microcomputer consulting and services corporation. Allen likes to spend his spare time doing "family stuff" with his wife, Debra, and his three children.

OVERVIEW

TABLE OF CONTENTS

Introduction

Here we are at the beginning. "The beginning of what?" you may ask. If you take a few moments to scan this introduction, you should get a good idea of what is in store for you in this book.

I wrote this book because I find that I learn faster and progress further when I have examples I can digest and understand. Not many books take this approach, particularly in the assembly language area. Most books attempt to teach you the fundamentals, and then leave you high and dry to apply those fundamentals in whatever way you can. I believe that the fundamentals are only a small portion of what programmers need. Learning the fundamentals is relatively easy compared to the gigantic task of applying them to real-world problems.

So, welcome to the real world. It sounds strange to say, but many authors don't always seem to live there. Many times, I doubt whether *I* do! (See the section at the end of this introduction about talking back to me.) What does assembly language programming have to do with the real world? It seems to be a reasonable question, especially if you have a high-level language background. The fact of the matter, though, is that you can't beat assembly language for speed, compactness, and the ability to get to down-and-dirty details.

Who Needs This Book?

This book was written for those who recognize that assembly language still has an active, vital, vibrant role in developing programs for the PC. In this book, you will find many programs and ideas you can use as the basis for your own applications. Or, you can gut the programs here and use them as sub-routines in your high-level language programs. (If you have any doubt about how to interface to high-level languages, refer to my other book, *Using Assembly Language*, 3rd Edition, published by Que Corporation. Its detailed instructions and examples explain interfacing.)

This book assumes that you understand how to program in assembly language. It provides some practical, hands-on applications you can sink your teeth into. I hope that these programs either solve a problem you have faced or provide ideas to enhance your existing programs. I believe that everyone has had that need from time to time.

How Was This Book Developed?

This book was written based on personal experience and many, many months of research. The programming examples assume that you are programming with Microsoft Macro Assembler (MASM) and take advantage of language advances introduced in version 6.0.

I have been questioned about why I don't use examples expressly for Borland's Turbo Assembler (TASM), and you deserve an answer. The answer is multi-faceted:

- The majority of the assembler market is owned by MASM.

- Virtually every assembly language programmer knows MASM.

- The typical reader of this book can make a switch between MASM code and TASM code with a minimum of trouble.

- Borland has abandoned the stand-alone assembly language market.

This last statement may seem rather strong, but that is not my intention. Borland simply no longer markets a stand-alone assembler; if you want TASM, you must purchase it as part of the professional development packages sold with Borland's high-level languages. The people in the product development department at Borland indicate that the reason for this situation is that they believe most TASM users only use TASM to augment their high-level language development. Borland apparently does not believe that people program with TASM as their primary language. This belief very well may be true, but I would bet that a relatively large number of folks use assembly language because they know and love it, in addition to the other advantages it offers.

The programs in this book are designed to work with DOS 5 and with the latest versions of specifications such as EMS, XMS, VCPI, and DPMI. Differences between versions are pointed out where relevant.

Finally, every program in this book was tested and run by Greg Guntle, a very competent technical editor. Points and nuances that escaped me in developing the original text were caught and pointed out (nicely) by him. I'm sure that each reader will appreciate the pretested nature of these programs.

As you read through this book, you probably will notice that I refuse to get caught up in such topics as clock cycles, op code optimization, and so on. Although these subjects have their place (and they invariably are connected with assembly language programming), I doubt whether they impinge much on "the real world" of day-to-day programming concerns.

How Should You Use This Book?

You definitely should jump right into the subjects presented in this book. I believe that the best way to learn is by observing what others do, applying it to your situation, and adapting proven methods to your needs. With that in mind, the programs in this book were developed to be accessible. I attempted to document them well and not use some of the more esoteric assembly language instructions.

Organizing this book was a particularly difficult task, due in large part to the interrelated nature of PC programming topics. The approach almost has to be circular; you learn about topic A so that you can learn about topic B, which in turn teaches you more about topic A. That's the way it is with this book. The topics in some chapters rely on information presented in other chapters. I tried, as much as possible, to write each chapter so that it can be considered a stand-alone unit, but a few notable exceptions exist.

So, what is in this book? The remainder of this section gives you a brief rundown.

Chapter 1, "Interrupt Handlers," is the foundation for virtually everything that happens in the PC.

Chapter 2, "Controlling the Keyboard," teaches you more than you probably thought you needed to know about this most common input device. The chapter relies heavily on the information in Chapter 1.

Chapter 3, "Serial Communications," also relies on the concepts in Chapter 1. In this chapter, you eventually learn how to craft an interrupt-driven serial communications program.

Chapter 4, "Critical Error Handlers," are a specialized form of interrupt handlers. As such, they rely on the information in Chapter 1.

Chapter 5, "TSR Programming," delves into this complex topic with gusto. You learn how to program both passive and active TSRs.

Chapter 6, "Expanded and Extended Memory," makes you switch gears a little from the general thread that runs through the first five chapters. In this chapter, you learn all about memory and why memory management on the PC has become such a confusing issue. The chapter discusses conventional, expanded, and extended memory, as well as the XMS, XMA, VCPI, and DPMI specifications.

Chapter 7, "Working with Disk Files and Directories," leads you through a discussion of how DOS views these most basic elements. Several useful utilities are presented in the chapter to help you understand what can and cannot be done with files and directories.

Chapter 8, "Using IOCTL," describes the basics of a special classification of DOS functions. You learn about character and block devices and how they are viewed and controlled by DOS.

Chapter 9, "Device Drivers," takes the information in Chapter 8 one step further. You write your own device drivers, which are added as system resources when DOS loads. Some of the topics from Chapter 6 are helpful here.

Chapter 10, "Programming for the Mouse," describes how to control the mouse within your programs. A series of examples leads you through how to work with various mouse cursors. One program even enables you to pick information from the screen with the mouse.

Chapter 11, "Using the EXEC Function," discusses how your programs can spawn little children of their own. You learn how to start the child process and how to return successfully.

Chapter 12, "Protected Mode Programming," introduces the basics of this brave new world. You learn about the promise held by protected mode, as well as how far you must go to get there. Understanding the information presented in Chapter 6 is necessary to understand the concepts in Chapter 12.

Finally, several appendixes present reference information that you may find helpful.

What Is on the Companion Disk?

The disk that accompanies this book includes every listing in the book. These listings are provided in source code, OBJ, LST, and executable formats. More than 11,300 lines of source code in 43 programs comprise at least 420K of disk space. It sure beats having to type it all in. (I should know—I typed them originally.)

Talk Back to the Author

I don't have all the answers to the programming questions you face. I know that I don't have all the answers to the ones *I* face. And, I've been around the block too many times to believe in my own infallibility or to think that I have all the knowledge I'll ever need. However, just as I would bet that you can learn a thing or two from me, I also know that I can learn from you.

So, how about it? Drop me a line or send me a message. Throw a rock, if you want. I particularly wouldn't mind knowing the following:

- What do you like most about this book? The least?

- Did the programs help you?

- Do you think that I'm living in the real world?

- What computer-related problems do you face that aren't addressed by books currently on the market?

You can contact me directly at the following addresses:

Allen L. Wyatt
Discovery Computing, Inc.
P.O. Box 88
Riverton, UT 84065

CompuServe: 72561,2207

I hope you enjoy . . ..

Interrupt Handlers

What are interrupts, and why should you be concerned about them? Honestly, they are at the heart of everything that happens within your computer, and it is virtually impossible to do any assembly language programming in a DOS environment without them.

Depending on what you are reading, you may see interrupts referred to as *exceptions* or as *faults*. Although the terminology is the same, all three—interrupts, exceptions, and faults—result in the occurrence of the same actions.

Let's start with what interrupts are and how they work. Conceptually, an interrupt is just that—an interruption of the work being done by the CPU. It means simply that the CPU is diverted for a moment to do some work, and then it is returned to exactly where it was before the interruption. The program that was interrupted continues as though there never had been an interruption. This concept is illustrated in Figure 1.1.

The details of what happens during an interrupt are discussed later in this chapter, in the section "What Happens During an Interrupt?" The programming code executed during the interrupt condition is called an *interrupt handler*, or an *interrupt service routine* (ISR). It is generally short and concise and performs a well-defined task. This is because the original program (the one that was interrupted) might be time-sensitive in nature, and a long interrupt therefore might disrupt the overall performance of the program.

But, what happens if an interrupt occurs while an interrupt handler is running? It doesn't matter to the CPU what type of program it was running when the interrupt occurred; the CPU processes the interrupt. Therefore, interrupt handlers can be interrupted, which in turn can be interrupted, and so on. The architecture of the CPU and the system help to keep everything straight.

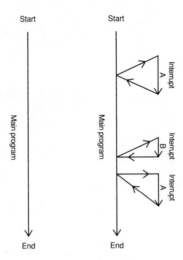

Sources of Interrupts

The CPU can detect an interrupt in several ways. First, a device can send an electrical signal on the NMI (non-maskable interrupt) pin of the CPU. The CPU cannot ignore this interrupt signal; it is used to signal the occurrence of a catastrophic event. In human terms, it is analogous to slapping a person to get his attention.

The next way to signal an interrupt to the CPU is to send an electrical signal on the INTR pin of the CPU. Sending this signal is handled by a *programmable interrupt controller* (PIC), a chip that handles external, non-catastrophic (maskable) interrupt requests for the CPU. This chip is typically an Intel 8259A or equivalent chip.

Interrupts that are signaled in either of these first two ways are referred to as *hardware*, or *external*, interrupts.

The third method of signaling an interrupt is internally to the CPU, and generally is known as a *software*, or *internal*, interrupt. This type of interrupt generally occurs when the CPU executes an INT instruction, but it can occur when the INTO, DIV, or IDIV instructions are executed, or when the single-step (trap) flag is set. Every time you use a BIOS or DOS system service, you are initiating a software interrupt. For instance, the following program fragment uses a software interrupt:

```
MOV   AH,51h
INT   21h
MOV   PSP_Seg,BX
```

With all these sources for interrupts, how does the CPU prioritize the interrupts it might receive? Table 1.1 indicates the priority level assigned to interrupts by the CPU.

Table 1.1. CPU priority level by interrupt source (1 is the highest priority; 4 is the lowest).

Interrupt Source	Type	Priority
Divide by 0	Internal	1
INT	Internal	1
INTO	Internal	1
NMI line	External	2
INTR line	External	3
Single-step	Internal	4

Hardware, or External, Interrupts

Interrupts that are signaled through use of the NMI or INTR pins of the CPU are hardware, or external, interrupts. As an example, a hardware interrupt occurs every time you press a key on your keyboard—the interrupt is generated by the hardware of your keyboard, through the interrupt controller.

As already mentioned, interrupts signaled through the NMI pin cannot be disabled. They generally indicate the occurrence or imminent occurrence of a catastrophic event. These events can include memory parity errors or some other system failure. These interrupts receive higher priority than those signaled through the INTR pin.

Interrupts signaled through the INTR pin are governed by the PIC. The PIC works in closely with the CPU to control the INTR line. The job of the PIC is to receive interrupt requests from external devices (such as the keyboard, printer, or communications port), determine which interrupt has the highest priority, and then signal the CPU to pay attention. The CPU then responds, based on the setting of the interrupt-enable flag (IF). The relation of this flag to what actions the CPU takes is discussed later in this chapter, in the section "What Happens During an Interrupt?"

When the CPU has responded to the PIC that it is ready to acknowledge the interrupt, the PIC sends a 1-byte code indicating the interrupt number the PIC has assigned to the interrupt. The interrupt handler branched to by the CPU is controlled by the code relayed by the PIC.

Software, or Internal, Interrupts

There are several sources of internal interrupts. The most common source is through use of the INT instruction, as mentioned earlier. But there are other ways as well.

For instance, if you are using the DIV or IDIV instructions to perform a division and the divisor is 0, then an internal interrupt, level 0, is generated. Likewise, if an operation results in the overflow flag (OF) being set, then a level 4 interrupt is generated when an INTO instruction is encountered. These conditions are the same as using the INT 0 or INT 4 commands.

You can also cause the CPU to generate a level 1 interrupt if the trap flag (TF) is set. Generating an interrupt in this manner is often used in debugging, and is referred to as the *single-step interrupt*. When the flag is set, this internal interrupt is generated after the execution of every instruction.

What Happens During an Interrupt?

How does your CPU and supporting circuitry handle interrupts? After the CPU knows the interrupt code, or level, for the interrupt, it behaves exactly the same regardless of the interrupt source. If the interrupt is internal, this level either is specified by the INT instruction or is assumed by the CPU, based on predefined interrupt levels. If the interrupt is external, the level is supplied by the PIC.

The CPU will respond to an interrupt only between executing program instructions. Although this may seem straightforward, it is not strictly adhered to when the CPU is executing repetitive string instructions. In these instances, the interrupt is serviced between repetitions. Interrupts therefore are handled in the most expeditious manner possible.

The first task the CPU performs is to push the value of the flags register on the stack. Then the CPU clears the interrupt and trap flags. The value of the CS register then is pushed, followed by the IP register.

Next, the interrupt level is multiplied by 4 to determine a value that is used as an offset to segment 0000, where the *vector* of the desired interrupt is located. In this context, a vector is nothing more than an address—it is a pointer to where the interrupt handler resides in memory. First, IP (the offset address) is loaded, and then CS (the segment address). Then, with CS:IP containing the address of the interrupt handler, the CPU begins execution of that handler.

When the interrupt handler has completed processing, it sends a signal to the interrupt controller (if it was a hardware interrupt), and the IRET instruction is executed. This action restores the contents of CS:IP, as well as the flags register. From this point on, the CPU continues as though the interrupt never occurred.

Figure 1.2 is a detailed flowchart that shows what happens during an interrupt.

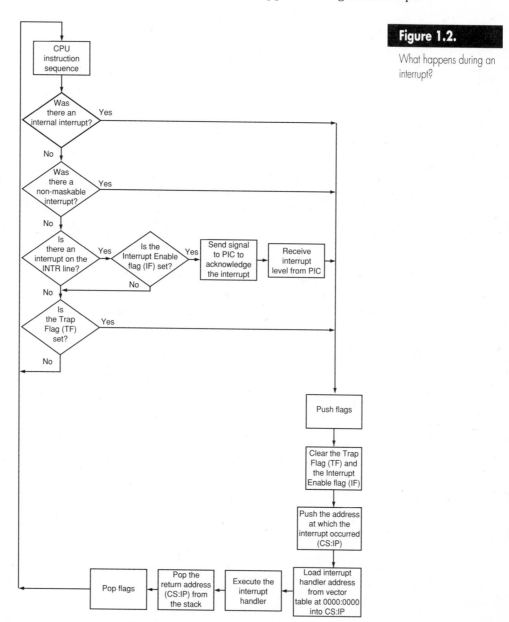

Figure 1.2.

What happens during an interrupt?

When you look at Figure 1.2, remember that interrupts can occur after the execution of any CPU instruction—including those being executed within an interrupt handler. If you want to limit the interrupts that can occur, you should use the CLI instruction disable maskable interrupts.

System Interrupts

As you have learned already, the PC can have as many as 256 interrupt vectors (0 through 255) stored in the first page of memory. A portion of these are reserved for use by the Intel CPU. When Intel first introduced the 8086, it reserved the first 32 vectors (0 through 31) for internal use. Some were used, and others were reserved for future use. In Table 1.2, interrupts without an X in the CPU column are reserved on that CPU; interrupts 0Fh and 12h through 1Fh are reserved for future use.

Table 1.2. Internal interrupts as defined by Intel.

Int	Vector Table Offset	Name	Processors Using the Interrupts			
			86/88	286	386	486
00h	00h	Divide by zero	X	X	X	X
01h	04h	Single step	X	X	X	X
02h	08h	Non-maskable	X	X	X	X
03h	0Ch	Breakpoint	X	X	X	X
04h	10h	Overflow	X	X	X	X
05h	14h	BOUND exceeded		X	X	X
06h	18h	Invalid opcode		X	X	X
07h	1Ch	NPX unavailable		X	X	X
08h	20h	Interrupt table limit too small		X	X	
08h	20h	Double fault				X
09h	24h	CPU extension segment overrun		X		
0Ah	28h	Invalid task-state segment				X
0Bh	2Ch	Segment not present				X
0Ch	30h	Stack exception				X

Int	Vector Table Offset	Name	Processors Using the Interrupts 86/88	286	386	486
0Dh	34h	Segment overrun		X	X	
0Dh	34h	General protection fault			X	
0Eh	38h	Page fault				X
10h	40h	NPX error		X	X	X
11h	44h	Alignment check				X

Notice in Table 1.2 that several interrupts are defined for different purposes on different CPUs. Note also that these interrupts have meaning only when they are working in real mode. In any other operating mode, the location and composition of the interrupt table vary.

What about on the IBM PC family of computers? The interrupts used differ slightly. When the PC first was introduced, IBM did not pay attention to Intel's reserving interrupts 0 through 1Fh and redefined some interrupt numbers in the first part of the vector table. Table 1.3 indicates the interrupt vector meanings on the PC family of computers.

Table 1.3. The standard interrupt list for the PC.

Int	Vector Table Offset	Applicable —Systems— PC	AT	PS/2	Used by	Name
00h	00h	X	X	X	System	Divide by zero
01h	04h	X	X	X	System	Single step
02h	08h	X	X	X	System	Non-maskable
03h	0Ch	X	X	X	System	Breakpoint
04h	10h	X	X	X	System	Overflow
05h	14h	X	X	X	BIOS	Print screen
			X	X	System	BOUND exceeded
06h	18h		X	X	System	Invalid opcode
07h	1Ch		X	X	System	NPX unavailable
08h	20h	X	X	X	Hardware	Timer tick (IRQ0)
			X	X	System	Double fault

continues

Table 1.3. Continued

Int	Vector Table Offset	Applicable —Systems— PC	AT	PS/2	Used by	Name
09h	24h	X	X	X	Hardware	Keyboard (IRQ1)
			X	X	System	CPU extension segment overrun
0Ah	28h		X	X	Hardware	IRQ2
0Bh	2Ch	X	X	X	Hardware	COM2 (IRQ3)
0Ch	30h	X	X	X	Hardware	COM1 (IRQ4)
0Dh	34h	X			Hardware	Fixed disk (IRQ5)
			X	X	Hardware	LPT2 (IRQ5)
			X	X	System	Segment overrun
0Eh	38h	X	X	X	Hardware	Diskette (IRQ6)
0Fh	3Ch	X	X	X	Hardware	LPT1 (IRQ7)
10h	40h	X	X	X	BIOS	Video
			X	X	Hardware	NPX error
11h	44h	X	X	X	BIOS	Equipment check
12h	48h	X	X	X	BIOS	Memory size
13h	4Ch	X	X	X	BIOS	Disk I/O
14h	50h	X	X	X	BIOS	Communications
15h	54h	X			BIOS	Cassette services
			X	X	BIOS	Extended services
16h	58h	X	X	X	BIOS	Keyboard I/O
17h	5Ch	X	X	X	BIOS	Printer I/O
18h	60h	X			BIOS	ROM BASIC
			X	X	BIOS	Boot failure
19h	64h	X	X	X	BIOS	Boot routines
1Ah	68h		X	X	BIOS	Time of day
1Bh	6Ch	X	X	X	BIOS	Ctrl-C/Ctrl-Break
1Ch	70h	X	X	X	BIOS	Timer tick
1Dh	74h	X	X	X	BIOS	Video parameters vector

Int	Vector Table Offset	Applicable —Systems—			Used by	Name
		PC	AT	PS/2		
1Eh	78h	X	X	X	BIOS	Diskette parameters vector
1Fh	7Ch	X	X	X	BIOS	Video graphics fonts vector
20h	80h				DOS	Program termination
21h	84h				DOS	General DOS services
22h	88h				DOS	Terminate address
23h	8Ch				DOS	Ctrl-C vector
24h	90h				DOS	Critical error vector
25h	94h				DOS	Absolute disk read
26h	98h				DOS	Absolute disk write
27h	9Ch				DOS	TSR
28h	A0h				DOS	Idle routines
29h	A4h				DOS	Fast console routines
2Ah	A8h				DOS	Network redirector
2Eh	B8h				DOS	COMMAND.COM reload transient
2Fh	BCh				DOS	Multiplex
30h	C0h				DOS	Entry point storage
31h	C4h				DOS	Entry point storage
40h	100h	X	X	X	BIOS	Diskette driver
41h	104h	X	X	X	BIOS	Fixed disk parameters (drive 0)
42h	108h	X	X	X	BIOS	Video driver
43h	10Ch	X	X	X	BIOS	EGA/MCGA/VGA character table
46h	118h		X	X	BIOS	Fixed disk parameters (drive 1)
4Ah	128h		X	X	BIOS	Alarm handler
50h	140h		X	X	BIOS	Alarm

continues

ADVANCED ASSEMBLY LANGUAGE

Table 1.3. Continued

Int	Vector Table Offset	Applicable —Systems— PC	AT	PS/2	Used by	Name
5Ah	168h	X	X		BIOS	Cluster adapter
5Bh	16Ch	X	X		BIOS	Cluster adapter
5Ch	170h		X	X	BIOS	Networking
67h	19Ch	X	X	X	System	LIM/EMS functions
70h	1C0h		X	X	BIOS	Real-time clock (IRQ8)
71h	1C4h		X	X	BIOS	IRQ2 redirect (IRQ9)
72h	1C8h		X	X	BIOS	IRQ10
73h	1CCh		X	X	BIOS	IRQ11
74h	1D0h		X		BIOS	IRQ12
				X	BIOS	Mouse (IRQ12)
75h	1D4h		X	X	BIOS	Coprocessor (IRQ13)
76h	1D8h		X	X	BIOS	Fixed disk (IRQ14)
77h	1DCh		X	X	BIOS	IRQ15

Notice that only a portion of the 256 possible interrupt vectors are defined for specific purposes. The rest are unassigned, and you can use them within your own programs. For instance, you can use them in a TSR program so that they always are available, or you can set up interrupts in one program and use them to define routines used by other, related programs. You should be aware, however, that the interrupts in use vary from system to system. Your hardware, firmware, or software might use interrupt vectors not listed in Table 1.3. If a vector is unassigned, it will contain zeros.

How do you see what interrupts are defined on your system, and what the actual interrupt vectors are? The program in Listing 1.1, VECTORS.ASM, lists the vectors from the interrupt table in your system.

Listing 1.1. VECTORS.ASM

```
Page 60,132

Comment ¦
******************************************************************

File:      VECTORS.ASM
Author:    Allen L. Wyatt
Date:      3/25/92
Assembler: MASM 6.0

Purpose:   Display the contents of the interrupt vectors.

Format:    VECTORS


******************************************************************¦
          .MODEL   small
          .STACK                       ;Default 1 KB stack is OK
          .DATA
Row       DB       02
Column    DB       00
IntCount  DB       00

Output    DB       'Int '
IntNum    DW       0000
          DB       'h $'
Address   EQU      THIS BYTE
SegNum    DW       0000,0000
          DB       ':'
OffNum    DW       0000,0000
          DB       '$'
Unused    DB       '[unused]$'

TopLine   DB       '                        System Interrupt Vectors$'
Pause     DB       'Press any key to continue...$'

          .CODE
          .STARTUP
Vectors   PROC
```

continues

Listing 1.1. Continued

```
              CALL    NewScreen           ;Go do a new screen setup
              MOV     BX,0                ;Point to vector table
              MOV     ES,BX
              MOV     IntCount,0
              MOV     CX,255              ;Want to go all the way round

Vloop:        MOV     AL,IntCount
              CALL    ConHex
              MOV     IntNum,AX
              MOV     AX,ES:[BX]
              CALL    ConHexLong
              MOV     OffNum[0],AX
              MOV     OffNum[2],DX
              INC     BX
              INC     BX
              MOV     AX,ES:[BX]
              CALL    ConHexLong
              MOV     SegNum[0],AX
              MOV     SegNum[2],DX
              INC     BX
              INC     BX
              CALL    ShowVector          ;Go show the vector
              INC     IntCount            ;Next interrupt
              JNE     Vloop               ;Keep going until IntCount = 0
again
              CALL    PagePause           ;Go wait for a keypress
              CALL    Cls                 ;Clear the screen

              .EXIT
Vectors       ENDP


; The following routine displays the individual vectors on the screen

ShowVector    PROC    USES AX BX DX
              MOV     DH,Row
              MOV     DL,Column
              MOV     BH,0                ;Assume page 0
              MOV     AH,2                ;Set cursor position
              INT     10h
```

```
              MOV     DX,OFFSET Output     ;Point to start of screen display
              MOV     AH,9                 ;Display a string using DOS
              INT     21h
              MOV     DX,OFFSET Address    ;Point to output string
              CMP     SegNum[0],3030h      ;Is this set to zeros?
              JNE     SV1
              CMP     SegNum[2],3030h      ;Is this set to zeros?
              JNE     SV1
              CMP     OffNum[0],3030h      ;Is this set to zeros?
              JNE     SV1
              CMP     OffNum[2],3030h      ;Is this set to zeros?
              JNE     SV1
              MOV     DX,OFFSET Unused     ;Unused vector

SV1:          MOV     AH,9                 ;Display a string using DOS
              INT     21h

              INC     Row                  ;Point to next row
              CMP     Row,21               ;At bottom of column?
              JLE     SVok                 ;No, continue
              MOV     Row,2                ;Yes, set to top of column
              ADD     Column,20            ;Move to next column
              CMP     Column,80            ;Is the screen full?
              JL      SVok                 ;No, continue
              MOV     Column,0             ;Set to leftmost column
              CALL    PagePause            ;Go wait for a keypress
              CALL    NewScreen            ;Go do a new screen setup

SVok:         RET
ShowVector    ENDP


; The following routine sets up the standard screen info

NewScreen     PROC    USES AX BX DX
              Call    Cls                  ;Clear the screen
              MOV     DX,0                 ;Set up to print page title
              MOV     BH,0                 ;Assume page 0
              MOV     AH,2                 ;Set cursor position
              INT     10h
              MOV     DX,OFFSET TopLine    ;Point to start of header
              MOV     AH,9                 ;Display a string using DOS
              INT     21h
```

continues

Listing 1.1. Continued

```
                RET
NewScreen       ENDP


; The following routine clears the screen

Cls             PROC    USES AX BX CX DX
                MOV     AH,6                    ;Scroll window up
                MOV     AL,0                    ;Scroll full screen
                MOV     BH,7                    ;Normal white on black
                MOV     CX,0                    ;Upper left corner of screen
                MOV     DH,24                   ;Bottom right
                MOV     DL,79
                INT     10h
                RET
Cls             ENDP


; The following routine pauses at the bottom of a page

PagePause       PROC    USES AX BX DX
                MOV     DH,23                   ;Set up to print pause message
                MOV     DL,0
                MOV     BH,0                    ;Assume page 0
                MOV     AH,2                    ;Set cursor position
                INT     10h
                MOV     DX,OFFSET Pause         ;Point to start of pause message
                MOV     AH,9                    ;Display a string using DOS
                INT     21h
                MOV     AH,0                    ;Read keyboard character
                INT     16h
                RET
PagePause       ENDP


; The following routine converts the number in AL into an ASCII
; representation of the hex value, with a leading zero. Value
; is returned in AX as well.

ConHex          PROC    USES CX
                MOV     CL,10h                  ;What you will be dividing by
                MOV     AH,0
                DIV     CL                      ;Divide by 16
```

```
              ADD      AL,30h
              ADD      AH,30h
              CMP      AL,'9'           ;Is it greater than 9?
              JBE      CA4              ;No, so continue
              ADD      AL,7             ;Make into hex digit
CA4:          CMP      AH,'9'           ;Is it greater than 9?
              JBE      CA5              ;No, so continue
              ADD      AH,7             ;Make into hex digit
CA5:          RET
ConHex        ENDP

; The following uses ConHex to convert a long number (AX) into its ASCII
; equivalent in DX:AX.

ConHexLong    PROC
              PUSH     AX
              CALL     ConHex
              MOV      DX,AX
              POP      AX
              MOV      AL,AH
              CALL     ConHex
              RET
ConHexLong    ENDP

              END
```

The program simply grabs each vector from the table in the first page of memory, converts it to hexadecimal, and displays it on the screen. If the vector contents are equal to 0, then the interrupt is not used and the program indicates that fact in the display. When you assemble this program and execute it, you see a display similar to Figure 1.3.

Again, the addresses shown on your system will differ from those shown here.

Changing Interrupt Vectors

There are two ways you can change interrupt vectors. Both ways work fine, but one is easier to use than the other. Let's look at the direct route first, which happens to be the more difficult of the two methods.

```
                        System Interrupt Vectors

Int 00h 011C:108A    Int 14h 0E85:04D6    Int 28h 0E85:0583    Int 3Ch 011C:10DA
Int 01h 0070:06F4    Int 15h 0E85:04E8    Int 29h CC01:0503    Int 3Dh 011C:10DA
Int 02h F000:E2C3    Int 16h 0E85:0502    Int 2Ah 011C:10DA    Int 3Eh 011C:10DA
Int 03h 0070:06F4    Int 17h 1955:2351    Int 2Bh 011C:10DA    Int 3Fh 011C:10DA
Int 04h 0070:06F4    Int 18h F000:983A    Int 2Ch 011C:10DA    Int 40h F000:EC59
Int 05h 0E85:0334    Int 19h 09A1:002F    Int 2Dh 011C:10DA    Int 41h C800:3E50
Int 06h F000:CC0A    Int 1Ah F000:FE6E    Int 2Eh 09A6:0140    Int 42h F000:F065
Int 07h F000:CC0A    Int 1Bh CC01:019F    Int 2Fh 0B12:3081    Int 43h C000:610C
Int 08h 0E85:0346    Int 1Ch F000:FF53    Int 30h 1C10:D0EA    Int 44h F000:CC0A
Int 09h 1955:56BB    Int 1Dh F000:F0A4    Int 31h F000:CC01    Int 45h F000:CC0A
Int 0Ah F000:CC0A    Int 1Eh 0000:0522    Int 32h 011C:10DA    Int 46h F000:E401
Int 0Bh F000:CC0A    Int 1Fh C000:650C    Int 33h 0E85:05C2    Int 47h F000:CC0A
Int 0Ch 031F:02B8    Int 20h 1955:261D    Int 34h 011C:10DA    Int 48h F000:CC0A
Int 0Dh F000:CC0A    Int 21h 1955:24F4    Int 35h 011C:10DA    Int 49h F000:CC0A
Int 0Eh F000:EF57    Int 22h 09A6:01DC    Int 36h 011C:10DA    Int 4Ah F000:CC0A
Int 0Fh 0E85:03DC    Int 23h 09A6:014B    Int 37h 011C:10DA    Int 4Bh 025D:04D5
Int 10h 17CD:0049    Int 24h 09A6:0156    Int 38h 011C:10DA    Int 4Ch F000:CC0A
Int 11h F000:F84D    Int 25h 011C:10A8    Int 39h 011C:10DA    Int 4Dh F000:CC0A
Int 12h F000:F841    Int 26h 011C:10B2    Int 3Ah 011C:10DA    Int 4Eh F000:CC0A
Int 13h 0E85:04C0    Int 27h 011C:10BC    Int 3Bh 011C:10DA    Int 4Fh F000:CC0A

Press any key to continue...
```

Changing the Vector Table Directly

It would seem to be a simple enough task to change the values in the interrupt
table directly. This process presents potential problems, however. Suppose
that you are changing the keyboard interrupt vector, Int 09h at 0000:0024. You
change the first part of the vector, and change only the segment address, and
an Int 09h is generated because someone has pressed a key. Suddenly the
computer branches to the wrong area of memory—an area pointed to by the
new segment address and the old offset address.

This scenario may seem like a trivial example—after all, what are the chances
of someone pressing a key at exactly the same moment an interrupt vector is
being changed? The problem becomes more pronounced, however, if you are
changing other vectors. For instance, it is impossible to successfully change
the clock tick interrupt, Int 08h, because it is called 18.2 times a second.

To overcome this situation, you must always disable interrupts before changing a vector, and enable them afterward. You could use the following code,
therefore, for safely changing the keyboard interrupt vector:

```
; This code is used to change the keyboard interrupt vector directly
        PUSH    ES
        PUSH    DS
        MOV     AX,CS              ;Point to current code segment
        MOV     DS,AX
```

```
MOV     AX,0                    ;Point to the vector table
MOV     ES,AX
MOV     BX,24h                  ;Point to the keyboard interrupt
MOV     AX,OFFSET NewInt        ;Get offset of new routine
CLI                             ;Disable interrupts
MOV     ES:[BX],AX              ;Put offset in place
MOV     AX,SEG NewInt           ;Get segment of new interrupt
INC     BX
INC     BX
MOV     ES:[BX],AX              ;Put segment in place
STI                             ;Enable interrupts again
POP     DS
POP     ES
```

This code easily can be changed into a subroutine to enable the changing of any interrupt vector. Why go through all this hassle, however, when there is an easier method available?

Using the DOS Functions for Interrupt Vectors

Because of the problems typically associated with changing interrupt vectors directly, DOS provides two functions that take care of all the "gotchas" automatically. These routines simply do what was done in the last section, where you changed the vector table directly. The DOS routines make sure that both the segment and offset addresses in the vector table are changed without interruption.

The first DOS function enables you to set an interrupt vector. As an example, consider the following programming code, which accomplishes the same task as the code in the preceding section:

```
PUSH    DS                      ;Store data segment
MOV     AX,CS                   ;New segment address
MOV     DS,AX
MOV     DX,OFFSET NewInt        ;New offset address
MOV     AL,9h                   ;Change keyboard vector
MOV     AH,25h                  ;to point to new handler
INT     21h
POP     DS                      ;Restore data segment
```

DOS function 25h uses the contents of AL to indicate which interrupt should be changed, and then the vector is changed to DS:DX. You don't have to worry about calculating offsets into the vector table or about disabling and enabling interrupts—DOS does this for you.

Another DOS function related to interrupts is also very important. Int 21h, function 35h enables you to determine what an interrupt vector is currently set to. You can use this function, therefore, to determine an interrupt vector and save it before you change it. Then, when your program is done, you can restore the interrupt vector to its original condition.

Consider the following program code:

```
MOV     AL,09h              ;Get keyboard interrupt
MOV     AH,35h
INT     21h
MOV     KeyInt[0],BX        ;Offset address
MOV     KeyInt[2],ES        ;Segment address

PUSH    DS                  ;Store data segment
MOV     AX,CS               ;New segment address
MOV     DS,AX
MOV     DX,OFFSET NewInt    ;New offset address
MOV     AL,9h               ;Change keyboard vector
MOV     AH,25h              ;to point to new handler
INT     21h
POP     DS                  ;Restore data segment
```

This code expands the previously presented code to first save the current vector for the keyboard interrupt. Int 21h, function 35h expects AL to contain the interrupt number for which you want a vector. On return, ES:BX contains the requested address.

Both of these functions, because of their ease of use, are used extensively in programs later in this book.

Summary

Interrupts are an integral part of programming for the PC environment. Understanding them is fundamental to doing any meaningful programming. This chapter has presented the basics of interrupts—what they are, how they work, and how you can modify them.

In the following chapters, this information is put to use. Various programs intercept and use the standard DOS interrupt handlers to add functions and expand capabilities.

Controlling the Keyboard

M ost computer programs, at one time or another, involve the use of the keyboard, the primary method of user interaction. There obviously are other methods of input, including mice, light pens, pucks, digitizing tablets, and communications ports. Still, the majority of interaction happens through the keyboard.

How is the keyboard connected to the computer? Depending on whom you ask, you may get wildly different responses. If you ask an engineer, he may tell you about the bus structure and chips and how the keyboard relates to them. A programmer, on the other hand, generally is interested in only what information is transmitted from the keyboard to a program and how it can be retrieved and used. This is not to say that an understanding of the hardware interface for the keyboard is unnecessary. To the contrary, such an understanding greatly enhances a programmer's appreciation of how the components of a computer system work with each other.

With this in mind, let's look quickly at the hardware behind the keyboard. The following section shows exactly what happens when you press a key and how BIOS functions retrieve information from this essential part of the system. This chapter does not dwell on any DOS keyboard functions because the keyboard, as viewed by DOS, is rather limited. This statement may sound funny, but DOS basically relies on the BIOS to handle all the nitty-gritty details of working with the keyboard and retrieving characters from the keyboard buffer.

The Keyboard: A Hardware View

At the physical level, the keyboard is nothing but a series of on-off switches. The number of physical switches depends on the type of keyboard in use and is irrelevant to how the keyboard functions. Suffice it to say that when you press a key on the keyboard, a circuit is closed that sends a signal, known as a *make signal*, to the keyboard's controlling firmware. When you release the key (which opens the circuit), another signal, called a *break signal*, is generated.

Both make and break signals can be represented in a single byte called a *key code*. The only difference between them is the setting of the high-order bit. Therefore, a make signal may be 05h and the corresponding break signal is 85h. Because the key code value provided in technical documentation is synonymous with the make signal, if the make signal is 05h, the key code is 05h also. The key code indicates only the key that was pressed or released, not the value that may be assigned to the key. The translation of the key code to an ASCII value occurs at a later step within your computer system. The keyboard itself deals only with key codes.

The key codes used internally by your keyboard depend on the type of keyboard you are using. If you are interested in the key codes used by different keyboards, see Appendix A, "Keyboard Interpretation Tables."

Your keyboard has a built-in microprocessor that intercepts the key codes generated each time you press a key. The microprocessor is responsible for several operations, including testing the operation and integrity of the keyboard and communicating with your computer. The type of microprocessor used depends on the type of computer you are using. The older PC- and XT-class machines use an Intel 8048 or equivalent, and an Intel 8042 or equivalent is used in AT-class machines. These chips relieve your main CPU from the necessity of managing what goes on in your keyboard. They control both the sending of key codes to your computer and the repeating of key codes if a key is held down long enough.

The microprocessor in your keyboard communicates with your computer using a handshaking serial protocol in which every byte sent to the computer requires an acknowledgment signal, and every byte sent to the keyboard is answered with an acknowledgment. On the computer end of the keyboard cable, the communication is handled by a *keyboard controller*. In the older PC- and XT-class machines, this controller is an Intel 8255A-5 or equivalent; in the AT-class machines, it is an Intel 8042 or equivalent.

The basic difference between these keyboard controllers is what they do with the key codes received from the keyboard. The Intel 8255A-5 does nothing but convert the key codes from the serial format in which they are received into a complete byte that is presented to your computer through an I/O port. These key codes then are called *scan codes* and are used by your computer in further translations, described in the section "The BIOS Keyboard Buffer."

The Intel 8042 performs an additional step. It converts the key codes into scan codes that are backward-compatible with the codes generated by the older XT-class keyboards. In this way, the positional values, which are the key codes, are converted into standard scan codes that software in your computer can transform into ASCII values. These scan codes are detailed in Appendix A, "Keyboard Interpretation Tables."

Regardless of which keyboard controller your system uses, when a complete byte of data has been received, an IRQ 1 is generated that invokes the BIOS Int 09h routine. This discussion leads directly into the following section, which discusses the keyboard from a BIOS perspective.

The Keyboard: A BIOS View

After the Int 09h interrupt handler has been invoked, the BIOS takes over. This handler fetches the incoming byte from the output port of the keyboard controller (memory mapped to I/O port 60h) and determines what to do with it. This interrupt handler does quite a bit of work, depending on the value of the byte sent, as the following list shows.

- If a keyboard control code has been received, such as an acknowledgment, request for resend, or error code, the interrupt handler responds to it.

- If a system key such as Shift, Alt, Ctrl, Caps Lock, Num Lock, or Scroll Lock is being depressed or released, an internal flag is set to indicate the current state of the key. If one of the Lock keys is depressed, the interrupt handler sends the proper commands to the keyboard to turn on the LED indicators on the keyboard.

- If the Pause key or Ctrl-Num Lock key is pressed, a waiting condition within Int 09h begins. The condition ends when any key other than Caps Lock, Scroll Lock, Num Lock, Sys Request, Alt, or Ctrl is pressed.

- If the Sys Request key is pressed, Int 15/85/00 is invoked. If the key is released, Int 15/85/01 is invoked.

- If the Del key is pressed while Ctrl and Alt also are being pressed, the system reboots.

- If the Break key is pressed while Ctrl is depressed, a flag in the BIOS data area is set, the BIOS keyboard buffer is cleared, and Int 1Bh is invoked. This interrupt typically invokes the DOS Ctrl-Break handler.

- If the Print Screen key or the Shift-Print Screen key combination is pressed, Int 05h is invoked.

- If the keypad numbers are pressed while the Alt key is depressed, the numbers are accumulated to create an ASCII code that is returned when Alt is released.

■ If any other key is pressed, it is translated to the appropriate ASCII value or scan code depending on the state of the Ctrl, Alt, or Shift flags. These values then are deposited in the BIOS keyboard buffer.

In communicating with the keyboard controller, the Int 09h handler uses several I/O ports. In computers that use the 8255A-5, I/O ports 60h and 61h are used. Port 60h is the data output buffer for the keyboard controller; you can read incoming keyboard data from it. The use of the term *buffer* in this instance is a little misleading because the I/O port can contain only one character at a time. Port 61h is the 8255A-5 output register that is used to control the keyboard controller.

In systems using the 8042 keyboard controller, I/O ports 60h and 64h are used. Port 60h is the data output buffer for the controller. Port 64h is used by the keyboard controller to indicate the status of any incoming data, and is used also as an input buffer for information you may want to send to the controller.

The Int 09h handler also uses several important memory locations in the BIOS data area, beginning at 0040:0000. The offsets for these locations are shown in Table 2.1.

Table 2.1. Offset locations used by Int 09h within the BIOS data area beginning at 0040:0000.

Offset	Length	Use
17h	1 byte	Keyboard shift flags
18h	1 byte	Keyboard shift flags
19h	1 byte	Alt-key work area
1Ah	1 word	Pointer to head in the BIOS keyboard buffer (oldest character in the buffer)
1Ch	1 word	Pointer to tail in the BIOS keyboard buffer (next place for a keypress to be deposited)
1Eh	16 words	Keyboard input buffer
71h	1 byte	Ctrl-Break flag
80h	1 word	Offset in BIOS data segment (0040h) of beginning of the keyboard buffer
82h	1 word	Offset in BIOS data segment (0040h) of end of the keyboard buffer
96h	1 byte	Keyboard status byte
97h	1 byte	Keyboard status byte

The following section looks at the major data areas detailed in Table 2.1.

The Keyboard Shift Flags

The shift flags are two bytes located at 0040:0017 and 0040:0018. Every time you press or release the Shift, Alt, Ctrl, Ins, Caps Lock, Num Lock, Shift Lock, or Sys Request keys, the Int 09h handler changes bits within these flags. Table 2.2 shows the meaning of the bits at 0040:0017; Table 2.3 shows the meaning of the bits at 0040:0018.

Table 2.2. The keyboard shift flags at 0040:0017.

Bit settings 76543210	Meaning
1	Insert is active.
0	Insert is inactive.
1	Caps Lock is active.
0	Caps Lock is inactive.
1	Num Lock is active.
0	Num Lock is inactive.
1	Scroll Lock is active.
0	Scroll Lock is inactive.
1	The Alt key is being depressed (the make code has been received).
0	The Alt key is not being depressed (the break code has been received).
1	The Ctrl key is being depressed (the make code has been received).
0	The Ctrl key is not being depressed (the break code has been received).
1	The left Shift key is being depressed (the make code has been received).
0	The left Shift key is not being depressed (the break code has been received).
1	The right Shift key is being depressed (the make code has been received).
0	The right Shift key is not being depressed (the break code has been received).

Table 2.3. The keyboard shift flags at 0040:0018.

Bit settings 76543210	Meaning
1	The Ins key is being depressed (the make code has been received).
0	The Ins key is not being depressed (the break code has been received).
1	The Caps Lock key is being depressed (the make code has been received).
0	The Caps Lock key is not being depressed (the break code has been received).
1	The Num Lock key is being depressed (the make code has been received).
0	The Num Lock key is not being depressed (the break code has been received).
1	The Scroll Lock key is being depressed (the make code has been received).
0	The Scroll Lock key is not being depressed (the break code has been received).
1	A Pause (Ctrl-Num Lock) condition is in effect.
0	No Pause (Ctrl-Num Lock) condition is in effect.
1	The Sys Request key is being depressed (the make code has been received; available on only enhanced keyboards).
0	The Sys Request key is not being depressed (the break code has been received; available on only enhanced keyboards).
1	The left Alt key is being depressed (the make code has been received; available on only enhanced keyboards).
0	The left Alt key is not being depressed (the break code has been received; available on only enhanced keyboards).
1	The left Ctrl key is being depressed (the make code has been received; available on only enhanced keyboards).
0	The left Ctrl key is not being depressed (the break code has been received; available on only enhanced keyboards).

You should note that these bytes are internal to the BIOS; they are separate from the keyboard. For example, if the LED for Caps Lock is illuminated on your keyboard, the BIOS does not recognize the Caps Lock key as being depressed unless the appropriate bit in the keyboard shift flags is set. If your programs will change the bits in these registers, you may want to remember to send the proper commands to the keyboard controller to turn the LEDs on or off.

Notice also a few other interesting items about these keyboard flags. First, you can directly determine whether the left or right Shift keys are being depressed. If you are using an enhanced keyboard, you also can determine directly whether the left Alt or Ctrl keys are being depressed. If you have an enhanced keyboard and you want to determine whether the right Alt or Ctrl keys are being depressed, you first must check whether the Alt or Ctrl flags are set in the flags at 0040:0017. If they are set, you then must check whether the left Alt or Ctrl key flags are set in the flags at 0040:0018. If they are not, you know that the right Alt or Ctrl keys are being depressed.

Also, the flag for the Sys Request key is a bit extraneous. Because pressing Sys Request results in the invocation of Int 15/85/00, it is best to hook into that interrupt to use the key rather than continually look at this flag.

Finally, if you do not want to let the user press Pause or Ctrl-Num Lock to pause your program, you periodically can check bit 3 of the flags at 0040:0018. If it is set to 1, you can reset it to 0 and the Pause condition will end. You should note that this action does not disable any pause the user may have invoked by pressing Ctrl-S.

The Alt-Key Work Area

The Alt-key work area is made up of a single byte at 0040:0019. This byte is used by the Int 09h handler to construct an ASCII value when the keypad numbers are pressed while the Alt key is being held down. When you first press Alt, this work area is zeroed out. When you press a keypad number, the work area is multiplied by 10, and the value of the keypad number is added to the work area. When you release the Alt key, the value in the keypad is placed in the keyboard buffer as an ASCII value; the scan code is set to 0. If you press any other key while the Alt key is being held down, the work area is zeroed out again. If you press Alt-1-2-1, therefore, the ASCII value 121 (y) is placed in the keyboard buffer. If you press Alt-1-2-q-1, the ASCII value 1 (Ctrl-A) is placed in the keyboard buffer.

The BIOS Keyboard Buffer

Whenever you press a key that does not have a special meaning to the Int 09h handler, your keypress is translated into a pair of bytes that are deposited in the BIOS keyboard buffer. This circular buffer begins at the offset address pointed to by the word at 0040:0080. By default, the address in this word points to 001E, which is the default start of the BIOS keyboard buffer (0040:001E). The pointer at 0040:0082 is the offset address of 1 byte past the end of the keyboard buffer. By default, this is set to 003Eh. The default buffer area therefore is 32 bytes, or 16 words, long.

Each keypress deposited in the buffer occupies an entire word. The high-order byte contains the scan code for the keypress, and the low-order byte contains the ASCII value of the keypress. You should not confuse the scan code deposited in the buffer with the scan code retrieved from I/O port 60h by the Int 09h handler. It is possible for them to be the same, but there are numerous times when they are not. The Int 09h handler is free to change the scan code as necessary to a coding that is consistent with what it understands the state of the keyboard interface to be.

Because the keyboard buffer is circular in nature, the BIOS maintains both a head and tail pointer to addresses within the keyboard buffer. The tail pointer is maintained at 0040:001C, and represents the next offset memory address at which a keypress can be deposited. The head pointer, found at 0040:001A, is a pointer to the oldest character in the buffer.

The head and tail pointers are relatively simple in their operation. The flow-charts in Figures 2.1 and 2.2 show how these pointers are used.

Figure 2.1.

How the keyboard buffer head and tail pointers work when adding a character.

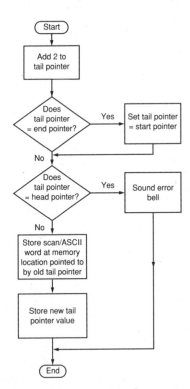

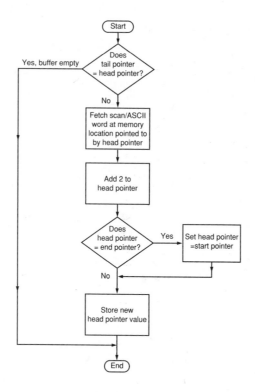

Figure 2.2.

How the keyboard buffer head and tail pointers work when deleting a character.

This section has mentioned that each keystroke deposited in the keyboard buffer consumes one word of space. Simple math would suggest that a 16-word buffer (such as the default keyboard buffer) can hold 16 keystrokes. This statement is not correct, however. Look at Figure 2.1 again. The logic diagrammed there shows that the tail pointer always points to where the *next* keystroke will be deposited. Before a keystroke is deposited, the routine checks to make sure that the tail will not be equal to the head. This action is important because whenever the head and tail are equal, the buffer is assumed to be empty. The 16th keystroke never can be stored, therefore, because the tail and head pointers would be equal after the algorithm was complete. A circular keyboard buffer can hold one less keystroke than the number of words set aside for the buffer.

The programs presented later in this chapter let you view and manipulate the keyboard buffer.

Other Data Areas

The BIOS uses several more data areas in relation to the keyboard. The Ctrl-Break flag at 0040:0071 is set to 80h by the Int 09h handler whenever you press Ctrl-Break. This flag is not set when you press Ctrl-C, nor is it ever reset after it has been set. It is simply a flag to indicate whether Ctrl-Break has ever been pressed.

The Ctrl-Break flag can come in handy. Suppose that you are writing a full-blown program that intercepts the normal Ctrl-Break interrupt, Int 1Bh, so that critical processing is not disturbed. You have two choices. You can simply disable Int 1Bh so that it returns to your program immediately, or you can write for the interrupt handler some code that sets your own internal flags so that the Ctrl-Break can be handled later. If you choose the first method, you can check the flag at 0040:0071 later to see whether Ctrl-Break was entered. If it was, you can reset the flag and handle the condition in any way you want. This method may seem great, but it has one drawback: When a user enters Ctrl-C, DOS eventually will chain to the Int 1Bh handler, but the Int 09h handler will not have set the Ctrl-Break flag. This flag is set only if Ctrl-Break—not Ctrl-C—is entered. The value of the flag therefore is limited, and the second method of handling Ctrl-Break in your full-blown program may be more beneficial.

The final remaining data areas, at 0040:0096 and 0040:0097, are used by the Int 09h handler to maintain information internal to its workings. The availability of these flags varies depending on your BIOS version, but Tables 2.4 and 2.5 detail the meaning of the flags.

Table 2.4. The keyboard status byte at 0040:0096.

Bit settings 76543210	Meaning
1	A read of the keyboard ID is in process.
0	The keyboard ID is not being read.
1	The last keyboard code received was the first ID code.
0	The last keyboard code received was not part of an ID code.
1	Forced Num Lock condition.
0	Num Lock is not active.
1	Enhanced keyboard is in use.
0	A standard keyboard is in use.
1	The right Alt key is being depressed (the make code has been received; available on only enhanced keyboards).

Bit settings 76543210	Meaning
0	The right Alt key is not being depressed (the make code has been received; available on only enhanced keyboards).
1	The right Ctrl key is being depressed (the make code has been received; available on only enhanced keyboards).
0	The right Ctrl key is not being depressed (the make code has been received; available on only enhanced keyboards).
1	The last keyboard code received was E0.
0	The last keyboard code received was not E0.
1	The last keyboard code received was E1.
0	The last keyboard code received was not E1.

Table 2.5. The keyboard status byte at 0040:0097.

Bit settings 76543210	Meaning
1	An error has occurred during a command to the keyboard.
0	No keyboard error has occurred.
1	The LEDs on the keyboard are being updated.
0	The LEDs on the keyboard are not being updated.
1	A resend request was received from the keyboard.
0	The last keyboard transmission was OK; no resend request was received.
1	An acknowledge code was received from the keyboard.
0	The last keyboard code received was not an acknowledge code.
x	Reserved; not defined.
1	The Caps Lock LED is illuminated.
0	The Caps Lock LED is dark.
1	The Num Lock LED is illuminated.
0	The Num Lock LED is dark.
1	The Scroll Lock LED is illuminated.
0	The Scroll Lock LED is dark.

In one respect, these status bytes are similar to the shift flags discussed earlier in this chapter. These bytes are internal to the BIOS; they are separate from the keyboard. The LED illumination status flags, therefore, can be out of sync with the condition of the LEDs on the keyboard. Your program must make sure that this does not happen.

The BIOS Keyboard Functions

Now that you understand how the keyboard works, and how the BIOS works with the keyboard, you should understand that the BIOS provides several functions which enable you to get information from the keyboard (see Table 2.6). These functions are not described in great detail here, but you can refer to *Using Assembly Language*, 3rd Edition (Que Corporation), the companion to this book, for detailed BIOS function information.

Table 2.6. The BIOS keyboard functions.

Int	Service	Purpose
16h	00h	Read keyboard character
16h	01h	Read keyboard status
16h	02h	Read keyboard shift status
16h	03h	Adjust repeat rate
16h	04h	Key-click control
16h	05h	Write to keyboard buffer
16h	10h	Get extended keystroke
16h	11h	Get extended keyboard status
16h	12h	Get extended keyboard status flags

On older PC and XT systems, only the first three functions shown in Table 2.6 are available.

The remaining sections of this chapter explain how to use these functions in conjunction with other programming techniques to modify the way the keyboard works with your system.

Understanding the Keyboard Buffer Better

Earlier in this chapter, you learned about the keyboard buffer and how it works. You learned, conceptually, how Int 09h places information in the buffer and how Int 16h removes information. In this section, you use an assembly language program to gain an even better understanding of the buffer.

Remember that you learned in Chapter 1 about interrupts and interrupt handlers. The program in Listing 2.1 expands on techniques presented in Chapter 1 to intercept the Int 09h handler and act on certain keypresses. This technique is not unlike those employed by some terminate-and-stay-resident (TSR) programs discussed in Chapter 3, "Serial Communications," but this program is not TSR in nature. It assembles to an EXE file that displays the contents of the keyboard buffer and dynamically enables you to see how it works.

Listing 2.1. KEYLOOK1.ASM

```
Page 60,132


Comment ¦
*********************************************************************

File:       KEYLOOK1.ASM
Author:     Allen L. Wyatt
Date:       3/21/92
Assembler:  MASM 6.0

Purpose:    Display the status of the keyboard buffer. This program
            intercepts Int 09 and examines the keypresses there.

Format:     KEYLOOK1


*********************************************************************¦


DataPort    EQU     60h
StatusPort  EQU     64h
InputFull   EQU     02h
```

continues

Listing 2.1. Continued

```
Head        EQU     01Ah
Tail        EQU     01Ch
Buffer      EQU     01Eh
BuffStart   EQU     080h
BuffEnd     EQU     082h

EscScan     EQU     01h             ;Keypress to exit program
DelScan     EQU     3Bh             ;Keypress to delete from buffer
ClrScan     EQU     3Ch             ;Keypress to clear buffer

            .MODEL  small
            .STACK                  ;Default 1K stack is OK
            .DATA
ExitFlag    DB      00
ClearFlag   DB      00
PopFlag     DB      00
OldDiff     DW      0000
Screen      DB      'Pair # 0 1 2 3 4 5 6 7 8 9 A B C D E F '
            DB      '                                       '
            DB      'Byte 1                                 '
            DB      'Byte 2                                 '
            DB      ' ASCII                                 '
            DB      '                                       '

Info        DB      'Byte 1 is the ASCII value of the keypress, Byte 2 is the'
            DB      'scan code. The ASCII row is the ASCII representation of '
            DB      'Byte 1.  Special keys:      Esc  to Exit                '
            DB      '                            F1   to Grab from buffer    '
            DB      '                            F2   to Clear buffer        '

            .CODE
            .STARTUP

KEYLOOK     PROC

; Check that keyboard buffer is in proper place; exit if not
            PUSH    DS
            MOV     AX,040h          ;Point to BIOS data area
            MOV     DS,AX
            MOV     BX,BuffStart
```

```
              CMP    WORD PTR [BX],Buffer  ;Does the buffer begin at the default?
              POP    DS                    ;Restore DS before branching
              JE     BufferOK             ;Yes, so continue
              JMP    FinalExit

BufferOK:     MOV    AL,09h               ;Get keyboard interrupt
              MOV    AH,35h
              INT    21h
              MOV    CS:KeyInt[0],BX      ;Offset address
              MOV    CS:KeyInt[2],ES      ;Segment address

              PUSH   DS                   ;Store data segment
              MOV    AX,CS                ;New segment address
              MOV    DS,AX
              MOV    DX,OFFSET NewInt     ;New offset address
              MOV    AL,9h                ;Change keyboard vector
              MOV    AH,25h               ;to point to new handler
              INT    21h
              POP    DS                   ;Restore data segment

              CALL   Cls                  ;Clear the screen
              CALL   ShowScreen           ;Paint the original screen
              CALL   ShowHex              ;Show the buffer data in hex
              CALL   ShowASCII            ;Show the buffer data in ASCII
              CALL   ShowPtrs             ;Show the buffer pointers

              MOV    AX,040h
              MOV    ES,AX                ;Point to BIOS data area

M1:           MOV    AX,[ES:Head]         ;Get head pointer
              SUB    AX,[ES:Tail]         ;Difference to tail
              CMP    AX,OldDiff           ;Any change?
              JE     M2                   ;No, so continue
              MOV    OldDiff,AX

              CALL   ShowHex              ;Show the buffer data in hex
              CALL   ShowASCII            ;Show the buffer data in ASCII
              CALL   ShowPtrs             ;Show the buffer pointers

M2:           CMP    ExitFlag,1           ;Has the exit key been pressed?
              JE     Exit
```

continues

Listing 2.1. Continued

```
            CMP     PopFlag,1               ;Should a key be popped?
            JNE     M3
            CALL    DelKey
            MOV     PopFlag,0

M3:         CMP     ClearFlag,1             ;Should the buffer be cleared?
            JNE     M4
            CALL    ClrBuff
            MOV     ClearFlag,0

M4:         JMP     M1                      ;Do it continually

Exit:       PUSH    DS                      ;Store for later
            MOV     DX,CS:KeyInt[0]         ;Get offset address
            MOV     AX,CS:KeyInt[2]         ;Get segment address
            MOV     DS,AX
            MOV     AL,9h                   ;Change keyboard vector
            MOV     AH,25h                  ;to point to old interrupt
            INT     21h
            POP     DS                      ;Restore data segment

FinalExit:  CALL    ClrBuff                 ;Clear the buffer before leaving
            CALL    Cls                     ;Clear the screen
            .EXIT
KEYLOOK     ENDP


; The following routine displays the static portion of
; the display screen

ShowScreen  PROC    USES AX BX CX DX SI
            MOV     SI,OFFSET Screen        ;Point to start of screen display
            CLD                             ;Make sure the direction flag is OK
            MOV     BH,0                    ;Assume page 0 (for next BIOS calls)
            MOV     DH,6                    ;Starting on row 7 (increment later)
            MOV     DL,12                   ;Always use column 12
            MOV     CX,11                   ;Have 11 rows to paint
Paint1:     PUSH    CX                      ;Outside loop
            INC     DH                      ;Point to proper row
            CMP     CX,5                    ;Only 5 rows left?
```

```
            JNE     P1A             ;No, continue
            ADD     DH,4            ;Yes, so put some blank rows in
P1A:        MOV     AH,2            ;Set cursor position
            INT     10h
            MOV     AH,0Eh          ;Teletype output
            MOV     CX,56           ;71 characters wide

Paint2:     LODSB                   ;Get character
            INT     10h
            LOOP    Paint2          ;Continue for row
            POP     CX              ;Get outside loop back
            LOOP    Paint1          ;Continue for all rows
            RET
ShowScreen  ENDP
```

; The following routine displays on the screen, in hex, the
; contents of the keyboard buffer

```
ShowHex     PROC    USES AX BX CX DX DS SI
            MOV     DL,17           ;Set column
            MOV     AX,040h
            MOV     DS,AX           ;Point to BIOS data area
            MOV     SI,Buffer       ;Point to keyboard buffer
            MOV     CX,16           ;Have 16 iterations to do

SB1:        LODSB                   ;Get the first byte of the pair
            CALL    ConHex          ;Go convert byte to hex ASCII
            PUSH    AX              ;Store value
            ADD     DL,3            ;Point to the next column
            MOV     AH,2            ;Set cursor position
            MOV     BH,0            ;Assume video page 0
            MOV     DH,9            ;Set row
            INT     10h
            POP     AX              ;Get value back
            PUSH    AX              ;Store it again
            MOV     AH,0Eh          ;Teletype output
            INT     10h
            POP     AX              ;Get value back
            MOV     AL,AH           ;Move ASCII value into proper place
            MOV     AH,0Eh          ;Teletype output
            INT     10h
```

continues

Listing 2.1. Continued

```
                LODSB                           ;Get the second byte of the pair
                CALL    ConHex                  ;Go convert byte to hex ASCII
                PUSH    AX                      ;Store value
                MOV     AH,2                    ;Set cursor position
                MOV     DH,10                   ;Set row
                INT     10h
                POP     AX                      ;Get value back
                PUSH    AX                      ;Store it again
                MOV     AH,0Eh                  ;Teletype output
                INT     10h
                POP     AX                      ;Get value back
                MOV     AL,AH                   ;Move ASCII value into proper place
                MOV     AH,0Eh                  ;Teletype output
                INT     10h
                LOOP    SB1                     ;Do it all again
                RET
ShowHex         ENDP


; The following routine displays on the screen, in ASCII, the
; contents of the keyboard buffer

ShowASCII       PROC    USES AX BX CX DX DS SI
                MOV     DL,18                   ;Set column
                MOV     BH,0                    ;Assume video page 0
                MOV     AX,040h
                MOV     DS,AX                   ;Point to BIOS data area
                MOV     SI,Buffer               ;Point to keyboard buffer
                MOV     CX,16                   ;Have 16 iterations to do

SA1:            ADD     DL,3                    ;Point to the next column
                MOV     DH,11                   ;Set row
                MOV     AH,2                    ;Set cursor position
                INT     10h
                LODSB                           ;Get the first byte of the pair
                MOV     AH,0Eh                  ;Teletype output
                INT     10h
                INC     SI                      ;Throw away the scan code
                LOOP    SA1                     ;Do it all again
                RET
ShowASCII       ENDP
```

```
; The following routine displays on the screen the position of the
; keyboard buffer pointers

ShowPtrs    PROC      USES AX BX CX DX ES
            MOV       AH,6              ;Scroll window up
            MOV       AL,1              ;Scroll only one line
            MOV       BH,7              ;Normal white on black
            MOV       CH,13             ;Row
            MOV       CL,0              ;Start at left column
            MOV       DH,13             ;Row
            MOV       DL,79             ;End at right side
            INT       10h

            MOV       AX,040h
            MOV       ES,AX             ;Point to BIOS data area
            MOV       AX,[ES:Head]      ;Get head pointer
            SUB       AX,Buffer         ;Subtract start of buffer location
            SHR       AX,1              ;Divide by 2 to find right offset
            MOV       BL,3              ;Want to multiply by this
            MUL       BL                ;Adjust for screen position
            ADD       AL,20             ;Point to screen column

            MOV       DL,AL             ;Put column in proper place
            MOV       DH,13             ;Always will be this row
            MOV       AH,2              ;Set cursor position
            MOV       BH,0              ;Assume page 0
            INT       10h

            MOV       AH,0Eh            ;Teletype output
            MOV       AL,'H'
            INT       10h

            MOV       AX,[ES:Tail]      ;Get tail pointer
            SUB       AX,Buffer         ;Subtract start of buffer location
            SHR       AX,1              ;Divide by 2 to find right offset
            MOV       BL,3              ;Want to multiply by this
            MUL       BL                ;Adjust for screen position
            ADD       AL,21             ;Point to screen column

            MOV       DL,AL             ;Put column in proper place
            MOV       DH,13             ;Always will be this row
```

continues

Listing 2.1. Continued

```
                MOV     AH,2            ;Set cursor position
                MOV     BH,0            ;Assume page 0
                INT     10h

                MOV     AH,0Eh          ;Teletype output
                MOV     AL,'T'
                INT     10h
                RET
ShowPtrs        ENDP


; The following routine removes a key from the buffer

DelKey          PROC    USES AX
                MOV     AH,1            ;Read keyboard status
                INT     16h
                JZ      DKExit          ;Sorry, no key, so exit
                MOV     AH,0            ;Read keyboard character
                INT     16h
DKExit:         RET
DelKey          ENDP


; The following routine clears the entire keyboard buffer

ClrBuff         PROC    USES AX
CB1:            MOV     AH,1            ;Read keyboard status
                INT     16h
                JZ      CBExit          ;No key, so exit
                MOV     AH,0            ;Read keyboard character
                INT     16h
                JMP     CB1             ;Go do it all again
CBExit:         RET
ClrBuff         ENDP


; The following routine clears the screen

Cls             PROC    USES AX BX CX DX
                MOV     AH,6            ;Scroll window up
                MOV     AL,0            ;Scroll full screen
                MOV     BH,7            ;Normal white on black
                MOV     CX,0            ;Upper left corner of screen
```

```
            MOV     DH,24                   ;Bottom right
            MOV     DL,79
            INT     10h
            RET
Cls         ENDP


; The following routine converts the number in AL into an ASCII
; representation of the hex value, with a leading 0. Value
; is returned in AX as well.

ConHex      PROC    USES CX
            MOV     CL,10h                  ;What we will be dividing by
            MOV     AH,0
            DIV     CL                      ;Divide by 16
            ADD     AL,30h
            ADD     AH,30h
            CMP     AL,'9'                  ;Is it greater than 9?
            JBE     CA4                     ;No, so continue
            ADD     AL,7                    ;Make into hex digit
CA4:        CMP     AH,'9'                  ;Is it greater than 9?
            JBE     CA5                     ;No, so continue
            ADD     AH,7                    ;Make into hex digit
CA5:        RET
ConHex      ENDP


; The following is the new keyboard interrupt to replace Int 09h

NewInt      PROC
            PUSH    CX
            PUSH    BX
            PUSH    AX
            PUSH    DS
            MOV     AX,SEG ExitFlag         ;Set up addressing
            MOV     DS,AX

            CLI                             ;Disable interrupts
GetStat:    IN      AL,StatusPort           ;Get keyboard status
            TEST    AL,InputFull            ;Is the coding complete?
            LOOPNZ  GetStat                 ;No, so continue waiting
            IN      AL,DataPort             ;Yes, so get code
            STI                             ;Enable interrupts
```

continues

Listing 2.1. Continued

```
Process:    MOV     BX,AX                   ;Will put break flag here
            AND     BX,80h                  ;Mask out all others
            MOV     CL,7                    ;Want to shift this far
            SHR     BL,CL                   ;Set in rightmost position
            AND     AL,7Fh                  ;Turn off if a break key
            CMP     AL,EscScan              ;Was Esc pressed?
            JNE     NI1
            MOV     ExitFlag,BL             ;Set only if break
            JMP     Ignore

NI1:        CMP     AL,DelScan              ;Want to delete a key?
            JNE     NI2
            MOV     PopFlag,BL              ;Set only if break
            JMP     Ignore

NI2:        CMP     AL,ClrScan              ;Want to clear the buffer?
            JNE     Pass
            MOV     ClearFlag,BL            ;Set only if break
            JMP     Ignore

Pass:       POP     DS
            POP     AX
            POP     BX
            POP     CX
            JMP     DWORD PTR CS:KeyInt  ;Skip to original INT 9 routine

Ignore:     MOV     AL,20h                  ;Signify end of interrupt
            OUT     20h,AL
            POP     DS
            POP     AX
            POP     BX
            POP     CX
            IRET

; The following bytes are for the original Int 09 routine. It is necessary
; for it to be here because of the JMP hook at the end of the Pass section
; of the new interrupt handler.
```

```
KeyInt     DW       0000,0000           ;Address for old keyboard routine

NewInt     ENDP

           END
```

When you are running the program, make sure that your keyboard buffer is set to the default 16-word BIOS buffer. If you are using a keyboard extender or any other program that changes the keyboard buffer, KEYLOOK1.EXE detects it and refuses to run.

When you are using the program, you can type any keys you want and see how Int 09h deposits the scan code and ASCII value in the keyboard buffer. You see also the tail and head pointers maintained by the BIOS. You can press F1 to use Int 16/0 to grab a keystroke from the buffer. When you do, you will notice the movement of the head pointer. If you press F2, a series of Int 16/0 services is called to empty the buffer. This part of the program just as easily could have been written to simply set the head and tail pointers to the same value. The BIOS then would have assumed that the buffer was empty.

When you are finished using the program, you can press Esc to exit.

KEYLOOK1 intercepts the Int 09h handler so that Esc, F1, and F2 control functions of the program rather than get put in the buffer. If you are using an AT-class machine, chances are that you can use the program in Listing 2.2, KEYLOOK2.ASM, instead. It is basically the same as KEYLOOK1, but the interrupt servicing routine has been replaced with one that hooks into a different interrupt.

Listing 2.2. KEYLOOK2.ASM

```
Page 60,132

Comment ¦
******************************************************************


File:      KEYLOOK2.ASM
Author:    Allen L. Wyatt
Date:      3/21/92
Assembler: MASM 6.0
```

continues

Listing 2.2. Continued

```
Purpose:     Display the status of the keyboard buffer, but use
             Int 15/4F to intercept keys, instead of intercepting
             Int 09.

Format:      KEYLOOK2


******************************************************************|

Head          EQU      01Ah
Tail          EQU      01Ch
Buffer        EQU      01Eh
BuffStart     EQU      080h
BuffEnd       EQU      082h

EscScan       EQU      01h                ;Keypress to exit program
DelScan       EQU      3Bh                ;Keypress to delete from buffer
ClrScan       EQU      3Ch                ;Keypress to clear buffer

              .MODEL   small
              .STACK                      ;Default 1K stack is OK
              .DATA
ExitFlag      DB       00
ClearFlag     DB       00
PopFlag       DB       00
OldDiff       DW       0000



Screen        DB       'Pair #  0  1  2  3  4  5  6  7  8  9  A  B  C  D  E  F '
              DB       '
              DB       'Byte 1
              DB       'Byte 2
              DB       ' ASCII
              DB       '

Info          DB       'Byte 1 is the ASCII value of the keypress, Byte 2 is the'
              DB       'scan code. The ASCII row is the ASCII representation of '
              DB       'Byte 1.  Special keys:       Esc  to Exit
              DB       '                             F1   to Grab from buffer
              DB       '                             F2   to Clear buffer
```

```
                .CODE
                .STARTUP

KEYLOOK         PROC

; Check that keyboard buffer is in proper place; exit if not
                PUSH    DS
                MOV     AX,040h                 ;Point to BIOS data area
                MOV     DS,AX
                MOV     BX,BuffStart
                CMP     WORD PTR [BX],Buffer  ;Does the buffer begin at the default?
                POP     DS                      ;Restore DS before branching
                JE      BufferOK                ;Yes, so continue
NoWay:          JMP     FinalExit

; To make sure that Int 15/4F is usable on this machine, call Int 15/C0. Bit
; 4 of the byte at offset 05 of the returned table indicates whether 15/4F is
; chained from Int 09h. If Int 15/C0 is not available on the system, then
; 80h or 86h should be returned in AH.

BufferOK:       MOV     AH,0C0h
                INT     15h
                CMP     AH,80h                  ;Available?
                JE      NoWay                   ;Nope
                CMP     AH,86h                  ;
                JE      NoWay                   ;Sorry

                MOV     AL,ES:[BX+5]            ;Get the byte
                AND     AL,10h                  ;Interested only in bit 4
                CMP     AL,0                    ;Is it there?
                JE      NoWay                   ;No, so exit

; Everything is OK.  Now hook in the intercept and start the program.

                MOV     AL,15h                  ;Get keyboard interrupt
                MOV     AH,35h
                INT     21h
                MOV     CS:KeyInt[0],BX         ;Offset address
                MOV     CS:KeyInt[2],ES         ;Segment address

                PUSH    DS                      ;Store data segment
                MOV     AX,CS                   ;New segment address
```

continues

Listing 2.2. Continued

```
        MOV     DS,AX
        MOV     DX,OFFSET NewInt    ;New offset address
        MOV     AL,15h              ;Change keyboard vector
        MOV     AH,25h              ;to point to new handler
        INT     21h
        POP     DS                  ;Restore data segment

        CALL    Cls                 ;Clear the screen
        CALL    ShowScreen          ;Paint the original screen
        CALL    ShowHex             ;Show the buffer data in hex
        CALL    ShowASCII           ;Show the buffer data in ASCII
        CALL    ShowPtrs            ;Show the buffer pointers

        MOV     AX,040h
        MOV     ES,AX               ;Point to BIOS data area

M1:     MOV     AX,[ES:Head]        ;Get head pointer
        SUB     AX,[ES:Tail]        ;Difference to tail
        CMP     AX,OldDiff          ;Any change?
        JE      M2                  ;No, so continue
        MOV     OldDiff,AX

        CALL    ShowHex             ;Show the buffer data in hex
        CALL    ShowASCII           ;Show the buffer data in ASCII
        CALL    ShowPtrs            ;Show the buffer pointers

M2:     CMP     ExitFlag,1          ;Has the exit key been pressed?
        JE      Exit

        CMP     PopFlag,1           ;Should a key be popped?
        JNE     M3
        CALL    DelKey
        MOV     PopFlag,0

M3:     CMP     ClearFlag,1         ;Should the buffer be cleared?
        JNE     M4
        CALL    ClrBuff
        MOV     ClearFlag,0
```

```
M4:          JMP      M1                  ;Do it continually

Exit:        PUSH     DS                  ;Store for later
             MOV      DX,CS:KeyInt[0]     ;Get offset address
             MOV      AX,CS:KeyInt[2]     ;Get segment address
             MOV      DS,AX
             MOV      AL,15h              ;Change keyboard vector
             MOV      AH,25h              ;to point to old interrupt
             INT      21h
             POP      DS                  ;Restore data segment

FinalExit:   CALL     ClrBuff             ;Clear the buffer before leaving
             CALL     Cls                 ;Clear the screen
             .EXIT
KEYLOOK      ENDP


; The following routine displays the static portion of
; the display screen

ShowScreen   PROC     USES AX BX CX DX SI
             MOV      SI,OFFSET Screen    ;Point to start of screen display
             CLD                          ;Make sure the direction flag is OK
             MOV      BH,0                ;Assume page 0 (for next BIOS calls)
             MOV      DH,6                ;Starting on row 7 (increment later)
             MOV      DL,12               ;Always use column 12
             MOV      CX,11               ;Have 11 rows to paint
Paint1:      PUSH     CX                  ;Outside loop
             INC      DH                  ;Point to proper row
             CMP      CX,5                ;Only 5 rows left?
             JNE      P1A                 ;No, continue
             ADD      DH,4                ;Yes, so put in some blank rows
P1A:         MOV      AH,2                ;Set cursor position
             INT      10h
             MOV      AH,0Eh              ;Teletype output
             MOV      CX,56               ;71 characters wide

Paint2:      LODSB                        ;Get character
             INT      10h
```

continues

Listing 2.2. Continued

```
                LOOP    Paint2              ;Continue for row
                POP     CX                  ;Get outside loop back
                LOOP    Paint1              ;Continue for all rows
                RET
ShowScreen      ENDP


; The following routine displays on the screen, in hex, the
; contents of the keyboard buffer

ShowHex         PROC    USES AX BX CX DX DS SI
                MOV     DL,17               ;Set column
                MOV     AX,040h
                MOV     DS,AX               ;Point to BIOS data area
                MOV     SI,Buffer           ;Point to keyboard buffer
                MOV     CX,16               ;Have 16 iterations to do

SB1:            LODSB                       ;Get the first byte of the pair
                CALL    ConHex              ;Go convert byte to hex ASCII
                PUSH    AX                  ;Store value
                ADD     DL,3                ;Point to the next column
                MOV     AH,2                ;Set cursor position
                MOV     BH,0                ;Assume video page 0
                MOV     DH,9                ;Set row
                INT     10h
                POP     AX                  ;Get value back
                PUSH    AX                  ;Store it again
                MOV     AH,0Eh              ;Teletype output
                INT     10h
                POP     AX                  ;Get value back
                MOV     AL,AH               ;Move ASCII value into proper place
                MOV     AH,0Eh              ;Teletype output
                INT     10h

                LODSB                       ;Get the second byte of the pair
                CALL    ConHex              ;Go convert byte to hex ASCII
                PUSH    AX                  ;Store value
                MOV     AH,2                ;Set cursor position
                MOV     DH,10               ;Set row
                INT     10h
```

```
                POP     AX                      ;Get value back
                PUSH    AX                      ;Store it again
                MOV     AH,0Eh                  ;Teletype output
                INT     10h
                POP     AX                      ;Get value back
                MOV     AL,AH                   ;Move ASCII value into proper place
                MOV     AH,0Eh                  ;Teletype output
                INT     10h
                LOOP    SB1                     ;Do it all again
                RET
ShowHex         ENDP


; The following routine displays on the screen, in ASCII, the
; contents of the keyboard buffer

ShowASCII       PROC    USES AX BX CX DX DS SI
                MOV     DL,18                   ;Set column
                MOV     BH,0                    ;Assume video page 0
                MOV     AX,040h
                MOV     DS,AX                   ;Point to BIOS data area
                MOV     SI,Buffer               ;Point to keyboard buffer
                MOV     CX,16                   ;Have 16 iterations to do

SA1:            ADD     DL,3                    ;Point to the next column
                MOV     DH,11                   ;Set row
                MOV     AH,2                    ;Set cursor position
                INT     10h
                LODSB                           ;Get the first byte of the pair
                MOV     AH,0Eh                  ;Teletype output
                INT     10h
                INC     SI                      ;Throw away the scan code
                LOOP    SA1                     ;Do it all again
                RET
ShowASCII       ENDP


; The following routine displays on the screen the position of the
; keyboard buffer pointers

ShowPtrs        PROC    USES AX BX CX DX ES
                MOV     AH,6                    ;Scroll window up
                MOV     AL,1                    ;Scroll only one line
```

continues

Listing 2.2. Continued

```
        MOV     BH,7            ;Normal white on black
        MOV     CH,13           ;Row
        MOV     CL,0            ;Start at left column
        MOV     DH,13           ;Row
        MOV     DL,79           ;End at right side
        INT     10h

        MOV     AX,040h
        MOV     ES,AX           ;Point to BIOS data area
        MOV     AX,[ES:Head]    ;Get head pointer
        SUB     AX,Buffer       ;Subtract start of buffer location
        SHR     AX,1            ;Divide by 2 to find right offset
        MOV     BL,3            ;Want to multiply by this
        MUL     BL              ;Adjust for screen position
        ADD     AL,20           ;Point to screen column

        MOV     DL,AL           ;Put column in proper place
        MOV     DH,13           ;Always will be this row
        MOV     AH,2            ;Set cursor position
        MOV     BH,0            ;Assume page 0
        INT     10h

        MOV     AH,0Eh          ;Teletype output
        MOV     AL,'H'
        INT     10h

        MOV     AX,[ES:Tail]    ;Get tail pointer
        SUB     AX,Buffer       ;Subtract start of buffer location
        SHR     AX,1            ;Divide by 2 to find right offset
        MOV     BL,3            ;Want to multiply by this
        MUL     BL              ;Adjust for screen position
        ADD     AL,21           ;Point to screen column

        MOV     DL,AL           ;Put column in proper place
        MOV     DH,13           ;Always will be this row
        MOV     AH,2            ;Set cursor position
        MOV     BH,0            ;Assume page 0
        INT     10h
```

```
                MOV      AH,0Eh              ;Teletype output
                MOV      AL,'T'
                INT      10h
                RET
ShowPtrs        ENDP


; The following routine removes a key from the buffer

DelKey          PROC     USES AX
                MOV      AH,1                ;Read keyboard status
                INT      16h
                JZ       DKExit              ;Sorry, no key, so exit
                MOV      AH,0                ;Read keyboard character
                INT      16h
DKExit:         RET
DelKey          ENDP


; The following routine clears the entire keyboard buffer

ClrBuff         PROC     USES AX
CB1:            MOV      AH,1                ;Read keyboard status
                INT      16h
                JZ       CBExit              ;No key, so exit
                MOV      AH,0                ;Read keyboard character
                INT      16h
                JMP      CB1                 ;Go do it all again
CBExit:         RET
ClrBuff         ENDP


; The following routine clears the screen

Cls             PROC     USES AX BX CX DX
                MOV      AH,6                ;Scroll window up
                MOV      AL,0                ;Scroll full screen
                MOV      BH,7                ;Normal white on black
                MOV      CX,0                ;Upper left corner of screen
                MOV      DH,24               ;Bottom right
                MOV      DL,79
                INT      10h
                RET
Cls             ENDP
```

continues

Listing 2.2. Continued

```
; The following routine converts the number in AL into an ASCII
; representation of the hex value, with a leading 0. Value
; is returned in AX as well.

ConHex      PROC    USES CX
            MOV     CL,10h                  ;What we will be dividing by
            MOV     AH,0
            DIV     CL                      ;Divide by 16
            ADD     AL,30h
            ADD     AH,30h
            CMP     AL,'9'                  ;Is it greater than 9?
            JBE     CA4                     ;No, so continue
            ADD     AL,7                    ;Make into hex digit
CA4:        CMP     AH,'9'                  ;Is it greater than 9?
            JBE     CA5                     ;No, so continue
            ADD     AH,7                    ;Make into hex digit
CA5:        RET
ConHex      ENDP


; The following is the new keyboard interrupt to replace Int 15/4F

NewInt      PROC
            CMP     AH,4Fh                  ;Is it the keyboard intercept?
            JE      Process                 ;Yes, so continue
            JMP     DWORD PTR CS:KeyInt     ;Skip to original interrupt handler

Process:    PUSH    DS
            PUSH    AX
            MOV     AX,SEG ExitFlag         ;Set up addressing
            MOV     DS,AX
            POP     AX                      ;Now get the key back
            PUSH    AX                      ;Store again

            CMP     AL,EscScan              ;Was Esc pressed?
            JNE     NI1
            MOV     ExitFlag,1
            JNC     Ignore                  ;Carry is clear from equality

NI1:        CMP     AL,DelScan              ;Want to delete a key?
            JNE     NI2
            MOV     PopFlag,1
            JNC     Ignore                  ;Carry is clear from equality
```

```
NI2:        CMP     AL,ClrScan          ;Want to clear the buffer?
            JNE     Pass
            MOV     ClearFlag,1
            JNC     Ignore              ;Carry is clear from equality

Pass:       STC                         ;Go ahead, put key in buffer
Ignore:     POP     AX
            POP     DS
            RETF    2                   ;Don't want IRET because it restores
                                        ;the flags register

; The following bytes are for the original Int 15 routine. It is necessary
; for it to be here because of the JMP hook at the end of the Pass section
; of the new interrupt handler.

KeyInt      DW      0000,0000           ;Address for old keyboard routine

NewInt      ENDP

            END
```

On AT-class machines, the Int 09h handler automatically calls Int 15/4F before completion. In the normal BIOS, this routine does nothing. In KEYLOOK2.ASM, however, a routine was written that uses Int 15/4F to test for the presence of the Esc, F1, or F2 keys. When they were found, the carry flag was cleared, and control returned to Int 09h. The result is that the keys were not placed in the keyboard buffer.

The advantage of using the technique shown in KEYLOOK2 is that initial programming is much easier. You don't have to worry about communicating properly with the keyboard controller—a huge advantage in almost every programming circumstance.

Changing the Keyboard Buffer Size

The easiest way to change the keyboard buffer size is to change the pointers in the BIOS system data area that control where the buffer is located. As stated earlier in this chapter, the pointers that control this buffer location are as follows:

Offset	Length	Use
1Ah	1 word	Pointer to head in the BIOS keyboard buffer (oldest character in the buffer)
1Ch	1 word	Pointer to tail in the BIOS keyboard buffer (next place for a keypress to be deposited)
80h	1 word	Offset in BIOS data segment (0040h) of beginning of the keyboard buffer
82h	1 word	Offset in BIOS data segment (0040h) of end of the keyboard buffer

These four pointers are used by both Int 09h and Int 16h to indicate where characters should be both stored and retrieved. A pointer size of one word means that you can specify a buffer anywhere within 64K of memory, beginning at 0040:0000. The problem is finding somewhere that isn't already in use or that will not be "trampled on" by other programs. With complex programs and memory managers, finding such an area is harder than you might think.

The program in Listing 2.3, although very short, relocates the keyboard buffer to the 256 bytes of memory between 0040:0200 and 0040:02FF. This area of memory seems to be unused after your system initially boots. The operative word here is *seems*. You should remember that the use of memory varies greatly from one system to another. In other words, *this program might not work on your computer*. It should, but it might not. If it does not work, you may have to work around it. Perhaps you could develop your own keyboard device driver (see Chapter 9, "Device Drivers," for information about device drivers).

Listing 2.3. BUFFMOVE.ASM

```
Page 60,132

Comment ¦
*******************************************************************


File:       BUFFMOVE.ASM
Author:     Allen L. Wyatt
Date:       3/21/92
Assembler:  MASM 6.0

Purpose:    Moves the keyboard buffer pointers to new location
            in the 64K of memory beginning at 0040:0000.

Format:     BUFFMOVE


*******************************************************************¦
```

```
Head         EQU     01Ah
Tail         EQU     01Ch
OrigBuff     EQU     01Eh
BuffStart    EQU     080h
BuffEnd      EQU     082h

NewBuff      EQU     200h
NewEnd       EQU     300h

             .MODEL  small
             .STACK                     ;Default 1K stack is OK

             .CODE
             .STARTUP

BUFFMOVE     PROC

             PUSH    DS
             MOV     AX,040h             ;Point to BIOS data area
             MOV     DS,AX

             MOV     AX,NewBuff          ;Set start of buffer
             MOV     BX,BuffStart
             MOV     [BX],AX
             MOV     BX,Head
             MOV     [BX],AX             ;Move head and tail into
             MOV     BX,Tail             ;the new buffer area
             MOV     [BX],AX

             MOV     AX,NewEnd           ;Set end of buffer
             MOV     BX,BuffEnd
             MOV     [BX],AX

             POP     DS
             .EXIT
BuffMove     ENDP

             END
```

Give the program a try. It quickly and easily expands your keyboard buffer to 127 characters, which should make even the fastest typists happy. You can try this program without decreasing your available memory.

Stuffing the Keyboard Buffer

Now that you have enlarged the keyboard buffer, you can't let all that room go to waste, right? Right. One of the new BIOS keyboard functions enables you to stuff the keyboard buffer with keypresses. You can add to your programs the capability to put information directly into the keyboard buffer, which is executed by DOS when you exit from your program. For a somewhat trivial example of this capability, enter the program in Listing 2.4.

Listing 2.4. BUFFSTUF.ASM

```
Page 60,132


Comment ¦
*********************************************************************


File:      BUFFSTUF.ASM
Author:    Allen L. Wyatt
Date:      3/21/92
Assembler: MASM 6.0

Purpose:   Stuff characters into the keyboard buffer, which will
           be executed by DOS when the program is completed.

Format:    BUFFSTUF.ASM


*********************************************************************¦


           .MODEL  small
           .STACK                      ;Default 1K stack is OK
           .DATA

OKMsg      DB      'BUFFSTUF has completed working. Now returning to DOS...$'
FullMsg    DB      'Sorry; the keyboard buffer is full. Flushing buffer...$'
```

```
; The following line to be stuffed into the buffer works with DOS 5. It can
; be changed with no ill effects to the program. All commands will be
; stuffed until a NULL character is reached. The 0Dh is a carriage return
; and will cause DOS to execute the line before it.

Stuffer     DB        'dir',0Dh
            DB        'cls',0Dh
            DB        'type buffstuf.asm',0Dh
            DB        'Well, that',27h,'s about it. (Now for an Esc)',1Bh
            DB        00

            .CODE
            .STARTUP

BUFFSTUF    PROC

            MOV       SI,OFFSET Stuffer    ;Point to start of stuffing
            CLD                            ;Make sure the direction flag is OK
St1:        LODSB                          ;Get the character
            CMP       AL,0                 ;Is it the ending signal?
            JE        StDone               ;Yes, so exit
            MOV       CL,AL                ;Put ASCII in proper place
            MOV       CH,0                 ;Don't care about the scan code
            MOV       AH,5                 ;Stuffing routine
            INT       16h
            CMP       AL,1                 ;If the buffer is full, AL=1
            JNE       St1
            CALL      ClrBuff              ;Go clear the buffer
            MOV       DX,Offset FullMsg    ;Point to full message
            JMP       Exit

StDone:     MOV       DX,Offset OKMsg      ;Point to Everything OK message
Exit:       MOV       AH,9                 ;Display a string using DOS
            INT       21h

            .EXIT
BUFFSTUF    ENDP

; The following routine clears the entire keyboard buffer
```

continues

Listing 2.4. Continued

```
ClrBuff    PROC    USES AX
CB1:       MOV     AH,1              ;Read keyboard status
           INT     16h
           JZ      CBExit            ;No key, so exit
           MOV     AH,0              ;Read keyboard character
           INT     16h
           JMP     CB1               ;Go do it all again
CBExit:    RET
ClrBuff    ENDP

           END
```

This program uses Int 16/05 to stuff characters into the keyboard buffer. This function returns with AL=0 if it was able to stuff the character. If not, AL=1 on return.

Notice that BUFFSTUF stuffs a rather long string (beginning at Stuffer in the listing). If you have not expanded your keyboard buffer as described earlier in this chapter, you may run out of buffer space. If this is the case, you receive an error message when you run BUFFSTUF. To run the program successfully, you must either shorten the string being stuffed or expand your buffer with a program such as BUFFMOVE.

Summary

This chapter has covered keyboard-related issues in depth. You have learned what is involved in programming the keyboard at various levels, including writing your own interrupt handlers. You can produce, on your own, any number of utilities using the techniques presented in this chapter.

In Chapter 3, you learn about another integral part of your daily work with computers: how to work with disk files.

Serial Communications

Two general types of communication occur between computers or between a computer and a peripheral: *Parallel communications* involve sending information one byte at a time across eight different data lines; *serial communications* involve sending information one bit at a time across one data line. As you probably already know, information travels across a parallel channel much more quickly than across a serial channel. This faster parallel speed often is cited as the biggest advantage to using parallel communications between computer devices.

Perhaps the biggest advantage to serial communications, however, is that they typically are bidirectional; parallel communications are not. You can send information to a remote device or computer as it is sending information to you. Sounds easy, but it can be very complicated and tricky. This is one reason that many programmers choose to steer clear of programming for serial communications.

Before getting into actual programming, you should understand a few of the underlying concepts of serial communications on the PC. This invaluable preliminary information is intended as a quick introduction. If you want more detailed information, refer to *C Programmer's Guide to Serial Communications*, by Joe Campbell (Howard W. Sams & Co., 1987).

Some Basic Terminology

Computer use and programming are rife with many terms that make up (or so it seems) a peculiar language. Nowhere is this more evident than in the world of serial communications. There are several terms you must understand before discussing serial programming topics in depth.

The communication link between two devices is known as the *channel*. The device that is sending information is the *transmitter*. It is the transmitter's responsibility to break down the information into individual bits that can be sent over the channel. The device that is receiving information, the *receiver*, is responsible for reassembling the bits coming across the channel into a byte that matches the one sent by the transmitter.

As mentioned, information travels across a serial channel as series of bits. The collection of bits that make up a single byte are sent in a *data packet*. The exact composition of this packet depends on the type of serial communication taking place.

There are two types of serial communication. *Synchronous communication* occurs when the intercharacter timing across the channel is exactly synchronized between the transmitter and the receiver. Periodically, a sync character is transmitted across the channel to ensure that both transmitter and receiver are exactly synchronized. Otherwise, only the bits that make up the data being transmitted are sent across the channel. These types of communication channels are expensive to maintain, and typically involve leased data lines.

Asynchronous communication occurs when the transmitter and the receiver do not have to be exactly synchronized. The transmitter can send information as it is available, and the receiver decodes it as received, with no regard to the time period in which they appear. Asynchronous communication channels are much cheaper to establish and maintain than are synchronous channels. For this reason, virtually all the serial communications that occur in PCs are asynchronous.

To communicate asynchronously, the transmitter has the added responsibility of transmitting complete data packets, which consist of a *start bit, data bits,* a *parity bit,* and *stop bits*. Figure 3.1 illustrates a typical asynchronous data packet.

Figure 3.1.

A typical data packet.

When the transmitter and receiver are communicating asynchronously, it is important that they both know exactly how the data packets will be constructed. Therefore, you will hear nomenclature such as N81, which means no parity, 8 data bits, and 1 stop bit. The beginning of each data packet always has 1 stop bit. The rest of the parameters are open to modification.

Communicating over the Channel

How does the asynchronous communication occur? It begins by establishing communication between the transmitter and receiver. The primary component of establishing successful communication is the *data rate*, typically expressed as the *baud rate*. It is more accurate, however, to refer to the data rate in terms of *bits per second*, or *bps*. The data rate indicates how many bits the transmitter can place over the channel each second, and how many bits the receiver should expect. Common data rates are 1200, 2400, and 9600 bps.

When a channel has been established between the transmitter and receiver, the receiver sits idle and waits for an electronic signal to appear on the channel to indicate that a bit is being sent. When a bit is detected, the receiver synchronizes itself to the timing of the first bit—and for this reason is called a start bit. The start bit is used by the receiver only to prepare to receive the data bits that follow. After the data bits are synchronized, they are received and processed into a single byte.

The parity bit, which follows the data bits, is used to determine whether an error occurred during transmission. If an error is detected, a request is sent to the transmitter asking for the data packet to be resent. If the parity is not being ignored (remember that the *N* in N81 means no parity) or if no error was detected, the byte is stored for use by the main computer. The stop bits signal the end of the data packet, which puts the receiver in the mode to begin looking for the start of the next data packet.

Sound simple? It really is a much more simple process than in the early days of computers when it had to be managed by software. Now it is handled by hardware, the topic of the following section.

The Hardware

The computer chip that makes the procedure discussed in the preceding section possible is a *Universal Asynchronous Receiver/Transmitter*, or *UART*. The first UART in wide use in PCs was the National Semiconductor 8250. Other chips from other manufacturers are used in some PCs, but they all effectively operate in the same way. Regardless of the make and part number, the UART handles the translation of bytes into bits, by framing them into data packets, sending them over the channel, and reassembling them at the other end of the link. The UART is the heart of all serial communications in PCs.

You communicate with the UART through a series of memory ports mapped directly to the UART's registers. There are ten single-byte registers accessed through seven memory port addresses. Most of the ports are used for initializing and programming the UART; only a few are used to transfer data. Table 3.1

shows the registers and ports that have meaning for the UART. The registers are shown as offsets of the base memory address, which varies depending on the serial port being used. These base addresses are shown in Table 3.2.

Table 3.1. The UART registers and PC memory ports.

Offset	LSR Setting	Name	Use
0	0	THR	Transmitter holding register
	0	RDR	Receiver data register
	1	BRDL	Low byte, baud rate divisor
1	0	IER	Interrupt enable register
	1	BRDH	High byte, baud rate divisor
2		IIR	Interrupt ID register
3		LCR	Line control register
4		MCR	Modem control register
5		LSR	Line status register
6		MSR	Modem status register

Table 3.2. The PC serial port base addresses.

Base Address	Port Name
03F8h	COM1:
02F8h	COM2:
03E8h	COM3:
02E8h	COM4:

From Tables 3.1 and 3.2, you can determine that if you want to access the LSR for COM3:, you access the port at memory address 03EDh. Notice in Table 3.1 that only seven ports control ten registers on the UART. This section discusses each UART register and how each one works in relation to the ports.

Transmitter Holding Register (THR)

The transmitter holding register is accessible when bit 7 of the line status register (LSR) is clear. You output to this port the information you want the UART to transmit across the channel. You should write information to the THR port only when bit 5 of the line status register (LSR) is clear.

Receiver Data Register (RDR)

The receiver data register is accessible when bit 7 of the line status register (LSR) is clear. When bit 0 of the LSR is set, you can input information from the RDR port. The byte you receive from this port is the freshly received data from the UART.

Baud Rate Divisor (BRDL and BRDH)

The baud rate divisor is accessed through two registers and two data ports. You must set bit 7 of the line status register (LSR) first, and then you can set the BRD. The BRD specifies the bit transfer rate the UART will use. The BRD is determined by dividing the clock speed used by the UART by 16 times the desired transfer rate:

$$BRD = \frac{UART\ clock\ speed}{16 \times bps}$$

Notice that the UART clock speed is used—not your CPU's clock speed. The UART clock speed is always 1.8432 MHz, the clock speed of the original IBM PC. Therefore, to determine the baud rate divisor for a 2400 bps transfer rate, you use this formula:

$$BRD = \frac{1,843,200}{16 \times 2,400} = \frac{1,843,200}{38,400} = 48$$

The baud rate divisor therefore is 48, or 30h. The BRDH value is 0, and the BRDL value is 30h. Table 3.3 shows different baud rate divisor values for some common data-transfer rates.

Table 3.3. Baud rate divisors for common data-transfer rates.

Data Rate	BRD	BRDH	BRDL
300	0180h	01h	80h
1200	0060h	00h	60h
2400	0030h	00h	30h
9600	000Ch	00h	0Ch
19200	0006h	00h	06h
38400	0003h	00h	03h

Interrupt Enable Register (IER)

The interrupt enable register is accessible when bit 7 of the line status register (LSR) is clear. The IER controls the type of interrupts the IER can generate. Table 3.4 shows the possible settings for this register.

Table 3.4. Interrupt enable register settings.

Bit Settings 76543210	Action Resulting in an Interrupt
1	Data available in RDR
1	THR is empty
1	Data error or receipt of break
1	MSR has changed
xxxx	Unused (always 0)

To develop an interrupt-driven serial communications routine, as you do later in this chapter, in the section "Writing an Interrupt-Driven Program," you must set the desired bits of the IER so that the interrupt will be generated.

Interrupt Identification Register (IIR)

The contents of the interrupt identification register are used to indicate the type of interrupt generated by the UART. When an interrupt occurs, you should examine the contents of the IIR register to determine the type of interrupt that occurred. Table 3.5 shows the bit meanings for this register.

Table 3.5. Interrupt identification register bit settings.

Bit settings 76543210	Meaning
1	More than one interrupt occurred
00	MSR has changed
01	THR is empty
10	Data available in RDR
11	Data error or receipt of break
xxxxx	Unused

Line Control Register (LCR)

The line control register is used to set the communications parameters used by the UART. Table 3.6 shows the bit settings for the LCR register.

Table 3.6. Line control register bit settings.

Bit settings 76543210	Meaning
00	5-bit character length
01	6-bit character length
10	7-bit character length
11	8-bit character length
0	1 stop bit
1	1.5 stop bits if using 5-bit character length; 2 stop bits if using 6-, 7-, or 8-bit character length
000	Ignore parity
100	ODD parity
110	EVEN parity
101	MARK parity

continues

Table 3.6. Continued

Bit settings 76543210	Meaning
111	SPACE parity
0	Break disabled
1	Break enabled
0	Normal use of port offsets 0 and 1
1	Alternative use of port offsets 0 and 1

Modem Control Register (MCR)

The modem control register is used to directly control the DTR and RTS signal lines, and to control other modem functions. Table 3.7 lists the bit settings for the MCR register.

Table 3.7. Modem control register settings.

Bit settings 76543210	Meaning
1	Activate DTR line
1	Activate RTS line
1	Activate user output line #1
1	Enable interrupts (user output line #2)
1	Enable UART loopback testing
xxx	Unused (always 0)

Line Status Register (LSR)

The line status register is used to determine the status of the communications channel. Generally it is inspected if your program detects an error during transmission, or if you are not using interrupt-driven software. Table 3.8 shows the bit meanings for the LSR register.

Table 3.8. Line status register bit meanings.

Bit settings 76543210	Meaning
1	Data available in RDR
1	Overrun error
1	Parity error
1	Framing error
1	Break detect
1	THR is empty
1	TSR is empty
x	Unused

Modem Status Register (MSR)

The last register discussed in this section, the modem status register, is used to signal the status of modem control lines. Table 3.9 lists the meanings of the bits in the MSR register.

Table 3.9. Modem status register bit meanings.

Bit settings 76543210	Meaning
1	Clear to send (CTS) status has changed
1	Data set ready (DSR) status has changed
1	Ring indicator (RI) status has changed
1	Data carrier detect (DCD) status has changed
1	CTS is active
1	DSR is active
1	RI is active
1	DCD is active

The BIOS Serial Communications Functions

Six different BIOS functions control serial communications. All these functions are accessible through interrupt 14h; they are summarized in Table 3.10.

Table 3.10. The BIOS serial communication functions.

Function	Name
00h	Initialize port
01h	Write character to port
02h	Read character from port
03h	Request port status
04h	PS/2 extended initialization
05h	Extended port control

Most of these functions have been included in every version of the BIOS shipped with every version of the IBM PC. The exceptions are functions 04h and 05h, available only in the PS/2 line. Because those computers represent a relatively small portion of the programming platform (I assume that you are programming for the widest possible platform), these extended functions are not discussed in this book.

Let's look at each basic BIOS serial communications function.

Initializing the Port

To initialize the communications port, you use interrupt 14h, function 00h. You simply load the AL register with an initialization parameter (see Table 3.11) and load the DX register with the communications port to initialize, where 0=COM1, 1=COM2, and so on.

Table 3.11. BIOS communications function 00h initialization values.

Bit settings 76543210	Meaning
10	7 data bits
11	8 data bits
0	1 stop bit
1	2 stop bits
00	No parity
01	Odd parity
10	No parity
11	Even parity
000	110 baud
001	150 baud
010	300 baud
011	600 baud
100	1200 baud
101	2400 baud
110	4800 baud
111	9600 baud

When the BIOS function is invoked, the initialization value in AL is split between the different serial port registers necessary to effect the initialization. When the function returns, it provides information about the port status (AH) and the modem status (AL). The modem status returned in AL corresponds to the bit values in Table 3.9. The port status values returned in AH are similar to the line status values in Table 3.8, with one exception: As you can see in Table 3.12, the line status register's unused seventh bit is used by this function to indicate whether a time-out occurred during the operation.

Table 3.12. Port status register bit meanings.

Bit settings 76543210	Meaning
1	Data available in RDR
1	Overrun error
1	Parity error

continues

Table 3.12. Continued

Bit settings 76543210	Meaning
1	Framing error
1	Break detect
1	THR is empty
1	TSR is empty
1	Time-out

The following code fragment is an example of how to use this function:

```
.CODE
MOV    AH,0                ;Initialize port
MOV    DX,0                ;Using COM1:
MOV    AL,10100111b        ;Set for N81, 2400 baud
INT    14h
```

This code fragment does not show anything being done with the status values returned by the initialization function, but you can examine them and take appropriate actions.

Outputting a Character to the Port

Interrupt 14h, function 01h is used to output a character to a communications port. You should be sure that the port has been initialized previously using function 00h. When your program calls this function, AL must contain the character you want output through the port, and DX contains the port number to use (0=COM1, 1=COM2, and so on).

On return, AH contains the port status detailed in Table 3.12. By examining bit 7, you can determine whether a time-out occurred. If a time-out occurred, the values in bits 0 through 6 indicate the reason.

The following code fragment shows how to use this function:

```
.CODE
MOV    AH,1                ;Write character to port
LODSB                      ;Load AL from DS:[SI]
MOV    DX,0                ;Using COM1:
INT    14h
TEST   AH,10000000b        ;Test if bit 7 set
JNZ    XmitError           ;Yes, error occurred
```

Reading a Character from the Port

After you have initialized the communications port (see function 00h), you can use interrupt 14h, function 02h to read a character from the port. As with the other communications functions, you must load DX with the communications port you want (0=COM1, 1=COM2, and so on) before you call the function.

When this function is called, it waits until a character is ready at the serial port. If the time-out period expires before a character is received, the function returns anyway. On return, examine the contents of the AH register. This port status register is detailed in Table 3.12. If bit 7 is clear, the character read from the port is in the AL register. If bit 7 is set, you can examine bits 0 through 6 to determine the cause of the error.

The following code shows how to use this function:

```
.CODE
MOV     AH,1                    ;Write character to port
MOV     DX,0                    ;Using COM1:
INT     14h
TEST    AH,10000000b            ;Test if bit 7 set
JNZ     XmitError               ;Yes, error occurred
STOSB                           ;Store AL at ES:[DI]
```

Determining the Port Status

Interrupt 14, function 03h is used to determine the status of the communications port. It returns the same information returned by function 00h. When you load the DX register with the communications port you want to query (0=COM1, 1=COM2, and so on), the function returns the port status register in AH (refer to Table 3.12) and the modem status register in AL (refer to Table 3.9).

You should use this function when you are curious about the status of the port, and when you don't want the extra overhead involved in initializing the port.

Polling Versus Interrupt-Driven Routines

Polling is a process by which your program examines the serial port for incoming data when your program is ready, rather than when the serial port has information ready for your program. Therefore, you can retrieve information only if both your program and the serial port are ready at the same time.

An interrupt-driven program enables your program to accomplish tasks and then be interrupted when the serial port has information available for processing.

Because the polling process can be hit-and-miss in nature, you must be eminently concerned with timing. For instance, you must make sure that your program does not perform any task that takes so long that the serial port receives more than a single character without being polled. Doing so can be more difficult than it sounds. For instance, what if your program is handling a massive screen update or writing information to disk? If the video hardware or the disk drive is slower than you anticipated, you may miss a polling cycle and lose incoming data.

Typically, this timing is not a problem; through careful programming, you can dedicate large periods of time to polling the serial port so that no data is lost. A timing problem becomes more likely, however, as the communications speed used for your serial port increases. At 2400 baud, you receive approximately 240 characters each second on an active channel. This number of characters can be readily serviced for short periods. The next step in modems, however—9600 baud—sends information at 960 characters per second. It is virtually impossible for your computer to keep up with this volume of data, particularly if your program must also *do something* with the data received.

At higher speeds, you must, for the sake of data integrity, use interrupt-driven techniques to receive data. Fortunately, the UART included in your PC makes this process relatively painless, as shown later in this chapter, when you develop an interrupt-driven program.

Writing a Polling Program

Before this section discusses writing an interrupt-driven program, you may find it useful to examine an example of a polling program. The program in this section, POLL.ASM, uses the BIOS functions described earlier to accomplish the following steps:

1. Initialize the communications port.

2. Check for a keypress in the keyboard buffer; retrieve and transmit it if it is present.

3. Check for an incoming character from the serial port; retrieve and print it if it is present.

4. Continue steps 2 and 3 until the Esc key is pressed.

This basic procedure is followed in all polling programs. Check for the occurrence of one event, and then check for another. If the checked-for event has occurred, ignore everything else until processing of that event is completed. The program in Listing 3.1, POLL.ASM, implements these steps.

Listing 3.1. POLL.ASM

```
Page 60,132


Comment ¦
*********************************************************************


File:       POLL.ASM
Author:     Allen L. Wyatt
Date:       6/27/92
Assembler:  MASM 6.0

Purpose:    A mini-terminal program. Displays on the screen all the
            info coming into the modem. Anything typed is sent to
            the modem. Uses polling techniques and BIOS functions
            for all communications access. Program is exited when
            Esc is pressed.

Format:     POLL


*********************************************************************¦

; The following equates are modem configuration settings.
ComPort     EQU     01h                 ;0=COM1, 1=COM2, 2=COM3, 3=COM4

; The following equates are for data format settings
DF_N81      EQU     10100011b           ;2400 bps, 8 data bits, 1 stop bit, no parity
DF_E71      EQU     10111010b           ;2400 bps, 7 data bits, 1 stop bit, even parity

            .MODEL  small
            .STACK                      ;Default 1K stack is OK

            .CODE
            .STARTUP
```

continues

Listing 3.1. Continued

```
Poll        PROC
            MOV     AH,00h              ;Initialize communications port
            MOV     AL,DF_E71           ;2400 bps, E71
            MOV     DX,ComPort          ;Using this port
            INT     14h
            CALL    Cls

InputLoop:  MOV     AH,1                ;Check keyboard status
            INT     16h
            JZ      NoKey               ;No key there

            MOV     AH,0                ;Get key
            INT     16h
            CMP     AH,1                ;Was the key Escape? (scan code=1)
            JE      AllDone             ;Yes, so exit
            MOV     AH,01h              ;No, so write character in AL to port
            MOV     DX,ComPort          ;Send to this port
            INT     14h

NoKey:      MOV     AH,03h              ;Get port status
            MOV     DX,ComPort          ;From this port
            INT     14h
            TEST    AH,00000001b        ;Is data ready?
            JZ      InputLoop           ;No, so go back in loop

            MOV     AH,02h              ;Read character from port
            MOV     DX,ComPort          ;From this port
            INT     14h
            TEST    AH,10000000b        ;Was there a time-out?
            JZ      NoTimeout           ;No, continue
            TEST    AH,00011110b        ;If not these errors, then data not ready
            JZ      InputLoop
            MOV     AL,'!'              ;Indicate data loss
NoTimeout:  MOV     DL,AL
            MOV     AH,02h              ;Output a character
            INT     21h
            JMP     InputLoop

AllDone:    .EXIT
Poll        ENDP
```

```
; The following routine clears the screen and homes the cursor.

Cls        PROC    USES AX BX CX DX
           MOV     AH,6                  ;Scroll window up
           MOV     AL,0                  ;Scroll full screen
           MOV     BH,7                  ;Normal white on black
           MOV     CX,0                  ;Upper left corner of screen
           MOV     DH,24                 ;Bottom right
           MOV     DL,79
           INT     10h

           MOV     DX,0                  ;Upper left corner of screen
           MOV     BH,0                  ;Assume page 0
           MOV     AH,2                  ;Set cursor position
           INT     10h
           RET
Cls        ENDP

           END
```

Through use of the BIOS communications functions, the program is relatively short. The main polling loop begins at the label InputLoop, and continues through fully handling any event that may occur when a character is ready at the serial port.

The communications parameters for this program are set through a series of equates near the start of the program. The baud rate is set at 2400 bps, which is relatively low by today's standards. Even so, this program is unreliable for catching all data coming into the serial port. I assembled and ran this program on a 33 MHz 386 machine, and it still lost data.

Such unreliability in a program is unacceptable by any standard. It is difficult to fault the program, however, when the blame can be laid squarely on the methodology used in the program. Let's start the process of learning how to program the UART directly and then develop an interrupt-driven program that will not lose data.

Programming the UART

Before you can write an interrupt-driven program, you must understand how to program the UART. Most of the programming fundamentals were discussed early in this chapter, in the section "The Hardware," when the registers and port addresses were discussed. This section, however, describes the way you must program each of the UART elements in order to use them properly.

This list shows the tasks that must be accomplished:

■ Determine the port addresses to use.

■ Set the data format.

■ Set the data speed (baud rate).

■ Set DTR/RTS values.

■ Turn on interrupts.

The order in which you complete these items is not particularly important, with the exception of the first and last items on the list. You must know the port addresses you want to use to accomplish the other tasks on the list. It is a good idea to enable interrupts after you have set the rest of your communication parameters.

Determining the Port Addresses to Use

The first step in programming the UART is to determine which communications port you will use; on the PC, these ports typically are COM1, COM2, COM3, or COM4. For illustration, let's assume that you will work with COM2. Based on your understanding of the information in Tables 3.1 and 3.2, therefore, the register addresses for COM2 are as shown in Table 3.13.

Table 3.13. The UART registers for COM2.

Port Address	LSR Setting	Name	Use
2F8h	0	THR	Transmitter holding register
	0	RDR	Receiver data register
	1	BRDL	Low byte, baud rate divisor
2F9h	0	IER	Interrupt enable register
	1	BRDH	High byte, baud rate divisor
2FAh		IIR	Interrupt ID register
2FBh		LCR	Line control register
2FCh		MCR	Modem control register
2FDh		LSR	Line status register
2FEh		MSR	Modem status register

Setting the Data Format

Now that you know which port addresses you will use, the next step is to set the data format you want to use. You do this through the line control register. Remember, from Table 3.6, that the line control register is used to set the number of data bits, stop bits, and parity. For example, suppose that you want to set the data format for COM2 to 8 data bits, no parity, and 1 stop bit (often referred to simply as N81). The following code accomplishes this task:

```
MOV     DX,2FBh             ;Point to line control register
MOV     AL,00000011b        ;Set for N81
OUT     DX,AL               ;Send byte
```

Setting the Data Speed

The data speed, known also as the baud rate, is set in a two-step process. The first step, setting bit 7 of the line control register, enables the baud rate divisor registers to be addressed. Then you set the low-order and high-order baud rate divisors to the proper value for the data speed you want.

Table 3.3 showed also that the setting of the BRDH register is always 0 at higher data speeds. The value of the BRDL varies depending on the data speed. For example, let's assume that you want to set the data speed for COM2 to 9600 bps. The following code accomplishes this task:

```
MOV     DX,2FBh             ;Point to line control register
IN      AL,DX               ;Get what is there
OR      AL,10000000b        ;Set bit 7 to enable alternate registers
OUT     DX,AL               ;Send the byte

DEC     DX                  ;Point to MSB of baud rate divisor
DEC     DX
MOV     AL,0
OUT     DX,AL

DEC     DX                  ;Point to LSB of baud rate divisor
MOV     AL,0Ch
OUT     DX,AL

ADD     DX,3                ;Point to line control register
IN      AL,DX               ;Get what is there
AND     AL,01111111b        ;Clear bit 7 to enable normal registers
OUT     DX,AL               ;Send the byte
```

Set the DTR/RTS Values

Setting the DTR/RTS values is optional depending on your modem. If your modem pays no attention to the DTR or RTS lines, you can skip this step. Most newer, high-speed modems require the use of the RTS line to indicate when it is OK for the modem to send information to the computer. Turning the line on indicates that it is OK to send information; turning it off inhibits any data transfer to the computer.

The DTR line, on the other hand, typically is considered the "master switch" for the modem. Without asserting the line (turning it on), the modem could not go or remain on-line. DTR, an acronym for *data terminal ready*, is a signal that everything is ready for operation of the modem.

The DTR and RTS are set using the modem control register. Refer to Table 3.7 to see that bits 0 and 1 of the register control these lines. The following code is used to accomplish the task of asserting DTR and RTS:

```
MOV     DX,2FCh                 ;Point to modem control register
IN      AL,DX                   ;Get what is there
AND     AL,00001100b            ;Turn off loopback testing
OR      AL,00000011b            ;Turn on DTR/RTS
OUT     DX,AL                   ;Send it back out
```

Notice that an additional step has been added to this code. This step makes sure (for good measure) that the UART loopback test control bit (bit 4) is cleared. This code also leaves bits 2 and 3 in their original state.

Turn on the Interrupts

The final step in programming the UART is to turn on the interrupts. The execution of this step assumes two things: that you already have set the interrupt vector for your modem interrupt handler and that you have finished setting up the UART as described in previous sections.

You must complete several steps and manipulate several registers to enable interrupts. The first step concerns the modem control register. Bit 3 of this register must be turned on. This action enables the UART to generate interrupts; if this bit is not turned on, the UART never generates an interrupt.

The following code sets bit 3 of the modem control register:

```
MOV     DX,2FCh                 ;Point to modem control register
IN      AL,DX                   ;Get what is there
OR      AL,00001000b            ;Enable interrupts
OUT     DX,AL                   ;Send it back out
```

Because this task involves manipulating the modem control register, most programmers combine this step with the previous step that turned on the DTR and RTS signals.

The next task is to enable the interrupts for the COM ports. Remember from Chapter 1, "Interrupt Handlers," that it is the responsibility of a programmable interrupt controller, or PIC, to manage system interrupts. Port 21h contains the interrupt mask register used by the PIC. Each bit of this register corresponds to a specific IRQ that can be generated by the system. This information is summarized in Table 3.14.

Table 3.13. The PIC interrupt mask register bit meanings. (Setting the bit disables the associated IRQ.)

Bit settings 76543210	Interrupt	Meaning
x	IRQ0	System timer tick
x	IRQ1	Keyboard
x	IRQ2	Cascade to secondary PIC
x	IRQ3	COM2/COM4
x	IRQ4	COM1/COM3
x	IRQ5	LPT2
x	IRQ6	Diskette controller
x	IRQ7	LPT1

To enable system interrupts for a particular device, the corresponding bit in the interrupt mask register must be cleared. To enable interrupts for the com ports, therefore, it is necessary to clear bits 3 and 4. It is acceptable to enable only a specific port, but clearing both bits works also. The following code accomplishes this task:

```
IN      AL,21h              ;Get current contents of interrupt mask
AND     AL,11100111b        ;Make sure that both COMs are enabled
OUT     21h,AL
```

The final step in enabling interrupts is to set the bits in the interrupt enable register corresponding to the events for which you want interrupts enabled. To keep matters simple, in most cases you enable interrupts only for when data is available from the serial port. Refer to Table 3.4 to see that this statement means that bit 0 must be set. All other bits in the register can remain clear. The following code performs this task:

```
MOV     DX,ComAddr+1        ;Point to interrupt enable register
MOV     AL,00000001b        ;Turn on bit 0
OUT     DX,AL               ;Set it
```

Now that you know all the steps in programming the UART, you are ready to pull them together to create an entire interrupt-driven program.

Writing an Interrupt-Driven Program

Recall from Chapter 1 that interrupts are an efficient method of working with the computer. After you set up your interrupts, you can do virtually any task, and your interrupt handlers can monitor and service external events. Because of this efficiency and capability, interrupt handlers are well-suited to serial communications routines.

This section discusses how to write a simple terminal program that is interrupt-driven. The tasks performed by this program include the following:

- Hook in the interrupt handler

- Set up the modem

- Clear the screen

- Check for input from the keyboard; if available, send it to the modem.

- Check the input buffer to see whether any data has arrived from the modem; print it if it has.

- Continue steps 4 and 5 until the Esc key is pressed.

The main difference between this program approach and the one used in the polling example is that there is no explicit step to check the serial port. This step is handled by the interrupt handler mentioned in the first task. It does only one thing—stores any information it receives in a memory buffer where it later can be processed independently of when it was received across the communications channel.

The program presented in this section relies on a circular buffer to hold information that is received. You decide the size of this circular buffer; this example uses a 2K buffer. In other words, it holds almost an entire screen of data. This buffer area is administered in much the same way as the circular keyboard buffer discussed in Chapter 2, "Controlling the Keyboard."

Why do you put received information in a buffer? Because, if you print directly to the screen, the BIOS or DOS functions slow down the program enough that you can lose data coming into the line. The idea behind an interrupt handler is to do the minimum amount of processing necessary to ensure that the received data is not lost.

Earlier, this chapter mentioned that POLL.ASM is unreliable in receiving data because the program cannot process the received information quickly enough. With the interrupt-driven program, however, data can be received at much higher data speeds. I have tested TERM.ASM at 9600 bps, for real communications purposes (that is, CompuServe). It performed admirably, without losing a single byte.

At the beginning of TERM.ASM are several equate statements for the labels ComInt, ComAddr, BRDMSB, and BRDLSB. These labels must be set to the values that match your modem's capabilities and the needs of your communication session. You also must set the data format in the Hookin subroutine. The easiest way to do so is to set equates at the beginning of the program and then change the equate name in the routine. Two data format equates, DF_N81 and DF_E71, already are defined at the beginning of the program. The complete listing for TERM.ASM is shown in Listing 3.2.

Listing 3.2. TERM.ASM

```
Page 60,132

Comment ¦
******************************************************************


File:       TERM.ASM
Author:     Allen L. Wyatt
Date:       6/27/92
Assembler:  MASM 6.0

Purpose:    A mini-terminal program. Displays on the screen all the
            info coming into the modem. Anything typed is sent to
            the modem. Uses interrupt-driven techniques for all
            communications access. Program is exited when Esc is
            pressed.

Format:     TERM


******************************************************************¦
                                                                 ¦

TimeOut    EQU    364                ;20 seconds (18.2 * 20)
NormWait   EQU    18                 ;1 second
BuffSize   EQU    2048               ;Size of incoming buffer (in bytes)
```

continues

Listing 3.2. Continued

```
; The following equates are modem configuration settings
ComInt     EQU     0Bh                 ;COM1/COM3=0Ch, COM2/COM4=0Bh
ComAddr    EQU     2F8h                ;COM1=3F8h, COM2=2F8h, COM3=3E8h, COM4=2E8h
BRDMSB     EQU     0                   ;See book for common BRD values
BRDLSB     EQU     0Ch

; The following equates are for data format settings
DF_N81     EQU     00000011b           ;8 data bits, 1 stop bit, no parity
DF_E71     EQU     00011010b           ;7 data bits, 1 stop bit, even parity

           .MODEL  small
           .STACK                      ;Default 1K stack is OK
           .DATA

VectorSeg  DW      0000
VectorOff  DW      0000
XmitCount  DW      0000
CTMax      DW      0000

SetUpMsg   DB      'Setting up modem information ...',13,10,0
MemMsg     DB      'Could not allocate buffer space',13,10,0
RemindMsg  DB      'Press ESC to exit program',13,10,13,10,0

           .CODE
           .STARTUP
Term       PROC

; The following memory allocation code works because it is known that MASM
; sets DS and SS to the same segment address in the start-up code. Also, ES
; is set to the PSP for the program on entry.

           MOV     BX,DS               ;Point to start of data segment
           MOV     AX,ES               ;Point to start of PSP
           SUB     BX,AX               ;Number of segments for code and data
           MOV     AX,SP               ;SP is pointing to top of stack area
           MOV     CL,4                ;Dividing by 16
           SHR     AX,CL
           ADD     BX,AX               ;BX=paragraphs needed
           MOV     AH,4Ah              ;Modify memory allocation
           INT     21h
```

```
            MOV     AH,48h                  ;Allocate memory
            MOV     BX,BuffSize/16          ;Paragraphs to request
            INT     21h
            JNC     MemOK                   ;No errors
            MOV     SI,OFFSET MemMsg
            CALL    PrtString
            JMP     AllDone

MemOK:      MOV     CS:BuffSeg,AX           ;Store segment address
            CALL    HookIn                  ;Go hook interrupt information
            CALL    Cls
            MOV     SI,OFFSET RemindMsg     ;Reminder about how to exit
            CALL    PrtString

InputLoop:  MOV     AH,1                    ;Check keyboard status
            INT     16h
            JZ      NoKey                   ;No key there
            MOV     AH,0                    ;Get key
            INT     16h
            CMP     AH,1                    ;Was the key Escape? (scan code=1)
            JE      AllDone                 ;Yes, so exit
            CALL    XmitChar                ;Send the character in AL to modem
            JNC     NoKey                   ;No error, so continue
            MOV     DL,'!'                  ;Indication there was a time-out
            MOV     AH,02h                  ;Output a character
            INT     21h

NoKey:      CALL    BuffChar                ;Go see if anything in buffer to display
            JMP     InputLoop

AllDone:    MOV     ES,CS:BuffSeg
            MOV     AH,49h                  ;Release memory block at ES
            INT     21h
            CALL    HookOut
            .EXIT
Term        ENDP
```

```
; The following routine hooks in the interrupt routine and sets up the
; data format and communications parameters
```

continues

Listing 3.2. Continued

```
HookIn      PROC    USES AX DX SI

            MOV     SI,OFFSET SetUpMsg
            CALL    PrtString

            PUSH    ES
            MOV     AL,ComInt
            MOV     AH,35h              ;Get interrupt vector
            INT     21h
            MOV     VectorOff,BX        ;Store original offset
            MOV     VectorSeg,ES        ;Store original segment
            POP     ES

            MOV     AL,ComInt
            PUSH    DS
            PUSH    CS
            POP     DS
            MOV     DX,OFFSET IntHandler
            MOV     AH,25h              ;Set interrupt vector
            INT     21h
            POP     DS

            CLI
            MOV     DX,ComAddr+3        ;Point to line control register
            MOV     AL,DF_E71
            OUT     DX,AL               ;Send byte
            INC     DX                  ;Point to modem control register
            MOV     AL,00001011b
            OUT     DX,AL               ;Set it for interrupts

            IN      AL,21h              ;Get current contents of interrupt request mask
            AND     AL,11100111b        ;Make sure that both COMs are enabled
            OUT     21h,AL

            MOV     DX,ComAddr+1        ;Point to interrupt enable register
            MOV     AL,00000001b        ;Turn on bit 0
            OUT     DX,AL               ;Set it
            STI

            CALL    SetBRD              ;Go set for desired baud rate
```

```
          RET
HookIn    ENDP


; The following routine unhooks the interrupt handler

HookOut   PROC    USES AX DX SI
          MOV     DX,ComAddr+1        ;Point to interrupt enable register
          MOV     AL,0               ;Disable the interrupts
          OUT     DX,AL              ;Set it

          MOV     DX,ComAddr+1        ;Point to interrupt enable register
          MOV     AL,00000000b       ;Turn off all bits
          OUT     DX,AL              ;Set it

          IN      AL,21h             ;Get current contents of interrupt request mask
          OR      AL,00011000b       ;Make sure that both COMs are disabled
          OUT     21h,AL

          PUSH    DS                 ;Hold current data segment
          MOV     DS,VectorSeg       ;Get original segment
          MOV     DX,VectorOff
          MOV     AL,ComInt
          MOV     AH,25h             ;Set interrupt vector
          INT     21h
          POP     DS                 ;Get the data segment back

          RET
HookOut   ENDP


; Routine to check input buffer for info and display it if there

BuffChar  PROC    USES AX DX SI ES
          MOV     SI,CS:Tail
          CMP     SI,CS:Head         ;Any characters there?
          JE      NoInput            ;No, so continue

          MOV     ES,CS:BuffSeg      ;Point to buffer area
          CLD
BCLoop:   MOV     DL,ES:[SI]         ;Get character
          INC     SI                 ;Point to next character
```

continues

Listing 3.2. Continued

```
                MOV     AH,02h          ;Output character in DL
                INT     21h
                CMP     SI,BuffSize     ;End of buffer?
                JNE     NotAtEnd        ;No, continue
                MOV     SI,0            ;Point to beginning
NotAtEnd:       CMP     SI,CS:Head      ;At end of buffered data yet?
                JNE     BCLoop          ;No, grab another
                MOV     CS:Tail,SI      ;Update pointer

NoInput:        RET
BuffChar        ENDP


; Routine to transmit the character in AL out the rs232 port

XmitChar        PROC    USES AX BX DX
                PUSH    AX              ;Save character for a moment
                MOV     AH,0
                INT     1Ah             ;Get clock ticks
                MOV     XmitCount,DX    ;Store ticks for later

XC1:            MOV     DX,ComAddr+5    ;Point to line status register
                IN      AL,DX           ;Get status byte
                TEST    AL,00100000b    ;Test if ready to transmit character
                JNZ     XC2             ;Yes, so continue
                MOV     BX,XmitCount
                MOV     AX,NormWait     ;Wait 1 second
                CALL    CheckTime       ;Go see if time expired
                JNC     XC1             ;Time not up, wait in loop
                POP     AX              ;Get back character
                JMP     XCBad           ;Time up, exit with error

XC2:            POP     AX              ;Get character back
                MOV     DX,ComAddr      ;Point to port
                OUT     DX,AL
                CLC
                JNC     XCExit
XCBad:          STC
XCExit:         RET
XmitChar        ENDP
```

```
; Routine to check whether time has elapsed
; Enter with original clock ticks in BX and maximum wait (in ticks) in AX
; Returns with carry set if time is expired; all other registers intact

CheckTime   PROC    USES AX BX CX DX
            MOV     CTMax,AX                ;Store maximum ticks
            MOV     AH,0
            INT     1Ah                     ;Check for time-out
            CMP     BX,DX                   ;Check for wrap around
            JG      CT1                     ;Yep, it was there
            SUB     DX,BX                   ;Now we have elapsed ticks in DX
            JMP     CT2
CT1:        MOV     AX,0FFFFh
            SUB     AX,BX
            ADD     DX,AX
CT2:        CMP     DX,CTMax                ;Is our time up?
            JA      TimeUp                  ;Yes, so exit accordingly
            CLC                             ;No, no error
            JNC     CTExit
TimeUp:     STC                             ;Set for time up
CTExit:     RET
CheckTime   ENDP


; Set the baud rate divisor at chip level to 2400 baud

SetBRD      PROC    USES AX DX
            MOV     DX,ComAddr+3            ;Point to line control register
            IN      AL,DX                   ;Get what is there
            OR      AL,10000000b            ;Going to set bit 7 high
            OUT     DX,AL                   ;Send the byte

            DEC     DX                      ;Point to MSB of baud rate divisor
            DEC     DX
            MOV     AL,BRDMSB
            OUT     DX,AL

            DEC     DX                      ;Point to LSB of baud rate divisor
            MOV     AL,BRDLSB
            OUT     DX,AL
```

continues

Listing 3.2. Continued

```
        ADD     DX,3                ;Point to line control register
        IN      AL,DX               ;Get what is there
        AND     AL,01111111b        ;Going to set bit 7 low
        OUT     DX,AL               ;Send the byte

        RET
SetBRD  ENDP


; The following routine clears the screen and homes the cursor

Cls     PROC    USES AX BX CX DX
        MOV     AH,6                ;Scroll window up
        MOV     AL,0                ;Scroll full screen
        MOV     BH,7                ;Normal white on black
        MOV     CX,0                ;Upper left corner of screen
        MOV     DH,24               ;Bottom right
        MOV     DL,79
        INT     10h

        MOV     DX,0                ;Upper left corner of screen
        MOV     BH,0                ;Assume page 0
        MOV     AH,2                ;Set cursor position
        INT     10h
        RET
Cls     ENDP


; The following routine prints the ASCIIZ string pointed to by DS:SI

PrtString PROC  USES AX DX SI
PS1:    MOV     DL,[SI]             ;Get character
        INC     SI                  ;Point to next one
        CMP     DL,0                ;End of string?
        JE      PS2                 ;Yes, so exit
        MOV     AH,02h              ;Output a character
        INT     21h
        JMP     PS1                 ;Keep doing it
```

```
PS2:        RET
PrtString   ENDP


; Interrupt handler - process byte coming in on serial channel (COM)

IntHandler  PROC    FAR
            PUSH    AX
            PUSH    DX

; The following bit diddling turns off RTS so that the modem stops sending info
            MOV     DX,ComAddr+4        ;Point to modem control register
            IN      AL,DX
            AND     AL,11111101b        ;Sets bit 1 to 0 (turn off RTS)
            OUT     DX,AL               ;Set it

            PUSH    DS
            PUSH    ES
            PUSH    DI

            MOV     AX,CS
            MOV     DS,AX
            MOV     ES,BuffSeg
            MOV     DI,Head
            CLD

Receive:    MOV     DX,ComAddr          ;Get COM base address
            IN      AL,DX               ;Get the character
            STOSB                       ;Store character in buffer
            CMP     DI,BuffSize         ;At end?
            JNE     NoWrap              ;No, so continue
            MOV     DI,0                ;Point to start
NoWrap:     MOV     Head,DI

            MOV     DX,ComAddr+2        ;Point to interrupt identification
register
            IN      AL,DX               ;Get the value that is there
                                        ;Bit 0 will contain 1 if nothing there
                                        ;Will contain 0 if pending
            TEST    AL,1                ;Is another request pending?
            JZ      Receive             ;Yes, so go handle again
```

continues

Listing 3.2. Continued

```
                MOV     AL,20h                  ;Send end-of-interrupt code
                OUT     20h,AL

                POP     DI
                POP     ES
                POP     DS

; This turns RTS back on
                MOV     DX,ComAddr+4            ;Point to modem control register
                IN      AL,DX
                OR      AL,00000010b           ;Sets bit 1 to 1
                OUT     DX,AL                  ;Set it

                POP     DX
                POP     AX
                IRET

BuffSeg         DW      0000
Head            DW      0000
Tail            DW      0000


IntHandler      ENDP

                END
```

Notice that three data elements—BuffSeg, Head, and Tail—are maintained as part of the code segment. Maintaining them is necessary because these pointers are needed by the interrupt handler to do its job. The only offset register whose value you can count on when entering the interrupt handler is the CS register. All other registers may point to the wrong segments to access this information if it remained in the data segment.

The main work area of TERM.ASM is the code between InputLoop and NoKey. If you want to add additional functionality to the program—for example, checking for special keypresses to send information to the printer or a disk file—then this is the place to do it. You decide how much to develop TERM.ASM; it is only the beginning of a full-featured communications program.

Summary

This chapter has provided a quick tutorial in the basics of data communications. You have learned about the UART and how to program it, as well as how to create and implement an interrupt handler.

I should end this chapter by saying that it is impossible to discuss everything possible about data communications in a single chapter. Indeed, data communications is a topic for many complete books. If you want more information on data communications, your local bookstore should be able to direct you to several good sources. Because each book on the market takes a different approach to data communications, you should browse through the books to determine which one best fits your needs. Or, if you want your bookstore manager to remember you at Christmas, purchase all the store's books on the topic.

In Chapter 4, you learn how to program critical error handlers—another topic that expands your knowledge of interrupt handlers.

Critical Error Handlers

What is a critical error? Technically, it is an error of such magnitude that the operating system cannot fully recover or compensate. A critical error usually does not hang the computer, but it does mean that your program cannot finish working.

DOS classifies many defined events as critical errors. On a typical computer system, critical errors are exclusively generated when you are accessing the disk or the printer. For example, DOS considers each of the following to be critical errors:

- Attempting to write information to a disk that is write-protected

- Trying to access a drive that is "not ready," for example, one in which the drive door is open or a disk is not available

- A disk sector with an invalid CRC

- An unknown type of disk in the drive

- An invalid request for a sector, or a disk sector that cannot be located

- The printer is out of paper

This list shows the bulk of the errors that DOS considers critical. There are other types of critical errors, but they will become apparent as you work through the code later in this chapter.

Why You Should Write a Critical Error Handler

Unfortunately, the critical error handler often is either ignored by programmers or not written until the last moment. An argument can be made that your program is never complete until you have considered every eventuality (as much as possible), which includes anticipating and programming for critical errors.

The first reason for writing your own critical error handler is integrity of your user interface. Programmers often spend countless hours on the user interface for their programs. When DOS discovers a critical error, it doesn't care one whit about your interface. It immediately initiates an interrupt 24h, for which the default handler is the infamous Abort, Retry, Ignore, Fail prompt. This type of error can wreak havoc, and the error message alone can confuse an unseasoned computer user.

Perhaps the most important reason for writing a critical error handler, however, is simply housekeeping. A rich, dynamic program uses files and computer resources dynamically. Because critical errors occur predominantly while you are accessing disk drives, there is a good chance that you have disk files open or information that must be saved to disk. If the default critical-error prompt appears on-screen and the user chooses to abort, then your program is rudely terminated. Open files are closed with no regard to their condition, and interrupt vectors can remain pointing to code that is no longer protected in memory. Your computer system therefore is unstable. The best solution to this problem is to write your own handler that facilitates, wherever possible, the orderly shutdown of your program.

What Happens During a Critical Error

When DOS detects a critical error, it does the following things:

- Disables interrupts
- Makes the user program stack the active stack
- Copies to the stack the contents of the registers as they were when the DOS function that caused the error was invoked
- Pushes the flags and return address on the stack, as is expected when invoking an interrupt
- Loads the AH, AL, DI, BP, and SI registers with error values

- Set the InDOS flag (see Chapter 5) to 0 so that a few DOS functions can be called by the critical error handler

- Set the ErrorMode flag to 1 so that the critical error handler cannot be reentered

- Jumps to the critical interrupt handler pointed to by interrupt 24h

When the critical error handler is entered, the stack appears as shown in Figure 4.1.

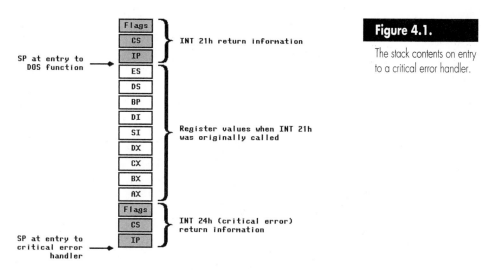

Figure 4.1.

The stack contents on entry to a critical error handler.

Table 4.1 shows the register meanings on entry to the critical error handler.

Table 4.1. Registers on entry to a critical error handler.

Register	Meaning
AH	Error type and proximity
AL	Drive number for error (A=0, B=1, and so on)
DI	Error code
BP:SI	Pointer to device header

Let's look at each of the registers and what they mean.

Error Type and Proximity (AH)

When you enter the critical error interrupt handler, each bit in the AH register has a special meaning. Table 4.2 details the information contained in this byte.

Table 4.2. Bit meanings for the AH register.

Bit settings 76543210	Meaning
0	Error occurred while reading data
1	Error occurred while writing data
00	Error in reserved sector
01	Error in FAT
10	Error in directory
11	Error in data area
0	The DOS function that generated the error cannot be terminated
1	The DOS function that generated the error can be terminated
0	The DOS function that generated the error cannot be retried
1	The DOS function that generated the error can be retried
0	The error cannot be ignored by the DOS function that generated the error
1	The error can be ignored by the DOS function that generated the error
x	Reserved
0	Error occurred on a block device
1	Error occurred on a character device or in a memory image of the FAT

You should examine bit 7 of AH first. This bit indicates whether the error occurred on a character device (the printer) or on a block device (a disk drive). Determining on which device the error occurred is necessary because it affects how the rest of the error data is interpreted.

As an example, bits 1 and 2 have relevance only for block devices. If the error occurred on a character device (for instance, the printer was out of paper), you can ignore the setting of these bits.

Bit 7 has a potentially confusing aspect, however. The status of this bit either indicates outright that the device in error is a block device (if bit 7 is clear) or indicates that it *may be* a character device. If bit 7 is set, you must check also the device header information, pointed to by BP:SI, to determine whether the device is a character device or whether the error occurred while accessing the memory image of a block device FAT.

Bits 3, 4, and 5 of the AH register indicate what valid actions your program can take when leaving the critical error handler. The significance of these bits becomes clearer later in this chapter.

Drive Number (AL)

The value in AL indicates the drive number where the error occurred. A value of 0 indicates drive A, 1 is B, 2 is C, and so on. Before acting on the information in AL, you should determine whether the error occurred on a block or charac-ter device. See the preceding section for further information.

Error Code (DI)

The value in DI indicates the actual error that occurred. Table 4.3 shows the possible error codes and their meanings.

Table 4.3. Critical error codes and their meanings.

Value	Meaning
00h	Disk is write-protected
01h	Unknown unit
02h	Drive not ready
03h	Unknown command
04h	CRC error
05h	Invalid request structure length
06h	Seek error
07h	Unknown media type
08h	Invalid sector (sector not found)
09h	Printer out of paper
0Ah	Write fault
0Bh	Read fault
0Ch	General failure

Device Header Pointer (BP:SI)

The BP:SI register pair points to the device header structure used by the device responsible for the error. Table 4.4 shows the structure of this header.

Table 4.4. The device header structure layout (offset and length are in bytes).

Offset	Length	Meaning
00h	4	Pointer to the next device driver header
04h	2	Device attribute
06h	2	Device strategy
08h	2	Interrupt routine offset
0Ah	Variable	Name or number of units

The device header structure is contained in the device driver. For detailed information on this structure, see Chapter 9, "Device Drivers."

The only information of immediate interest in this header is the device attributes field. Bit 15 of this field is used to confirm absolutely that the error occurred on a character device. If bit 15 is set and bit 7 of AH is set, then the error occurred on a character device. If bit 15 is clear and bit 7 of AH is set, then the error occurred while accessing a memory image of a block device FAT.

If it is determined that the error occurred on a character device, the device name beginning at header offset 0Ah is useful in notifying the user what is happening.

Limits on a Critical Error Handler

The first thing you should do when creating your critical error handler is to save the BX, CX, DX, DS, ES, SS, and SP registers. These registers are unused in passing error information to the handler and must remain unchanged by your code. In addition, you should not change the device driver header structure pointer in BP:SI.

When a critical error occurs, DOS is considered to be in a relatively unstable condition. You can call only a limited number of DOS functions in your handler (see Table 4.5). These functions include the DOS character I/O functions and a few informational functions.

Table 4.5. DOS functions allowed within a critical error handler.

Function	Name
01h	Character Input with Echo
02h	Output Character
03h	Auxiliary Input
04h	Auxiliary Output
05h	Printer Output
06h	Direct Console I/O
07h	Direct Character Input without Echo
08h	Character Input without Echo
09h	Output Character String
0Ah	Buffered Input
0Bh	Check for Character Waiting
0Ch	Clear Buffer and Get Input
30h	Get DOS Version Number
3300h	Get Ctrl-Break Flag
3301h	Set Ctrl-Break Flag
3305h	Get Boot Drive Code
3306h	Get DOS Version Number
50h	Set PSP Address
51h	Get PSP Address
59h	Get Extended Error Information
62h	Get Program Segment Prefix (PSP) Address

The character I/O functions (01h through 0Ch) are the basic functions that allow output of individual ASCII characters and ASCII strings terminated with a dollar sign ($). If you have written your own output routines that do not take advantage of any DOS functions other than those shown in Table 4.5, it's safe to use them. For instance, if you use output routines that produce output directly to the video memory area, they should be OK to use.

The reason you shouldn't use any other DOS functions is that DOS is not reentrant: If you call any other DOS functions, you can mess up data areas already in use by the function that generated the critical error. Play it safe, and stick to the approved list of functions.

Keep in mind that many BIOS functions also can be used safely from within your interrupt handler. Generally, you should use only those functions available through interrupt 10h, which deal with the screen. BIOS functions that access information on the disk run the same risk of messing up data areas on the disk as do their DOS function counterparts.

Exiting a Critical Error Handler

You can exit a critical error handler the way you exit any other interrupt handler, by using the IRET instruction, except for one difference: DOS uses the contents of the AL register to determine what to do next. You should set AL according to the information shown in Table 4.6.

Table 4.6. Settings for register AL when exiting a critical error handler.	
Value	**Meaning**
00h	Ignore the error
01h	Retry the operation
02h	Abort (terminate) the program
03h	Fail the operation

The retry code is self-explanatory, but what about the other codes? When you return the ignore code (AL=0), DOS ignores the error, and acts as though the original DOS function call that generated the error was successful.

If you use the abort code (AL=2), then the process (program) that was executing when the error occurred is terminated. DOS initiates an interrupt 21h, function 4Ch with the return code set to 2 to indicate that the program terminated with a critical error.

The fail code (AL=3) is the opposite of the ignore code. It causes DOS to return to your program, from the DOS function that caused the error, with an error. Your program then can continue processing as though a normal DOS error had occurred.

Before finally exiting the critical error handler, you should check whether the return code you want to use is permissible for the type of error that occurred. If you remember correctly, on entry to the critical error handler, the condition of bits 3, 4, and 5 of the AH register determines whether return codes 0, 1, and 3 are allowable. Bit 3 indicates whether return code 3 is allowable, bit 4 determines whether return code 1 is allowable, and bit 5 determines whether a return code of 0 is allowable.

The information provided about the allowable return codes should be used to determine the strategy you use in handling a critical error. If you do not check the return code and provide one that is not allowed, DOS enforces the following strategies:

- If you specify a return code of 0 and it is not allowed, a return code of 3 is substituted.

- If you specify a return code of 1 and it is not allowed, a return code of 3 is substituted.

- If you specify a return code of 3 and it is not allowed, a return code of 2 is substituted.

Notice that there is never a substitution for return code 2. DOS always tries to terminate the program as a measure of last resort.

Writing a Critical Error Handler

As with any program you write, the first thing you should do in writing a critical error handler is to determine what you want to accomplish. Generally, you will want to inform the user that an error has occurred and then take an appropriate action. Sometimes, however, you can take an action without user intervention.

For instance, you may actually have wanted a critical error to be generated. An example of this is when your program expects the disk in the drive to be write-protected. You can try writing to the disk to see whether it is write-protected. If the write is successful, then you know that the disk is not protected, and you can prompt the user to write-protect the disk. If a critical error occurs, the disk is protected and you can continue processing.

For the sake of illustration, however, assume that critical errors are the exception. You do not expect them to happen, but you must be prepared in case they do. In such an instance, your handler must accomplish the following tasks:

- Save all registers

- Determine whether the error occurred on a block device or a character device

- If the error occurred on a character device, prompt the user to correct the situation

- If the error occurred on a block device, determine whether the user can correct the situation

- If the user can correct the situation, prompt the user to do so
- If the user cannot correct the situation, inform the user
- Restore the registers
- Exit with the appropriate exit code

The program code in Listing 4.1 implements these steps.

Listing 4.1. CRITERR.ASM

```
Page 60,132

Comment ¦
*******************************************************************

File:       CRITERR.ASM
Author:     Allen L. Wyatt
Date:       7/3/92
Assembler:  MASM 6.0

Purpose:    A basic critical error handler. This routine
            is designed to be used within another program.


*******************************************************************¦


            .CODE

CritErr     PROC    FAR
            PUSH    BX
            PUSH    CX
            PUSH    DX
            PUSH    BP
            PUSH    DI
            PUSH    DS
            PUSH    ES

            MOV     BX,CS               ;Set up addressing for data segment
            MOV     DS,BX

            PUSH    AX                  ;Save current value
            MOV     AH,03h              ;Get cursor position
```

```
        MOV     BH,0                    ;Assume page 0
        INT     10h
        MOV     Coord,DX                ;Save cursor position
        MOV     AH,06h                  ;Scroll window up
        MOV     AL,2                    ;by two lines
        MOV     BH,07h                  ;Attribute to use
        MOV     CX,1700h                ;Upper left corner (23:00)
        MOV     DX,184Fh                ;Lower right corner (24:79)
        INT     10h
        MOV     AH,02h                  ;Set cursor position
        MOV     BH,0                    ;Assume page 0
        MOV     DX,1700h                ;Row and column (23:00)
        INT     10h
        POP     AX                      ;Get error info back

        MOV     BL,AH                   ;Set up valid exit code info
        MOV     CL,3
        SHR     BL,CL
        AND     BL,00000001b
        MOV     TermOK,BL
        MOV     BL,AH
        MOV     CL,4
        SHR     BL,CL
        AND     BL,00000001b
        MOV     RetryOK,BL
        MOV     BL,AH
        MOV     CL,5
        SHR     BL,CL
        AND     BL,00000001b
        MOV     IgnoreOK,BL

        TEST    AH,10000000b            ;Test bit 7
        JZ      BlockDev                ;Happened on a block device
        MOV     ES,BP
        MOV     BX,ES:[SI+4]            ;Get attribute from header
        TEST    BH,10000000b            ;Test bit 15
        JZ      BlockDev                ;Happened in memory FAT

; By this point, it has been determined that the error occurred on a
; character device
```

continues

Listing 4.1. Continued

```
                MOV     AH,09h              ;Display string
                MOV     DX,OFFSET CharMsg1
                INT     21h
                ADD     SI,0Ah              ;Point to device name
                MOV     CX,8               ;Maximum number of characters
NameLoop:       MOV     DL,ES:[SI]          ;Get character
                INC     SI                 ;Point to next one
                CMP     DL,' '             ;Is it a space?
                JE      EndOfName          ;Yes, so end name
                MOV     AH,02h             ;Display a character
                INT     21h
                LOOP    NameLoop
EndOfName:      MOV     AH,09h             ;Display string
                MOV     DX,OFFSET CharMsg2
                INT     21h
                JMP     Common

BlockDev:       ADD     AL,'A'             ;Make it ASCII
                MOV     Drive,AL           ;Put in string
                MOV     AH,09h             ;Display string
                MOV     DX,OFFSET BlockMsg
                INT     21h

Common:         MOV     SI,DI
                SHL     SI,1               ;Multiply by 2
                ADD     SI,OFFSET ErrTable
                MOV     DX,[SI]            ;Get address from error table
                MOV     AH,09h             ;Display string
                INT     21h

                CMP     DI,01h             ;Unknown unit?
                JE      NonRecover         ;Yes, so exit
                CMP     DI,03h             ;Unknown command?
                JE      NonRecover         ;Yes, so exit
                CMP     DI,04h             ;Bad CRC?
                JE      NonRecover         ;Yes, so exit
                CMP     DI,05h             ;Bad request structure length?
                JE      NonRecover         ;Yes, so exit
                CMP     DI,06h             ;Seek error?
                JE      NonRecover         ;Yes, so exit
```

```
CMP     DI,07h                  ;Unknown media?
JE      NonRecover              ;Yes, so exit
CMP     DI,08h                  ;Sector not found?
JE      NonRecover              ;Yes, so exit
CMP     DI,0Ah                  ;Write fault?
JE      NonRecover              ;Yes, so exit
CMP     DI,0Bh                  ;Read fault?
JE      NonRecover              ;Yes, so exit
CMP     DI,0Ch                  ;Was it a general failure?
JE      NonRecover              ;Yes, so exit

MOV     AH,02h                  ;Set cursor position
MOV     BH,0                    ;Assume page 0
MOV     DX,1800h                ;Row and column (24:00)
INT     10h
MOV     AH,09h                  ;Display string
MOV     DX,OFFSET Prompt
INT     21h
MOV     AH,01h                  ;Character input with echo
INT     21h

PUSH    AX                      ;Save the keypress
MOV     AH,06h                  ;Scroll window up
MOV     AL,2                    ;by two lines
MOV     BH,07h                  ;Attribute to use
MOV     CX,1700h                ;Upper left corner (23:00)
MOV     DX,184Fh                ;Lower right corner (24:79)
INT     10h
MOV     AH,02h                  ;Set cursor position
MOV     BH,0                    ;Assume page 0
MOV     DX,Coord                ;Original row and column
INT     10h
POP     AX                      ;Get the keypress back

CMP     AL,'X'                  ;Was X pressed?
JE      NonRecover              ;Yes, so exit with error
CMP     AL,'x'                  ;Was x pressed?
JE      NonRecover              ;Yes, so exit with error
MOV     AL,01h                  ;Exit with retry
CMP     RetryOK,1               ;Is it OK to retry the function?
JE      ExitCrit                ;Yes, so continue
```

continues

Listing 4.1. Continued

```
NonRecover: MOV     AL,03h                  ;Terminate function (let parent
                                            ;      program handle the error)
            CMP     TermOK,1                ;Is it OK to terminate the function?
            JE      ExitCrit                ;Yes, so continue
            MOV     AL,02h                  ;No, force termination of program

ExitCrit:   POP     ES
            POP     DS
            POP     DI
            POP     BP
            POP     DX
            POP     CX
            POP     BX
            IRET

TermOK      DB      00
RetryOK     DB      00
IgnoreOK    DB      00
Coord       DW      0000
CharMsg1    DB      'Error with the $'
CharMsg2    DB      ' device - $'
BlockMsg    DB      'Error with drive '
Drive       DB      '?: - $'
Prompt      DB      'Press X to stop trying, or correct and press another '
            DB      'key to try again...$'

ErrTable    DW      OFFSET Err00
            DW      OFFSET Err01
            DW      OFFSET Err02
            DW      OFFSET Err03
            DW      OFFSET Err04
            DW      OFFSET Err05
            DW      OFFSET Err06
            DW      OFFSET Err07
            DW      OFFSET Err08
            DW      OFFSET Err09
```

```
                DW       OFFSET Err0A
                DW       OFFSET Err0B
                DW       OFFSET Err0C

Err00           DB       'disk is write-protected$'
Err01           DB       'unknown unit$'
Err02           DB       'drive not ready$'
Err03           DB       'unknown command$'
Err04           DB       'CRC error$'
Err05           DB       'bad drive-request structure length$'
Err06           DB       'seek error$'
Err07           DB       'unknown media type$'
Err08           DB       'sector not found$'
Err09           DB       'out of paper$'
Err0A           DB       'error while writing$'
Err0B           DB       'error while reading$'
Err0C           DB       'general failure$'

CritErr         ENDP

                END
```

This handler is basic in nature; no fancy processing occurs. It tests for the type of error and then presents a message to the user. If you want more in-depth error messages or if you want to provide even more information to the user, you can use DOS function 59h, which returns extended error information.

Notice where the data used by the routine is located—in the code segment after the end of the handler. This approach is consistent with the one used for the interrupt handler in Chapter 3, "Serial Communications." It is necessary because the CS register is the only offset register whose value you can count on when entering the interrupt handler.

This routine starts by saving the cursor position on the screen. Then the cursor is repositioned to the bottom of the screen. This error handler assumes that it has control of the bottom two lines of the video screen. In a program that uses those lines for other purposes, you must change this routine accordingly. You can either cause the routine to print its messages elsewhere or save the information on the bottom two lines and restore it when the error handler is completed.

Enabling and Disabling a Critical Error Handler

Enabling a critical error handler is a simple, straightforward process. You simply use DOS function 25h to reset the interrupt vector for interrupt 24h.

One of the nice things about a critical error handler is that if you spawn any child processes (see Chapter 11, "Using the EXEC Function"), they also continue to use the critical error handler you have invoked. You can develop individual critical error handlers for each of the child processes, however.

When your program is complete, it is not necessary to set the interrupt vector back to its previous value. DOS does this for you as part of its termination process, but only for the critical error vector. Any other interrupts you have changed must be changed back to their previous value. The critical error vector is restored from the value stored in offset 12h of the PSP for the program.

Testing the Critical Error Handler

So, how do you test your critical error handler? You put it in your program and try to cause critical errors. I used the program in Listing 4.2 to test the CritErr handler presented earlier in this chapter:

Listing 4.2. CRITTEST.ASM

```
Page 60,132

Comment |
*********************************************************************

File:       CRITTEST.ASM
Author:     Allen L. Wyatt
Date:       7/3/92
Assembler:  MASM 6.0

Purpose:    A test program for the critical error handler. Run
            this program with no disk in drive A:. The program
            attempts to open a file on drive A:. When it
            cannot (no disk is there), a critical error is
            generated. Then you can insert a disk, and the
            program continues.
```

```
Format:    CRITTEST


**********************************************************************!
                                                                      '
           .MODEL   small
           .STACK                        ;Default 1K stack is OK
           .DATA

Filename   DB       'A:\TEST.DAT',0
Message    DB       'This is a test file',13,10
           DB       'created by CRITTEST.EXE.',13,10,13,10
           DB       'It can safely be deleted.'
CRLF       DB       13,10,0
Status     DB       'There was an error and the file could',13,10
           DB       'not be created.  Upon trying, the DOS',13,10
           DB       'function returned an error code of ',0

           .CODE
           .STARTUP
CritTest   PROC
           MOV      AL,24h                ;Resetting interrupt handler
           PUSH     DS
           PUSH     CS
           POP      DS
           MOV      DX,OFFSET CritErr
           MOV      AH,25h                ;Set interrupt vector
           INT      21h
           POP      DS

           MOV      AH,3Ch                ;Create/truncate file
           MOV      CX,0                  ;Normal file
           MOV      DX,OFFSET Filename    ;Point to name
           INT      21h                   ;This should generate error
           JNC      Continue              ;No error, continue
           MOV      SI,OFFSET Status
           CALL     PrtString
           CALL     PrtDec
           MOV      SI,OFFSET CRLF
           CALL     PrtString
           JMP      AllDone
```

continues

Listing 4.2. Continued

```
Continue:    MOV     BX,AX                  ;Put handle in proper place
             MOV     AH,40h                 ;Write to file
             MOV     CX,76                  ;Number of bytes
             MOV     DX,OFFSET Message
             INT     21h
             MOV     AH,3Eh                 ;Close file (handle in BX)
             INT     21h


AllDone:     .EXIT
CritTest     ENDP


; The following routine prints the ASCIIZ string pointed to by DS:SI

PrtString    PROC    USES AX DX SI
PS1:         MOV     DL,[SI]                ;Get character
             INC     SI                     ;Point to next one
             CMP     DL,0                   ;End of string?
             JE      PS2                    ;Yes, so exit
             MOV     AH,02h                 ;Output a character
             INT     21h
             JMP     PS1                    ;Keep doing it
PS2:         RET
PrtString    ENDP


; The following routine prints the value in AX as a decimal number

PrtDec       PROC    USES AX CX DX
             MOV     CX,0FFFFh              ;Ending flag
             PUSH    CX
             MOV     CX,10
PD1:         MOV     DX,0
             DIV     CX                     ;Divide by 10
             ADD     DL,30h                 ;Convert to ASCII
             PUSH    DX                     ;Store remainder
             CMP     AX,0                   ;Are we done?
             JNE     PD1                    ;No, so continue
```

```
PD2:        POP     DX                  ;Character is now in DL
            CMP     DX,0FFFFh           ;Is it the ending flag?
            JE      PD3                 ;Yes, so continue
            MOV     AH,02h              ;Output a character
            INT     21h
            JMP     PD2                 ;Keep doing it

PD3:        RET
PrtDec      ENDP


; Critical error handler (from the file CRITERR.ASM)

CritErr     PROC    FAR
            PUSH    BX
            PUSH    CX
            PUSH    DX
            PUSH    BP
            PUSH    DI
            PUSH    DS
            PUSH    ES

            MOV     BX,CS               ;Set up addressing for data segment
            MOV     DS,BX

            PUSH    AX                  ;Save current value
            MOV     AH,03h              ;Get cursor position
            MOV     BH,0                ;Assume page 0
            INT     10h
            MOV     Coord,DX            ;Save cursor position
            MOV     AH,06h              ;Scroll window up
            MOV     AL,2                ;by two lines
            MOV     BH,07h              ;Attribute to use
            MOV     CX,1700h            ;Upper left corner (23:00)
            MOV     DX,184Fh            ;Lower right corner (24:79)
            INT     10h
            MOV     AH,02h              ;Set cursor position
            MOV     BH,0                ;Assume page 0
            MOV     DX,1700h            ;Row and column (23:00)
            INT     10h
            POP     AX                  ;Get error info back
```

continues

Listing 4.2. Continued

```
            MOV     BL,AH                   ;Set up valid exit code info
            MOV     CL,3
            SHR     BL,CL
            AND     BL,00000001b
            MOV     TermOK,BL
            MOV     BL,AH
            MOV     CL,4
            SHR     BL,CL
            AND     BL,00000001b
            MOV     RetryOK,BL
            MOV     BL,AH
            MOV     CL,5
            SHR     BL,CL
            AND     BL,00000001b
            MOV     IgnoreOK,BL

            TEST    AH,10000000b            ;Test bit 7
            JZ      BlockDev                ;Happened on a block device
            MOV     ES,BP
            MOV     BX,ES:[SI+4]            ;Get attribute from header
            TEST    BH,10000000b            ;Test bit 15
            JZ      BlockDev                ;Happened in memory FAT

; By this point, it has been determined that the error occurred on a
; character device

            MOV     AH,09h                  ;Display string
            MOV     DX,OFFSET CharMsg1
            INT     21h
            ADD     SI,0Ah                  ;Point to device name
            MOV     CX,8                    ;Maximum number of characters
NameLoop:   MOV     DL,ES:[SI]              ;Get character
            INC     SI                      ;Point to next one
            CMP     DL,' '                  ;Is it a space?
            JE      EndOfName               ;Yes, so end name
            MOV     AH,02h                  ;Display a character
            INT     21h
            LOOP    NameLoop
EndOfName:  MOV     AH,09h                  ;Display string
            MOV     DX,OFFSET CharMsg2
```

```
            INT     21h
            JMP     Common

BlockDev:   ADD     AL,'A'                  ;Make it ASCII
            MOV     Drive,AL                ;Put in string
            MOV     AH,09h                  ;Display string
            MOV     DX,OFFSET BlockMsg
            INT     21h

Common:     MOV     SI,DI
            SHL     SI,1                    ;Multiply by 2
            ADD     SI,OFFSET ErrTable
            MOV     DX,[SI]                 ;Get address from error table
            MOV     AH,09h                  ;Display string
            INT     21h

            CMP     DI,01h                  ;Unknown unit?
            JE      NonRecover              ;Yes, so exit
            CMP     DI,03h                  ;Unknown command?
            JE      NonRecover              ;Yes, so exit
            CMP     DI,04h                  ;Bad CRC?
            JE      NonRecover              ;Yes, so exit
            CMP     DI,05h                  ;Bad request structure length?
            JE      NonRecover              ;Yes, so exit
            CMP     DI,06h                  ;Seek error?
            JE      NonRecover              ;Yes, so exit
            CMP     DI,07h                  ;Unknown media?
            JE      NonRecover              ;Yes, so exit
            CMP     DI,08h                  ;Sector not found?
            JE      NonRecover              ;Yes, so exit
            CMP     DI,0Ah                  ;Write fault?
            JE      NonRecover              ;Yes, so exit
            CMP     DI,0Bh                  ;Read fault?
            JE      NonRecover              ;Yes, so exit
            CMP     DI,0Ch                  ;Was it a general failure?
            JE      NonRecover              ;Yes, so exit

            MOV     AH,02h                  ;Set cursor position
            MOV     BH,0                    ;Assume page 0
            MOV     DX,1800h                ;Row and column (24:00)
            INT     10h
```

continues

Listing 4.2. Continued

```
        MOV     AH,09h              ;Display string
        MOV     DX,OFFSET Prompt
        INT     21h
        MOV     AH,01h              ;Character input with echo
        INT     21h

        PUSH    AX                  ;Save the keypress
        MOV     AH,06h              ;Scroll window up
        MOV     AL,2                ;by two lines
        MOV     BH,07h              ;Attribute to use
        MOV     CX,1700h            ;Upper left corner (23:00)
        MOV     DX,184Fh            ;Lower right corner (24:79)
        INT     10h
        MOV     AH,02h              ;Set cursor position
        MOV     BH,0                ;Assume page 0
        MOV     DX,Coord            ;Original row and column
        INT     10h
        POP     AX                  ;Get the keypress back

        CMP     AL,'X'              ;Was X pressed?
        JE      NonRecover          ;Yes, so exit with error
        CMP     AL,'x'              ;Was x pressed?
        JE      NonRecover          ;Yes, so exit with error
        MOV     AL,01h              ;Exit with retry
        CMP     RetryOK,1           ;Is it OK to retry the function?
        JE      ExitCrit            ;Yes, so continue

NonRecover: MOV  AL,03h             ;Terminate function (let parent
                                    ;    program handle the error)
        CMP     TermOK,1            ;Is it OK to terminate the function?
        JE      ExitCrit            ;Yes, so continue
        MOV     AL,02h              ;No, force termination of program

ExitCrit: POP   ES
        POP     DS
        POP     DI
        POP     BP
        POP     DX
        POP     CX
        POP     BX
        IRET
```

```
TermOK      DB      00
RetryOK     DB      00
IgnoreOK    DB      00
Coord       DW      0000
CharMsg1    DB      'Error with the $'
CharMsg2    DB      ' device - $'
BlockMsg    DB      'Error with drive '
Drive       DB      '?: - $'
Prompt      DB      'Press X to stop trying, or correct and press another '
            DB      'key to try again...$'

ErrTable    DW      OFFSET Err00
            DW      OFFSET Err01
            DW      OFFSET Err02
            DW      OFFSET Err03
            DW      OFFSET Err04
            DW      OFFSET Err05
            DW      OFFSET Err06
            DW      OFFSET Err07
            DW      OFFSET Err08
            DW      OFFSET Err09
            DW      OFFSET Err0A
            DW      OFFSET Err0B
            DW      OFFSET Err0C

Err00       DB      'disk is write-protected$'
Err01       DB      'unknown unit$'
Err02       DB      'drive not ready$'
Err03       DB      'unknown command$'
Err04       DB      'CRC error$'
Err05       DB      'bad drive-request structure length$'
Err06       DB      'seek error$'
Err07       DB      'unknown media type$'
Err08       DB      'sector not found$'
Err09       DB      'out of paper$'
Err0A       DB      'error while writing$'
Err0B       DB      'error while reading$'
Err0C       DB      'general failure$'

CritErr     ENDP

            END
```

This program sets up an easy-to-use critical error condition. You should run the program without a disk in the A: drive. Because the program tries to create a file on the A: drive and no disk is there, a critical error is generated.

When the error is generated, a message is presented at the bottom of the screen that prompts the user to correct the condition and press a key, or to press *X* to stop retrying. Try it both ways: Correct the condition by putting a formatted disk in drive A:, and then press a key. The program continues as though nothing happened. Also try pressing the X key. When you do, the DOS function that generated the critical error fails, and the test program displays the results.

This example of a test program is very limited in nature. Because many different situations can cause a critical error, you will have to write similar test programs for each condition that you reasonably expect your users to encounter.

Summary

Like it or not, critical errors are a part of everyday use of programs. As simple as your program may be, if it involves disk file or printer access, there is a reasonable chance that your users can generate an error for which the operating system cannot compensate.

This chapter has described what a critical error is and how you can allow for them in your programs. You have learned the do's and don'ts of writing the special type of interrupt handler that can serve as a critical error handler.

You probably have noticed that the information in this chapter built on routines, principles, and concepts presented in the earlier chapters of this book. Like many things in the DOS environment, many programming solutions and application areas seem to be interwoven.

Chapter 5 discusses how to do TSR programming.

TSR Programming

By now, you should be aware of what a TSR program is. (If not, where have you been the past decade?) A TSR program is loaded into memory and left there, by exiting from the program with the TSR function, which is interrupt 21h, function 31h. This function is similar to other DOS exiting functions, but you can specify the amount of memory you want to reserve as you exit.

Types of TSR Programs

TSR programs have been used for virtually everything. There are two general types of TSR programs: passive and active. *Passive* TSR programs do nothing but wait in memory until they are called by another program. *Active* TSR programs are constantly running and monitoring the actions taking place on the computer until a set of conditions causes them to take action.

The type of TSR program you use depends on your needs. Passive TSRs generally are used to develop an application program interface (API), which you can use across a variety of programs to control common system functions. Passive TSRs are loaded into memory one time, and then can be used as needed within other programs.

Active TSRs are generally used to accomplish periodic or specialized tasks. Perhaps the most famous example of an active TSR is the SideKick program, published by Borland International. SideKick, as is the case with virtually all active TSRs, is loaded into memory and activated by pressing a specific keystroke. Other active TSRs may, depending on their purpose, monitor the disk drives, video card, or serial and parallel ports.

The monitoring done by active TSRs is implemented by intercepting and processing information passed to interrupt vectors. The interrupt vectors intercepted depend on the purpose and complexity of the TSR. Some TSRs even intercept the DOS interrupt (21h) to reroute some basic DOS functions.

If a certain set of conditions or a specific set of information is detected, the main code of the TSR is executed to perform a specific function. If the key information or conditions are not detected, processing is passed on to the original interrupt vector for regular system processing.

Problems with TSR Programs

Because of the variety of tasks that can be accomplished with TSR programs, they have proliferated wildly over the years. This proliferation means that it is possible (and likely) that any user can have several TSR programs loaded at one time. With passive TSRs, this situation is not much of a problem. Active TSRs, however, present a much more complex situation.

For instance, assume that you have a TSR installed that monitors the serial port for periodic incoming data. This data is gathered from an analog device, such as a weather station or a phone system. The purpose of the TSR is to receive the data and store it to disk. What happens, however, if your main program is in the middle of a directory search, and incoming data is detected? The TSR, in true form, exerts control over the computer to save the incoming information. Everyone knows that DOS is not a reentrant system. The disk information being used by the main program may be lost, therefore, when control is grabbed by the TSR. When the TSR finishes, the original program no longer has the information it needs to run correctly. The program may crash or exhibit erratic behavior.

Later, this chapter describes how to overcome the conflict problems presented by TSRs. First, however, let's look at the elements of a TSR program and a couple of examples.

TSR Program Elements

Regardless of the type of TSR you develop, by nature it contains two sections: a resident section and a transient section. As the names suggest, the *resident section* remains in memory, and the *transient section* does not. The transient section generally accomplishes the following tasks:

- Determines whether the TSR can be installed
- Initializes data areas

- Redirects interrupt vectors
- Frees memory no longer required
- Exits from the program by way of the TSR function

In contrast, the resident portion does the meat of the work after it has been installed by the transient portion. The resident portion remains in memory to be used when the TSR is activated.

The programmer has the responsibility to keep the memory used by the resident portion of the TSR as inconspicuous as possible. Many larger TSR programs segment the memory used and transfer large portions of the program to extended or expanded memory, or even to disk. These portions of the program then are accessed only when needed.

Writing and Using a Passive TSR Program

Passive TSR programs are usually much easier to write than are active TSRs. Passive TSRs do not run into conflict problems, as is typical with active TSRs. Look at an example of a passive TSR. The program in Listing 5.1, TSRVIDEO.ASM, installs a passive TSR that can be used from your other programs. When the passive TSR is installed, it occupies 384 bytes of memory. It hooks into the interrupt vector for interrupt 78h, which typically is unused. The transient portion of this program detects whether the vector is unused and, if it is in use, does not install itself.

If you have questions about which vectors are in use in your system, refer to Chapter 1, "Interrupt Handlers," and use the VECTORS.EXE program to determine which ones are available.

Listing 5.1. TSRVIDEO.ASM

```
Page 60,132

Comment ¦
*********************************************************************

File:      TSRVIDEO.ASM
Author:    Allen L. Wyatt
Date:      7/10/92
Assembler: MASM 6.0
```

continues

Listing 5.1. Continued

```
Purpose:    A TSR program that acts as a function dispatcher for
            various video-related subroutines. This implementation
            contains only two functions, as follows:
                AH        Function
                0         Clear screen, home cursor
                1         Print string at DS:SI
            This TSR is passive. It can be used from other
            programs by invoking an INT 78h with AH loaded with
            the function number wanted.

Format:     TSRVIDEO


*********************************************************************|
                                                                    ¦

            .MODEL  tiny                    ;Creating a COM file
            .STACK                          ;Default 1K stack is OK
            .DATA

IntUse      EQU     78h                     ;Interrupt to use
EnvBlock    EQU     2Ch
ErrMsg      DB      'Sorry, that vector is already in use',13,10,0

            .CODE
            .STARTUP
TSRVideo    PROC
            CALL    Hookin                  ;Start TSR, no return
TSRVideo    ENDP              ,

; The following is the new interrupt routine for Int 78h. It clears the
; screen and homes the cursor.

NewInt:     CMP     AH,0                    ;Want to clear screen?
            JNE     NI1                     ;No, continue
            CALL    Cls
            JMP     NI9
NI1:        CMP     AH,1                    ;Want to print string?
            JNE     NI9                     ;No, continue
            CALL    PrtString

NI9:        IRET
```

```
; Clear the screen and home the cursor

Cls        PROC     USES AX BX CX DX
           MOV      AH,8                  ;Read character and attribute
           MOV      BH,0                  ;Assume page 0
           INT      10h
           MOV      BH,AH                 ;Put attribute in right place

           MOV      AH,6                  ;Scroll window up
           MOV      AL,0                  ;Scroll full screen
           MOV      CX,0                  ;Upper left corner of screen
           MOV      DH,24                 ;Bottom right
           MOV      DL,79
           INT      10h

           MOV      DX,0                  ;Upper left corner of screen
           MOV      BH,0                  ;Assume page 0
           MOV      AH,2                  ;Set cursor position
           INT      10h

           RET
Cls        ENDP

; The following routine prints the ASCIIZ string pointed to by DS:SI

PrtString  PROC     USES AX DX SI
PS1:       MOV      DL,[SI]               ;Get character
           INC      SI                    ;Point to next one
           CMP      DL,0                  ;End of string?
           JE       PS2                   ;Yes, so exit
           MOV      AH,02h                ;Output a character
           INT      21h
           JMP      PS1                   ;Keep doing it
PS2:       RET
PrtString  ENDP

; The following is the transient portion of the TSR. It is discarded
; after the start-up procedure takes place.

Hookin     PROC
           POP      AX                    ;Throw away the return address
```

continues

Listing 5.1. Continued

```
                MOV     AL,IntUse               ;Get keyboard interrupt
                MOV     AH,35h
                INT     21h
                MOV     AX,ES
                ADD     AX,BX                   ;See if all zero
                CMP     AX,0
                JE      AllOK                   ;Nothing there, continue
                MOV     SI,OFFSET ErrMsg        ;Point to error message
                CALL    PrtString
                MOV     AH,4Ch                  ;Terminate with code
                MOV     AL,1
                INT     21h

AllOK:          MOV     DX,OFFSET NewInt        ;New offset address
                MOV     AL,IntUse               ;Redirect this vector
                MOV     AH,25h                  ;to point to new handler
                INT     21h

                MOV     ES,DS:[EnvBlock]        ;Get environment block segment
                MOV     AH,49h                  ;Free memory block (don't need it)
                INT     21h

                MOV     DX,OFFSET Hookin        ;End of resident area
                MOV     CL,4                    ;Divide by 16
                SHR     DX,CL                   ;No in paragraphs
                INC     DX                      ;Add 1 for good measure
                MOV     AL,0                    ;Return code is OK
                MOV     AH,31h                  ;TSR function
                INT     21h
Hookin          ENDP

                END
```

Notice how the transient portion of TSRVIDEO is implemented. The start-up portion of the program does only one thing: makes a call to Hookin, which is located physically at the end of the source code file. This call is made primarily to satisfy MASM, which does not allow routines to be nested. Hookin is located at the end of the file so that it can be discarded as the transient when the TSR function is invoked.

Hookin is designed as a routine that does not return to the caller. Because TSRVIDEO assembles and links to a COM file, you know that only the offset return address is pushed on the stack. The first thing Hookin does is to discard the return address. It is then free to end the program in any way it sees fit.

As the transient portion of the program, Hookin does several things. First, it checks to see whether the interrupt you want is in use. If it is, an error message is displayed and the program ends. If not, it establishes the correct interrupt vector, releases the memory used by the environment block for the program, and then uses the TSR function to exit.

If the environment block memory area were not released, the 512 bytes of memory occupied by the environment block would remain unavailable to other programs. Because the memory area is not needed after TSRVIDEO is a TSR program, it is safe to release it.

TSRVIDEO.ASM is set up to use interrupt 78h. If you want to use a different interrupt, all you do is change the equate value at IntUse.

TSRVIDEO.ASM is a very simple program, but it presents a rudimentary API. It seems almost laughable to refer to it that way, but it does do what any honest-to-goodness API does, albeit very simplistically. The program in Listing 5.2, TESTVID.ASM, enables you to test the functionality of this TSR. Make sure that you run TSRVIDEO.COM before executing TESTVID.EXE. The program tests to make sure that you have installed TSRVIDEO; if you have not, you see an error message and the program ends.

Listing 5.2. TESTVID.ASM

```
Page 60,132

Comment |
*********************************************************************


File:      TESTVID.ASM
Author:    Allen L. Wyatt
Date:      7/10/92
Assembler: MASM 6.0

Purpose:   Fill the screen with information, wait for a keypress,
           and then invoke Int 78h to clear the screen and home
           the cursor. Requires that TSRVIDEO.COM has been run
           before execution.

Format:    TESTVID


*********************************************************************|
                                                                    |
```

continues

Listing 5.2. Continued

```
            .MODEL  small
            .STACK                      ;Default 1K stack is OK
            .DATA

IntUse      EQU     78h                 ;Interrupt to use
Upper       EQU     'z'
Lower       EQU     ' '

ErrMsg      DB      'TSRVIDEO.COM has not been run$'
Pause       DB      13,10,'Press any key to clear screen...',0

            .CODE
            .STARTUP
TestVid     PROC
            MOV     AL,IntUse           ;Get keyboard interrupt
            MOV     AH,35h
            INT     21h
            MOV     AX,ES
            ADD     AX,BX               ;See if all zero
            CMP     AX,0
            JNE     ItsThere            ;Assume that it is there, continue
            MOV     DX,OFFSET ErrMsg    ;Point to error message
            MOV     AH,9                ;Display a string using DOS
            INT     21h
            JMP     Done

ItsThere:   MOV     CX,25*80            ;Full screen
            MOV     DL,Upper            ;Get top character
TC1:        MOV     AH,02h              ;Output a character
            INT     21h
            DEC     DL                  ;Next character down
            CMP     DL,Lower
            JAE     TC2
            MOV     DL,Upper            ;Get top character
TC2:        LOOP    TC1

            MOV     SI,OFFSET Pause     ;Point to start of pause message
            MOV     AH,1                ;Display string at DS:SI
            INT     IntUse              ;Invoke the TSR
```

```
             MOV      AH,0                    ;Read keyboard character
             INT      16h

             MOV      AH,0                    ;Clear the screen
             INT      IntUse                  ;Invoke the TSR

Done:        .EXIT
TestVid      ENDP
             END
```

This program first checks to make sure that TSRVIDEO has been installed. If it has not been installed, an error message is displayed and the program ends. If it has been installed, processing continues. Remember that if you change the interrupt number used in TSRVIDEO, you must change also the IntUse equate in this program.

Next, the screen is filled with information that subsequently is cleared by the TSR routines. CX contains the number of characters being written to the screen, in this case 2000, or 25 lines of 80 characters each.

The TSR function is then used to display a prompt message, and the program pauses until the user presses a key. Finally, the screen is cleared using the TSR function, and the program ends.

The benefit of using passive TSRs is that, if you have an entire group of programs you will be running, the TSRs can reduce the amount of common code that must be in each individual program. The drawback is that you must provide some forethought to make sure that you select an interrupt not in use by some other program or device driver.

Writing and Using an Active TSR Program

Active TSRs by their nature are more complex than passive ones. The program in Listing 5.3, TSRHELP, is a simple implementation of an active TSR. It uses a technique first introduced in Chapter 2, "Controlling the Keyboard," to hook to the back end of the keyboard interrupt to detect a keypress. In this case, if the F1 key is pressed, the program does the following:

- Clears the keyboard buffer
- Stuffs an escape character (1Bh) in the keyboard buffer, followed by the characters H-E-L-P and a carriage return
- Discards the F1 character that was pressed

The effect of this TSR is to provide an active (albeit simplistic) help system. You do this by abandoning any command on the command line and invoking the HELP command, available with DOS 5.

Listing 5.3. TSRHELP.ASM

```
Page 60,132

Comment ¦
*********************************************************************


File:       TSRHELP.ASM
Author:     Allen L. Wyatt
Date:       7/10/92
Assembler:  MASM 6.0

Purpose:    A TSR program that monitors the keyboard interrupt.
            When a user presses the F1 key, the DOS HELP command
            is executed.

Format:     TSRHELP


*********************************************************************!


            .MODEL  tiny                ;Creating a COM file
            .STACK                      ;Default 1K stack is OK
            .DATA

F1Scan      EQU     3Bh
EnvBlock    EQU     2Ch
ErrMsg      DB      'Sorry, this program cannot be used',13,10,'$'

            .CODE
            .STARTUP
TSRHelp     PROC
            CALL    Hookin              ;Go start the program
TSRHelp     ENDP


; The following is the new keyboard interrupt to replace Int 15/4F.

NewInt:     CMP     AH,4Fh              ;Is it the keyboard intercept?
```

```
                JE        Process                  ;Yes, so continue
                JMP       DWORD PTR CS:KeyInt      ;Skip to original interrupt handler

Process:        CMP       AL,F1Scan                ;Was F1 pressed?
                JNE       NoProc                   ;No, so return

                PUSH      DS
                PUSH      AX
                PUSH      CX
                PUSH      SI
                MOV       AX,CS                    ;New segment address
                MOV       DS,AX

ClrLoop:        MOV       AH,1                     ;Read keyboard status
                INT       16h
                JZ        Empty                    ;No key, so exit
                MOV       AH,0                     ;Read keyboard character
                INT       16h
                JMP       ClrLoop                  ;Go do it all again

Empty:          MOV       SI,OFFSET DOSCmd         ;Point to start of stuffing
                CLD                                ;Make sure that the direction flag is OK
St1:            LODSB                              ;Get the character
                CMP       AL,0                     ;Is it the ending signal?
                JE        StDone                   ;Yes, so exit
                MOV       CL,AL                    ;Put ASCII in proper place
                MOV       CH,0                     ;Don't care about the scan code
                MOV       AH,5                     ;Stuffing routine
                INT       16h
                JMP       St1

StDone:         POP       SI
                POP       CX
                POP       AX
                POP       DS
                CLC                                ;Ignore character
                JNC       Done

NoProc:         STC                                ;Process character as normal
Done:           RETF      2                        ;Don't want IRET because it restores
                                                   ;the flags register
```

continues

Listing 5.3. Continued

```
; The following data elements are here because they must be included in
; the memory reserved by the TSR call. If they are in the normal .DATA area,
; then they are placed AFTER all the code. That would place them in the
; transient program area, which is discarded. That would cause a run-time
; error.


DOSCmd      DB      1Bh,'help',0Dh
            DB      00
KeyInt      DW      0000,0000            ;Address for old keyboard routine



; This is the routine to hook in the interrupt

; To make sure that Int 15/4F is usable on this machine, call Int 15/C0. Bit
; 4 of the byte at offset 05 of the returned table indicates whether 15/4F is
; chained from Int 09h. If Int 15/C0 is not available on the system, then
; 80h or 86h should be returned in AH.


Hookin      PROC
            POP     AX                  ;Throw away the return address

            MOV     AH,0C0h
            INT     15h
            CMP     AH,80h              ;Available?
            JE      NoWay               ;Nope
            CMP     AH,86h
            JE      NoWay               ;Sorry

            MOV     AL,ES:[BX+5]        ;Get the byte
            TEST    AL,00010000b        ;Interested in only bit 4
            JNZ     AllOK               ;Function supported, so continue

NoWay:      MOV     DX,OFFSET ErrMsg    ;Point to error message
            MOV     AH,9                ;Display a string using DOS
            INT     21h
            MOV     AH,4Ch              ;Terminate with code
            MOV     AL,1
            INT     21h
```

```
; Everything is OK. Now hook in the intercept and start the program

AllOK:      MOV     AL,15h              ;Get keyboard interrupt
            MOV     AH,35h
            INT     21h
            MOV     KeyInt[0],BX        ;Offset address
            MOV     KeyInt[2],ES        ;Segment address

            MOV     DX,OFFSET NewInt    ;New offset address
            MOV     AL,15h              ;Change keyboard vector
            MOV     AH,25h              ;to point to new handler
            INT     21h

            MOV     ES,DS:[EnvBlock]    ;Get environment block segment
            MOV     AH,49h              ;Free memory block (don't need it)
            INT     21h

            MOV     DX,OFFSET Hookin    ;End of resident area
            MOV     CL,4                ;Divide by 16
            SHR     DX,CL               ;No in paragraphs
            INC     DX                  ;Add 1 for good measure
            MOV     AL,0                ;Return code is OK
            MOV     AH,31h              ;TSR function
            INT     21h

Hookin      ENDP

            END
```

TSRHELP uses the same start-up and Hookin techniques described for
TSRVIDEO. The tasks that must be accomplished to establish TSRHELP,
however, are more detailed. First, you must determine that the extended
keyboard functions are available. This technique was introduced in Chapter 2,
"Controlling the Keyboard." Because the TSR depends on BIOS interrupt 15h,
function 4Fh, steps must be taken to determine whether the function is supported. This is done by calling interrupt 15h, function C0h. This function
returns a pointer to a table. You are interested in bit 4 of byte 5 of this table.
If the bit is set, interrupt 15h, function 4Fh is supported.

After the supported functions have been determined, Hookin retrieves and
stores the old interrupt vector for interrupt 15h. Storing this address is critical
because it is used by the TSR program to pass control when function 4Fh is

not being called. Then, as with TSRVIDEO, the new interrupt vector is saved, the environment block is released, and the TSR function is used to exit from the program.

TSRHELP is then active. It occupies slightly more than 300 bytes in memory, and springs into action only when the F1 key is pressed. This step differentiates it from a passive TSR—it constantly examines the keys being pressed and acts only when a certain key is detected.

When F1 is pressed, the keyboard buffer is cleared and the information at DOSCmd is stuffed in the keyboard buffer. This action has the effect of aborting anything already on the command line and issuing the HELP command.

You should note that TSRHELP is a bare-bones TSR. Because it does not check to see whether it previously has been loaded, TSRHELP can be loaded more than once. Each loading consumes additional memory. Because TSRHELP is simplistic by design, you must reboot your computer to remove TSRHELP from memory. Later in this chapter, you learn how to determine whether a TSR is already loaded, thereby preventing multiple loadings of the same program.

The functions provided by TSRHELP sound very straightforward, and they are—as long as TSRHELP is the only TSR in the system. What happens, however, if the system on which TSRHELP is working has several different TSR programs installed, and all of them intercept the keyboard interrupt? In this case, conflicts can occur. The user may press F1 and expect to see the help screen, but it already was intercepted and modified by the preceding TSR. The net result is that your TSR has no effect in the system, and the user has a system on which he cannot depend.

The situation becomes even more complex if your TSR provides disk services. For instance, what if DOS is already accessing a disk when your TSR interrupts? The result can be chaos, and a resolution must be found.

Peaceful Coexistence

How do you program your TSRs to operate peacefully and safely with other TSRs and programs that may be running? The answer, unfortunately, is not easy. You must monitor what DOS is doing and act only when it is safe to do so. Several key DOS variables and techniques help you do this successfully:

■ *Monitor the InDOS flag.* This internal DOS flag, located at the address returned by DOS function 34h, indicates when it is safe to call DOS.

■ *Determine when DOS is idle.* You must monitor when DOS is in an idle period and awaiting keyboard input. During such conditions, it is safe to execute your TSR.

- *Don't interfere with video or disk operations.* Depending on what your TSR is doing, you should not grab control when the video (interrupt 10h) or disk (interrupt 13h) BIOS functions are operational.

- *Identify your TSR.* You should link into the multiplex interrupt (2Fh) and provide a way for your TSR to determine whether it is loaded already.

- *Pass control when done.* Always chain to previous interrupt vectors when you have completed your processing to enable other TSRs (if any) to do their work.

- *Make no assumptions about the stack.* If you will use the stack for more than a few words, use your own stack. You never can count on the size of the stack in effect when your TSR is invoked.

This section looks at each of these points in more depth.

Monitor the *InDOS* Flag

Every programmer probably is aware that numerous DOS function calls are undocumented. Countless other variables that DOS uses for its operations also remain undocumented. Until DOS 5, the InDOS flag was one such variable. Information about this flag was available and it was used before DOS 5, but Microsoft Corporation did not release information about it until DOS 5 was released.

The InDOS flag is used by DOS to indicate when it is busy. This flag is set to a nonzero value when a DOS function starts, and is set to zero when the DOS function is completed.

Your program should check the condition of the InDOS flag. If it is set and DOS is not idling (see the following section, "When DOS Is Idle"), it is not safe for your TSR to operate. If the InDOS flag is clear, it is safe to continue.

The address of the InDOS flag is determined with DOS function 34h. The following code retrieves the flag:

```
PUSH    ES                      ;Save for later
MOV     AH,34h                  ;Get InDOS flag address
INT     21h
MOV     AL,ES:[BX]              ;Get InDOS flag
POP     ES                      ;Restore segment
CMP     AL,0                    ;Is it safe?
JNE     Unsafe                  ;No, so skip routine
```

Notice that the address is returned in ES:BX, and the flag itself is only a single byte.

Determine When DOS Is Idle

If the idle condition is in effect, it is safe to operate, even if the InDOS flag indicates that DOS is busy. This safety zone is operational when DOS invokes interrupt 28h. By intercepting this vector, you can determine when DOS is idling and it is safe to continue.

Normally, the interrupt vector for interrupt 28h points to an IRET instruction. It is invoked whenever DOS is awaiting completion of character I/O functions (00h through 0Ch). It is highly possible that the vector for interrupt 28h has been changed by other programs, such as PRINT. Therefore, you never should exit your interrupt 28h handler with an IRET instruction; you always should chain to the old interrupt vector.

Don't Interfere with Video or Disk Operations

Not interfering with video or disk operations is simple. You just increment a variable whenever an interrupt 10h or 13h is invoked, and decrement the same variable when it is completed. When the following code is used to replace the original interrupt 10h vector, it does the trick:

```
INC     VidFlag             ;Increment the video flag
CALL    DWORD PTR OldVideo  ;Call the old INT 10h routine
DEC     VidFlag             ;Decrement the video flag
IRET
```

Your main TSR code then can check the condition of VidFlag (or DiskFlag) to determine whether it is safe to proceed. Although this type of safeguard is not necessary for all TSRs, you may find it necessary for yours, depending on whether you run into trouble in debugging your program.

Identify Your TSR

DOS provides interrupt 2Fh, the multiplex interrupt, for use by TSRs in establishing an interface by which other progams can interact with it. Any multiplex function higher than 0C00h is available for use.

To take advantage of the multiplex function, you intercept the interrupt 2Fh vector and test for the expected function code in AH (and possibly AL). If it is found, you act on it. To return, you should chain to the preceding vector for the multiplex interrupt.

Pass Control When Done

Passing control when done is common courtesy. You do not want another TSR to grab control and not pass information to your TSR, yet that happens all the time with ill-behaved programs. As you can tell from the previous sections, numerous interrupts are intercepted. Because it is safe to assume that multiple programs intercept each of these vectors, it is imperative that all of them pass control to the old interrupt vector when your TSR code is complete.

Make No Assumptions About the Stack

When DOS is in the middle of performing a function, it switches to an internal stack. DOS uses two different stacks, depending on which functions are being executed. It uses one stack for character I/O functions (00h through 0Ch) and another for all other DOS functions.

Because the size of these stacks is unpredictable, if you are using routines that push more than a word or two on the stack, you should set up and use your own stack. You must restore SS:SP when you are done.

A Full-Fledged Active TSR Program

As you probably have gathered from this chapter, writing a full-fledged TSR program can be daunting at times. This section presents the largest-scale TSR program in this chapter. You may want to use this TSRLOCK utility on your computer all the time. From the user's perspective, it does the following:

- Monitors the keyboard to see when a hot key is pressed (in this program, it is F12)
- If the hot key is pressed, clears the screen and prompts the user for a password
- When the user presses Enter, restores the original screen
- Ignores input until user again presses the hot key; otherwise, keyboard is locked
- When the hot key is pressed again, clears the screen and prompts the user for the password
- If the correct password is entered, restores the system to a fully functioning state
- If the wrong password is entered, informs the user and keeps the keyboard locked

To simplify the work that it must do, TSRLOCK makes the following assumptions:

- The user is operating in text mode, on video page 0.
- The user has an enhanced keyboard.

The latter assumption is necessary because the program, as written, uses an F12 hot key. This key can be changed easily, as discussed later in this section.

The program in Listing 5.4, TSRLOCK.ASM, is the source code for the utility.

Listing 5.4. TSRLOCK.ASM

```
Page 60,132

Comment ¦
********************************************************************

File:       TSRLOCK.ASM
Author:     Allen L. Wyatt
Date:       7/11/92
Assembler:  MASM 6.0

Purpose:    A TSR program that monitors the keyboard interrupt.
            When a user presses a designated function key, the TSR
            is activated. Allows the user to lock the keyboard
            until a user-defined password is entered.

Format:     TSRLOCK


********************************************************************!

            .MODEL  tiny                ;Creating a COM file
            .STACK                      ;Default 1K stack is OK
            .DATA

TRUE        EQU     -1
FALSE       EQU     0
DataPort    EQU     60h
StatusPort  EQU     64h
InputFull   EQU     02h
FuncScan    EQU     58h                 ;Using F12
EnvBlock    EQU     2Ch                 ;Offset of pointer in PSP
StkSize     EQU     256                 ;Stack size for TSR
```

```
AlreadyIn    DB         'Sorry, TSRLock is already installed$'
Hooked       DB         'TSRLock is now installed$'

             .CODE
             .STARTUP
TSRLock      PROC
             CALL     Hookin                  ;Go start the program
TSRLock      ENDP


; The following is the new keyboard interrupt to replace Int 09h,

NewKeyInt:   PUSH     CX
             PUSH     BX
             PUSH     AX
             PUSH     DS
             PUSH     ES
             MOV      AX,CS                   ;Set up addressing
             MOV      DS,AX

             CLI                              ;Disable interrupts
GetStat:     IN       AL,StatusPort          ;Get keyboard status
             TEST     AL,InputFull           ;Is the coding complete?
             LOOPNZ   GetStat                ;No, so continue waiting
             IN       AL,DataPort            ;Yes, so get code
             STI                              ;Enable interrupts

             AND      AL,7Fh                 ;Turn off if a Break key
             CMP      AL,FuncScan            ;Was the function key pressed?
             JE       GotFunc                ;Yes, go handle
             CMP      LockState,TRUE         ;Is the keyboard locked?
             JNE      Pass                   ;No, so continue
             CMP      TSRActive,TRUE         ;Yes, but are you in the TSR?
             JE       Pass                   ;Yes, so let it through
             JNE      Ignore                 ;No, so ignore keystroke

GotFunc:     CMP      TSRActive,TRUE         ;Already in TSR?
             JE       Ignore                 ;Yes, so ignore key and continue
             MOV      RequestFlag,TRUE       ;Turn on the flag
             JMP      Ignore                 ;Drop the key (don't need it)

Pass:        POP      ES
```

continues

Listing 5.4. Continued

```
                POP     DS
                POP     AX
                POP     BX
                POP     CX
                JMP     DWORD PTR CS:KeyInt ;Skip to original INT 9 routine

Ignore:         MOV     AL,20h                  ;Signify end of interrupt
                OUT     20h,AL
                POP     ES
                POP     DS
                POP     AX
                POP     BX
                POP     CX
                IRET
```

```
; The following is the new handler for the idler interrupt.
; Only effect on stack is to push one word (return address for DoTSR).
```

```
Idler:          PUSHF                           ;Want to save original flags
                CMP     CS:TSRActive,TRUE   ;Already in TSR?
                JE      ExitIdle            ;Yes, so exit
                CMP     CS:RequestFlag,TRUE ;Was TSR requested?
                JNE     ExitIdle            ;No, so exit
                MOV     CS:TSRActive,TRUE
                CALL    DoTSR               ;Yes, go handle TSR
                MOV     CS:TSRActive,FALSE
ExitIdle:       POPF
                JMP     DWORD PTR CS:IdleInt ;Skip to original interrupt handler
```

```
; The following is the new handler for the timer interrupt.
```

```
Timer:          PUSHF                           ;Save original flags
                CALL    DWORD PTR CS:TimeInt ;Call original interrupt handler
                PUSH    AX
                PUSH    BX
                PUSH    DS
                PUSH    ES
                MOV     AX,CS
```

```
            MOV     DS,AX
            CMP     TSRActive,TRUE        ;Already in TSR?
            JE      ExitTime             ;Yes, so exit
            CMP     RequestFlag,TRUE     ;Was TSR requested?
            JNE     ExitTime             ;No, so exit
            LES     BX,DWORD PTR InDOSPtr
            CMP     BYTE PTR ES:[BX],0   ;OK to process?
            JNE     ExitTime             ;No, so set exit

            MOV     TSRActive,TRUE
            MOV     AL,20h               ;Signify end of interrupt
            OUT     20h,AL
            CALL    DoTSR                ;Yes, go handle TSR
            MOV     TSRActive,FALSE

ExitTime:   POP     ES
            POP     DS
            POP     BX
            POP     AX
            IRET


; The following is the new handler for the multiplex interrupt.
; Implements the following functions:
;       D700h      Installation state   AX=TRUE, Carry clear if installed
;       D701h      Current lock state   AX=TRUE, Carry set if locked
;       D702h      Lock keyboard
;       D703h      Unlock keyboard

Multiplex:  CMP     AH,0D7h              ;Is it our interrupt?
            JE      MPin                 ;Yes, so continue
            JMP     DWORD PTR CS:MultiInt ;Skip to original interrupt handler

MPin:       PUSH    DS                   ;Set up addressability
            PUSH    AX
            MOV     AX,CS
            MOV     DS,AX
            POP     AX

            CMP     AL,0                 ;Want to know installation state?
            JNE     MP1                  ;No, so look at next option
```

continues

Listing 5.4. Continued

```
            MOV     AX,TRUE
            JMP     RetCC                   ;Return with carry clear

MP1:        CMP     AL,1                    ;Want to know lock state?
            JNE     MP2
            MOV     AX,LockState
            CMP     AX,TRUE
            JE      RetCS                   ;Return with carry set
            JMP     RetCC                   ;Otherwise, return with carry clear

MP2:        CMP     AL,2                    ;Want to lock keyboard?
            JNE     MP3
            MOV     LockState,TRUE
            MOV     RequestFlag,FALSE       ;No request pending
            JMP     RetCC

MP3:        CMP     AL,3                    ;Want to unlock keyboard?
            JNE     MPErr
            MOV     LockState,FALSE
            MOV     RequestFlag,FALSE       ;No request pending

RetCC:      CLC
            JNC     MPDone
MPErr:      MOV     AX,1
RetCS:      STC                             ;Return with error
MPDone:     POP     DS                      ;Restore data segment
            RETF    2                       ;Don't want IRET because it restores
                                            ;the flags register


; The following routine is the main pop-up part of the TSR

DoTSR       PROC
            CLI
            MOV     CS:OrigSS,SS            ;Swap stack information
            MOV     CS:OrigSP,SP
            MOV     SS,CS:StkSeg
            MOV     SP,CS:StkPtr
            STI
```

```
            PUSH    AX
            PUSH    BX
            PUSH    CX
            PUSH    DX
            PUSH    SI
            PUSH    DI
            PUSH    DS
            PUSH    ES

            MOV     AX,CS               ;New segment address
            MOV     DS,AX

            MOV     AH,05h              ;Select active display page
            MOV     AL,01h              ;Want to use page 1
            INT     10h
            CALL    Cls                 ;Clear video page 1

            MOV     AX,0D701h           ;Get current state of lock
            INT     2Fh
            JC      TryUnlock           ;Locked, so try to unlock

            MOV     SI,OFFSET LPrompt   ;Point to locking prompt
            CALL    PrtString           ;Display it
            CALL    GetString           ;Go get input
            JCXZ    ResetVid            ;No password, exit early
            MOV     PWlength,CX         ;Store the length
            MOV     AX,CS
            MOV     ES,AX
            CLD
            MOV     SI,OFFSET InBuff
            MOV     DI,OFFSET Password
            REP     MOVSB               ;Move to password field
            MOV     AX,0D702h           ;Lock keyboard
            INT     2Fh
            CALL    ClrBuff             ;Clear the keyboard buffer
            JMP     ResetVid            ;And exit

TryUnlock:  MOV     SI,OFFSET UPrompt   ;Point to unlocking prompt
            CALL    PrtString           ;Display it
            CALL    GetString           ;Go get input
```

continues

Listing 5.4. Continued

```
              JCXZ    ResetVid            ;No password, exit early
              CMP     CX,PWlength         ;Same length as current one?
              JNE     BadMatch            ;No, so exit early

              MOV     AX,CS
              MOV     ES,AX
              CLD
              MOV     SI,OFFSET InBuff
              MOV     DI,OFFSET Password
              REPE    CMPSB               ;Compare strings
              JNE     BadMatch            ;Didn't match
              MOV     AX,0D703h           ;Unlock keyboard
              INT     2Fh
              JMP     ResetVid            ;And exit

BadMatch:     MOV     SI,OFFSET BadPass   ;Point to error message
              CALL    PrtString
              MOV     AH,10h              ;Wait for keypress from keyboard
              INT     16h

ResetVid:     MOV     AH,05h              ;Select active display page
              MOV     AL,00h              ;Set back to original page
              INT     10h
              MOV     RequestFlag,FALSE   ;Reset request flag
              POP     ES
              POP     DS
              POP     DI
              POP     SI
              POP     DX
              POP     CX
              POP     BX
              POP     AX

              CLI
              MOV     SS,CS:OrigSS        ;Swap stack information
              MOV     SP,CS:OrigSP
              STI
              RET
DoTSR         ENDP
```

```
; The following routine clears the entire keyboard buffer.

ClrBuff     PROC      USES AX
CB1:        MOV       AH,1              ;Read keyboard status
            INT       16h
            JZ        CBExit            ;No key, so exit
            MOV       AH,0              ;Read keyboard character
            INT       16h
            JMP       CB1               ;Go do it all again
CBExit:     RET
ClrBuff     ENDP


; Clear the screen and home the cursor. WORKS ON VIDEO PAGE 1 ONLY.

Cls         PROC      USES AX BX CX DX
            MOV       AH,8              ;Read character and attribute
            MOV       BH,1              ;Assume page 1
            INT       10h
            MOV       BH,AH             ;Put attribute in right place

            MOV       AH,6              ;Scroll window up
            MOV       AL,0              ;Scroll full screen
            MOV       CX,0              ;Upper left corner of screen
            MOV       DH,24             ;Bottom right
            MOV       DL,79
            INT       10h

            MOV       DX,0              ;Upper left corner of screen
            MOV       BH,1              ;Assume page 1
            MOV       AH,2              ;Set cursor position
            INT       10h


            RET
Cls         ENDP


; The following routine prints the ASCIIZ string pointed to by DS:SI.
; Writes only to video page 1.

PrtString   PROC      USES AX BX SI
            MOV       BH,01h            ;Write only to video page 1
PS1:        MOV       AL,[SI]           ;Get character
```

continues

Listing 5.4. Continued

```
                INC     SI                      ;Point to next one
                CMP     AL,0                    ;End of string?
                JE      PS2                     ;Yes, so exit
                MOV     AH,0Eh                  ;Write text
                INT     10h
                JMP     PS1                     ;Keep doing it
PS2:            RET
PrtString       ENDP


; The following routine gets a string at the current cursor position.
; Accumulates as many as 10 characters at InBuff. String entry halted
; by carriage return. Will handle backspace character. Otherwise, only
; printable characters are handled. Returns with CX set to the number
; of characters in the buffer. All other registers unchanged. Video
; output is to page 1.

GetString       PROC    USES AX BX DI DS ES
                MOV     AX,CS
                MOV     DS,AX
                MOV     ES,AX
                CLD
                MOV     DI,OFFSET InBuff        ;Point to start of buffer
                MOV     CX,10
                MOV     AL,0
                REP     STOSB                   ;Zero out the buffer

                MOV     DI,OFFSET InBuff        ;Point to start of buffer
                MOV     CX,0                    ;Character count
GS1:            MOV     AH,10h                  ;Get keystroke
                INT     16h
                CMP     CX,10                   ;At length limit?
                JE      GS2                     ;Yes, don't accept any other
                CMP     AL,' '                  ;Within lower range?
                JL      GS2                     ;No
                CMP     AL,'~'                  ;Within upper range?
                JA      GS2                     ;No
                STOSB
                INC     CX
                JMP     GS4                     ;Ready for next character
```

```
GS2:        CMP     AL,8                    ;Was it Backspace?
            JNE     GS3                     ;No, continue
            CMP     CX,0                    ;Already at left side?
            JE      GS5                     ;Yes, so ignore
            DEC     CX
            DEC     DI
            MOV     BYTE PTR ES:[DI],0      ;Zero it out
            MOV     AH,0Eh                  ;Write text
            MOV     BH,1                    ;Using video page 1
            INT     10h
            MOV     AL,' '                  ;Overwrite with space
            MOV     AH,0Eh                  ;Write text
            MOV     BH,1                    ;Using video page 1
            INT     10h
            MOV     AL,8                    ;Load with backspace again
            JMP     GS4
GS3:        CMP     AL,13                   ;Was it C/R?
            JE      GSDone                  ;Yes, so exit
            MOV     AL,7                    ;Bell character for error
GS4:        MOV     AH,0Eh                  ;Write text
            MOV     BH,1                    ;Using video page 1
            INT     10h
GS5:        JMP     GS1                     ;Do it all again

GSDone:     RET
GetString   ENDP
```

```
; The following data elements are here because they must be included in
; the memory reserved by the TSR call. If they are in the normal .DATA
; area, they are placed AFTER all the code. That would place them in the
; transient program area, which is discarded. That would cause a run-time
; error.
```

```
RequestFlag DW      0000
TSRActive   DW      0000
KeyInt      DW      0000,0000               ;Address for old keyboard routine
IdleInt     DW      0000,0000               ;Address for old idle routine
TimeInt     DW      0000,0000               ;Address for old timer tick
MultiInt    DW      0000,0000               ;Address for old multiplex interrupt
InDOSPtr    DW      0000,0000               ;Pointer to InDOS flag
LockState   DW      0000
```

continues

Listing 5.4. Continued

```
OrigSS       DW      0000                    ;Calling program SS:SP
OrigSP       DW      0000
LPrompt      DB      'Enter password to use: ',0
UPrompt      DB      'Enter password to unlock keyboard: ',0
BadPass      DB      13,10,'Incorrect password!  Press a key to continue...',7,0
InBuff       DB      11 DUP (0)
Password     DB      11 DUP (0)
PWlength     DW      0000
Temp         DW      0000                    ;Used as temporary area


; The following area is for the stack used by the TSR.

StkSeg       DW      0000
StkPtr       DW      0000
TSRStack     DB      StkSize DUP(0)


; This is the routine to hook in the interrupt intercepts

Hookin       PROC
             POP     AX                      ;Throw away the return address

AllOK:       MOV     AX,0D700h               ;Want to get state of TSR
             INT     2Fh
             JC      NotThere                ;Not there, so continue
             CMP     AX,TRUE                 ;Is it installed?
             JNE     NotThere                ;No, so continue
             MOV     DX,OFFSET AlreadyIn     ;Point to error message
             MOV     AH,09h                  ;Display string
             INT     21h
             MOV     AH,4Ch                  ;Terminate with code
             MOV     AL,1                    ;Error code=1
             INT     21h

NotThere:    MOV     AL,09h                  ;Changing this vector
             MOV     DI,OFFSET KeyInt        ;Storing old address here
             MOV     DX,OFFSET NewKeyInt     ;New offset address
             CALL    ChgInt                  ;Go change it

             MOV     AL,28h                  ;Changing this vector
             MOV     DI,OFFSET IdleInt       ;Storing old address here
```

```
        MOV     DX,OFFSET Idler       ;New offset address
        CALL    ChgInt                ;Go change it

        MOV     AL,1Ch                ;Changing this vector
        MOV     DI,OFFSET TimeInt     ;Storing old address here
        MOV     DX,OFFSET Timer       ;New offset address
        CALL    ChgInt                ;Go change it

        MOV     AL,2Fh                ;Changing this vector
        MOV     DI,OFFSET MultiInt    ;Storing old address here
        MOV     DX,OFFSET Multiplex   ;New offset address
        CALL    ChgInt                ;Go change it

        MOV     AX,0D703h             ;Unlock keyboard
        INT     2Fh
        MOV     TSRActive,FALSE       ;Indicate not in TSR right now

        MOV     AH,34h                ;Get InDOS flag
        INT     21h
        MOV     InDOSPtr[0],BX        ;Offset address
        MOV     InDOSPtr[2],ES        ;Segment address

        MOV     AX,CS
        MOV     StkSeg,AX             ;Store for later use
        MOV     AX,OFFSET TSRStack+StkSize ;Set top of stack
        MOV     StkPtr,AX

        MOV     ES,DS:[EnvBlock]      ;Get environment block segment
        MOV     AH,49h                ;Free memory block (don't need it)
        INT     21h

        MOV     DX,OFFSET Hooked      ;Point to initial message
        MOV     AH,09h                ;Display string
        INT     21h

        MOV     DX,OFFSET Hookin      ;End of resident area
        MOV     CL,4                  ;Divide by 16
        SHR     DX,CL                 ;No in paragraphs
        INC     DX                    ;Add 1 for good measure
        MOV     AL,0                  ;Return code is OK
        MOV     AH,31h                ;TSR function
        INT     21h
```

continues

Listing 5.4. Continued

```
Hookin      ENDP

; Set the interrupt pointed to by AL to the address in DS:DX
; Stores the old address in DS:DI.

ChgInt      PROC    USES AX DI
            MOV     AH,35h                ;Get interrupt address
            INT     21h
            MOV     DS:[DI],BX            ;Offset address
            MOV     DS:[DI+2],ES         ;Segment address

            MOV     AH,25h                ;Set interrupt vector to DS:DX
            INT     21h
            RET
ChgInt      ENDP

            END
```

When this program is compiled and linked to a COM file, it occupies slightly more than 1,300 bytes of memory when it is run. This amount of memory is relatively small for what TSRLOCK does. For TSRLOCK to do its work, the following interrupts are intercepted and monitored:

- Keyboard (09h, vectored to NewKeyInt)
- System timer (1Ch, vectored to Timer)
- DOS idle (28h, vectored to Idler)
- Multiplex (2Fh, vectored to Multiplex)

Each of these interrupts was discussed earlier in this chapter; the routines used as interrupt handlers are discussed later in this section.

This chapter has stated that a couple of assumptions are made by this program. You can easily modify one of the assumptions by changing the function key used as the hot key. You change the FuncScan equate at the beginning of the program. Just change it to the scan code of the key you want to use as the hot key. If your purpose in making the change is to make the program work on a wider variety of keyboards, you should also change the BIOS function called immediately after the BadMatch label. This function, one of the extended keyboard functions, waits for a keypress. You can change this function so that function 01h is called, and the program will work just as well.

You can make many other refinements or changes to TSRLOCK. For instance, you can make it work with all video modes. Or, you can make upper- and lowercase passwords the same (as written, TSRLOCK treats upper- and lower-case differently). The number of changes you make are limited only by your imagination and skill.

You should be aware that because of the way the keyboard interrupt is intercepted and monitored, this routine even disables Ctrl-Alt-Del when the keyboard is locked. Therefore, if you lock the keyboard and forget the password, the only way you can regain control of your system is to turn the computer off and then on again or use the hard-reset button available on some computers.

The remainder of this chapter looks at each of the subroutines in the program. They are presented in alphabetical order, not in order of appearance in the program.

ChgInt

The ChgInt routine is used by Hookin to save the current interrupt vectors and reset them to the new interrupt handlers. This is done with DOS functions 35h and 25h.

ClrBuff

The ClrBuff routine clears the keyboard buffer by reading information from the keyboard buffer until BIOS indicates that there is no more to read. This routine was used in some programs in Chapter 2, "Controlling the Keyboard."

Cls

The Cls routine clears the screen and homes the cursor. This version of the same routine used elsewhere in this book is modified to work only with video page 1. Only BIOS screen-control functions are used from this routine.

DoTSR

DoTSR, the main code for the TSR, controls password entry and verification. DoTSR does the following:

```
Swap the stack
Save all registers
```

```
Establish addressibility of variables
Change to video page 1
Clear the screen
Determine whether the keyboard is already locked
If unlocked:
     Prompt the user for a password
     If a password was entered:
          Save the length of the password
          Transfer the password to long-term storage
          Lock the keyboard
          Clear the keyboard buffer
If locked:
     Prompt the user for the password
     If a password was entered:
          Check the length of the entered password
          If correct length:
               Compare password against saved password
               If they are identical:
                    Unlock the keyboard
               If they are different:
                    Display a message
                    Wait for the user to press a key
          If incorrect length
               Display a message
               Wait for the user to press a key
Change to video page 0
Turn off hot key flag
Restore all registers
Swap the stack back
```

The size of the stack used by the TSR is controlled at compile time by the StkSize equate. In this listing, it is set to 256, which is the number of bytes set aside for the stack. This number should be plenty for most purposes. If you have numerous other TSR programs or software that uses the stack extensively, you may need to increase the stack size.

GetString

The GetString routine enables the user to enter a string. The information the user types is echoed to the screen at the current cursor location. This approach to this task is minimalistic—you can write a routine that is much more universal and powerful. If you do so, however, use BIOS functions only for all I/O. DOS character I/O functions are unstable in TSRs and therefore should not be used.

GetString accumulates as many as ten characters and places them in the variable InBuff. When the user presses Enter, the routine is exited. The only control key supported is the Backspace key; when it is pressed, the character to the left of the cursor is removed from the buffer and deleted from the screen.

When GetString returns to the calling routine, all registers are unchanged except CX, which is set to the number of characters in the buffer at InBuff.

As with other character I/O routines in this TSR, all output is to video page 1.

Hookin

The transient portion of the TSR is Hookin. It is called once, by TSRLock, and then it discards itself before returning to DOS by way of the TSR function. Hookin performs the following tasks:

- Checks the multiplex interrupt (D700h) to see whether TSRLOCK was previously installed; if it was, a message is displayed and the program is exited

- Sets the four vectors intercepted by the TSR, by using the ChgInt routine

- Makes sure that the keyboard is unlocked and the main TSR code flag is cleared

- Gets and saves the pointer to the InDOS flag

- Stores the pointers used by DoTSR to set the TSR stack

- Releases the memory reserved by the environment block

- Displays a welcome message

- Determines the memory that should be reserved and then returns to DOS by way of the TSR function

Idler

Idler is the interrupt handler for the DOS idle interrupt (28h). It is set up in the Hookin routine. When this interrupt is invoked by DOS, the routine checks to see whether the main TSR code (DoTSR) is active. If it is, or if the request flag has not been set (done in NewKeyInt), control is passed to the preceding DOS idle interrupt routine.

If the main TSR code is not active and the request flag has been set, the TSRActive flag is set and the main TSR code is called (DoTSR). When this routine returns, the TSRActive flag is cleared. Control then is passed to the preceding DOS idle interrupt routine.

Multiplex

The multiplex interrupt (2Fh) is used by TSR programs to provide an API to programs and to communicate with each other. You can determine the function values you want to use for your routines. Be aware, however, that Microsoft has reserved all multiplex functions below C000h for use by their TSRs (such as PRINT or SHARE or DOSVER). For TSRLOCK, I used the function D7h, with subfunctions 0 through 3. The functions provided for in TSRLOCK are shown in the following list:

Function	Purpose
D700h	Returns the installation state. Returns with AX=–1 (TRUE) and the carry flag clear if the multiplex functions are installed. If they are not installed, there is no change in AX.
D701h	Returns the current keyboard lock state. Returns AX=–1 (TRUE) and the carry flag set if the keyboard is locked. Returns AX=0 (FALSE) and the carry flag clear if the keyboard is unlocked.
D702h	Locks the keyboard. Sets the LockStatus variable to TRUE.
D703h	Unlocks the keyboard. Sets the LockStatus variable to FALSE.

If any other subfunction is specified, the carry flag is set on return and all other registers remain unchanged.

NewKeyInt

NewKeyInt is the interrupt handler for the keyboard interrupt (09h). It is set up in the Hookin procedure. In pseudocode, NewKeyInt does the following:

```
Wait for a complete keypress
Determine whether the keypress is the hot key
If no:
        Determine whether the keyboard is locked
        If no, process the keystroke in a normal manner
        If yes:
```

```
            Determine whether the main TSR code is active
            If yes, process the keystroke in a normal manner
            If no, ignore the keystroke
If yes:
     Determine whether the main TSR code is active
     If yes, ignore the keystroke
     If no:
            Set the request flag
            Ignore the keystroke
```

This routine does not invoke the main TSR code because, when this interrupt is invoked, the computer typically is busy doing something else and the InDOS flag usually is set. Therefore, invocation of the main routine is left to the Timer or Idler routines.

PrtString

PrtString is a modified version of the PrtString routine used elsewhere in this book. This version prints to the video screen the string pointed to by DS:SI. Other versions in this book use DOS function 02h to do this. This version uses BIOS functions to do effectively the same thing, because DOS character I/O functions are unstable in TSR programs and should not be called.

Timer

Timer is the interrupt handler for the system timer interrupt (1Ch). This routine is established and set up in the Hookin routine. Timer performs the following tasks:

```
Call the previous interrupt handler for the system timer.
Determine whether the main TSR code is active
If no:
     Determine if the hot key has been pressed
     If yes:
            Determine the status of the InDOS flag
            If clear:
                   Set the TSRActive flag
                   Enable interrupts
                   Call the main TSR code (DoTSR)
                   Clear the TSRActive flag
Return from interrupt
```

The flag that indicates whether a hot key has been pressed is RequestFlag; it is set in the NewKeyInt routine.

TSRLock

TSRLock is the main function used to start the program. It simply makes a call to Hookin.

Summary

TSR programming has been around for some time, and the techniques peculiar to these types of programs have baffled many programmers for just as many years. TSRs fall into two main categories: passive and active. The category of TSR depends on how much control it exerts on your computer system.

You can find or write TSRs that perform any number of tasks, but they all follow the same basic steps. All TSRs have a transient portion (which sets up the TSR and then is discarded) and a resident portion (which remains in memory). The number of interrupts a TSR must monitor and control is directly related to the complexity of the task being accomplished.

I can't close without noting that if DOS were a reentrant system, TSR programming would be much easier and "programmer friendly." But that is a big *if*. DOS is not reentrant, and likely never will be. Future operating systems may solve this shortcoming, but until then TSR programmers must learn and apply the principles covered in this chapter.

Expanded and Extended Memory

This chapter discusses one of the areas that, as a programmer, you must understand in order to effectively use and control your computer: memory. It sounds simple enough, but it really isn't. Memory and its use has grown from humble beginnings to one of the most complex areas of computers.

In the '80s, when the PC was young and no one realized the market that was opening, the PC had what seemed then to be numerous capabilities. One of the PC's key selling points was that it was supplied with 16 kilobytes of memory, and you could upgrade it to 256 kilobytes. Although that amount was sufficient for a while, within a relatively short time, program requirements for the new business computer market dictated the need for increasingly more memory. That was okay, however, because the CPU used in the PC could handle as much as 1,024 kilobytes—one megabyte—of memory. Not all of that amount was available to programmers, however; some was used by hardware components and other parts by the operating system. The net result was that programmers had about 640 kilobytes of memory at their disposal.

Now, just a few years later, 640 kilobytes doesn't seem like that much memory. Program needs have evolved to where many programs require 2 megabytes or more to run. Some require even 4 or 8 megabytes, and the need for more memory probably will not abate. How did we get from 640 kilobytes (or 1 megabyte) to the multi-megabyte system requirements of many of today's programs? The answer is almost simple: expanded and extended memory.

To understand expanded and extended memory, you must understand also all the other types of memory available in your system. Let's take a broad look at the memory use on a PC. Figure 6.1 shows the general breakdown of the memory areas in your system.

Figure 6.1.

Memory areas and classifications within the PC.

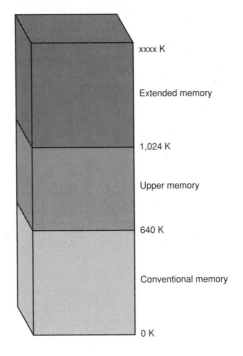

xxxx K

Extended memory

1,024 K

Upper memory

640 K

Conventional memory

0 K

The area between 0 and 640 kilobytes is termed *conventional memory* because it is simply the work area set aside for general programs by the designers of the original PC. The area between 640 kilobytes and 1,024 kilobytes (1 megabyte) is called *upper memory* because it resides at the upper boundary of what the original 8086/8088 could address. The area above the 1-megabyte boundary is called *extended memory* because it extended the original memory space available on the PC.

These three types of linear memory are the ones available on the PC. Both conventional and upper memory can be addressed by the PC in *real mode*, in which the CPU uses a traditional 20-bit address register, expressed in the familiar segment:offset format. The extended memory area can be addressed by only 80286 or later CPUs, and then only if they are operating in protected mode.

In Figure 6.1, a major memory term is missing. What about expanded memory? This type of memory was an outgrowth of the need that users of the original PC had for more memory. It employs an old computing technique called *bank switching*, which involves mapping portions of a large memory space (the expanded part) into a memory area that can be readily addressed by the CPU. These portions are called *banks* (of memory); the *switching* part is that you can selectively map which ones are available at any time. Because the mapping occurred in the upper memory area, in either 16K or 64K chunks, the CPU can easily address the memory.

The following list summarizes the major memory areas:

- Conventional memory: 0 to 640 kilobytes

- Upper memory: 640 kilobytes to 1 megabyte

- Expanded memory: additional memory swapped into holes in the upper memory area

- Extended memory: 1 megabyte and up

This chapter does not dwell on the history of memory approaches or standards or on what typically resides in each memory area on your computer. Plenty of available sources provide much more information on these areas than what can be addressed here. This book does discuss how to use the memory you have. It examines methods and standards that have been developed to aid in your exploitation of these different memory areas, and then briefly shows you how to use them.

Using Expanded Memory

The expanded memory specification abided by today was developed by Lotus, Intel, and Microsoft (LIM), in conjunction with other software and hardware vendors. Several versions of the LIM Expanded Memory Specification (LIM EMS) have been created (the most recent version is 4.0).

To begin understanding how you can work with expanded memory, you should be able to visualize the way this type of memory works. LIM EMS divides the PC's upper memory area into *page frames*. Each page frame begins at a memory segment address that ends in three zeros (see Figure 6.2).

Because three of the six page frames are occupied or reserved, three page frames in upper memory are available for use. A program called an *expanded memory manager* (EMM) can swap blocks of data in and out of these page frames (see Figure 6.3).

LIM EMS stipulates that each page frame, which is 64 kilobytes in length, is broken down into four individual 16-kilobyte pages. These individual pages are what the EMM swaps in and out of upper memory as needed. LIM EMS is the set of guidelines that dictate how all this is supposed to work.

Figure 6.2.

The six page frames in the PC's upper memory area.

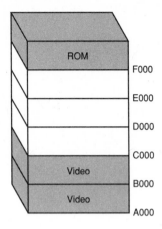

ROM
F000
E000
D000
C000
Video
B000
Video
A000

Figure 6.3.

An expanded memory manager swaps data in and out of page frames in the upper memory area.

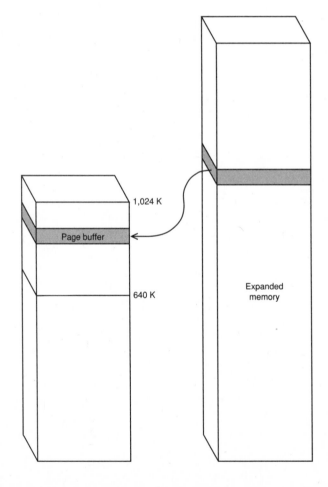

1,024 K

Page buffer

640 K

Expanded memory

The interface you use to work with the EMM is a series of function calls available through interrupt 67h. These function calls are used in the programs in this chapter (and elsewhere in this book), and are detailed in Appendix C, "The EMS Functions."

Determining Whether Expanded Memory Is Present

How can you determine whether expanded memory is installed in a system, and how much is there? There are a couple of ways to do it, and the easiest involves the following two steps:

1. Open the device name EMMXXXX0 as a file using DOS function 3Dh. If there is an error, the EMM is not present.

2. Test whether the open device is ready for output, using IOCTL function 07h. If the return value is not –1, the EMM is not present.

If your program successfully completes both these tasks, you can close the file and assume that the EMM is present. You then are free to access the EMM through the standard Int 67h functions.

The program in Listing 6.1, EMSINFO.ASM, tests to see whether the EMM is present and then displays a small amount of information about expanded memory in your system.

Listing 6.1. EMSINFO.ASM

```
Page 60,132

Comment ¦
*****************************************************************


File:       EMSINFO.ASM
Author:     Allen L. Wyatt
Date:       7/29/92
Assembler:  MASM 6.0

Purpose:    Display information about expanded memory

Format:     EMSINFO


*****************************************************************¦
```

continues

Listing 6.1. Continued

```
            .MODEL  small
            .STACK                          ;Default 1K stack is OK
            .DATA

EMSName     DB      'EMMXXXX0',0
InMsg       DB      'An expanded memory manager is installed',13,10,0
NoneMsg     DB      'No expanded memory manager detected',13,10,0
Version     DB      'Supports EMS version '
Major       DB      00,'.'
Minor       DB      00,'.'
CRLF        DB      13,10,0
PageMsg     DB      'Using page frame address: ',0
TotalMsg    DB      'Total expanded memory:       ',0
FreeMsg     DB      'Expanded memory available: ',0

            .CODE
            .STARTUP
EMSinfo     PROC

            CALL    ChkEMS              ;See if EMM present
            JNC     ItsThere
            MOV     SI,OFFSET NoneMsg
            CALL    PrtString
            JMP     AllDone

ItsThere:   MOV     SI,OFFSET InMsg
            CALL    PrtString

            MOV     AH,46h              ;Get EMS version
            INT     67h
            MOV     AH,AL
            AND     AH,1111b            ;Minor version
            MOV     CL,4
            SHR     AL,CL               ;Major version
            OR      AX,3030h            ;Turn to ASCII
            MOV     Major,AL
            MOV     Minor,AH
            MOV     SI,OFFSET Version
            CALL    PrtString

            MOV     SI,OFFSET PageMsg   ;Page frame message
            CALL    PrtString
```

```
            MOV     AH,41h              ;Get page frame address
            INT     67h
            MOV     AX,BX              ;This is the page frame base
            CALL    PrtHex
            MOV     SI,OFFSET CRLF
            CALL    PrtString
            CALL    PrtString

            MOV     SI,OFFSET TotalMsg  ;Total memory message
            CALL    PrtString
            MOV     AH,42h
            INT     67h
            MOV     AX,DX
            MOV     DX,0
            MOV     CX,4000h
            MUL     CX
            CALL    PrtDec
            MOV     SI,OFFSET CRLF
            CALL    PrtString

            MOV     SI,OFFSET FreeMsg   ;Available memory message
            CALL    PrtString
            MOV     AX,BX
            MOV     DX,0
            MOV     BX,4000h
            MUL     BX
            CALL    PrtDec
            MOV     SI,OFFSET CRLF
            CALL    PrtString

AllDone:
            .EXIT
EMSinfo     ENDP


; The following routine checks to see whether an EMM is installed.
; If one is not, the carry flag is set on return.
; If one is, the carry flag is cleared on return.

ChkEMS      PROC    USES AX BX DX ES
            MOV     DX,OFFSET EMSName   ;Device driver name
            MOV     AH,3Dh              ;Open file
            MOV     AL,0                ;Access/file sharing mode
```

continues

Listing 6.1. Continued

```
                INT     21h
                JC      NotThere2
                MOV     BX,AX              ;Put handle in proper place
                MOV     AH,44h             ;IOCTL
                MOV     AL,07h             ;Get output status
                INT     21h
                JC      NotThere1
                CMP     AL,0FFh
                JNE     NotThere1
                MOV     AH,3Eh             ;Close file
                INT     21h
                CLC                        ;Set for no error
                JNC     Done

NotThere1:      MOV     AH,3Eh             ;Close file
                INT     21h
NotThere2:      STC
Done:           RET
ChkEMS          ENDP


; The following routine prints the ASCIIZ string pointed to by DS:SI

PrtString       PROC    USES AX DX SI
PS1:            MOV     DL,[SI]            ;Get character
                INC     SI                 ;Point to next one
                CMP     DL,0               ;End of string?
                JE      PS2                ;Yes, so exit
                MOV     AH,02h             ;Output a character
                INT     21h
                JMP     PS1                ;Keep doing it
PS2:            RET
PrtString       ENDP


; The following routine prints the value in AX as a hex number

PrtHex          PROC    USES AX CX DX
                MOV     CX,0FFFFh          ;Ending flag
                PUSH    CX
                MOV     CX,10h             ;Divide by 16
PH1:            MOV     DX,0
```

```
                DIV     CX                  ;Divide by 16
                ADD     DL,30h              ;Convert to ASCII
                PUSH    DX                  ;Store remainder
                CMP     AX,0                ;Are we done?
                JNE     PH1                 ;No, so continue

PH2:            POP     DX                  ;Character is now in DL
                CMP     DX,0FFFFh           ;Is it the ending flag?
                JE      PH4                 ;Yes, so continue
                CMP     DL,'9'              ;Greater than 9?
                JBE     PH3
                ADD     DL,7                ;Convert to hex
PH3:            MOV     AH,02h              ;Output a character
                INT     21h
                JMP     PH2                 ;Keep doing it

PH4:            RET
PrtHex          ENDP


; The following routine prints the value in DX:AX as a decimal number
; Will accept numbers up to 655,359,999. Anything larger will not print.

                .DATA
Temp            DW      0000

                .CODE
PrtDec          PROC    USES AX BX CX DX

                MOV     CX,0FFFFh           ;Ending flag
                PUSH    CX

PD0:            MOV     CX,10000            ;Divide by 10,000
                DIV     CX
                MOV     Temp,AX             ;Store whole portion
                MOV     BX,0                ;Count for this iteration

                MOV     AX,DX
                MOV     CX,10
PD1:            MOV     DX,0
                DIV     CX                  ;Divide by 10
                ADD     DL,30h              ;Convert to ASCII
```

continues

Listing 6.1. Continued

```
              PUSH    DX                      ;Store remainder
              INC     BX                      ;Cycle count
              CMP     AX,0                    ;Are we done?
              JNE     PD1                     ;No, so continue
              MOV     DX,0
              MOV     AX,Temp                 ;Get back part above 10,000
              CMP     AX,0
              JE      PD3
              MOV     CX,'0'
PD2:          CMP     BX,4                    ;Did we push 4 numbers?
              JE      PD0                     ;Yes, continue
              PUSH    CX                      ;No, so push it
              INC     BX                      ;Push counter
              JMP     PD2

PD3:          POP     DX                      ;Character is now in DL
              CMP     DX,0FFFFh               ;Is it the ending flag?
              JE      PD4                     ;Yes, so continue
              MOV     AH,02h                  ;Output a character
              INT     21h
              JMP     PD3                     ;Keep doing it

PD4:          RET
PrtDec        ENDP

              END
```

The EMM detection work occurs in the subroutine ChkEMS. This program uses other EMS functions also to determine the EMS version number supported, the page frame address, and the amount of memory available.

Allocating and Using Expanded Memory

After you have determined that an expanded memory manager is in your system and that expanded memory is available, you must follow a few more steps to use expanded memory:

1. Allocate the memory using EMS function 43h. Make sure that you save the EMS handle returned by the function.

2. Map the memory to a page frame using EMS function 44h. You will have to use the handle you received in step 1.

3. Get the page frame address using EMS function 41h. This function gives you the segment address to access the memory.

After you complete these steps, you can determine the address of the pages of memory within the page frame and access it like regular conventional memory. The program in Listing 6.2, EMSTEST.ASM, is an example of implementing these steps.

Listing 6.2. EMSTEST.ASM

```
Page 60,132

Comment ¦
*******************************************************************


File:       EMSTEST.ASM
Author:     Allen L. Wyatt
Date:       7/30/92
Assembler:  MASM 6.0


Purpose:    Allocate a block of expanded memory, write to it,
            read the information from there, and then display it.


Format:     EMSTEST


*******************************************************************¦

            .MODEL   small
            .STACK                    ;Default 1K stack is OK
            .DATA

EMSName     DB       'EMMXXXX0',0
EMPhandle   DW       0000
FillMsg     DB       'Filling expanded memory pages',13,10,0
ReadMsg     DB       'Reading expanded memory pages',13,10,0
TestMsg     DB       'This is test message '
Count       DB       '   1',13,0

EMsg1       DB       'Expanded memory manager not installed',13,10,0
EMsg2       DB       'Could not allocate memory requested',13,10,0
EMsg3       DB       'Error mapping memory',13,10,0
EMsg4       DB       'Could not determine page frame',13,10,0
EMsg5       DB       'Error releasing EMS handle',13,10,0
```

continues

Listing 6.2. Continued

```
            .CODE
            .STARTUP
EMSTest     PROC

            CALL    ChkEMS              ;See if EMM present
            JC      Error1              ;Not there

            MOV     AH,43h              ;Allocate pages
            MOV     BX,2                ;Get 2 pages (32K)
            INT     67h
            CMP     AH,0                ;Was there an error?
            JNE     Error2              ;Yes, so handle
            MOV     EMPhandle,DX        ;No, save handle

            MOV     AH,44h              ;Map memory
            MOV     AL,0                ;First EMS page
            MOV     BX,0                ;Want this part of my memory
            MOV     DX,EMPhandle        ;Assigned to this handle
            INT     67h
            CMP     AH,0                ;Was there an error?
            JNE     Error3              ;Yes, so handle
            MOV     AH,44h              ;Map memory
            MOV     AL,1
            MOV     BX,1
            INT     67h
            CMP     AH,0                ;Was there an error?
            JNE     Error3              ;Yes, so handle

            MOV     AH,41h              ;Get page frame address
            INT     67h
            CMP     AH,0                ;Was there an error?
            JNE     Error4              ;Yes, so handle
            MOV     ES,BX               ;Make page frame addressable

            MOV     SI,OFFSET FillMsg
            CALL    PrtString
            MOV     CX,1213             ;27-character message fits this
            CLD                         ;  many times in 32K
            MOV     DI,0000             ;Start of page buffer
InLoop:     PUSH    CX
            MOV     SI,OFFSET TestMsg
```

```
            MOV     CX,27               ;Length of message
            REP     MOVSB
            CALL    IncMsg              ;Increment the counter
            POP     CX
            LOOP    InLoop
            MOV     AL,0FFh
            STOSB

            MOV     SI,OFFSET ReadMsg
            CALL    PrtString
            MOV     SI,0
            PUSH    DS                  ;Set up addressing
            PUSH    ES
            POP     DS
OutLoop:    CALL    PrtString
            CMP     BYTE PTR [SI],0FFh
            JNE     OutLoop
            POP     DS

            MOV     AH,45h              ;Release EMS handle
            MOV     DX,EMPhandle        ;This handle
            INT     67h
            CMP     AH,0                ;Was there an error
            JNE     Error5
            JMP     AllDone

Error1:     MOV     SI,OFFSET EMsg1     ;No EMM in system
            JMP     ErrCommon
Error2:     MOV     SI,OFFSET EMsg2
            JMP     ErrCommon
Error3:     MOV     SI,OFFSET EMsg3
            JMP     ErrCommon
Error4:     MOV     SI,OFFSET EMsg4
            JMP     ErrCommon
Error5:     MOV     SI,OFFSET EMsg5
ErrCommon:  CALL    PrtString

AllDone:
            .EXIT
EMSTest     ENDP
```

continues

Listing 6.2. Continued

```
; The following routine checks to see whether an EMM is installed.
; If one is not, the carry flag is set on return.
; If one is, the carry flag is cleared on return.

ChkEMS     PROC    USES AX BX DX ES
           MOV     DX,OFFSET EMSName     ;Device driver name
           MOV     AH,3Dh               ;Open file
           MOV     AL,0                 ;Access/file sharing mode
           INT     21h
           JC      NotThere2
           MOV     BX,AX                ;Put handle in proper place
           MOV     AH,44h               ;IOCTL
           MOV     AL,07h               ;Get output status
           INT     21h
           JC      NotThere1
           CMP     AL,0FFh
           JNE     NotThere1
           MOV     AH,3Eh               ;Close file
           INT     21h
           CLC                          ;Set for no error
           JNC     Done

NotThere1: MOV     AH,3Eh               ;Close file
           INT     21h
NotThere2: STC
Done:      RET
ChkEMS     ENDP



; Increment the message being stored in memory

IncMsg     PROC    USES SI
           MOV     SI,OFFSET Count
           ADD     SI,3
IM1:       INC     BYTE PTR [SI]
           CMP     BYTE PTR [SI],':'    ;Out of number range?
           JNE     IM3                  ;No, so continue
           MOV     BYTE PTR [SI],'0'    ;Reset to 0
           DEC     SI
           CMP     BYTE PTR [SI],' '    ;Filled in yet?
```

```
            JNE     IM2
            MOV     BYTE PTR [SI],'0'    ;Reset to 0
IM2:        JMP     IM1
IM3:        RET
IncMsg      ENDP


; The following routine prints the ASCIIZ string pointed to by DS:SI.
; The only register affected by this routine is SI.

PrtString   PROC    USES AX DX
PS1:        MOV     DL,[SI]              ;Get character
            INC     SI                  ;Point to next one
            CMP     DL,0                 ;End of string?
            JE      PS2                  ;Yes, so exit
            MOV     AH,02h               ;Output a character
            INT     21h
            JMP     PS1                  ;Keep doing it
PS2:        RET
PrtString   ENDP

            END
```

It is important to remember to release any EMS memory you allocate in your programs. In EMSTEST.ASM, this release is performed, using EMS function 45h, immediately after OutLoop is finished executing. If you do not remember to release the EMS memory, the memory will not be available to other programs you run later.

Accessing Extended Memory

Extended memory is the area of memory above the 1-megabyte boundary. This type of memory cannot be accessed by programs running in real mode, including MS-DOS. To access extended memory, your program must be operating in protected mode. When your programs are operating in protected mode, they cannot access BIOS, DOS, or other system functions that are readily accessible from real mode. This limitation can be a drag. Extended memory opens up new vistas for programmers because you can have as much as 4 *gigabytes* of extended memory on an 80386 or 80486 computer. It is wasted ground, however, if you can't use the system support functions you need.

To use all that extended memory and still use the operating system we all know and love, your program must be able, therefore, to switch between real mode and protected mode. With each switch, your view of the environment changes because you relate to the memory around you in entirely different ways. In effect, it is impossible to discuss using extended memory without discussing protected mode programming also.

Only a few methods and tools are available to make the job of switching operating modes easier. These tools, which all have advantages and disadvantages, include writing the context-switching algorithms yourself, using the limited BIOS support available, or using a commercial DOS extender. Not all of these tools are discussed fully here because several excellent books already describe them in much more depth. This chapter briefly describes the BIOS routines available and the extended memory access specifications that have been developed. This discussion should give you a taste for access to extended memory. See Chapter 12 also for information about protected-mode programming.

BIOS Extended-Memory Functions

If you have an 80286-, 80386-, or 80486-class machine, there is an excellent chance that you have two BIOS functions available to access extended mode from real mode. Interrupt 15h, function 88h enables you to determine how much extended memory you have, and interrupt 15h, function 87h enables you to move a block of memory anywhere within conventional or extended memory.

To illustrate quickly and simply the use of interrupt 15h, function 88h, look at the program in Listing 6.3, EXTSIZE.ASM.

Listing 6.3. EXTSIZE.ASM

```
Page 60,132

Comment ¦
*****************************************************************


        File:       EXTSIZE.ASM
        Author:     Allen L. Wyatt
        Date:       7/30/92
        Assembler:  MASM 6.0

        Purpose:    Display size of extended memory installed

        Format:     EXTSIZE


*****************************************************************¦
```

```
            .MODEL   small
            .STACK                       ;Default 1K stack is OK
            .DATA

EMsg1       DB       'BIOS function not available'
CRLF        DB       13,10,0
TotalMsg    DB       'Total extended memory:  ',0

            .CODE
            .STARTUP
ExtSize     PROC

            MOV      AH,88h               ;Get extended memory size
            INT      15h
            JC       Error                ;Function not available

            MOV      SI,OFFSET TotalMsg   ;Total memory message
            CALL     PrtString
            MOV      DX,0
            MOV      CX,400h
            MUL      CX
            CALL     PrtDec
            MOV      SI,OFFSET CRLF
            CALL     PrtString
            JMP      AllDone

Error:      MOV      SI,OFFSET EMsg1
            CALL     PrtString

AllDone:
            .EXIT
ExtSize     ENDP


; The following routine prints the ASCIIZ string pointed to by DS:SI

PrtString   PROC     USES AX DX SI
PS1:        MOV      DL,[SI]              ;Get character
            INC      SI                   ;Point to next one
            CMP      DL,0                 ;End of string?
            JE       PS2                  ;Yes, so exit
            MOV      AH,02h               ;Output a character
            INT      21h
            JMP      PS1                  ;Keep doing it
```

continues

Listing 6.3. Continued

```
PS2:        RET
PrtString   ENDP


; The following routine prints the value in DX:AX as a decimal number.
; Will accept numbers up to 655,359,999. Anything larger will not print.


            .DATA
Temp        DW      0000

            .CODE
PrtDec      PROC    USES AX BX CX DX

            MOV     CX,0FFFFh               ;Ending flag
            PUSH    CX

PD0:        MOV     CX,10000                ;Divide by 10,000
            DIV     CX
            MOV     Temp,AX                 ;Store whole portion
            MOV     BX,0                    ;Count for this iteration

            MOV     AX,DX
            MOV     CX,10
PD1:        MOV     DX,0
            DIV     CX                      ;Divide by 10
            ADD     DL,30h                  ;Convert to ASCII
            PUSH    DX                      ;Store remainder
            INC     BX                      ;Cycle count
            CMP     AX,0                    ;Are we done?
            JNE     PD1                     ;No, so continue
            MOV     DX,0
            MOV     AX,Temp                 ;Get back part above 10,000
            CMP     AX,0
            JE      PD3
            MOV     CX,'0'
PD2:        CMP     BX,4                    ;Did we push 4 numbers?
            JE      PD0                     ;Yes, continue
            PUSH    CX                      ;No, so push it
            INC     BX                      ;Push counter
            JMP     PD2

PD3:        POP     DX                      ;Character is now in DL
```

```
          CMP     DX,0FFFFh           ;Is it the ending flag?
          JE      PD4                 ;Yes, so continue
          MOV     AH,02h              ;Output a character
          INT     21h
          JMP     PD3                 ;Keep doing it

PD4:      RET
PrtDec    ENDP

          END
```

This simple program does only one thing: prints the number of bytes of extended memory available in your system. The value returned in AX is the amount of *extended* memory—the memory above 1 megabyte—in 1-kilobyte increments. If you want to adjust for the total memory in your system, add 1,024 to AX and multiply by 1,024.

You should understand that this program may not (at first) appear to work correctly on your system. If you have a full-blown memory manager installed, such as HIMEM.SYS, from Microsoft, or QEMM386, from Quarterdeck, the program returns zero bytes of extended memory available because the memory manager manages all the extended memory itself. To see how the program really works, remove the memory manager and try again.

The Extended Memory Specification (XMS)

Early attempts to provide consistent interfaces to extended memory led to the development of the extended memory specification (XMS) and, later, to VCPI and DPMI. This section discusses XMS; the following two sections discuss VCPI and DPMI.

The same people who brought us the EMS got together with other major software and hardware companies in 1988 and published the extended memory specification. It was one of the first efforts to access extended memory and also enabled the management of upper memory and high memory. *High memory* is the first 64 kilobytes of extended memory (less 16 bytes), the area effectively between 1024K and 1088K.

Wait! You might ask how a real mode program, which is limited to the 20-bit addresses, can access any memory above 1 megabyte. It's a good question. This chapter has indicated that programs running in real mode cannot access any memory above the 1-megabyte boundary because the addresses you load in a segment:offset pair cannot translate to a physical address above FFFFFh. Any addresses that translated above this boundary will wrap, resulting in the segment register being set to 0. Therefore, the address FFFF:FFFFh would wrap to 0000:FFEFh.

This boundary was stretched, however, by 64 kilobytes when Microsoft introduced Windows 2.1. Microsoft discovered that, on 80286 or greater machines, it could stretch the boundary by enabling the A20 line on the CPU, which turns on 21-bit physical addresses. Because there were then 21 bits, no more wrapping would occur. The address FFFF:FFFFh would correctly translate to 10FFEFh because it fit in the address register. On 80286 or greater machines, therefore, with the A20 line enabled, you could access addresses between FFFFh and 10FFEFh from real mode. But that was the absolute limit, because FFFF:FFFFh was the largest segment:offset pair that could be constructed.

What does this have to do with XMS? As indicated earlier, the specification allowed for the management of upper memory (640K to 1024K), high memory (1024K to 1088K), and extended memory (all memory above that amount).

Implementation of the XMS specification means that you must have an extended memory manager (XMM) installed in your system. HIMEM.SYS from Microsoft is an example of such a device driver. Other, more sophisticated memory managers are available that support expanded (LIM EMS) and extended (XMS) function calls.

The XMS function calls are accessed not through any particular interrupt, but through an entry point. You can determine whether an XMS-compliant driver is loaded by using interrupt 2Fh, function 4300h. Assuming that this function indicates that the driver is present, the entry point for the XMS driver is discovered by using interrupt 2Fh, function 4310h. The program in Listing 6.4, XMSINFO.ASM, displays information about extended memory derived through the XMS driver.

Listing 6.4. XMSINFO.ASM

```
Page 60,132

Comment |
******************************************************************


File:       XMSINFO.ASM
Author:     Allen L. Wyatt
Date:       7/30/92
Assembler:  MASM 6.0

Purpose:    Display information about extended memory using XMS functions

Format:     XMSINFO


******************************************************************|
```

```
            .MODEL  small
            .STACK                      ;Default 1K stack is OK
            .DATA

XMSentry    DD      00000000
InMsg       DB      'An XMS-compliant extended memory manager is installed',13,10,0
Version     DB      'Supports XMS version '
Major       DB      00,'.'
Minor       DB      00,'.'
CRLF        DB      13,10,0
EnabMsg     DB      'The A20 line is enabled',13,10,0
DisMsg      DB      'The A20 line is disabled',13,10,0

TotalMsg    DB      'Total extended memory:      ',0
FreeMsg     DB      'Extended memory available:  ',0

EMsg1       DB      'No XMS-compliant expanded memory manager detected',13,10,0
EMsg2       DB      'Error checking on A20 line',13,10,0


            .CODE
            .STARTUP
XMSinfo     PROC

            CALL    ChkXMS              ;See if EMM present
            JC      Error1              ;Not there
            MOV     SI,OFFSET InMsg
            CALL    PrtString

            MOV     AH,0                ;Get XMS version
            CALL    XMSentry
            OR      AX,3030h            ;Turn to ASCII
            MOV     Major,AH
            MOV     Minor,AL
            MOV     SI,OFFSET Version
            CALL    PrtString

            MOV     AH,07h              ;Get status of A20 line
            CALL    XMSentry
```

continues

Listing 6.4. Continued

```
           MOV     SI,OFFSET EnabMsg    ;Assume enabled
           CMP     AX,1                 ;Was it enabled?
           JE      Enabled              ;Yes, continue
           CMP     BL,0                 ;Was there really an error?
           JNE     Error2               ;Yes, so handle
           MOV     SI,OFFSET DisMsg     ;No, so it is disabled
Enabled:   CALL    PrtString

           MOV     SI,OFFSET TotalMsg   ;Total extended memory message
           CALL    PrtString
           MOV     AH,08h               ;Query free extended memory
           CALL    XMSentry

           PUSH    AX                   ;Save available
           MOV     AX,DX                ;Move total amount
           MOV     DX,0
           MOV     CX,400h
           MUL     CX
           CALL    PrtDec
           MOV     SI,OFFSET CRLF
           CALL    PrtString

           MOV     SI,OFFSET FreeMsg    ;Available memory message
           CALL    PrtString
           POP     AX                   ;Get back amount
           MOV     DX,0
           MOV     BX,400h
           MUL     BX
           CALL    PrtDec
           MOV     SI,OFFSET CRLF
           CALL    PrtString
           JMP     AllDone

Error1:    MOV     SI,OFFSET EMsg1
           JMP     ErrCommon
Error2:    MOV     SI,OFFSET EMsg2
ErrCommon: CALL    PrtString

AllDone:
           .EXIT
XMSinfo    ENDP
```

```
; The following routine checks to see whether an XMM is installed.
; If one is not, the carry flag is set on return.
; If one is, the address is stored and the carry flag is cleared on return.

ChkXMS      PROC      USES AX BX ES
            MOV       AX,4300h                ;Get XMS installed state
            INT       2Fh
            CMP       AL,0
            JE        NotThere
            MOV       AX,4310h                ;Get entry point
            INT       2Fh
            MOV       WORD PTR XMSentry[0],BX
            MOV       WORD PTR XMSentry[2],ES
            CLC                               ;Set for no error
            JNC       Done
NotThere:   STC
Done:       RET
ChkXMS      ENDP


; The following routine prints the ASCIIZ string pointed to by DS:SI.

PrtString   PROC      USES AX DX SI
PS1:        MOV       DL,[SI]                 ;Get character
            INC       SI                      ;Point to next one
            CMP       DL,0                    ;End of string?
            JE        PS2                     ;Yes, so exit
            MOV       AH,02h                  ;Output a character
            INT       21h
            JMP       PS1                     ;Keep doing it
PS2:        RET
PrtString   ENDP


; The following routine prints the value in DX:AX as a decimal number.
; Will accept numbers up to 655,359,999. Anything larger will not print.

            .DATA
Temp        DW        0000
```

continues

Listing 6.4. Continued

```
            .CODE
PrtDec      PROC    USES AX BX CX DX

            MOV     CX,0FFFFh           ;Ending flag
            PUSH    CX

PD0:        MOV     CX,10000            ;Divide by 10,000
            DIV     CX
            MOV     Temp,AX             ;Store whole portion
            MOV     BX,0                ;Count for this iteration

            MOV     AX,DX
            MOV     CX,10
PD1:        MOV     DX,0
            DIV     CX                  ;Divide by 10
            ADD     DL,30h              ;Convert to ASCII
            PUSH    DX                  ;Store remainder
            INC     BX                  ;Cycle count
            CMP     AX,0                ;Are we done?
            JNE     PD1                 ;No, so continue
            MOV     DX,0
            MOV     AX,Temp             ;Get back part above 10,000
            CMP     AX,0
            JE      PD3
            MOV     CX,'0'
PD2:        CMP     BX,4                ;Did we push 4 numbers?
            JE      PD0                 ;Yes, continue
            PUSH    CX                  ;No, so push it
            INC     BX                  ;Push counter
            JMP     PD2

PD3:        POP     DX                  ;Character is now in DL
            CMP     DX,0FFFFh           ;Is it the ending flag?
            JE      PD4                 ;Yes, so continue
            MOV     AH,02h              ;Output a character
            INT     21h
            JMP     PD3                 ;Keep doing it

PD4:        RET
PrtDec      ENDP

            END
```

All other XMS functions are accessed in this same way. If you are interested in more detail on the XMS functions available, see Appendix D, "The XMS Functions."

VCPI

At about the same time that the XMS specification emerged, another standard for the use of extended memory also was released. This standard addresses the conflicts that arise when EMS emulators and DOS extenders operate in the same machine. EMS emulators are memory managers that treat extended memory as though it were expanded memory; DOS extenders are programs that handle the complex task of allowing DOS programs full access to extended memory by way of protected mode context switching. This standard is called the *virtual control program interface*, or VCPI. It is effectively an extension of the LIM EMS 4.0 specification, and is applicable only to 80386 systems or greater. It was developed by Phar Lap Software, a vendor of DOS extenders, and Quarterdeck Office Systems, a vendor of an EMS-emulating memory manager.

The VCPI specification defines an interface, implemented by a series of function calls, that the client can use to request services from the server. Without such an arrangement, confusion over who would provide what services made coexistence between EMS emulators and DOS extenders impossible.

The VCPI function calls are accessed through interrupt 67h, the same interrupt used for EMS function calls. For more detailed information about the VCPI function calls, see Appendix D, "The XMS Functions."

VCPI deals with memory in a client/server relationship. The EMS emulator is the server, and the DOS extender is the client. Technically, according to the VCPI specification, any program that offers both EMS 4.0 and VCPI functions is considered a VCPI server, and any program that accesses those functions is considered a VCPI client. Because the majority of VCPI clients are DOS extenders, it is not unusual (although it is technically incorrect) to imply that the only VCPI clients are DOS extenders.

Even though the VCPI relationship is termed client/server, both parts of this pair are peers; neither one exerts control over the other. When the client is running in virtual 86 (V86) mode, the server has control of the system resources behind the scenes in protected mode. When the client requests a switch to protected mode, the server relinquishes total control to the clien the environment then belongs to the client. When the client requests a switch back to V86 mode, the server again asserts control and the client slinks into the background. Whichever part of the client/server pair has control at the time expects to own the entire protected-mode environment, and therefore exerts total control over all system tables and resources.

The VCPI arrangement, as described here, works well as long as the computer is a single-task machine. The arrangement gets messy (and sometimes downright impossible) if you want to implement true multitasking. This shortcoming was addressed with the DPMI standard, which is addressed in the next section.

The majority of programmers never will use VCPI function calls within programs. The VCPI function calls are taken care of by any DOS extender you use. If you decide to access VCPI function calls yourself, you should make sure that you have a VCPI master program running in your system. For the test program used in this section, I used QEMM386, version 6.

The program in Listing 6.5, VCPIINFO.ASM, is designed to give you just a taste of VCPI. VCPIINFO.ASM uses VCPI function DE00h to determine whether the VCPI master program is available. If it is available, the version information and available memory information are displayed.

Listing 6.5. VCPIINFO.ASM

```
Page 60,132


Comment ¦
********************************************************************


File:       VCPIINFO.ASM
Author:     Allen L. Wyatt
Date:       7/30/92
Assembler:  MASM 6.0

Purpose:    Display information about extended memory using VCPI functions

Format:     VCPIINFO


********************************************************************¦

            .MODEL  small
            .STACK                      ;Default 1K stack is OK
            .386                        ;Instructions require 80386
            .DATA

EMSName   DB        'EMMXXXX0',0
InMsg     DB        'A VCPI master program is installed',13,10,0
Version   DB        'Supports VCPI version '
Major     DB        00,'.'
```

```
Minor       DB      00,'.'
CRLF        DB      13,10,0
AvailMsg    DB      'Extended memory available:  ',0

EMsg1       DB      'No VCPI master program detected',13,10,0
EMsg2       DB      'Could not determine available 4K pages',13,10,0

            .CODE
            .STARTUP
VCPIinfo    PROC
            CALL    ChkVCPI             ;See whether master program is present
            JC      Error1              ;Not there
            MOV     SI,OFFSET InMsg
            CALL    PrtString
            MOV     SI,OFFSET Version
            CALL    PrtString

            MOV     AX,0DE03h           ;Get number of free 4K pages
            INT     67h
            CMP     AH,0                ;Any error?
            JNE     Error2              ;Yes, handle
            SHL     EDX,12              ;Multiply by 4,096 (4K pages)
            MOV     AX,DX               ;Low word
            SHR     EDX,16              ;Move high word into DX
            MOV     SI,OFFSET AvailMsg  ;Total available memory message
            CALL    PrtString
            CALL    PrtDec
            MOV     SI,OFFSET CRLF
            CALL    PrtString
            JMP     AllDone

Error1:     MOV     SI,OFFSET EMsg1
            JMP     ErrCommon
Error2:     MOV     SI,OFFSET EMsg2
ErrCommon:  CALL    PrtString

AllDone:
            .EXIT
VCPIinfo    ENDP
```

continues

Listing 6.5. Continued

```
; The following routine checks to see whether a VCPI master program is installed.
; If one is not, the carry flag is set on return.
; If one is, the version info is stored and the carry flag is cleared on return.

ChkVCPI       PROC       USES AX BX ES
              CALL       ChkEMS              ;Make sure that EMS is in first
              JC         NotThere            ;EMS not in, so VCPI can't be
              CALL       GrabPage            ;Make sure EMS initiated
              JC         NotThere            ;Exit if any hint of error

              MOV        AX,0DE00h           ;Get VCPI installed state
              INT        67h
              CMP        AL,0
              JNE        NotThere
              OR         BX,3030h            ;Turn to ASCII
              MOV        Major,BH
              MOV        Minor,BL
              CLC                            ;Set for no error
              JNC        Done

NotThere:     STC
Done:         RET
ChkVCPI       ENDP


; The following routine checks to see whether an EMM is installed.
; If one is not, the carry flag is set on return.
; If one is, the carry flag is cleared on return.

ChkEMS        PROC       USES AX BX DX ES
              MOV        DX,OFFSET EMSName   ;Device driver name
              MOV        AH,3Dh              ;Open file
              MOV        AL,0                ;Access/file sharing mode
              INT        21h
              JC         NotThere2
              MOV        BX,AX               ;Put handle in proper place
              MOV        AH,44h              ;IOCTL
              MOV        AL,07h              ;Get output status
              INT        21h
              JC         NotThere1
```

```
                CMP      AL,0FFh
                JNE      NotThere1
                MOV      AH,3Eh             ;Close file
                INT      21h
                CLC                         ;Set for no error
                JNC      Done

NotThere1:      MOV      AH,3Eh             ;Close file
                INT      21h
NotThere2:      STC
Done:           RET
ChkEMS          ENDP



; This function allocates an EMS page and then releases it. This is
; done to make sure that the EMS driver has switched the CPU to V86 mode.
; On return, the carry is set if there was any problem using the EMS
; functions. Carry is clear otherwise.

GrabPage        PROC
                MOV      AH,43h             ;Allocate pages
                MOV      BX,1               ;Get 1 page (16K)
                INT      67h
                CMP      AH,0               ;Was there an error?
                JNE      GPErr              ;Yes, so exit
                MOV      AH,45h             ;Release EMS handle
                INT      67h
                CMP      AH,0               ;Was there an error?
                JNE      GPErr              ;Yes, so exit
                CLC                         ;Mark for no error
                JNC      GPEnd
GPErr:          STC
GPEnd:          RET
GrabPage        ENDP



; The following routine prints the ASCIIZ string pointed to by DS:SI

PrtString       PROC     USES AX DX SI
PS1:            MOV      DL,[SI]            ;Get character
                INC      SI                 ;Point to next one
```

continues

Listing 6.5. Continued

```
                CMP     DL,0                    ;End of string?
                JE      PS2                     ;Yes, so exit
                MOV     AH,02h                  ;Output a character
                INT     21h
                JMP     PS1                     ;Keep doing it
PS2:            RET
PrtString       ENDP


; The following routine prints the value in DX:AX as a decimal number.
; Will accept numbers up to 655,359,999. Anything larger will not print.

                .DATA
Temp            DW      0000

                .CODE
PrtDec          PROC    USES AX BX CX DX

                MOV     CX,0FFFFh               ;Ending flag
                PUSH    CX

PD0:            MOV     CX,10000                ;Divide by 10,000
                DIV     CX
                MOV     Temp,AX                 ;Store whole portion
                MOV     BX,0                    ;Count for this iteration

                MOV     AX,DX
                MOV     CX,10
PD1:            MOV     DX,0
                DIV     CX                      ;Divide by 10
                ADD     DL,30h                  ;Convert to ASCII
                PUSH    DX                      ;Store remainder
                INC     BX                      ;Cycle count
                CMP     AX,0                    ;Are we done?
                JNE     PD1                     ;No, so continue
                MOV     DX,0
                MOV     AX,Temp                 ;Get back part above 10,000
                CMP     AX,0
                JE      PD3
                MOV     CX,'0'
```

```
PD2:        CMP     BX,4            ;Did we push 4 numbers?
            JE      PD0             ;Yes, continue
            PUSH    CX              ;No, so push it
            INC     BX              ;Push counter
            JMP     PD2


PD3:        POP     DX              ;Character is now in DL
            CMP     DX,0FFFFh       ;Is it the ending flag?
            JE      PD4             ;Yes, so continue
            MOV     AH,02h          ;Output a character
            INT     21h
            JMP     PD3             ;Keep doing it


PD4:        RET
PrtDec      ENDP


            END
```

Notice the use of the .386 directive near the beginning of this program. This directive is necessary because the VCPI functions use the extended registers available with the 80386 and 80486 computers. In this example, EDX is used as a return register for VCPI function DE03h.

Notice also that the program calls EMS functions as part of the check to see whether VCPI is available. This is because you should do the following to determine whether VCPI is available:

1. Determine whether EMS is available. If it is not, you know that VCPI can't be there because VCPI is an extension to EMS.

2. If EMS is available, allocate an EMS page and free it again. This step ensures that the CPU has been placed in V86 mode by the VCPI server.

3. Issue the VCPI installation check function (DE00h). If AH is 0 on return, VCPI is installed.

For more information about the ChkEMS function, refer to the EMS discussion earlier in the chapter.

DPMI

DPMI (DOS protected-mode interface) is a step past VCPI. It does primarily what VCPI does, but exerts total control over the machine in the client/server relationship. Under VCPI, both the client and the server are equals in the system (one passes off total control to the other during a mode switch), but

DPMI forces the client to be subservient to the server. A DPMI server always functions at a higher privilege level than does the client, and does not provide access to the global system resources reserved for the server.

A DPMI host provides a collection of 77 functions the client can call. The host provides functions to handle the following areas:

- DOS and extended memory management
- Context switching
- Interrupt management
- Page management
- LDT management
- Debugging

All functions are available through interrupts 2Fh and 31h. Detailed information on these functions is available in Appendix F, "The DPMI Functions."

Chances are, you never will use the DPMI services unless you are writing a DOS extender. Because of this, detailed information on how to use the DPMI interface is beyond the scope of this book. The program in Listing 6.6, however, at least tests for the presence of a DPMI host and displays a message about what it finds.

Listing 6.6. DPMIINFO.ASM

```
Page 60,132

Comment ¦
************************************************************************


File:       DPMIINFO.ASM
Author:     Allen L. Wyatt
Date:       7/31/92
Assembler:  MASM 6.0

Purpose:    Display information about extended memory using DPMI functions

Format:     DPMIINFO


************************************************************************¦
```

```
              .MODEL   small
              .STACK                     ;Default 1K stack is OK
              .386                       ;Instructions require 80386
              .DATA

InMsg         DB       'A DPMI host is installed'
CRLF          DB       13,10,0
Version       DB       'Supports DPMI version ',0
Divider       DB       '.',0
AvailMsg      DB       'Extended memory available:  ',0
Yes32         DB       '32-bit programs can be executed with this host',13,10,0
No32          DB       'Only 16-bit programs can be executed with this host',13,10,0
EntryMsg      DB       'The protected mode entry point is '
SegNum        DW       0000,0000
              DB       ':'
OffNum        DW       0000,0000
              DB       13,10,0

CPUTable      DW       OFFSET CPU286
              DW       OFFSET CPU386
              DW       OFFSET CPU486
              DW       OFFSET CPUUN

CPU286        DB       'Running on an 80286 CPU',13,10,0
CPU386        DB       'Running on an 80386 CPU',13,10,0
CPU486        DB       'Running on an 80486 CPU',13,10,0
CPUUN         DB       'Running on an unknown CPU',13,10,0

Flag32        DB       00
ProcType      DB       00
VerNum        DW       0000
DPMIentry     DW       0000,0000

EMsg1         DB       'No DPMI host detected',13,10,0

              .CODE
              .STARTUP
DPMIinfo      PROC
              CALL     ChkDPMI                  ;See if master program present
              JC       Error1                   ;Not there
              MOV      SI,OFFSET InMsg
```

continues

Listing 6.6. Continued

```
            CALL    PrtString
            MOV     SI,OFFSET Version
            CALL    PrtString
            MOV     BX,VerNum
            MOV     AH,0
            MOV     AL,BH              ;Major version number
            CALL    PrtDec
            MOV     SI,OFFSET Divider
            CALL    PrtString
            MOV     AL,BL              ;Minor version number
            CALL    PrtDec
            MOV     SI,OFFSET CRLF
            CALL    PrtString

            MOV     BH,0
            MOV     BL,ProcType
            DEC     BL
            DEC     BL
            SHL     BX,1
            ADD     BX,OFFSET CPUTable
            MOV     SI,[BX]
            CALL    PrtString

            MOV     SI,OFFSET No32     ;Assume can't do 32-bit
            MOV     BL,Flag32
            CMP     BL,1
            JNE     FlagPrt
            MOV     SI,OFFSET Yes32    ;32-bit is OK after all
FlagPrt:    CALL    PrtString

            MOV     AX,DPMIentry[2]
            CALL    ConHexLong
            MOV     SegNum[0],AX
            MOV     SegNum[2],DX
            MOV     AX,DPMIentry[0]
            CALL    ConHexLong
            MOV     OffNum[0],AX
            MOV     OffNum[2],DX
```

```
              MOV      SI,OFFSET EntryMsg   ;Entry point message
              CALL     PrtString
              JMP      AllDone

Error1:       MOV      SI,OFFSET EMsg1
              CALL     PrtString

AllDone:
              .EXIT
DPMIinfo      ENDP



; The following routine checks to see whether a DPMI master program is installed.
; If one is not, the carry flag is set on return.
; If one is, the stat info is stored and the carry flag is cleared on return.

ChkDPMI       PROC     USES AX BX CX DX SI DI ES
              MOV      AX,1687h              ;Get DPMI host address
              INT      2Fh                   ;Multiplex interrupt
              CMP      AX,0                  ;Was it there?
              JNE      NotThere              ;No, so exit

              AND      BL,00000001b          ;Test bit 1 (32-bit OK?)
              SETNE    AL
              MOV      Flag32,AL
              MOV      ProcType,CL
              MOV      VerNum,DX
              MOV      DPMIentry[0],DI
              MOV      DPMIentry[2],ES
              CLC                            ;Set for no error
              JNC      Done

NotThere:     STC
Done:         RET
ChkDPMI       ENDP



; The following routine prints the ASCIIZ string pointed to by DS:SI
```

continues

Listing 6.6. Continued

```
PrtString   PROC     USES AX DX SI
PS1:        MOV      DL,[SI]          ;Get character
            INC      SI               ;Point to next one
            CMP      DL,0             ;End of string?
            JE       PS2              ;Yes, so exit
            MOV      AH,02h           ;Output a character
            INT      21h
            JMP      PS1              ;Keep doing it
PS2:        RET
PrtString   ENDP


; The following routine prints the value in AX as a decimal number

PrtDec      PROC     USES AX CX DX
            MOV      CX,0FFFFh        ;Ending flag
            PUSH     CX
            MOV      CX,10
PD1:        MOV      DX,0
            DIV      CX               ;Divide by 10
            ADD      DL,30h           ;Convert to ASCII
            PUSH     DX               ;Store remainder
            CMP      AX,0             ;Are we done?
            JNE      PD1              ;No, so continue

PD2:        POP      DX               ;Character is now in DL
            CMP      DX,0FFFFh        ;Is it the ending flag?
            JE       PD3              ;Yes, so continue
            MOV      AH,02h           ;Output a character
            INT      21h
            JMP      PD2              ;Keep doing it

PD3:        RET
PrtDec      ENDP


; The following routine converts the number in AL into an ASCII
; representation of the hex value, with a leading 0. Value
; is returned in AX as well.
```

```
ConHex        PROC     USES CX
              MOV      CL,10h                ;What you will be dividing by
              MOV      AH,0
              DIV      CL                    ;Divide by 16
              OR       AX,3030h              ;Convert to ASCII
              CMP      AL,'9'                ;Is it greater than 9?
              JBE      CA4                   ;No, so continue
              ADD      AL,7                  ;Make into hex digit
CA4:          CMP      AH,'9'                ;Is it greater than 9?
              JBE      CA5                   ;No, so continue
              ADD      AH,7                  ;Make into hex digit
CA5:          RET
ConHex        ENDP

; The following uses ConHex to convert a long number (AX) into its ASCII
; equivalent in DX:AX

ConHexLong    PROC
              PUSH     AX
              CALL     ConHex
              MOV      DX,AX
              POP      AX
              MOV      AL,AH
              CALL     ConHex
              RET
ConHexLong    ENDP

              END
```

As with the VCPI example in the preceding section, this program must be assembled for 80386 instructions. If you run the program from the DOS prompt, chances are you will get a message indicating that a DPMI host could not be detected. If you want to see the full output of the program, you should run Microsoft Windows 3.0 or 3.1, bring up the DOS prompt from within Windows, and then run the program. Windows implements a DPMI host that is compliant with version 0.9 of the DPMI specification.

Summary

Memory, in all its permutations and flavors, is what programs and programmers use most. As you develop programs that load large files, use complex data structures, or simply process large amounts of data, there is a good chance you will outgrow the traditional 640 kilobytes available to programs. In that case, you must add capabilities to your programs to take advantage of EMS, XMS, VCPI, or even DPMI functions. The intended use and user of your program may even make this decision for you.

Working with extended memory is a particularly hot topic for the foreseeable future. In fact, by the time this book is published, some of the information in this chapter about extended memory may be out-of-date. Be that as it may, this information should give you a good starting point for where to look in your programming efforts.

Chapter 7 looks at another old bugaboo with programmers—working with disk files and directories.

Working with Disk Files and Directories

I f you have been programming in the DOS environment for even a short time, you already know *how* information is stored on a disk. Getting to the information with an assembly language program can sometimes be a difficult task. Combine that with traversing and manipulating directories, and you can face an even more daunting task.

This chapter discusses several different aspects of file and directory programming. Through the programs introduced in this chapter, you learn how to open, read, write, close, and delete disk files. You learn also how to rename files and how to use DOS functions to move through directory structures.

First, you should understand that there are two classes of file-access functions available on the PC. The first type uses file-control blocks, or FCBs. The second type uses file handles.

Understanding FCBs

Many functions available for accessing and manipulating files use a *file control block*. This data structure is used by DOS to determine what parameters should govern an action to be taken on a file. FCBs, a vestige of the early days of MS-DOS, are an outgrowth of the way files were handled in CP/M.

As originally introduced in DOS version 1.0, file control blocks consisted of a relatively straightforward data structure (see Figure 7.1). Table 7.1 shows the use of each field in the FCB.

Figure 7.1.

The normal FCB structure.

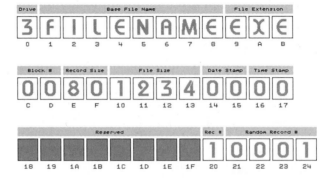

Table 7.1. FCB field use.

Offset	Length	Use
00h	1	Drive specification, where 0=default drive, 1=A, 2=B, 3=C, and so on
01h	8	Base file name, left-justified and padded with spaces
09h	3	File extension, left-justified and padded with spaces
0Ch	2	Current block number
0Eh	2	Record size, in bytes
10h	4	File size, in bytes
14h	2	Date created or updated
16h	2	Time created or updated
18h	8	Reserved by DOS
20h	1	Current record number
21h	4	Random record number

As DOS developed over the first few versions, new capabilities were added that the standard FCB layout could not adequately address. To meet the need to be able to specify file attributes for a file, Microsoft introduced the extended FCB (see Figure 7.2). Extended field use information is shown in Table 7.2.

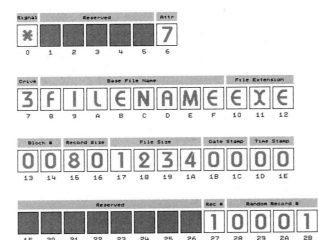

Figure 7.2.

The extended FCB
structure.

Table 7.2. Extended FCB field use.

Offset	Length	Use
00h	1	Flag to DOS (FFh) indicating this is an extended FCB
01h	5	Reserved by DOS
06h	1	File attribute
07h	1	Drive specification, where 0=default drive, 1=A, 2=B, 3=C, and so on
08h	8	Base file name, left-justified and padded with spaces
10h	3	File extension, left-justified and padded with spaces
13h	2	Current block number
15h	2	Record size, in bytes
17h	4	File size, in bytes
1Bh	2	Date created or updated
1Dh	2	Time created or updated
1Fh	8	Reserved by DOS
27h	1	Current record number
28h	4	Random record number

ADVANCED ASSEMBLY LANGUAGE

The extended FCB immediately was more useful for file-handling functions. If you examine the FCB structures, however, you discover that there is no way to specify the path name for a file because FCBs were developed for a filing system that did not use a hierarchical directory structure. Functions that use FCBs can function therefore only on files in the current directory.

This limitation of FCBs makes them unsatisfactory for most modern file-handling functions. They remain within DOS for compatibility with earlier versions of software, but their usefulness to programmers is still limited.

Understanding File Handles

With the introduction of DOS version 2.0 and the new hierarchical directory structure, a new concept in file handling was introduced. Actually, the concept was borrowed from the UNIX environment, where it had been in use for several years.

File handles enabled the program to specify the name of a file, along with any path, as an ASCIIZ string (a NULL-terminated string). DOS then set up its own internal data structure for the file and returned a number, known as the *file handle*, used for all subsequent references to the file.

Another interesting use of file handles, however, is that they can be used also for devices. Table 7.3 lists the devices commonly available on a PC. These devices can be opened, read from, written to, and closed in the same manner as actual files. It is possible, therefore, for your program to direct output to the screen (stdout), to the printer (stdprn), or to a file by simply changing the ASCIIZ string used to request a file handle.

Table 7.3. Common PC devices.

Name	Use
AUX	The standard auxiliary device, typically COM1:
CLOCK	Used to control the system clock
CON	The console unit (the keyboard and display monitor)
NUL	The "never-never land" device. Anything read from here returns nothing, and anything written here goes away.
PRN	The standard printer, typically LPT1:
LPT1:	The first parallel port
LPT2:	The second parallel port
LPT3:	The third parallel port

Name	Use
LPT4:	The fourth parallel port
COM1:	The first serial port
COM2:	The second serial port
COM3:	The third serial port
COM4:	The fourth serial port

Devices are discussed in more detail in Chapter 9, "Device Drivers," in which you learn how to write your own device driver.

Because of their ease of use and flexibility, file handles are typically the method of choice for accessing files. All the examples used in this chapter (and in this book) use this method.

Accessing Files

Accessing files with file handles is straightforward and easy. Which DOS function you use depends on whether the file already exists. If you want to create a file or truncate an existing file, you use function 3Ch. This function effectively deletes the file (if it already exists) and then opens it again. The following code segment illustrates the use of this function:

```
        .DATA
Filename  DB      'C:\TEST.DAT',0
Handle    DW      0000


        .CODE
        MOV    AH,3Ch                ;Create/truncate a file
MOV    CX,0                   ;Want normal file
MOV    DX,OFFSET Filename
INT    21h
JC     OpenErr                ;Could not open file
MOV    Handle,AX              ;Store file handle for later
```

Notice that before invoking function 3Ch, you load CX with the file attribute. This flag tells DOS the type of file you want the file to be. Table 7.4 shows the bit settings for CX.

ADVANCED ASSEMBLY LANGUAGE

Table 7.4. Attribute bit settings for the CX register in function 3Ch.

Value	File Type
0	Normal
2	Hidden
4	System
6	Hidden and system

To open a file that already exists, you use code similar to the following:

```
          .DATA
Filename  DB     'C:\AUTOEXEC.BAT',0
Handle    DW     0000

          .CODE
          MOV    AH,3Dh                ;Open file
          MOV    AL,2                  ;Want to read and write
          MOV    DX,OFFSET Filename
          INT    21h
          JC     OpenErr               ;Could not open file
          MOV    Handle,AX             ;Store file handle for later
```

DOS function 3Dh enables you to open a file. Just point DS:DX to the ASCIIZ string containing the full file name (including path, if any) and load AL with the access and file-sharing mode you want. Table 7.5 shows the meaning of bits in this byte.

Table 7.5. Access and file-sharing mode byte.

Bit settings 76543210	Meaning or Comment
000	Open file for read access
001	Open file for write access
010	Open file for read and write access
x	Reserved
000	Use compatibility sharing mode
001	Deny read/write access
010	Deny write access

Bit settings 76543210	Meaning or Comment
011	Deny read access
100	Allow full access
0	Allow this file to be inherited by a child process
1	Don't allow this file to be inherited by a child process

Notice in Table 7.5 that bits 0, 1, and 2 are used to specify the type of rights you want for the file—what you want to do with it. Bits 4, 5, and 6 are used to specify the type of rights you want to allow others to have if they try to open a file after you have opened it. Bit 7 determines whether child programs spawned by using the EXEC function (see Chapter 11, "Using the EXEC Function") will inherit any access to this file. The sharing and inheritance flags became available with DOS 3.0; the access flags, with DOS 2.0.

For most purposes, you probably will set AL to 2 in opening a file. This statement means that you allow the file to be inherited, that you want compatibility sharing mode, and that you want read and write access to the file. You should monitor and change the sharing rights flags when you are writing programs to be used predominantly in multi-user environments such as networks.

That's all there is to opening a file with file handles. You set a pointer and two registers, and you store the handle returned by DOS. This handle is used for all future functions (reading, writing, changing the pointer, and closing) that affect this file.

After a file is open, the file handle functions view it as a collection of bytes that are accessed sequentially. You can read or write beginning at any point in the file, as determined by the location of the internal file pointer. Let's look at writing, reading, and using the internal file pointer.

Writing a File

Writing to a file is as easy as opening it. You just specify the location and length of the data to be written, load the file handle, and then call a DOS function. The following code fragment illustrates this process:

```
        .DATA
Handle    DW    0000
NumBytes  DW    0000
Buffer    DB    80 DUP(0)
```

```
        .CODE
        MOV     AH,40h                  ;Write file
        MOV     BX,Handle
        MOV     CX,NumBytes             ;Bytes to write
        MOV     DX,OFFSET Buffer
        INT     21h
        JC      WriteErr                ;Could not write to file
        CMP     AX,CX                   ;Were all bytes written?
        JNE     Partial                 ;No, only partial buffer written
```

Notice the code after the return from the DOS call. The DOS file-writing function returns with the carry flag set if there was an error such as an invalid file
handle or if access to the file was denied. If you get an invalid file handle, it
means that either you did not open the file correctly or your file handle was
corrupted since you opened the file. If you get an "access denied" error, then
you requested only reading rights when you opened the file.

After it is determined that no error has occurred, you should compare the
number of bytes that were requested to write (CX) with the number that were
actually written (AX). If these two numbers are equal, then the entire block of
information you wanted written was written. If they are not equal, then only a
part of the block was written. Logically, this situation should occur only if your
disk ran out of space.

Earlier in this chapter, in the section "Understanding FCBs," you probably
noted that the FCB structures allowed for the specification of random record
numbers. No such specification is available with file handles, however. If you
want to write specific random record in a file, you must do the math yourself
to calculate where to begin writing. For instance, the following routine writes
to a specific random record on the disk:

```
            .DATA
Handle      DW      0000
NumBytes    DW      0000
Buffer      DB      80 DUP(0)
RecSize     DW      0000
RecNum      DW      0000
ErrorCode   DW      0000


            .CODE

; Routine to write to a specified record on the disk. Record size
; must be set in RecSize, and the desired record must be set in
; RecNum. It is assumed that record numbers are zero-based (there
; *IS* a record 0 in the file). On return, the carry flag is set
; if there was an error, and ErrorCode contains one of the following:
;     01h: invalid function
```

```
;     05h: access denied
;     06h: invalid handle
;     FFh: partial record written

PutRecord   PROC    USES AX BX CX DX
            MOV     AX,RecSize
            MOV     BX,RecNum
            MUL     AX,BX
            MOV     CX,DX               ;Most significant result
            MOV     DX,AX               ;Least significant result
            MOV     BX,Handle
            MOV     AH,42h              ;Move file pointer
            MOV     AL,0                ;From beginning of the file
            INT     21h
            MOV     ErrorCode,AX        ;Store any error code
            JC      PRExit              ;Exit if an error occurred

            MOV     AH,40h              ;Write file
            MOV     BX,Handle
            MOV     CX,NumBytes         ;Bytes to write
            MOV     DX,OFFSET Buffer
            INT     21h
            MOV     ErrorCode,AX        ;Store any error code
            JC      PRExit              ;Exit if an error occurred
            CMP     AX,CX               ;Were all bytes written?
            JNE     Partial             ;No, only partial buffer written
            MOV     ErrorCode,0         ;Reset error code
            CLC                         ;Signal no error
            JNC     PRExit
Partial:    MOV     ErrorCode,0FFh      ;Signal partial write
            STC                         ;Signal error
PRExit:     RET
PutRecord   ENDP
```

This code relies on DOS function 42h to work properly. Function 42h changes the location of the file pointer, which affects where the next file operation will occur. You learn more about the file pointer a little later in this chapter.

Reading a File

When you are using file handles, reading a file is as simple as writing to one. DOS function 3Fh enables you to read from a file. You just provide the file handle, the number of bytes to read, and a pointer to the buffer area that will contain the information read. The following code fragment illustrates this process:

```
            .DATA
Handle      DW          0000
NumBytes    DW          2048
Buffer      DB          2048 DUP(0)


            .CODE
            MOV         AH,3Fh              ;Read file
            MOV         BX,Handle
            MOV         CX,NumBytes         ;Bytes to read
            MOV         DX,OFFSET Buffer
            INT         21h
            JC          ReadErr             ;Could not read from file
            CMP         AX,CX               ;Were all bytes read?
            JNE         Partial             ;No, partial buffer; EOF reached
```

Of course, this code assumes that you previously have opened the file and stored the file handle number. When reading from a file, you must be careful to specify a buffer area large enough to hold the number of bytes you are reading. If you do not, it is possible to overwrite other data or your program, and you receive no error message or warning if this happens.

In the preceding section, you learned how to access random access files using file handles. The same techniques apply when you are reading from a file. Examine that section to discover the code that can be adapted for reading a random access file.

To illustrate more fully how to read a file, consider a rather simple program that reads from a file and displays the information on the computer screen. The program also should stop at the end of each screen and prompt the user to press a key. The steps involved in such a program are simple:

1. Examine the command line to determine the file name you want.

2. Open the specified file.

3. Read a block of information into the buffer.

4. Display a screenful of information.

5. Wait for a key to be pressed.

6. Repeat steps 4 and 5 until the end of the buffer is reached.

7. Repeat steps 3 through 6 until the end of the file is reached.

8. Close the file.

The program in Listing 7.1 implements these steps.

Listing 7.1. SHOWFILE.ASM

```
Page 60,132

Comment |
*******************************************************************

File:       SHOWFILE.ASM
Author:     Allen L. Wyatt
Date:       6/25/92
Assembler:  MASM 6.0

Purpose:    Display the contents of a file, one screen at a time

Format:     SHOWFILE filename.ext


*******************************************************************|

            .MODEL  small
            .STACK                          ;Default 1K stack is OK
            .DATA
TRUE        EQU     -1
FALSE       EQU     0
BufSize     EQU     2048

WorkDir     DB      129 DUP(0)
Handle      DW      0000
NumBytes    DW      0000
EOF         DB      00

Pause       DB      'Press any key to continue...',0
ErrMsg      DB      'Bad file name, path not found, or access denied',13,10,0

            .CODE
            .STARTUP
ShowFile    PROC

            MOV     AL,ES:[80h]     ;Get length of command tail
            CMP     AL,0            ;Is there a command tail?
            JE      Alldone         ;No, so exit completely
            CALL    Xfer            ;Go transfer command tail
```

continues

Listing 7.1. Continued

```
; The following memory allocation code works because it is known that MASM
; sets DS and SS to the same segment address in the start-up code. Also, ES
; is set to the PSP for the program on entry.

                MOV     BX,DS               ;Point to start of data segment
                MOV     AX,ES               ;Point to start of PSP
                SUB     BX,AX               ;Number of segments for code and data
                MOV     AX,SP               ;SP is pointing to top of stack area
                MOV     CL,4                ;Dividing by 16
                SHR     AX,CL
                ADD     BX,AX               ;BX=paragraphs needed
                MOV     AH,4Ah              ;Modify memory allocation
                INT     21h

                MOV     AH,3Dh              ;Open file
                MOV     AL,40h              ;Full sharing, read-only access
                MOV     DX,OFFSET WorkDir   ;Point to start of file name
                INT     21h
                JNC     FileOpen            ;No error, continue
                MOV     SI,OFFSET ErrMsg    ;Point to message to display
                CALL    PrtString           ;Display the string
                JMP     AllDone

FileOpen:       MOV     Handle,AX           ;Store handle for later
                MOV     AH,48h              ;Allocate memory
                MOV     BX,BufSize/16       ;Paragraphs to request
                INT     21h
                MOV     ES,AX               ;Point to memory block for later use
                MOV     EOF,FALSE
                CALL    Cls

DoLoop:         CALL    ReadFile
                CALL    DispBuffer
                CMP     EOF,FALSE
                JE      DoLoop
                MOV     BX,Handle           ;Get file handle
                MOV     AH,3Eh              ;Close file
                INT     21h

Done:           MOV     AH,49h              ;Release memory block at ES
                INT     21h
```

```
AllDone:    .EXIT
ShowFile    ENDP


; The following routine fills the buffer from the disk file
ReadFile    PROC    USES AX BX CX DX
            MOV     AH,3Fh              ;Read file
            MOV     BX,Handle
            MOV     CX,BufSize          ;Get a full buffer
            PUSH    DS                  ;Store data segment and point
            PUSH    ES                  ;       it to the right segment
            POP     DS                  ;       for the buffer area
            MOV     DX,0                ;Start of memory block
            INT     21h
            POP     DS
            JC      ReadErr             ;Could not read from file
            MOV     NumBytes,AX         ;Store number of bytes read
            CMP     AX,CX               ;Were all bytes read?
            JE      RFDone              ;Yes, so exit
SetEOF:     MOV     EOF,TRUE            ;No, so EOF reached
            JMP     RFDone
ReadErr:    CMP     AX,0                ;Was it because EOF was reached?
            JE      SetEOF              ;Yes, so set flag
RFDone:     RET
ReadFile    ENDP


; The following routine displays the buffer information. Assumes
; that ES points to the buffer segment.

DispBuffer  PROC    USES AX DX SI
            MOV     SI,0                ;Point to start of buffer
DB1:        MOV     DL,ES:[SI]          ;Get character
            MOV     AH,02h              ;Output a character
            INT     21h
            MOV     AH,03h              ;Read cursor position
            INT     10h
            CMP     DH,23               ;Rolled over to line 23 yet?
            JNE     DB2                 ;No, so continue
            CALL    PagePause           ;Yep, so display message
            CALL    Cls                 ;Clear screen
DB2:        INC     SI
```

continues

Listing 7.1. Continued

```
              CMP      SI,NumBytes         ;At end of buffer?
              JB       DB1                 ;No, so keep going
              RET
DispBuffer    ENDP

; Transfers the command tail into the work file area, and converts
; it into an ASCIIZ string. Assumes that ES points to PSP segment.

Xfer          PROC     USES AX CX SI DI ES DS
              PUSH     ES                  ;Swap ES and DS
              PUSH     DS
              POP      ES
              POP      DS
              MOV      SI,80h              ;Point to start of command tail
              MOV      CH,0
              MOV      CL,[SI]             ;Get length of command tail
              INC      SI                  ;Point to first character
              MOV      DI,OFFSET ES:WorkDir
X1:           LODSB
              CMP      AL,' '              ;Was it a space?
              JE       X4                  ;Yes, so skip it
              STOSB                        ;Store a byte
X4:           LOOP     X1                  ;Keep going to the end
              MOV      AL,0
              STOSB                        ;Make sure NUL at end of path
              RET
Xfer          ENDP

; The following routine clears the screen and homes the cursor

Cls           PROC     USES AX BX CX DX
              MOV      AH,6                ;Scroll window up
              MOV      AL,0                ;Scroll full screen
              MOV      BH,7                ;Normal white on black
              MOV      CX,0                ;Upper left corner of screen
              MOV      DH,24               ;Bottom right
              MOV      DL,79
              INT      10h

              MOV      DX,0                ;Upper left corner of screen
              MOV      BH,0                ;Assume page 0
```

```
            MOV     AH,2                ;Set cursor position
            INT     10h
            RET
Cls         ENDP


; The following routine pauses at the bottom of a page

PagePause   PROC    USES AX BX DX SI
            MOV     DH,24               ;Set up to print pause message
            MOV     DL,0
            MOV     BH,0                ;Assume page 0
            MOV     AH,2                ;Set cursor position
            INT     10h
            MOV     SI,OFFSET Pause     ;Point to start of pause message
            CALL    PrtString           ;Display the string
            INT     21h
            MOV     AH,0                ;Read keyboard character
            INT     16h
            RET
PagePause   ENDP


; The following routine prints the ASCIIZ string pointed to by DS:SI

PrtString   PROC    USES AX DX SI
PS1:        MOV     DL,[SI]             ;Get character
            INC     SI                  ;Point to next one
            CMP     DL,0                ;End of string?
            JE      PS2                 ;Yes, so exit
            MOV     AH,02h              ;Output a character
            INT     21h
            JMP     PS1                 ;Keep doing it
PS2:        RET
PrtString   ENDP


            END
```

After this file is compiled, you can use it to display the contents of a file quickly and simply in a manner similar to the TYPE command. SHOWFILE goes beyond TYPE, however, in that it pauses after each full screen of information and waits for you to press a key. To use the program, you just enter SHOWFILE followed by the name of the file you want to view. You can supply a full drive and path name.

Using the File Pointer

Earlier, this chapter mentioned that the file pointer can be used to position the location in a file where the next read or write will occur. Typically, the file pointer is manipulated to facilitate the random access of files. There are other valid uses, however.

The file pointer is adjusted through DOS function 42h. With this function, you can specify where you want to move the file pointer, and the movement can be relative to the start of the file, the current file pointer position, or the end of the file. You can even move the file pointer to a location before the beginning of the file or after the end of the file; neither action generates an error. You get an error, however, if you try to read or write with the file pointer positioned before the start of the file, or if you try to read with the file pointer positioned past the end of the file. If you write with the file pointer positioned past the end of the file, the file size is adjusted to encompass the new file pointer position.

As an example of how to use the file-positioning function, the following code fragment may be helpful:

```
        .DATA
Handle    DW      0000
FilePtrH  DW      0000
FilePtrL  DW      0000

        .CODE
        MOV     AH,42h          ;Move file pointer
        MOV     AL,00h          ;From beginning of file
        MOV     BX,Handle
        MOV     CX,FilePtrH     ;Get start of last read
        MOV     DX,FilePtrL
        INT     21h
```

Notice the value loaded into AL. This flag indicates how DOS should treat the offset loaded in CX:DX. If AL=0, then the offset is calculated from the start of the file; if AL=1, it is calculated from the current file pointer position; if AL=2, it is calculated from the end of the file.

Later, this chapter introduces a program (PURGE.ASM) that uses the file pointer positioning functions extensively.

Working with File Attributes

Each file stored on your disk has a group of attributes stored in its directory entry. These attributes serve as a flag to DOS to specify how the file should be treated. The six attributes are shown in Table 7.6.

Table 7.6. The file attributes and their meanings.

Attribute	Meaning
Read only	The file cannot be written to, deleted, or renamed
Hidden	The file is not displayed with the DIR command
System	A secondary type of hidden file designed to be used by DOS
Volume label	The name given to the disk
Directory	A file containing other directory entries; a subdirectory
Archive	A file that has been modified since the last BACKUP operation

Each type of attribute is controlled by a bit setting in the attribute byte of a file's directory entry. Table 7.7 lists the bit settings for an attribute byte.

Table 7.7. Bit settings for an attribute byte.

Bit settings 76543210	Attribute value
1	Read only
1	Hidden
1	System
1	Volume label
1	Directory
1	Archive
xx	Unused

You can mix and match most attribute values. For instance, a file can be both read only and hidden, or read only, hidden, and system. You cannot, however, mix the volume label or directory attribute values with other attribute values. If you mix them, the result has no practical meaning to DOS.

The two DOS subfunctions that control file attributes are controlled through DOS function 43h. Subfunction 0 enables you to retrieve the attribute byte for a file, and subfunction 1 enables you to set the attribute byte. Both subfunctions operate in a similar manner. To illustrate how they work, the following code reads the attribute byte of a file. If the hidden attribute value is set, the file changes to non-hidden; all other attribute values remain the same.

```
          .DATA
Filename  DB      'C:\TEST.DAT',0

          .CODE
          MOV     AH,43h              ;Get file attributes
          MOV     AL,0               ;Get file attributes
          MOV     DX,OFFSET Filename  ;Point at ASCIIZ string
          INT     21h
          MOV     BX,CX
          AND     BX,02h             ;Mask out all except hidden
          CMP     BX,0
          JE      NoChange
          AND     CX,3Dh             ;Turn off hidden attribute
          MOV     AL,1               ;Set file attributes
          INT     21h                ;All other parms still set
NoChange:
```

The function for setting file attributes is used extensively in DELDIR, the last program in this chapter (in the final section).

Working with Directories

When DOS V2.0 was introduced, a hierarchical directory structure was included that necessitated many new DOS functions. These functions enabled you to add and remove directories, and change the current directory. Another function enables you to find the path of the current directory. These four tasks are the only ones DOS lets you perform with directories.

DOS function 39h enables you to create a subdirectory. You just provide a pointer to an ASCIIZ string that defines the path to be created and then call the function, as in the following code fragment:

```
          .DATA
Directory DB      'C:\TESTDIR',0

          .CODE
          MOV     AH,39h             ;Create directory
```

```
        MOV     DX,OFFSET Directory ;Point to ASCIIZ name
        INT     21h
        JC      CreateErr          ;Could not create
```

This function returns an error (the carry flag is set and AX contains the error code) if the directory already exists, if you are creating the directory in the root and the root is full, or if an element in a multilevel path name does not exist.

The second task you can perform with directories is to remove them. There is virtually no difference between the code used to create a directory and the code used to remove one. The only difference is the function number called, which is DOS function 3Ah. The following code fragment shows the similarity in their use:

```
        .DATA
Directory   DB      'C:\TESTDIR',0

        .CODE
        MOV     AH,3Ah             ;Remove directory
        MOV     DX,OFFSET Directory ;Point to ASCIIZ name
        INT     21h
        JC      RemoveErr          ;Could not create
```

The only errors returned are if the directory does not exist, if it is not empty, or if it is the current directory. Because you can't be outside the directory structure (you must *always* operate within a directory), you cannot delete the root directory—the first and last directory to exist on a disk.

Next, you can change the current directory with the set directory function, 3Bh. The effect of this function is identical to the CD or CHDIR command. Again, it is similar in implementation to the functions that create and remove directories. The following program code is an example of how to use this function:

```
        .DATA
Directory   DB      'C:\TESTDIR',0

        .CODE
        MOV     AH,3Bh             ;Set directory
        MOV     DX,OFFSET Directory ;Point to ASCIIZ name
        INT     21h
        JC      RemoveErr          ;Could not create
```

In this case, only one error is possible—if the requested directory does not exist.

Finally, you can use DOS function 47h to determine the path name of the current directory. To call this function, you provide a pointer to a 65-byte buffer in which you want the current directory deposited. DOS fills this buffer with an ASCIIZ string that represents the path from the root to the current directory. The disk name and the leading backslash are not returned. If you want a full path name, therefore, you must use this function in the following manner:

```
        .DATA
FullDir  DB      '\'
DirBuff  DB      65 DUP(0)


        .CODE
        MOV     AH,47h              ;Get directory
        MOV     AL,0               ;This drive
        MOV     SI,OFFSET DirBuf    ;Point to buffer area
        INT     21h
```

After using the function in this manner, you can address the label FullDir as the full path name of the current directory. You should note that function 47h does not return a string (actually, it returns a NULL string) if the current directory is the root directory. Because of this, it is that much more important to use the path technique just illustrated.

Notice that a drive designator is loaded in the AL register before function 47h is invoked. Because DOS maintains information about the current directory on each drive, this code indicates in which drive you are interested. A code of 0 indicates the current drive, 1=A, 2=B, 3=C, and so on. If the drive you specify is invalid, function 47h returns an error code in AX and the carry flag is set.

These directory functions are used extensively in the final program presented later in this chapter.

Renaming and Deleting Files

DOS function 56h enables you to rename an existing file. It closely parallels the RENAME command. You provide a pointer to the current name of the file and a pointer to the new name and then invoke the function. On return, an error is generated if you have given invalid file names, invalid path names, or different drives in the current and new file names.

Why discuss renaming files *after* discussing directory structure? Because of one interesting capability of the rename function. Because you can specify full path names for both the old and new file names, you can use this function to move a file quickly from one directory structure to another without physically copying the file—only the directory entry location is modified. Because no copying takes place, you cannot move a file from one drive to another with this function, but you can move it from one directory to another on the same drive.

No DOS command implements this functionality. The program in Listing 7.2, however, does so. MOVE uses the same syntax as the RENAME command and either renames a file or moves it to another directory.

Listing 7.2. MOVE.ASM

```
Page 60,132

Comment ¦
******************************************************************


File:      MOVE.ASM
Author:    Allen L. Wyatt
Date:      6/26/92
Assembler: MASM 6.0


Purpose:   Full rename, including moving to another directory


Format:    MOVE oldfile.ext newfile.ext


******************************************************************¦


           .MODEL   small
           .STACK                        ;Default 1K stack is OK
           .DATA

WorkDir1   DB       129 DUP(0)
WorkDir2   DB       129 DUP(0)

Unknown    DB       'Unknown error occurred',0
BadFile    DB       'File not found',0
BadPath    DB       'Path not found',0
NoAccess   DB       'Access denied',0
BadDisk    DB       'File names must be on same disk',0

           .CODE
           .STARTUP
```

continues

Listing 7.2. Continued

```
MoveFile    PROC

            MOV      AL,ES:[80h]              ;Get length of command tail
            CMP      AL,0                     ;Is there a command tail?
            JE       Alldone                  ;No, so exit completely
            CALL     Xfer                     ;Go transfer command tail
            MOV      AL,WorkDir1              ;Get first byte of first name
            CMP      AL,0                     ;Is it NULL?
            JE       AllDone                  ;Yes, so exit
            MOV      AL,WorkDir2              ;Get first byte of second name
            CMP      AL,0                     ;Is it NULL?
            JE       AllDone                  ;Yes, so exit

            PUSH     DS
            POP      ES
            MOV      DX,OFFSET WorkDir1       ;Point to current file name
            MOV      DI,OFFSET WorkDir2       ;Point to new file name
            MOV      AH,56h
            INT      21h
            JNC      AllDone                  ;No error, so exit
            MOV      SI,OFFSET Unknown        ;Assume unknown error
            CMP      AX,02h                   ;File not found?
            JNE      E1
            MOV      SI,OFFSET BadFile

E1:         CMP      AX,03h                   ;Path not found?
            JNE      E2
            MOV      SI,OFFSET BadPath

E2:         CMP      AX,05h                   ;No access?
            JNE      E3
            MOV      SI,OFFSET NoAccess

E3:         CMP      AX,11h                   ;Not on same disk?
            JNE      E4
            MOV      SI,OFFSET BadDisk

E4:         CALL     PrtString

AllDone:    .EXIT
MoveFile    ENDP
```

```
; Transfers the command tail into the work file area, converting it
; into an ASCIIZ string. Assumes that ES points to PSP segment.

Xfer        PROC    USES AX CX SI DI ES DS
            PUSH    ES              ;Swap ES and DS
            PUSH    DS
            POP     ES
            POP     DS
            MOV     SI,80h          ;Point to start of command tail
            MOV     CH,0
            MOV     CL,[SI]         ;Get length of command tail
            INC     SI              ;Point to first character
            MOV     DI,OFFSET ES:WorkDir1
X1:         LODSB
            CMP     AL,' '          ;Was it a space?
            JNE     X2              ;No, so do first name
            LOOP    X1              ;Yes, so get next one
            JCXZ    XDone

X2:         DEC     SI              ;Point back to character
X3:         LODSB
            CMP     AL,' '          ;Was it a space?
            JNE     X4              ;No, so keep stuffing
            DEC     SI              ;Point back at space
            MOV     DI,OFFSET ES:WorkDir2
            JMP     X1
X4:         STOSB
            LOOP    X3
XDone:      RET
Xfer        ENDP


; The following routine prints the ASCIIZ string pointed to by DS:SI

PrtString   PROC    USES AX DX SI
PS1:        MOV     DL,[SI]         ;Get character
            INC     SI              ;Point to next one
            CMP     DL,0            ;End of string?
            JE      PS2             ;Yes, so exit
            MOV     AH,02h          ;Output a character
```

continues

Listing 7.2. Continued

```
            INT     21h
            JMP     PS1                     ;Keep doing it
PS2:        RET
PrtString   ENDP

            END
```

As an example of using MOVE, consider the following commands:

```
MOVE FILE.TXT FILE.ASC

MOVE FILE.ASC ..\FILE.ASC

MOVE ..\FILE.ASC \WORDPROC\TEXT\ALLEN\FILE.TXT
```

The first command does the same thing as the RENAME command—changes the name from the first file name to the second. The second command moves the file from the current directory to the parent directory. The file is not copied; it is simply moved. The third command moves the file from the first path name to the second, and renames the file in the process.

One note about MOVE.ASM. You should not confuse what this program does with the COPY command. MOVE is an extension of the RENAME command, not of the COPY command. It does not move a file by making a copy of it; it moves the file by changing its name—its complete name, including the path. Obviously, other enhancements can be made to MOVE to add features, but most of them involve physically copying the file. You may want to add some of this additional functionality to the program yourself.

Last, let's discuss the deletion of files. DOS function 41h enables you to remove an existing file that is not currently open, hidden, or marked as read-only. As with other file functions, you just provide a pointer to an ASCIIZ string for the file name (including complete path, if you want), and then invoke the function. The following code deletes a file:

```
            .DATA
Filename    DB      'C:\TEST.DAT',0

            .CODE
            MOV     AH,41h                  ;Delete file
            MOV     DX,OFFSET Filename      ;Pointer to ASCIIZ string
            INT     21h
            JC      Error                   ;File couldn't be deleted
```

This function works exactly as the DEL command does. It returns the disk sectors previously occupied by the file to the pool of available disk space and places a marker at the beginning of the directory entry for the file. This directory entry indicates to DOS that the file has been deleted. The actual information on the disk remains, however.

For some people and some applications, this remaining information can be a problem. You may need a program, therefore, that fully and completely deletes a file from the disk. The program in Listing 7.3 does just that. It writes spaces over the information previously in the file and then deletes the file in the normal way. In this way, even if the user employs a utility that undeletes files, the retrieved file is usable.

Listing 7.3. PURGE.ASM

```
Page 60,132

Comment ¦
********************************************************************


File:      PURGE.ASM
Author:    Allen L. Wyatt
Date:      6/25/92
Assembler: MASM 6.0

Purpose:   Erase the contents of a file, then delete the file

Format:    PURGE filename.ext


********************************************************************¦


           .MODEL  small
           .STACK                   ;Default 1K stack is OK
           .DATA
TRUE       EQU     -1
FALSE      EQU     0
BufSize    EQU     32768            ;Use large buffer

WorkDir    DB      129 DUP(0)
Handle     DW      0000
NumBytes   DW      0000
FilePtrH   DW      0000
```

continues

Listing 7.3. Continued

```
FilePtrL     DW       0000
Blocks       DW       0000
EOF          DB       00

ErrMsg       DB       'Bad file name, path not found, or access denied',13,10,0
DoneMsg      DB       'File is purged',0
WriteMsg     DB       'This file could not be written to',0
DelMsg       DB       'File has been overwritten, but was not deleted',0
MemMsg       DB       'Sorry, not enough memory could be allocated',13,10
             DB       'for this program',0
BlockMsg1    DB       'There are ',0
BlockMsg2    DB       ' blocks in this file',13,10,0
BlockMsgS    DB       'There is 1 block in this file',13,10,0
StatusMsg    DB       13,'Writing block ',0
ProcDone     DB       '... processing completed',13,10,0
Blank        DB       ' ',0

             .CODE
             .STARTUP
PurgeFile    PROC

             MOV      AL,ES:[80h]           ;Get length of command tail
             CMP      AL,0                  ;Is there a command tail?
             JE       Alldone               ;Nope, so exit completely
             CALL     Xfer                  ;Go transfer command tail

; The following memory allocation code works because it is known that MASM
; sets DS and SS to the same segment address in the start-up code. Also, ES
; is set to the PSP for the program on entry.

             MOV      BX,DS                 ;Point to start of data segment
             MOV      AX,ES                 ;Point to start of PSP
             SUB      BX,AX                 ;Number of segments for code and data
             MOV      AX,SP                 ;SP is pointing to top of stack area
             MOV      CL,4                  ;Dividing by 16
             SHR      AX,CL
             ADD      BX,AX                 ;BX=paragraphs needed
             MOV      AH,4Ah                ;Modify memory allocation
             INT      21h
```

```
                MOV     AH,3Dh                  ;Open file
                MOV     AL,42h                  ;Full sharing, read/write access
                MOV     DX,OFFSET WorkDir        ;Point to start of file name
                INT     21h
                JNC     FileOpen                ;No error, continue
                MOV     SI,OFFSET ErrMsg         ;Point to message to display
                CALL    PrtString               ;Display the string
                JMP     AllDone

FileOpen:       MOV     Handle,AX               ;Store handle for later
                MOV     AH,48h                  ;Allocate memory
                MOV     BX,BufSize/16           ;Paragraphs to request
                INT     21h
                JNC     MemOK                   ;No errors
                MOV     SI,OFFSET MemMsg
                CALL    PrtString
                JMP     AllDone

MemOK:          CALL    FindBlocks              ;Determine number of blocks in file
                MOV     ES,AX                   ;Point to memory block for later use
                MOV     EOF,FALSE

DoLoop:         CALL    ReadFile
                CALL    WriteFile
                JC      BadWrite
                CMP     EOF,FALSE
                JE      DoLoop
                JNE     CloseFile
BadWrite:       MOV     SI,OFFSET WriteMsg       ;Error message

CloseFile:      MOV     BX,Handle               ;Get file handle
                MOV     AH,3Eh                  ;Close file
                INT     21h
                CMP     EOF,FALSE               ;Was end of file reached?
                JE      Done                    ;No, exit with error message in SI

                MOV     AH,41h                  ;Delete file
                MOV     DX,OFFSET WorkDir        ;Point to start of file name
                INT     21h
                MOV     SI,OFFSET DoneMsg
```

continues

Listing 7.3. Continued

```
            JNC     Done                ;No error, file was deleted
            MOV     SI,OFFSET DelMsg    ;Point to error message

Done:       PUSH    SI
            MOV     SI,OFFSET ProcDone
            CALL    PrtString
            POP     SI
            CALL    PrtString
            MOV     AH,49h              ;Release memory block at ES
            INT     21h

AllDone:    .EXIT
PurgeFile   ENDP


; The following routine saves the current file pointer location,
; then fills the buffer from the disk file

ReadFile    PROC    USES AX BX CX DX
            MOV     AH,42h              ;Move file pointer
            MOV     AL,01h              ;Offset from current position
            MOV     BX,Handle
            MOV     CX,0                ;Stay where you are
            MOV     DX,0
            INT     21h
            MOV     FilePtrH,DX         ;Store current position
            MOV     FilePtrL,AX

            MOV     AH,3Fh              ;Read file
            MOV     CX,BufSize          ;Get a full buffer
            PUSH    DS                  ;Store data segment and point
            PUSH    ES                  ;      it to the right segment
            POP     DS                  ;      for the buffer area
            MOV     DX,0                ;Start of memory block
            INT     21h
            POP     DS
            JC      ReadErr             ;Could not read from file
            MOV     NumBytes,AX         ;Store number of bytes read
            CMP     AX,CX               ;Were all bytes read?
            JE      RFDone              ;Yes, so exit
```

```
SetEOF:      MOV     EOF,TRUE          ;No, so EOF reached
             JMP     RFDone
ReadErr:     CMP     AX,0              ;Was it because EOF was reached?
             JE      SetEOF            ;Yes, so set flag
RFDone:      RET
ReadFile     ENDP
```

```
; The following routine fills the buffer with spaces, sets the file
; pointer back to where the last read occurred, and then writes the
; buffer contents to disk.
```

```
WriteFile    PROC    USES AX BX CX DX
             MOV     CX,NumBytes       ;Need only this many
             MOV     AL,20h            ;Want to use spaces
             MOV     DI,0
             REP     STOSB

             MOV     AH,42h            ;Move file pointer
             MOV     AL,00h            ;From beginning of file
             MOV     BX,Handle
             MOV     CX,FilePtrH       ;Get start of last read
             MOV     DX,FilePtrL
             INT     21h

             MOV     AH,40h            ;Write file
             MOV     CX,NumBytes       ;Writing what was read earlier
             PUSH    DS                ;Store data segment and point
             PUSH    ES                ;     it to the right segment
             POP     DS                ;     for the buffer area
             MOV     DX,0              ;Start of memory block
             INT     21h
             POP     DS
             JC      WriteErr          ;Could not write to file
             CMP     AX,CX             ;Were all bytes written?
             JNE     WriteErr          ;No, so exit with error
             CALL    DoStatus
             CLC
             JNC     WFExit
WriteErr:    STC                       ;Return with error
WFExit:      RET
WriteFile    ENDP
```

continues

Listing 7.3. Continued

```
; Print a status message

DoStatus    PROC    USES AX SI
            MOV     SI,OFFSET StatusMsg
            CALL    PrtString
            MOV     AX,Blocks
            CALL    PrtDec
            MOV     SI,OFFSET Blank
            CALL    PrtString
            DEC     Blocks
            RET
DoStatus    ENDP


; Determine the number of blocks in the file

FindBlocks  PROC    USES AX BX CX DX SI
            MOV     AH,42h              ;Find file size
            MOV     AL,02h              ;From end of file
            MOV     BX,Handle
            MOV     CX,0                ;Keep at end
            MOV     DX,0
            INT     21h

            MOV     CX,BufSize
            DIV     CX
            CMP     DX,0
            JE      NoInc
            INC     AX
NoInc:      MOV     Blocks,AX
            CMP     AX,1               ;Only one block?
            JNE     FB1                ;No, so continue
            MOV     SI,OFFSET BlockMsgS ;Use singular message
            JMP     FB2
FB1:        MOV     SI,OFFSET BlockMsg1
            CALL    PrtString
            CALL    PrtDec
            MOV     SI,OFFSET BlockMsg2
FB2:        CALL    PrtString
```

```
                MOV     AH,42h              ;Find file size
                MOV     AL,00h              ;From start of file
                MOV     BX,Handle
                MOV     CX,0                ;Keep at start
                MOV     DX,0
                INT     21h
                RET
FindBlocks      ENDP


; Transfers the command tail into the work file area, converting it
; into an ASCIIZ string. Assumes that ES points to PSP segment.

Xfer            PROC    USES AX CX SI DI ES DS
                PUSH    ES                  ;Swap ES and DS
                PUSH    DS
                POP     ES
                POP     DS
                MOV     SI,80h              ;Point to start of command tail
                MOV     CH,0
                MOV     CL,[SI]             ;Get length of command tail
                INC     SI                  ;Point to first character
                MOV     DI,OFFSET ES:WorkDir
X1:             LODSB
                CMP     AL,' '              ;Was it a space?
                JE      X4                  ;Yes, so skip it
                STOSB                       ;Store a byte
X4:             LOOP    X1                  ;Keep going to the end
                MOV     AL,0
                STOSB                       ;Make sure NUL is at end of path
                RET
Xfer            ENDP


; The following routine prints the ASCIIZ string pointed to by DS:SI

PrtString       PROC    USES AX DX SI
PS1:            MOV     DL,[SI]             ;Get character
                INC     SI                  ;Point to next one
                CMP     DL,0                ;End of string?
                JE      PS2                 ;Yes, so exit
                MOV     AH,02h              ;Output a character
                INT     21h
```

continues

Listing 7.3. Continued

```
                JMP     PS1                     ;Keep doing it
PS2:            RET
PrtString       ENDP

; The following routine prints the value in AX as a decimal number

PrtDec          PROC    USES AX CX DX
                MOV     CX,0FFFFh               ;Ending flag
                PUSH    CX
                MOV     CX,10
PD1:            MOV     DX,0
                DIV     CX                      ;Divide by 10
                ADD     DL,30h                  ;Convert to ASCII
                PUSH    DX                      ;Store remainder
                CMP     AX,0                    ;Are we done?
                JNE     PD1                     ;No, so continue

PD2:            POP     DX                      ;Character is now in DL
                CMP     DX,0FFFFh               ;Is it the ending flag?
                JE      PD3                     ;Yes, so continue
                MOV     AH,02h                  ;Output a character
                INT     21h
                JMP     PD2                     ;Keep doing it

PD3:            RET
PrtDec          ENDP

                END
```

In examining the source code for PURGE, you may question why I didn't just find the size of the file and then write over the entire file. I read each block and then wrote over it to ensure that no read errors were in the file. I think that it's better to be safe than sorry; if you can read and write to the file, then you can be 100 percent sure that your overwriting was successful.

Putting It All Together

Now that you have learned how to work with files and directories, you may be interested in examining a useful program that applies all the information learned in this chapter. DELDIR is a program I developed in response to my frustration in working with directories. Many times, I have created an entire string of directories and subdirectories I want to remove from my drive. To do this, I traditionally had to descend to the lowest directory level, delete all files there, and ascend one level at a time to repeat the process. With a complex directory structure, this process can take considerable time.

That is where the following program, DELDIR, comes in handy. It enables you to specify a directory it deletes. If you don't specify a directory, it removes the current directory. DELDIR deletes not only that directory, but also every directory and file subordinate to that directory and even hidden and system files that reside in the directories to be deleted—all with one command.

Because this program is so powerful, you are asked to verify whether DELDIR should delete everything within and below the root directory. Answering No aborts the program. DELDIR performs the following steps:

1. Determines the directory to be removed.

2. Changes to that directory.

3. Searches for any directory entries.

4. If a directory entry is found and it is a file, changes the attributes to normal and deletes it.

5. If a directory entry is found and it is a directory, changes to that directory and repeats steps 2 through 7.

6. When the directory is empty, goes up one level in the directory structure.

7. Deletes the directory just left in step 6.

8. Changes back to the directory from which the program was called.

In step 5, DELDIR uses *recursion* to step down the directory structure until the last file at the lowest level is deleted and then works back up the structure. It does this by having a routine call itself multiple times to perform a repetitive task. The program listing for DELDIR is shown in Listing 7.4.

Listing 7.4. DELDIR.ASM

```
Page 60,132

Comment ¦
*******************************************************************

File:      DELDIR.ASM
Author:    Allen L. Wyatt
Date:      6/18/92
Assembler: MASM 6.0
```

continues

Listing 7.4. Continued

```
Purpose:    Delete specified directory and all subdirectories to it

Format:     DELDIR [path]


**********************************************************************!

            .MODEL  small
            .STACK                          ;Default 1K stack is OK
            .DATA

FileCount   DW      0
DirCount    DW      0

CurDrive    DB      'C:'
CurDir      DB      '\', 65 DUP(0)
WorkDrive   DB      'C:'
WorkOrig    DB      '\', 65 DUP(0)
WorkDir     DB      '\', 128 DUP(0)

MaxDrives   DB      0
Wild        DB      '*.*',0
Parent      DB      '..',0

DriveEMsg   DB      'Invalid drive',13,10,0
DirEMsg     DB      'Invalid directory',13,10,0
Sure        DB      'Delete everything on the '
SureDrive   DB      '?: drive (y/n)? ',0
RemDir      DB      'Removing ',0
DirMsgS     DB      ' directory was removed',13,10,0
DirMsgP     DB      ' directories were removed',13,10,0
FileMsgS    DB      ' file was deleted',13,10,0
FileMsgP    DB      ' files were deleted',13,10,0
DoneMsg     DB      'Program finished'
CRLF        DB      13,10,0

            .CODE
            .STARTUP
DelDir      PROC
```

```
; The following memory allocation code works because it is known that MASM
; sets DS and SS to the same segment address in the start-up code. Also, ES
; is set to the PSP for the program on entry.

            MOV     BX,DS               ;Point to start of data segment
            MOV     AX,ES               ;Point to start of PSP
            SUB     BX,AX               ;Number of segments for code and data
            MOV     AX,SP               ;SP is pointing to top of stack area
            MOV     CL,4                ;Dividing by 16
            SHR     AX,CL
            ADD     BX,AX               ;BX=paragraphs needed
            MOV     AH,4Ah              ;Modify memory allocation
            INT     21h

;    get the current drive and directory

            MOV     AH,19h              ;Get current drive
            INT     21h
            MOV     DL,AL               ;Move drive for next operation
            ADD     AL,'A'              ;Make it ASCII
            MOV     CurDrive,AL         ;Store it for later
            MOV     WorkDrive,AL
            MOV     SureDrive,AL

            MOV     AH,0Eh              ;Select default drive
            INT     21h
            MOV     MaxDrives,AL        ;Store number of drives

            MOV     DL,0                ;Use current drive
            MOV     AH,47h              ;Get current directory
            MOV     SI,OFFSET CurDir    ;Point to directory buffer
            INC     SI                  ;Point past leading backslash
            INT     21h
            MOV     DL,0                ;Use current drive
            MOV     AH,47h              ;Get current directory
            MOV     SI,OFFSET WorkDir   ;Point to working directory buffer
            INC     SI                  ;Point past leading backslash
            INT     21h

            CALL    Parse               ;Go parse command tail file name
```

continues

Listing 7.4. Continued

```
            MOV     DL,WorkDrive
            CMP     DL,CurDrive             ;Still working on same drive
            JE      DriveOK                 ;Yes, so continue
            SUB     DL,'A'                  ;Make drive zero-based
            CMP     DL,MaxDrives            ;Out of range?
            JA      DriveErr                ;Yes, exit with error
            MOV     AH,0Eh                  ;No, set current drive
            INT     21h

            MOV     DL,0                    ;Use current drive (new drive)
            MOV     AH,47h                  ;Get directory on new drive
            MOV     SI,OFFSET WorkOrig      ;Point to directory buffer
            INC     SI                      ;Point past leading backslash
            INT     21h

DriveOK:    MOV     AL,WorkDir
            CMP     AL,0                    ;Any directory to use?
            JE      GetDir                  ;No, so get where we are
            MOV     DX,OFFSET WorkDir       ;Point to new directory
            MOV     AH,3Bh                  ;Set directory to DS:DX
            INT     21h
            JC      DirBad                  ;Bad move

; Even though the directory was possibly just set, it is important to
; get the directory again because the command line could have used
; relative directory addressing. Getting the directory one more time
; ensures that absolute directory addressing is used.

GetDir:     MOV     DL,0                    ;Use current drive
            MOV     WorkDir,'\'
            MOV     SI,OFFSET WorkDir
            INC     SI                      ;Point past leading backslash
            MOV     AH,47h                  ;Get current directory
            INT     21h
            JMP     DirOK

DirBad:     MOV     SI,OFFSET DirEMsg
            JMP     ErrMsg
DriveErr:   MOV     SI,OFFSET DriveEMsg
ErrMsg:     CALL    PrtString               ;Display the string at DS:SI
            JMP     Done
```

```
DirOK:     CMP    WorkDir+1,0        ;At root directory?
           JNE    Start
           MOV    SI,OFFSET Sure
           CALL   PrtString
InLoop:    MOV    AH,0               ;Read keyboard character
           INT    16h
           OR     AL,20h             ;Convert to lowercase
           CMP    AL,'n'             ;Was it no?
           JE     GoodKey
           CMP    AL,'y'             ;Was it yes?
           JNE    InLoop
GoodKey:   MOV    SI,OFFSET CRLF
           CALL   PrtString
           CMP    AL,'n'             ;Was it no?
           JE     Done               ;Yes, so exit program

Start:     CALL   DoDir              ;Go erase this directory
           CMP    WorkDir+1,0        ;At root directory?
           JE     Stats              ;Yes, so don't try to remove

           MOV    DX,OFFSET Parent   ;Point to '..'
           MOV    AH,3Bh             ;Set directory to DS:DX
           INT    21h

           MOV    SI,OFFSET RemDir
           CALL   PrtString          ;Display the string at DS:SI
           MOV    SI,OFFSET WorkDir
           CALL   PrtString          ;Display the string at DS:SI
           MOV    SI,OFFSET CRLF
           CALL   PrtString

           MOV    DX,OFFSET WorkDir  ;Point to original directory
           MOV    AH,3Ah             ;Remove directory at DS:DX
           INT    21h
           JC     Stats              ;Couldn't remove directory
           INC    DirCount

Stats:     MOV    AX,DirCount
           CMP    AX,0               ;Any directories deleted?
           JE     Stats2             ;No, continue
```

continues

Listing 7.4. Continued

```
                CALL    PrtDec
                MOV     SI,OFFSET DirMsgS    ;Point to singular message
                CMP     AX,1                 ;Singular directories?
                JE      Stats1               ;Yes, so print singular message
                MOV     SI,OFFSET DirMsgP    ;Point to plural message
Stats1:         CALL    PrtString            ;Display the string at DS:SI

Stats2:         MOV     AX,FileCount
                CMP     AX,0                 ;Any files deleted?
                JE      Done                 ;No, so finish up
                CALL    PrtDec
                MOV     SI,OFFSET FileMsgS   ;Point to singular message
                CMP     AX,1                 ;Singular files?
                JE      Stats3               ;Yes, so print singular message
                MOV     SI,OFFSET FileMsgP   ;Point to plural message
Stats3:         CALL    PrtString            ;Display the string at DS:SI

Done:           MOV     DL,CurDrive          ;Move drive for next operation
                CMP     DL,WorkDrive         ;Same as original?
                JE      Done1                ;Yes, so continue
                MOV     DX,OFFSET WorkOrig   ;Original directory on target
drive
                MOV     AH,3Bh               ;Set current directory (if pos-
sible)
                INT     21h
                MOV     DL,CurDrive          ;Get calling drive
                SUB     DL,'A'               ;Make it zero-based
                MOV     AH,0Eh               ;Set current drive
                INT     21h

Done1:          MOV     DX,OFFSET CurDir     ;Point to new directory
                MOV     AH,3Bh               ;Set current directory
                INT     21h
                MOV     SI,OFFSET DoneMsg    ;Final message
                CALL    PrtString
                .EXIT
DelDir          ENDP
```

```
Comment ¦
=====================================================================
    The following routine performs these steps:
        1. Sets up a memory block and header information (see SetHdr)
        2. Deletes files in current directory one at a time
        3. Recursively calls DoDir when new subdirectories encountered
        4. Resets DTA to original area and releases memory block
        5. Returns to caller
=====================================================================¦


DoDir      PROC    USES AX BX CX DX SI DI ES
           CALL    SetHdr                  ;Allocate memory and set header info

           MOV     DX,OFFSET Wild          ;Point to *.*
           MOV     CX,16h                  ;Want normal, hidden, system, and vol
           MOV     AH,4Eh                  ;Search for first match
           INT     21h
           JC      NoFile                  ;No file found
           JNC     FoundOne                ;Go handle file found

NextFile:  MOV     AH,4Fh                  ;Search for next file
           INT     21h
           JC      NoFile                  ;No file found

FoundOne:  MOV     DX,1Eh                  ;ES:DX points to name in DTA
           MOV     AL,ES:[15h]             ;Get file attribute
           CMP     AL,10h                  ;Is it a directory?
           JNE     FoundFile               ;No, so go handle

           MOV     AL,ES:[1Eh]             ;Get first character of directory
           CMP     AL,'.'                  ;Is it . or ..?
           JE      NextFile                ;Yes, so ignore
           CALL    DirOut                  ;Go delete an entire directory
           JMP     NextFile                ;Go search for next entry

FoundFile: CALL    FileOut                 ;Go delete the file that was found
           JMP     NextFile                ;Go search for next entry


; By this point, there are no more files left. Switch back to original
; DTA and release memory block requested by SetHdr.
```

continues

Listing 7.4. Continued

```
NoFile:     PUSH    DS
            MOV     SI,128              ;Point to old DTA address
            MOV     AX,ES:[SI]          ;Get stored segment
            INC     SI
            INC     SI
            MOV     DX,ES:[SI]          ;Get stored offset
            MOV     DS,AX
            MOV     AH,1Ah              ;Set DTA address
            INT     21h
            POP     DS

            MOV     AH,49h              ;Release memory block at ES
            INT     21h

DDDone:     RET
DoDir       ENDP


Comment ¦
=====================================================================
    The following routine is used by DoDir to set up the new DTA and header
    area for this iteration of the deletion process. On exit, ES points to
    the segment of the memory area.  All other registers remain unchanged.

    Memory block structure:
       Start   Len     Use
           0   128     DTA for new directory work
         128     2     Segment pointer for old DTA
         130     2     Offset pointer for old DTA
         132    12     Unused area
=====================================================================¦


SetHdr      PROC    USES AX BX CX DI SI DS
            MOV     AH,48h              ;Allocate memory
            MOV     BX,09h              ;Requesting 144 bytes
            INT     21h
            MOV     ES,AX              ;Point to memory block for later use
            MOV     DS,AX              ;Point for current use

            MOV     AL,0               ;Zero out the newly acquired buffer
```

```
            MOV     DI,0
            CLD                             ;Make sure going in proper direction
            MOV     CX,144
            REP     STOSB

            PUSH    ES                      ;Store temporarily
            MOV     AH,2Fh                  ;Get DTA address
            INT     21h
            MOV     SI,128                  ;Point to address area in buffer
            MOV     AX,ES
            MOV     [SI],AX                 ;Store segment of DTA
            INC     SI
            INC     SI
            MOV     [SI],BX                 ;Store offset of DTA
            POP     ES                      ;Get back old ES

            MOV     DX,0                    ;DS:DX points to new DTA
            MOV     AH,1Ah                  ;Set DTA address
            INT     21h
            RET
SetHdr      ENDP

; Delete file pointed to by ES:DX, then increment counter

FileOut     PROC    USES AX CX DS
            PUSH    DS
            PUSH    ES
            POP     DS
            MOV     AH,43h                  ;Set file attributes of file at DS:DX
            MOV     AL,01h
            MOV     CX,0                    ;No attributes
            INT     21h
            MOV     AH,41h                  ;Delete file at DS:DX
            INT     21h
            POP     DS                      ;Reset DS
            JC      F09                     ;File was not deleted
            INC     FileCount
F09:        RET
FileOut     ENDP
```

continues

Listing 7.4. Continued

```
; Delete the directory pointed to by ES:DX, then increment counter

DirOut      PROC    USES AX BX SI DS
            PUSH    DS                      ;Store it
            PUSH    ES
            POP     DS
            MOV     AH,3Bh                  ;Set directory to DS:DX
            INT     21h
            POP     DS
            CALL    DoDir                   ;Recursive call for new dir
            MOV     DX,OFFSET Parent        ;Point to '..'
            MOV     AH,3Bh                  ;Set directory to DS:DX
            INT     21h

            MOV     SI,OFFSET RemDir
            CALL    PrtString               ;Display the string at DS:SI
            MOV     AH,2Fh                  ;Get DTA address into ES:BX
            INT     21h
            ADD     BX,1Eh                  ;Offset to file name (directory)
            PUSH    DS                      ;Store DS temporarily
            PUSH    ES
            POP     DS
            MOV     SI,BX
            CALL    PrtString               ;Display the string at DS:SI
            MOV     DX,BX
            MOV     AH,3Ah                  ;Remove directory at DS:DX
            INT     21h
            POP     DS
            JC      DO9                     ;Directory not removed
            INC     DirCount
DO9:        MOV     SI,OFFSET CRLF
            CALL    PrtString
            RET
DirOut      ENDP

; The following routine prints the value in AX as a decimal number

PrtDec      PROC    USES AX CX DX
            MOV     CX,0FFFFh               ;Ending flag
            PUSH    CX
```

```
        MOV     CX,10
PD1:    MOV     DX,0
        DIV     CX              ;Divide by 10
        ADD     DL,30h          ;Convert to ASCII
        PUSH    DX              ;Store remainder
        CMP     AX,0            ;Are we done?
        JNE     PD1             ;No, so continue

PD2:    POP     DX              ;Character is now in DL
        CMP     DX,0FFFFh       ;Is it the ending flag?
        JE      PD3             ;Yes, so continue
        MOV     AH,02h          ;Output a character
        INT     21h
        JMP     PD2             ;Keep doing it

PD3:    RET
PrtDec  ENDP

; The following routine prints the ASCIIZ string pointed to by DS:SI

PrtString  PROC     USES AX DX SI
PS1:       MOV      DL,[SI]       ;Get character
           INC      SI            ;Point to next one
           CMP      DL,0          ;End of string?
           JE       PS2           ;Yes, so exit
           MOV      AH,02h        ;Output a character
           INT      21h
           JMP      PS1           ;Keep doing it
PS2:       RET
PrtString  ENDP

; Parses a command line parameter into the file name work area

Parse   PROC     USES AX CX SI DI ES DS
        PUSH     ES              ;Swap ES and DS
        PUSH     DS
        POP      ES
        POP      DS
        MOV      SI,80h
        MOV      CL,[SI]         ;Get command tail length
```

continues

Listing 7.4. Continued

```
              MOV     CH,0
              JCXZ    PDone           ;Nothing there to parse
              INC     SI              ;Point to first character of command tail
              MOV     DI,OFFSET ES:WorkDir
P1:           LODSB
              CMP     AL,' '          ;Was it a space?
              JE      P4              ;Yes, so skip it
              CMP     AL,':'          ;Was it a drive designator?
              JNE     P3              ;No, so continue
              DEC     SI              ;Point to character before colon
              DEC     SI
              LODSB
              CALL    ToUC            ;Convert to uppercase
              INC     SI              ;Point past the colon
              MOV     ES:WorkDrive,AL
              MOV     ES:SureDrive,AL ;Store it for message
              MOV     DI,OFFSET ES:WorkDir ;Begin path again
              JMP     P4
P3:           CALL    ToUC            ;Convert to uppercase
              STOSB                   ;Store a byte
P4:           LOOP    P1              ;Keep going to the end
              MOV     AL,0
              STOSB                   ;Make sure NUL is at end of path
PDone:        RET
Parse         ENDP


; Converts the character in AL to uppercase. All other registers unchanged.


ToUC          PROC
              CMP     AL,'a'          ;Lowercase?
              JB      T9
              CMP     AL,'z'
              JA      T9
              SUB     AL,20h          ;Convert to uppercase
T9:           RET
ToUC          ENDP

              END
```

Because DELDIR is such a powerful command and erases files and directories quickly, make sure that you have a backup of your disk before you use DELDIR for the first time. Or, try it on floppy disks, where any errant behavior has minimal consequences—I have learned this the hard way.

Summary

In this chapter, you learned how to work with files to read and write information. You also learned how to traverse directories, even in a recursive manner. The techniques learned in this chapter are at the core of many powerful assembly language programs.

In Chapter 8, you learn about a commonly misunderstood area of programming: the IOCTL functions.

Using IOCTL

IOCTL is a collection of system routines accessed through DOS function 44h. IOCTL, which stands for *I/O control*, refers to the purpose of the routines. Each is intended to provide a standardized and consistent means to control any device that may be connected to the computer. The IOCTL routines provide a means of controlling device drivers, which in turn control the physical device.

Because the IOCTL routines provide a standard method of controlling device drivers, this chapter and Chapter 9, "Device Drivers," are closely related. This chapter examines the IOCTL routines and how they can be used to control standard devices connected to your computer—disk drives, monitor, and keyboard. Chapter 9, on the other hand, delves into how you can develop your own device drivers. The information in both chapters is necessary for a complete understanding of devices and how they are controlled by DOS.

Terminology surrounding the IOCTL routines can sometimes be confusing. The IOCTL routines often are referred to as IOCTL functions, even though they are subfunctions to DOS function 44h. These subfunctions have, in turn, their own subfunctions. To simplify terminology in this chapter (and in Chapter 9), the IOCTL routines are referred to as functions in their own right.

The IOCTL functions are used to control two general classifications of devices: character and block devices. *Character devices* process data one byte at a time. These devices include the keyboard, video monitor, mouse, modem, printer, and any other device that communicates through a serial or parallel channel. Files also are considered character devices.

Block devices can be broadly characterized as devices that deal with more than a single byte of information at a time. These devices include disk drives, disk files, CD-ROM drives, and RAM.

This chapter describes both classes of devices and pays particular attention to how they are accessed and manipulated by way of the IOCTL subfunctions of interrupt 21h, function 44h. Each type of device is treated individually. By way of introduction, Table 8.1 lists the 18 IOCTL functions and the types of devices to which they are applicable.

Table 8.1. The IOCTL subfunctions and device classification relevance.

Func	Sub	Name	Character	Block
00h		Get Device Information	X	
01h		Set Device Information	X	
02h		Read Character Device Control Information	X	
03h		Write Character Device Control Information	X	
04h		Read Block Device Control Information	X	
05h		Write Block Device Control Information		X
06h		Get Device Input Status	X	
07h		Get Device Output Status	X	
08h		Is Block Device Changeable?		X
09h		Is Block Device Remote?		X
0Ah		Is Handle Remote?	X	
0Bh		Set Sharing Retry Count	X	
0Ch		Generic IOCTL for Character Devices		
	45h	Set Iteration Count	X	
	4Ah	Select Code Page	X	
	4Ch	Start Code-Page Preparation	X	
	4Dh	End Code-Page Preparation	X	
	5Fh	Set Display Mode	X	
	65h	Get Iteration Count	X	
	6Ah	Query Selected Code Page	X	

Func	Sub	Name	Character	Block
	6Bh	Query Code-Page Prepare List	X	
	7Fh	Get Display Information	X	
0Dh		Generic IOCTL for Block Devices		
	40h	Set Device Parameters		X
	41h	Write Track		X
	42h	Format and Verify Track		X
	46h	Set Media ID		X
	47h	Set Access Flag		X
	60h	Get Device Parameters		X
	61h	Read Track		X
	62h	Verify Track		X
	66h	Get Media ID		X
	67h	Get Access Flag		X
	68h	Sense Media Type		X
0Eh		Get Logical Device Map		X
0Fh		Set Logical Device Map		X
10h		Query IOCTL Handle	X	
11h		Query IOCTL Device		X

Character Device Control

As mentioned, character devices access information a single byte at a time, or as a stream of bytes. Examples include the video display, serial and parallel ports, the mouse, and disk files. Each character device attached to a computer has a unique name, as much as eight characters long. Table 8.2 indicates some predefined DOS character devices and their names. Be aware that not all COM or LPT devices are available on all systems. It depends, in large part, on your system board and BIOS configuration.

Character devices can be accessed in one of two modes. In *raw mode*, characters received by or sent to the device are treated simply as binary values; no processing is done based on the ASCII value of those bytes. Raw mode sometimes is referred to as *binary mode*.

Table 8.2. Predefined character devices.

Name	Meaning
AUX	Auxiliary device; typically another name for the COM1 device
CLOCK$	The real-time system clock
COM1	Communications port 1; the first serial port
COM2	Communications port 2; the second serial port
COM3	Communications port 3; the third serial port
COM4	Communications port 4; the fourth serial port
CON	System console: for input, the keyboard; for output, the video monitor
LPT1	Line printer 1; the first parallel port
LPT2	Line printer 2; the second parallel port
LPT3	Line printer 3; the third parallel port
LPT4	Line printer 4; the fourth parallel port
NUL	Nonexistent input or output; input from this device is nonexistent, and output sent to it is discarded
PRN	Printer device; typically another name for the LPT1 device

In the other processing mode, *cooked mode*, DOS intervenes and does a limited amount of processing on the information being transmitted or received. In cooked mode, or *ASCII mode*, as it sometimes is called, the ASCII value of a byte determines what action DOS takes. Table 8.3 shows the control characters that DOS will intercept and what action it takes when they are detected.

Table 8.3. Cooked mode processing of characters.

ASCII Value	Name	Action Taken
03h	Ctrl-C	Passes program control to the Ctrl-C interrupt handler. Typically results in termination of your program unless you have developed your own Ctrl-C interrupt handler.
10h	Ctrl-P	Turns printer echo on or off. All characters, up to the next Ctrl-P, are copied to the printer.
13h	Ctrl-S	Pauses output. The next character received as input resumes output of characters.
1Ah	Ctrl-Z	Closes file.

In addition to the characters in Table 8.3, the exact nature of a character device may cause additional character interpretation in cooked mode. For example, if the output device you are using is the video monitor, a tab character causes DOS to insert the proper number of spaces to advance the cursor to the next tab stop. If the input character device is the keyboard, a backspace character causes the preceding character in the keyboard buffer to be deleted; pressing Enter causes DOS to substitute two characters: carriage return and line feed.

Applicable IOCTL Functions

Only some of the IOCTL functions are applicable to character devices. Table 8.1 indicates which functions can be used with character devices. Perhaps the most informative function is function 00h, which enables you to retrieve information about the device driver or about a file (because a file is viewed by DOS as a type of character device).

When you use IOCTL function 00h, you must already have opened the file or device using DOS function 3Dh. When you do this, DOS returns a numeric value, or handle, that you can use to refer to the device or file. When you specify this handle with IOCTL function 00h, DOS returns information in the DX register about the nature of the device or file. Table 8.4 shows what information is returned if the handle refers to a file; Table 8.5 indicates what information is returned if the handle belongs to a device.

Table 8.4. File-related information returned by IOCTL function 00h.

Bit settings FEDCBA98 76543210	Meaning
xxxxxx	Drive number (0=A, 1=B, 2=C, and so on)
1	File has not been written
0	File has been written
0	This handle belongs to a file
xxxxxxxx	Reserved

Table 8.5. Device-related information returned by IOCTL function 00h.

Bit settings FEDCBA98 76543210	Meaning
1	Standard input device
0	Not a standard input device
1	Standard output device
0	Not a standard output device
1	NUL device
0	Not a NUL device
1	Clock device
0	Not a clock device
1	Device supports Int 28h processing
0	Device does not support Int 28h processing
1	Processing in binary (raw) mode
0	Processing in ASCII (cooked) mode
1	Device does not signal EOF on input
0	Device signals EOF on input
1	This handle belongs to a device
xxxxxx	Reserved
1	IOCTL functions 02h and 03h are supported
0	IOCTL functions 02h and 03h are not supported
x	Reserved

If you compare Tables 8.4 and 8.5, you notice that the bit which indicates whether the handle belongs to a file or a device is bit 7. If bit 7 is set, the handle belongs to a device.

To show what happens when you use this function in a program, consider the program in Listing 8.1, IOINFO.ASM.

Listing 8.1. IOINFO.ASM

```
Page 60,132

Comment ¦
*******************************************************************


File:       IOINFO.ASM
Author:     Allen L. Wyatt
Date:       7/18/92
Assembler:  MASM 6.0


Purpose:    Using IOCTL functions, discover and display information
            about a character device


Format:     IOINFO


*******************************************************************¦


            .MODEL  small
            .STACK                          ;Default 1K stack is OK
            .DATA
WorkDir     DB      129 DUP(0)
Handle      DW      0000

NeedFile    DB      'You must supply a file or device name',0
EMsg1       DB      'Could not open device',0
EMsg2       DB      'Could not use IOCTL function 0',0

FileMsg1    DB      'You have specified a file on drive ',0
FileMsg2    DB      13,10,'The file has ',0
FileMsg3    DB      'not ',0
FileMsg4    DB      'been written',13,10,0

DeviceMsg   DB      'The following information about this device was',13,10
            DB      'returned by IOCTL function 00h:',13,10,0
StdOYes     DB      '    This is a standard input device',13,10,0
StdIYes     DB      '    This is a standard output device',13,10,0
NulYes      DB      '    This is a NUL device',13,10,0
ClockYes    DB      '    This is a clock device',13,10,0
Binary      DB      '    This device is operating in raw (binary) mode',13,10,0
ASCII       DB      '    This device is operating in cooked (ASCII) mode',13,10,0
```

continues

Listing 8.1. Continued

```
I28Yes      DB      '    This device supports Interrupt 28h',13,10,0
I28No       DB      '    This device does not support Interrupt 28h',13,10,0
EOFNo       DB      '    EOF is not returned when device is read',13,10,0
EOFYes      DB      '    EOF is returned when device is read',13,10,0
F23Yes      DB      '    IOCTL functions 02h and 03h are supported',13,10,0
F23No       DB      '    IOCTL functions 02h and 03h are not supported',13,10,0

DevTable    DB      01              ;Flag to test bit
            DW      OFFSET StdOYes
            DW      0000
            DB      01              ;Flag to test bit
            DW      OFFSET StdIYes
            DW      0000
            DB      01              ;Flag to test bit
            DW      OFFSET NulYes
            DW      0000
            DB      01              ;Flag to test bit
            DW      OFFSET ClockYes
            DW      0000
            DB      01              ;Flag to test bit
            DW      OFFSET I28Yes
            DW      OFFSET I28No
            DB      01              ;Flag to test bit
            DW      OFFSET Binary
            DW      OFFSET ASCII
            DB      01              ;Flag to test bit
            DW      OFFSET EOFNo
            DW      OFFSET EOFYes
            DB      00              ;No need to test
            DB      00              ;Reserved bit, do not test
            DB      00              ;Reserved bit, do not test
            DB      00              ;Reserved bit, do not test
            DB      00              ;Reserved bit, do not test
            DB      00              ;Reserved bit, do not test
            DB      00              ;Reserved bit, do not test
            DB      01              ;Flag to test bit
            DW      OFFSET F23Yes
            DW      OFFSET F23No
            DB      00              ;Reserved bit, do not test
```

```
            .CODE
            .STARTUP
IOInfo      PROC

            CALL    Xfer                    ;Move command tail into work area
            JNC     OpenFile
            MOV     SI,OFFSET NeedFile      ;Error message
            JMP     ErrCommon               ;And exit early

OpenFile:   MOV     AH,3Dh                  ;Open file
            MOV     AL,00000010b            ;Access mode
            MOV     DX,OFFSET WorkDir
            INT     21h
            JC      Error1
            MOV     Handle,AX               ;Store the handle

            MOV     AH,44h                  ;IOCTL
            MOV     AL,0                    ;Get device info
            MOV     BX,Handle
            INT     21h
            JC      Error2

            TEST    DL,10000000b            ;See whether it is a file
            JNZ     DoDevice                ;Indicates that it is a device

            MOV     SI,OFFSET FileMsg1
            CALL    PrtString
            PUSH    DX                      ;Save info word for a moment
            AND     DL,00111111b            ;Want only drive number
            ADD     DL,'A'                  ;Make it ASCII
            MOV     AH,02h                  ;Output a character
            INT     21h
            MOV     SI,OFFSET FileMsg2
            CALL    PrtString
            POP     DX                      ;Get back info word
            TEST    DL,01000000b            ;Test if written to
            JZ      File2                   ;Nope, not written
            MOV     SI,OFFSET FileMsg3
            CALL    PrtString
File2:      MOV     SI,OFFSET FileMsg4
            CALL    PrtString
            JMP     CloseFile
```

continues

Listing 8.1. Continued

```
DoDevice:   MOV    CX,16                      ;Testing 16 bits
            MOV    AX,DX                      ;Move word to test
            MOV    BX,OFFSET DevTable         ;Point to start of table

            MOV    SI,OFFSET DeviceMsg
            CALL   PrtString

TestLoop:   CMP    BYTE PTR DS:[BX],0    ;If 0, then skip
            JE     TL8
            INC    BX                         ;Point to first message
            CMP    WORD PTR DS:[BX],0    ;Is it a null message?
            JE     TL2                        ;Yes, so continue
            TEST   AX,01h
            JZ     TL2                        ;Bit is not set, don't do message
            MOV    SI,[BX]
            CALL   PrtString                  ;Go print the message
TL2:        INC    BX                         ;Point to the next message
            INC    BX
            CMP    WORD PTR DS:[BX],0    ;Is it a null message?
            JE     TL3                        ;Yes, so skip
            TEST   AX,01h
            JNZ    TL3                        ;Bit is set, don't do message
            MOV    SI,[BX]
            CALL   PrtString                  ;Go print the message
TL3:        INC    BX                         ;Point to start of next record
TL8:        INC    BX
TL9:        SHR    AX,1                       ;Move over one bit
            LOOP   TestLoop                   ;And do it again

CloseFile:  MOV    AH,3Eh                     ;Close file
            MOV    BX,Handle
            INT    21h
            JMP    AllDone

Error1:     MOV    SI,OFFSET EMsg1
            JMP    ErrCommon
Error2:     MOV    AH,3Eh                     ;Close file
            MOV    BX,Handle
            INT    21h
            MOV    SI,OFFSET EMsg2
```

```
ErrCommon:  CALL    PrtString

AllDone:    .EXIT
IOInfo      ENDP

; Transfers the command tail into the work file area, converting it
; into an ASCIIZ string. Assumes that ES points to PSP segment. Returns
; with carry set if there was no command tail.

Xfer        PROC    USES AX CX SI DI ES DS
            PUSH    ES              ;Swap ES and DS
            PUSH    DS
            POP     ES
            POP     DS
            MOV     SI,80h          ;Point to start of command tail
            MOV     CH,0
            MOV     CL,[SI]         ;Get length of command tail
            JCXZ    X8              ;No command tail, exit with error

            INC     SI              ;Point to first character
            MOV     DI,OFFSET ES:WorkDir
X1:         LODSB
            CMP     AL,' '          ;Was it a space?
            JE      X4              ;Yes, so skip it
            STOSB                   ;Store a byte
X4:         LOOP    X1              ;Keep going to the end
            MOV     AL,0
            STOSB                   ;Make sure NUL is at end of path
            CLC
            JNC     X9

X8:         STC
X9:         RET
Xfer        ENDP

; The following routine prints the ASCIIZ string pointed to by DS:SI.
; DOS routines for character output are used.

PrtString   PROC    USES AX DX SI
PS1:        MOV     DL,[SI]         ;Get character
            INC     SI              ;Point to next one
            CMP     DL,0            ;End of string?
```

continues

Listing 8.1. Continued

```
            JE      PS2                 ;Yes, so exit
            MOV     AH,02h              ;Output a character
            INT     21h
            JMP     PS1                 ;Keep doing it
PS2:        RET
PrtString   ENDP

            END
```

This program performs three primary tasks. First, it opens the device. Then it uses IOCTL function 00h to determine whether it is a file or an actual device, and displays the appropriate information. Finally, it closes the file or device associated with the handle.

As an example of how this program works, the following information is returned if you use IOINFO on the CON device:

```
C:\>IOINFO CON
The following information about this device was
returned by IOCTL function 00h:
    This is a standard input device
    This is a standard output device
    This device supports Interrupt 28h
    This device is operating in cooked (ASCII) mode
    EOF is not returned when device is read
    IOCTL functions 02h and 03h are supported
```

The information displayed is taken directly from the bit flags returned in DX by IOCTL function 00h. You can use IOINFO on any other device (NUL, LPT1, AUX, CLOCK$, and so on) simply by changing the parameter on the command line. You can use IOINFO also to return information about files, as the following example shows:

```
C:\>IOINFO IOINFO.ASM
You have specified a file on drive C
The file has not been written
```

In this case, much less information is displayed by the program because only two pieces of information about files are returned by IOCTL function 00h.

Controlling the Screen

Control over the screen depends on the device you are using. If you are using the built-in console device (CON), you can use any of the character IO functions. You can open the device, as you would a file, and write to it. Output appears on the screen instead of going to a file.

There is another way to control your screen if your display card requires a special device driver to function properly, as some high-level cards do. In this case, the chances are that you can control how that card functions through the IOCTL functions. Specific information about how to do so are beyond the scope of this book, however. Because the implementation of the IOCTL functions is up to whoever wrote the device driver, you have to refer to the programming documentation for the video card.

One screen-control device driver that many people use but rarely think about is ANSI.SYS. The reason that few people think about ANSI.SYS is that it in effect replaces the standard CON device; it has the same device name (CON), and therefore intercepts any commands that otherwise would have made it to the original CON device.

ANSI.SYS adds several functions and capabilities to the standard console device, however. The driver interprets codes passed to it in a different way than does a plain-vanilla console. This control is achieved through a series of escape codes that control device functions. Because other, in-depth sources are available, this book does not discuss using the ANSI.SYS commands.

Redirecting Character Output

One of the primary advantages of treating files and devices in the same manner is that they easily can be interchanged for output operations. You just open a file with either a real file name or a device name and then send output to it. DOS does not care whether the device is the console, a printer, or a disk file. It dutifully sends information in a device-independent manner. The program in Listing 8.2, IOWHERE.ASM, illustrates how this works.

Listing 8.2. IOWHERE.ASM

```
Page 60,132

Comment ¦
******************************************************************

File:     IOWHERE.ASM
Author:   Allen L. Wyatt
```

continues

Listing 8.2. Continued

```
Date:       7/18/92
Assembler:  MASM 6.0

Purpose:    Enable the user to decide where the output of a text
            string will be sent

Format:     IOWHERE

*********************************************************************!
                                                                    ¦

            .MODEL  small
            .STACK                          ;Default 1K stack is OK
            .DATA
Handle      DW      0000

EMsg1       DB      'Could not open device',0
EMsg2       DB      'Error while checking if ready for output',0
EMsg3       DB      'Timeout error',0

OutTable    DW      OFFSET Screen
            DW      OFFSET Printer
            DW      OFFSET FileName

Screen      DB      'CON',0
Printer     DB      'PRN',0
FileName    DB      'TEST.OUT',0

TestOut     DB      'This is a test string created with '
            DB      'the program IOWHERE.EXE. For more ',13,10
            DB      'information, please refer to the '
            DB      'book Advanced Assembly Language,',13,10
            DB      'by Allen L. Wyatt'
CRLF        DB      13,10,0

Prompt      DB      'Would you like the test string sent to:',13,10
            DB      '    1. The screen',13,10
            DB      '    2. The printer (PRN)',13,10
            DB      '    3. The file TEST.OUT',13,10,13,10
            DB      'Your choice: ',0
```

```
                .CODE
                .STARTUP
IOWhere         PROC

                CALL    Cls                 ;Clear the screen
                MOV     SI,OFFSET Prompt    ;Point to question
                CALL    PrtString
InLoop:         MOV     AH,0                ;Read keyboard character
                INT     16h
                CMP     AL,'1'              ;Less than minimum choice?
                JB      InLoop              ;Yes, so keep asking
                CMP     AL,'3'              ;Greater than maximum?
                JA      InLoop              ;Yes, so keep asking

                MOV     DL,AL               ;Print character
                MOV     AH,02h              ;Output a character
                INT     21h
                MOV     SI,OFFSET CRLF
                CALL    PrtString

                MOV     BH,0
                MOV     BL,AL
                AND     BL,00001111b        ;Convert to binary value
                DEC     BX                  ;Make it a zero offset
                SHL     BX,1                ;And multiply by 2
                ADD     BX,OFFSET OutTable  ;Point to proper table entry

                MOV     AH,6Ch              ;Extended file open
                MOV     AL,0
                MOV     SI,DS:[BX]          ;Point to name
                MOV     BX,02h              ;Open mode
                MOV     CX,0                ;Normal file
                MOV     DX,11h              ;Open or create
                INT     21h
                JC      Error1
                MOV     Handle,AX           ;Store the handle

                MOV     SI,OFFSET TestOut   ;Point to start of output data
OutLoop:        CMP     BYTE PTR DS:[SI],0  ;End of string?
                JE      CloseFile           ;Yes, so close device or file
                MOV     CX,20h              ;Number of times to try output
```

continues

Listing 8.2. Continued

```
WaitLoop:   MOV     AH,44h              ;IOCTL
            MOV     AL,07h              ;Test if ready for output
            MOV     BX,Handle
            INT     21h
            JC      Error2
            CMP     AL,0FFh             ;Ready for output?
            JE      CharOut             ;Yes, so send character
            LOOP    WaitLoop            ;No, so try another time
            JMP     Error3              ;Exit with error

CharOut:    MOV     AH,40h              ;Write file
            MOV     BX,Handle
            MOV     DX,SI               ;Pointer for info to write
            MOV     CX,1                ;Only 1 byte
            INT     21h
            INC     SI                  ;Point to next character
            JMP     OutLoop

CloseFile:  MOV     AH,3Eh              ;Close file
            MOV     BX,Handle
            INT     21h
            JMP     AllDone

Error1:     MOV     SI,OFFSET EMsg1
            JMP     ErrPrt
Error2:     MOV     SI,OFFSET EMsg2
            JMP     ErrCommon
Error3:     MOV     SI,OFFSET EMsg3
ErrCommon:  MOV     AH,3Eh              ;Close file
            MOV     BX,Handle
            INT     21h
ErrPrt:     CALL    PrtString

AllDone:    .EXIT
IOWhere     ENDP

    ; The following routine clears the screen and homes the cursor
```

```
Cls          PROC    USES AX BX CX DX
             MOV     AH,6                    ;Scroll window up
             MOV     AL,0                    ;Scroll full screen
             MOV     BH,7                    ;Normal white on black
             MOV     CX,0                    ;Upper left corner of screen
             MOV     DH,24                   ;Bottom right
             MOV     DL,79
             INT     10h

             MOV     DX,0                    ;Upper left corner of screen
             MOV     BH,0                    ;Assume page 0
             MOV     AH,2                    ;Set cursor position
             INT     10h
             RET
Cls          ENDP

; The following routine prints the ASCIIZ string pointed to by DS:SI.
; DOS routines for character output are used.

PrtString    PROC    USES AX DX SI
PS1:         MOV     DL,[SI]                 ;Get character
             INC     SI                      ;Point to next one
             CMP     DL,0                    ;End of string?
             JE      PS2                     ;Yes, so exit
             MOV     AH,02h                  ;Output a character
             INT     21h
             JMP     PS1                     ;Keep doing it
PS2:         RET
PrtString    ENDP

             END
```

This program is a simple one. All that happens is that you are presented with a menu of output choices, and then a test string (TestOut) is sent to wherever you direct. The beauty of the implementation, however, is that one command opens and accesses any of the three devices. You can use the same instructions, therefore, to output to all these recipients. The only thing that changes is the name of the device or file.

The only IOCTL function used in this program is function 07h, which tests to see whether the device being accessed is ready for more output. In reality, including this function is probably overkill—after all, the string being sent is very short. You should remember to include this function, however, if you are sending larger blocks of data or if you are dealing with a very slow printer.

Block Device Control

Early in this chapter, you learned that block devices access information in clusters—more than a single byte at a time. Block devices are considered mass storage devices, and typically the term "block device" is used synonymously with "disk drive." Block devices cover a wider range of peripherals, however. For instance, they also include devices such as tape drives.

Character devices are named with unique 8-character names, and block devices are referred to by unique drive letters or numbers. Block devices have familiar letters such as A:, B:, C:, and so on. In the IOCTL and DOS function world, however, these devices typically have a number attached. Most functions refer to drive A: as 1, B: as 2, C: as 3, and so on. In this case, drive number 0 designates the current drive—whatever DOS most recently accessed. With other functions, however, the drives are numbered beginning at 0. Because there is no universal rule about which number system is used when, it is best to refer to your DOS programming reference to keep all the functions straight.

Applicable IOCTL Functions

Not all of the IOCTL functions are applicable to block devices. In fact, in Table 8.1, the majority of the IOCTL functions apply to only character devices. A few of them, however, enable you to exert powerful control over block devices.

Let's start with the IOCTL function that provides the most information about block devices. Function 0Dh, generic I/O control for block devices, incorporates subfunction 60h, which returns information about a block device. To use this function, you must set up a parameter block to transfer information to and from the device driver. This parameter block has the format outlined in Table 8.6.

Table 8.6. Parameter block used by IOCTL function 0Dh, subfunctions 40h and 60h.

Offset	Length	Meaning
00h	1 byte	Special functions
01h	1 byte	Device type
02h	2 bytes	Device attributes
04h	2 bytes	Total cylinders

Offset	Length	Meaning
06h	1 byte	Media type
07h	1Fh bytes	Device BPB
26h	Varies	Track layout

Each of the fields in this parameter block deserves closer inspection.

Special Functions

The special functions field in the parameter block controls the type and quantity of information retrieved about the block device. Table 8.7 shows the bit meanings for the special functions byte.

Table 8.7. Bit meanings for the special function field of the device parameter block.

Bit settings 76543210	Meaning
1	Use existing BPB
0	Define new default BPB
1	Use track layout field only
0	Use all fields in device parameter block
1	Sectors in track all same size; numbering is sequential from sector 1
0	Sectors in track may be different sizes
xxxxx	Reserved

You set the bits that indicate what you intend to do. If you are trying to re-trieve information about a specific block device (using subfunction 60h), you probably will set bit 0, clear bit 1, and set bit 2. Other bit settings are used when you are attempting to exert control over the block device, as is done later in this chapter.

Device Type

The 1-byte device type field is used to indicate the type of block device being used. The possible values for this field are shown in Table 8.8.

Table 8.8. Possible values for the device type field of the device parameter block.

Value	Meaning
0	5 1/4 inch, 320K or 360K
1	5 1/4 inch, 1.2M
2	3 1/2 inch, 720K
3	8 inch, single density
4	8 inch, double density
5	Fixed disk
6	Tape drive
7	3 1/2 inch, 1.44M
8	3 1/2 inch, 2.88M
9	Other block device

If you are retrieving information about a block device (subfunction 60h), the information in this field is filled in by the IOCTL function.

Device Attributes

The 2-byte device attributes field is used to provide additional information about a device—information that is not capacity-related. Only the first 2 bits of the word currently have significance, as shown in Table 8.9.

Table 8.9. Bit meanings for the device attributes field of the device parameter block.

Bit settings FEDCBA98 76543210	Meaning
1	Media is not removable
0	Media is removable
1	Change line supported
0	Change line not supported
xxxxxxxx xxxxx	Reserved

By examining bit 0, you can determine whether the block device in question allows media (disks or tape) to be changed. If you are working with hard drives, this bit typically is set.

Bit 1 indicates whether the device can tell you that the media has been changed. Some newer disk drives have a *change support line*, which controls an electronic flag that indicates when the disk door has been opened and the media changed. If the device supports such a feature, this bit is set. Obviously, if bit 0 is set, bit 1 must be clear (there is no need to support a change line if the media is not removable).

Total Cylinders

The two bytes that comprise the total cylinders field are used to indicate the total number of cylinders on the device. This information is not supplied in the BPB field. Possible values in this field vary depending on the configuration and capacity of the block device.

Media Type

The 1-byte media type field is used to indicate whether the device supports multiple types of media. For example, a 5 1/4-inch drive usually can access both 1.2M and 360K or 320K disks. In this case, the IOCTL function returns a 1 for this field. A 0 is returned if the device accepts only a single type of media.

If the device does not use removable media (see the device attribute field), this field always is 0.

Device BPB

The 31-byte device BPB field is the BIOS parameter block (BPB) for the device. The layout of the BPB is shown in Table 8.10.

Table 8.10. BIOS parameter block layout.

Offset	Length	Meaning
00h	2 bytes	Bytes per sector
02h	1 byte	Sectors per allocation unit (cluster)
03h	2 bytes	Number of reserved sectors
05h	1 byte	Number of FATs

continues

Offset	Length	Meaning
06h	2 bytes	Maximum root directory entries
08h	2 bytes	Small total sectors
0Ah	1 byte	Media descriptor
0Bh	2 bytes	Sectors per FAT
0Dh	2 bytes	Sectors per track
0Fh	2 bytes	Number of heads
11h	4 bytes	Number of hidden sectors
15h	4 bytes	Large total sectors
19h	6 bytes	Reserved

The values in each of these fields vary based on the device type and capacity, as well as on the actual media in the device. Note that if the value at offset 08h (small total sectors) is 0, the total number of sectors on the media is stored at offset 15h (large total sectors).

Track Layout

The track layout field is used to indicate the composition of each track on the media in the device. The first word of this field indicates the total number of sectors in a track (the value of this field should match the value at offset 0Dh in the BPB). The length of the track layout field varies because, following this initial word, two words of data are required for each sector on a track. The first word indicates the sector number, and the second indicates the size of the sector.

As an example, on a device that has 9 sectors per track, the track layout field occupies a total of 38 bytes: 2 for the initial sector count and 4 for each of 9 sectors.

Examining Block Device Information

How do you make sense of this plethora of information? The best way is to look at each bit and build a profile of the media and the particular block device. The program in Listing 8.3, BLKINFO.ASM, does this, based on the information presented.

Listing 8.3. BLKINFO.ASM

```
Page 60,132

Comment ¦
*********************************************************************

File:       BLKINFO.ASM
Author:     Allen L. Wyatt
Date:       7/18/92
Assembler:  MASM 6.0

Purpose:    Using IOCTL functions, discover and display information
            about a block device

Format:     BLKINFO


*********************************************************************¦

            .MODEL   small
            .STACK                       ;Default 1K stack is OK
            .DATA
Drive       DB       00

NeedDrive   DB       'You must supply a valid drive name',0
EMsg1       DB       'Could not use IOCTL function 0D60h',0
EMsg2       DB       'Could not use IOCTL function 0Eh',0

OneDrive    DB       'There is only one logical drive assigned to this device',13,10,0
LastDrive   DB       'This drive was last referred to as drive '
CRLF        DB       13,10,0

DriveParams EQU      THIS BYTE
SpecialFunc DB       00
DeviceType  DB       00
DeviceAttr  DW       0000
Cylinders   DW       0000
MediaType   DB       00

BytesSect   DW       0000
SectClust   DB       00
ResvSect    DW       0000
```

continues

Listing 8.3. Continued

```
NumFATs     DB      00
RootDir     DW      0000
NumSect     DW      0000
MediaID     DB      00
SectFAT     DW      0000
SectTrack   DW      0000
NumHeads    DW      0000
NumHidden   DD      00000000
NumHuge     DD      00000000
Unused      DB      7 DUP (0)

TrackLayout DW      162 DUP (0)         ;Allow for as many as 80 sectors per track

TopMsg      DB      'Information derived with IOCTL function 0D60h:',13,10,13,10,0

DTTable     DW      0000h
            DW      OFFSET DT00
            DW      0001h
            DW      OFFSET DT01
            DW      0002h
            DW      OFFSET DT02
            DW      0003h
            DW      OFFSET DT03
            DW      0004h
            DW      OFFSET DT04
            DW      0005h
            DW      OFFSET DT05
            DW      0006h
            DW      OFFSET DT06
            DW      0007h
            DW      OFFSET DT07
            DW      0008h
            DW      OFFSET DT08
            DW      0009h
            DW      OFFSET DT09
            DW      0FFFFh
            DW      OFFSET DTUN

DT00        DB      ':  320K or 360K 5.25" disk',13,10,0
DT01        DB      ':  1.2M 5.25" disk',13,10,0
```

```
DT02        DB          ':  720K 3.5" disk',13,10,0
DT03        DB          ':  Single density 8" disk',13,10,0
DT04        DB          ':  Double density 8" disk',13,10,0
DT05        DB          ':  Fixed disk',13,10,0
DT06        DB          ':  Tape drive',13,10,0
DT07        DB          ':  1.44M 3.5" disk',13,10,0
DT08        DB          ':  2.88M 3.5" disk',13,10,0
DT09        DB          ':  Other block device',13,10,0
DTUN        DB          ':  Unknown device type code',13,10,0

MTTable     DW          0001h
            DW          OFFSET MT00
            DW          0002h
            DW          OFFSET MT01
            DW          0FFFFh
            DW          OFFSET MTUN

MT00        DB          ':  Drive accepts one type of media only',13,10,0
MT01        DB          ':  Drive accepts multiple media types',13,10,0
MTUN        DB          ':  Unknown media type',13,10,0

IDTable     DW          00F0h
            DW          OFFSET IDF0
            DW          00F8h
            DW          OFFSET IDF8
            DW          00F9h
            DW          OFFSET IDF9
            DW          00FAh
            DW          OFFSET IDFA
            DW          00FBh
            DW          OFFSET IDFB
            DW          00FCh
            DW          OFFSET IDFC
            DW          00FDh
            DW          OFFSET IDFD
            DW          00FEh
            DW          OFFSET IDFE
            DW          00FFh
            DW          OFFSET IDFF
            DW          0FFFFh
            DW          OFFSET IDUN
```

continues

Listing 8.3. Continued

```
IDF0      DB        ':  1.44M or 2.88M 3.5" disk, 1.2M 5.25" disk, or other',13,10,0
IDF8      DB        ':  Fixed disk',13,10,0
IDF9      DB        ':  720K 3.5" disk or 1.2M 5.25" disk',13,10,0
IDFA      DB        ':  320K 5.25" disk',13,10,0
IDFB      DB        ':  640K 3.5" disk',13,10,0
IDFC      DB        ':  180K 5.25" disk',13,10,0
IDFD      DB        ':  360K 5.25" disk or double-density 8" disk',13,10,0
IDFE      DB        ':  160K 5.25" disk or single-density 8" disk',13,10,0
IDFF      DB        ':  320K 5.25" disk',13,10,0
IDUN      DB        ':  Unknown media ID',13,10,0

MsgDT     DB        'Device type code ',0
MsgDA1    DB        'Drive supports removable media',13,10,0
MsgDA2    DB        'Drive does not support removable media',13,10,0
MsgDA3    DB        'Drive does not support change line status',13,10,0
MsgDA4    DB        'Drive supports change line status',13,10,0
MsgNC     DB        'Number of cylinders:  ',0
MsgMT     DB        'Media type code ',0
MsgBS     DB        'Bytes per sector:  ',0
MsgSC     DB        'Sectors per cluster:  ',0
MsgRS     DB        'Reserved sectors:  ',0
MsgFA     DB        'Number of FATs:  ',0
MsgRD     DB        'Maximum root directory entries:  ',0
MsgTS     DB        'Total sectors:  ',0
MsgID     DB        'Media ID type ',0
MsgSF     DB        'Sectors per FAT:  ',0
MsgST     DB        'Sectors per track:  ',0
MsgHD     DB        'Number of heads:  ',0
MsgHS     DB        'Hidden sectors:  ',0

          .CODE
          .STARTUP
BlkInfo   PROC

          CALL    GetDrive           ;Get drive from command tail
          JNC     GetInfo
          MOV     SI,OFFSET NeedDrive ;Error message
          JMP     ErrCommon          ;And exit early
```

```
GetInfo:    MOV     SpecialFunc,1         ;Want for current BPB
            MOV     AH,44h                ;IOCTL
            MOV     AL,0Dh                ;Generic block I/O
            MOV     BL,Drive
            MOV     CH,08h                ;Disk drive
            MOV     CL,60h                ;Get device parameters
            MOV     DX,OFFSET DriveParams
            INT     21h
            JC      Error1

            CALL    Cls
            MOV     SI,OFFSET TopMsg
            CALL    PrtString
            MOV     SI,OFFSET MsgDT
            CALL    PrtString
            MOV     DX,0
            MOV     AH,0
            MOV     AL,DeviceType
            CALL    PrtDec
            MOV     BX,OFFSET DTTable
            CALL    PrtTable              ;Go print from table

            MOV     SI,OFFSET MsgMT
            CALL    PrtString
            MOV     AL,MediaType
            CALL    PrtDec
            MOV     BX,OFFSET MTTable
            CALL    PrtTable              ;Go print from table

            MOV     SI,OFFSET MsgID
            CALL    PrtString
            MOV     AL,MediaID
            CALL    PrtDec
            MOV     BX,OFFSET IDTable
            CALL    PrtTable              ;Go print from table

            MOV     SI,OFFSET MsgDA1      ;Assume supports removable media
            MOV     AX,DeviceAttr
            TEST    AL,00000001b          ;Is media removable?
            JZ      PMedia                ;Yes, so go print
```

continues

Listing 8.3. Continued

```
          MOV     SI,OFFSET MsgDA2      ;No, does not support it
PMedia:   CALL    PrtString
          MOV     SI,OFFSET MsgDA3      ;Assume disk change line unsupported
          TEST    AL,00000010b         ;Is change line supported?
          JZ      PChange              ;No, so continue
          MOV     SI,OFFSET MsgDA4
PChange:  CALL    PrtString

          MOV     SI,OFFSET MsgHD
          CALL    PrtString
          MOV     AX,NumHeads
          CALL    PrtDec
          MOV     SI,OFFSET CRLF
          CALL    PrtString

          MOV     SI,OFFSET MsgNC
          CALL    PrtString
          MOV     AX,Cylinders
          CALL    PrtDec
          MOV     SI,OFFSET CRLF
          CALL    PrtString

          MOV     SI,OFFSET MsgTS
          CALL    PrtString
          MOV     AX,NumSect           ;Get number of sectors
          CMP     AX,0                 ;Is it 0?
          JNE     PSect                ;No, so print
          MOV     AX,WORD PTR NumHuge  ;Yes, so get huge sectors
          MOV     DX,WORD PTR NumHuge[2]
PSect:    CALL    PrtDec
          MOV     SI,OFFSET CRLF
          CALL    PrtString

          MOV     SI,OFFSET MsgBS
          CALL    PrtString
          MOV     DX,0
          MOV     AX,BytesSect
          CALL    PrtDec
          MOV     SI,OFFSET CRLF
          CALL    PrtString
```

```
MOV     SI,OFFSET MsgSC
CALL    PrtString
MOV     AH,0
MOV     AL,SectClust
CALL    PrtDec
MOV     SI,OFFSET CRLF
CALL    PrtString

MOV     SI,OFFSET MsgST
CALL    PrtString
MOV     AX,SectTrack
CALL    PrtDec
MOV     SI,OFFSET CRLF
CALL    PrtString

MOV     SI,OFFSET MsgRS
CALL    PrtString
MOV     AX,ResvSect
CALL    PrtDec
MOV     SI,OFFSET CRLF
CALL    PrtString

MOV     SI,OFFSET MsgHS
CALL    PrtString
MOV     AX,WORD PTR NumHidden
MOV     DX,WORD PTR NumHidden[2]
CALL    PrtDec
MOV     SI,OFFSET CRLF
CALL    PrtString
CALL    PrtString           ;Extra blank line

MOV     SI,OFFSET MsgFA
CALL    PrtString
MOV     DX,0
MOV     AH,0
MOV     AL,NumFATs
CALL    PrtDec
MOV     SI,OFFSET CRLF
CALL    PrtString
```

continues

Listing 8.3. Continued

```
          MOV     SI,OFFSET MsgSF
          CALL    PrtString
          MOV     AX,SectFAT
          CALL    PrtDec
          MOV     SI,OFFSET CRLF
          CALL    PrtString
          CALL    PrtString            ;Extra blank line

          MOV     SI,OFFSET MsgRD
          CALL    PrtString
          MOV     AX,RootDir
          CALL    PrtDec
          MOV     SI,OFFSET CRLF
          CALL    PrtString

          MOV     AH,44h               ;IOCTL
          MOV     AL,0Eh               ;Get logical device map
          MOV     BL,Drive
          INT     21h
          JC      Error2
          CMP     AL,0
          JNE     Block3
          MOV     SI,OFFSET OneDrive
          CALL    PrtString
          JMP     Block4
Block3:   MOV     SI,OFFSET LastDrive
          CALL    PrtString
          MOV     DL,AL
          ADD     DL,'@'               ;Make it printable ASCII
          MOV     AH,02h               ;Output a character
          INT     21h
          MOV     SI,OFFSET CRLF
          CALL    PrtString
Block4:   JMP     AllDone

Error1:   MOV     SI,OFFSET EMsg1
          JMP     ErrCommon
Error2:   MOV     SI,OFFSET EMsg2
ErrCommon: CALL   PrtString
```

```
AllDone:      .EXIT
BlkInfo       ENDP


; Transfers a drive name from the command tail, converting it into a
; drive number. Assumes that ES points to PSP segment. Returns with
; carry set if there was no command tail or the drive entered was not
; alphabetic.


GetDrive      PROC    USES AX CX SI
              MOV     SI,80h              ;Point to start of command tail
              MOV     CH,0
              MOV     CL,ES:[SI]          ;Get length of command tail
              JCXZ    X8                  ;No command tail, exit with error

              INC     SI                  ;Point to first character
X1:           MOV     AL,ES:[SI]          ;Get character
              INC     SI                  ;Point to next character
              CMP     AL,' '              ;Was it a space?
              JNE     X4                  ;No, so assume have drive
              LOOP    X1                  ;Keep going to the end
X4:           AND     AL,01011111b        ;Convert to uppercase
              CMP     AL,'A'              ;Check if in range
              JB      X8
              CMP     AL,'Z'
              JA      X8
              AND     AL,00011111b        ;Convert to drive code
              MOV     Drive,AL            ;And store for later
              CLC
              JNC     X9

X8:           STC
X9:           RET
GetDrive      ENDP


; The following routine clears the screen and homes the cursor

Cls           PROC    USES AX BX CX DX
              MOV     AH,6                ;Scroll window up
              MOV     AL,0                ;Scroll full screen
              MOV     BH,7                ;Normal white on black
```

continues

Listing 8.3. Continued

```
                MOV     CX,0                ;Upper left corner of screen
                MOV     DH,24               ;Bottom right
                MOV     DL,79
                INT     10h

                MOV     DX,0                ;Upper left corner of screen
                MOV     BH,0                ;Assume page 0
                MOV     AH,2                ;Set cursor position
                INT     10h
                RET
Cls             ENDP

; The following routine prints a message from an indexed table.
; Enter with AX set to the control value to match and BX set to
; the offset address of the table.

PrtTable        PROC    USES BX DX SI
PTLoop:         MOV     DX,[BX]             ;Get control word
                INC     BX                  ;Point to message
                INC     BX
                CMP     DX,0FFFFh           ;End of table?
                JE      PrintMsg            ;Yes, so force printing of message
                CMP     AX,DX               ;Proper code?
                JE      PrintMsg            ;Yes
                INC     BX                  ;Point past message
                INC     BX
                JMP     PTLoop              ;Do it again
PrintMsg:       MOV     SI,[BX]             ;Get pointer
                CALL    PrtString           ;Print it
                RET
PrtTable        ENDP

; The following routine prints the ASCIIZ string pointed to by DS:SI.
; DOS routines for character output are used.

PrtString       PROC    USES AX DX SI
PS1:            MOV     DL,[SI]             ;Get character
                INC     SI                  ;Point to next one
                CMP     DL,0                ;End of string?
                JE      PS2                 ;Yes, so exit
```

```
             MOV     AH,02h              ;Output a character
             INT     21h
             JMP     PS1                 ;Keep doing it
PS2:         RET
PrtString    ENDP
```

; The following routine prints the value in DX:AX as a decimal number.
; Will accept numbers up to 655,359,999. Anything larger will not print.

```
             .DATA
Temp         DW      0000


             .CODE
PrtDec       PROC    USES AX BX CX DX

             MOV     CX,0FFFFh           ;Ending flag
             PUSH    CX

PD0:         MOV     CX,10000            ;Divide by 10,000
             DIV     CX
             MOV     Temp,AX             ;Store whole portion
             MOV     BX,0                ;Count for this iteration

             MOV     AX,DX
             MOV     CX,10
PD1:         MOV     DX,0
             DIV     CX                  ;Divide by 10
             ADD     DL,30h              ;Convert to ASCII
             PUSH    DX                  ;Store remainder
             INC     BX                  ;Cycle count
             CMP     AX,0                ;Are we done?
             JNE     PD1                 ;No, so continue
             MOV     DX,0
             MOV     AX,Temp             ;Get back part above 10,000
             CMP     AX,0
             JE      PD3
             MOV     CX,'0'
PD2:         CMP     BX,4                ;Did we push 4 numbers?
             JE      PD0                 ;Yes, continue
             PUSH    CX                  ;No, so push it
             INC     BX                  ;Push counter
             JMP     PD2
```

continues

Listing 8.3. Continued

```
PD3:        POP     DX              ;Character is now in DL
            CMP     DX,0FFFFh       ;Is it the ending flag?
            JE      PD4             ;Yes, so continue
            MOV     AH,02h          ;Output a character
            INT     21h
            JMP     PD3             ;Keep doing it


PD4:        RET
PrtDec      ENDP


            END
```

This program enables you to specify on the command line a disk drive name about which you want to get information. IOCTL function 0Dh, subfunction 60h then is used to retrieve information about the device. This information is analyzed, and the proper status information is displayed.

After displaying this bulk of information, IOCTL function 0Eh is used to retrieve the logical drive map for the device. This map indicates whether more than one logical device is mapped to the physical device. The value in AL indicates this information. If it is 0, only one logical drive code is mapped to the device. If it is any other number, it indicates that the device is known by different logical names. This situation occurs most often in a system with a single floppy drive that is referred to as both A: and B:. If the value returned in AL is 1, the device was last referred to as A:. If it is 2, the last reference was as B:, and so on. As an example of the output from this program, the following information was displayed for my C: drive:

```
C:\>BLKINFO C
Information derived with IOCTL function 0D60h:

Device type code 5:  Fixed disk
Media type code 0:  Unknown media type
Media ID type 248:  Fixed disk
Drive does not support removable media
Drive does not support change line status
Number of heads:  16
Number of cylinders:  292
Total sectors:  294273
Bytes per sector:  512
Sectors per cluster:  8
```

```
Sectors per track:  63
Reserved sectors:  1
Hidden sectors:  63

Number of FATs:  2
Sectors per FAT:  144

Maximum root directory entries:  512
There is only one logical drive assigned to this device
```

Solving Single-Drive Hassles

The preceding section briefly described IOCTL function 0Eh, which returns the logical drive map for a block device. IOCTL function 0Fh is related to this one in that it enables you to set the logical drive map for a device. You can circumvent that annoying message that pops up on single-drive systems:

```
Insert diskette for drive B: and press any key when ready
```

You just call IOCTL function 0Fh with BL set to the drive code you want used when you access the drive the next time. The drive code is 1=A, 2=B, and so on. The program in Listing 8.4, LOGDRIVE.ASM, illustrates this process.

Listing 8.4. LOGDRIVE.ASM

```
Page 60,132

Comment ¦
*********************************************************************

File:      LOGDRIVE.ASM
Author:    Allen L. Wyatt
Date:      7/26/92
Assembler: MASM 6.0

Purpose:   Illustrates use of IOCTL function 0Eh and 0Fh. Always
           forces the desired drive into the logical mapping so
           that there is no prompt for "Insert disk for drive..."

Format:    LOGDRIVE


*********************************************************************¦
```

continues

Listing 8.4. Continued

```
            .MODEL  small
            .STACK                      ;Default 1K stack is OK
            .DATA
Msg1        DB      'Press any key to see directory of drive A:',13,10,0
Msg2        DB      'Press any key to see directory of drive B:',13,10,0
Msg3        DB      '*** Drive mapping techniques not being used ***',13,10,0
Msg4        DB      '*** Drive mapping techniques being used ***',13,10,0

OneDrive    DB      'There is only one logical drive assigned to this device'
CRLF        DB      13,10,0

EMsg1       DB      'Could not use IOCTL function 0Eh',0

DirA        DB      'A:\*.*',0
DirB        DB      'B:\*.*',0
NoMore      DB      'No more files on drive',13,10,13,10,0

            .CODE
            .STARTUP
LogDrive    PROC

; Check if running on system where A/B is one drive

            MOV     AH,44h              ;IOCTL
            MOV     AL,0Eh              ;Get logical device map
            MOV     BL,1                ;Drive A:
            INT     21h
            JC      Error1
            CMP     AL,0
            JNE     DoIt                ;Logical drives present, continue
            MOV     SI,OFFSET OneDrive
            CALL    PrtString
            JMP     AllDone

Doit:       CALL    Cls

; First, give an example of what normally happens

            MOV     SI,OFFSET Msg3
```

```
        CALL    PrtString
        MOV     SI,OFFSET Msg1
        CALL    KeyMsg              ;Display message, wait for keypress
        MOV     DX,OFFSET DirA
        CALL    ShowDir

        MOV     SI,OFFSET Msg2
        CALL    KeyMsg              ;Display message, wait for keypress
        MOV     DX,OFFSET DirB
        CALL    ShowDir

; Now give an example of what can happen

        MOV     SI,OFFSET Msg4
        CALL    PrtString
        MOV     SI,OFFSET Msg1
        CALL    KeyMsg              ;Display message, wait for keypress
        CALL    MakeItA
        MOV     DX,OFFSET DirA
        CALL    ShowDir

        MOV     SI,OFFSET Msg2
        CALL    KeyMsg              ;Display message, wait for keypress
        CALL    MakeItB
        MOV     DX,OFFSET DirB
        CALL    ShowDir
        JMP     AllDone

Error1: MOV     SI,OFFSET EMsg1
        CALL    PrtString
AllDone: .EXIT
LogDrive ENDP


; The following routine clears the screen and homes the cursor

Cls     PROC    USES AX BX CX DX
        MOV     AH,6                ;Scroll window up
        MOV     AL,0                ;Scroll full screen
        MOV     BH,7                ;Normal white on black
        MOV     CX,0                ;Upper left corner of screen
```

continues

Listing 8.4. Continued

```
                MOV     DH,24               ;Bottom right
                MOV     DL,79
                INT     10h

                MOV     DX,0                ;Upper left corner of screen
                MOV     BH,0                ;Assume page 0
                MOV     AH,2                ;Set cursor position
                INT     10h
                RET
Cls             ENDP

; The following routine displays the directory pointed to by DS:DX

ShowDir         PROC    USES AX BX CX DX SI ES
                MOV     AH,2Fh              ;Determine DTA
                INT     21h
                ADD     BX,1Eh              ;Point to ASCIIZ file name field

                MOV     AH,4Eh              ;Find first
                MOV     CX,37h              ;Show all except volume label
                INT     21h
                JC      Done
SDLoop:         CALL    ShowName            ;Print file name
                MOV     AH,4Fh              ;Find next
                INT     21h
                JNC     SDLoop
Done:           MOV     SI,OFFSET NoMore
                CALL    PrtString
                RET
ShowDir         ENDP

; Print ASCIIZ file name pointed to by ES:BX

ShowName        PROC    USES SI
                PUSH    DS                  ;Save for later
                PUSH    ES                  ;Set up addressing
                POP     DS
                MOV     SI,BX
                CALL    PrtString
                POP     DS
```

```
                MOV       SI,OFFSET CRLF
                CALL      PrtString
                RET
ShowName        ENDP


; Force drive to be assumed as A:

MakeItA         PROC      USES AX BX
                MOV       AH,44h               ;IOCTL
                MOV       AL,0Fh               ;Set logical drive map
                MOV       BL,1                 ;Drive A:
                INT       21h
                RET
MakeItA         ENDP


; Force drive to be assumed as B:

MakeItB         PROC      USES AX BX
                MOV       AH,44h               ;IOCTL
                MOV       AL,0Fh               ;Set logical drive map
                MOV       BL,2                 ;Drive A:
                INT       21h
                RET
MakeItB         ENDP


; The following routine prints the ASCIIZ string pointed to by DS:SI.
; DOS routines for character output are used.

PrtString       PROC      USES AX DX SI
PS1:            MOV       DL,[SI]              ;Get character
                INC       SI                   ;Point to next one
                CMP       DL,0                 ;End of string?
                JE        PS2                  ;Yes, so exit
                MOV       AH,02h               ;Output a character
                INT       21h
                JMP       PS1                  ;Keep doing it
PS2:            RET
PrtString       ENDP


; The following routine prints the message pointed to by SI and then
; waits for a keypress
```

continues

Listing 8.4. Continued

```
KeyMsg      PROC    USES AX
            CALL    PrtString           ;Message pointed to by SI
            MOV     AH,0                ;Read keyboard character
            INT     16h
            RET
KeyMsg      ENDP

            END
```

LOGDRIVE.EXE runs only on systems that view A: and B: as the same logical drive. IOCTL function 0Eh is used to determine whether A: is the only drive assigned to the corresponding physical drive. If it is, a message is displayed and the program ends. If not, the program first illustrates the normal way of dealing with drives A: and B: on a single-drive system. You are prompted to press a key to see the directory of drive A:, and then you are prompted to press a key to see the directory of drive B:. When you press a key, DOS prompts you to insert the disk for drive B:. If you have a program that uses carefully crafted screen displays, an unsolicited and unwanted message such as this one can cause havoc.

The next pass through the directories, however, prompts you to press a key to see the directory on drive A:, and then the directory on drive B:. When you press the key, there is no prompt for the disk for drive B: because of the subroutines at MakeItA and MakeItB. The code for these subroutines is virtually identical; in fact, you could code them as the same subroutine and simply pass a value in a register that indicates the drive you want. Regardless, the subroutines do the trick. The unwanted message is removed and DOS does what you want.

Formatting a Disk

If you have ever written a commercial program, chances are that you have at least wondered about how you could add routines to your program that enable users to format disks. This subject was addressed at some length in *Using Assembly Language,* 3rd Edition, but it deserves some follow-up here.

This section gives you a chance to examine a rather extensive program that enables you to format a disk in either the A: or B: drive. Because no other drives are supported, there is no possibility of erasing your hard drive. Unlike the formatting discussion and examples in *Using Assembly Language,* 3rd Edition, this example relies on the IOCTL formatting routines to do the disk formatting. The program therefore is not limited by the BIOS in your machine; it should work on all machines. It correctly formats 5 1/4-inch disks (360K and 1.2M) as well as 3 1/2-inch disks (720K and 1.44M).

The following pseudocode shows the major steps in the formatting program, FMT.ASM:

```
Determine whether user has a single-floppy system
    If so, make sure set as drive A:
    If not, ask user which drive to use
Determine whether user's drives support multiple formats
    If so, ask user which format to use
    If not, set for the format supported
Set up disk parameters to format disk properly
Format proper number of tracks
Write boot sector and media ID
Write FAT area
Write directory area
Restore disk parameters to original condition
```

Some of these steps use techniques described earlier in this chapter; others are new to this program. As far as IOCTL functions are concerned, six different functions are used. The functions accomplish virtually all the major disk interfacing necessary for the program. Table 8.11 shows the major program steps, along with the IOCTL functions used to support those steps. Listing 8.5 shows FMT.ASM.

Table 8.11. IOCTL functions and support in FMT.ASM.

Major Program Function	IOCTL Support
Determine whether user has a single-floppy system	Get Logical Device Map (function 0Eh)
If so, make sure set as drive A:	Set Logical Device Map (function 0Fh)
If not, ask user which drive to use	
Determine whether user's drives support multiple formats	Get Device Parameters (function 0Dh/60h)
If so, ask user which format to use If not, set for the format supported	
Set up disk parameters to format disk properly	Set Device Parameters (function 0Dh/40h)
Format proper number of tracks	Format and Verify Track (function 0Dh/42h)

continues

Table 8.11. Continued

Major Program Function	IOCTL Support
Write boot sector and media ID	Set Media ID (function 0Dh/46h)
Write FAT area	
Write directory area	
Restore disk parameters to original condition	Set Device Parameters (function 0Dh/40h)

Listing 8.5. FMT.ASM

```
Page 60,132


Comment ¦
*********************************************************************


File:      FMT.ASM
Author:    Allen L. Wyatt
Date:      7/26/92
Assembler: MASM 6.0

Purpose:   Illustrates use of IOCTL functions to format a drive.
           This program formats only drives A: or B:, so there
           is no danger of formatting the hard drive.

Format:    FMT


*********************************************************************¦


           .MODEL  small
           .STACK                     ;Default 1K stack is OK
           .DATA
Drive      DB      00
FormatType DB      00
CurHead    DB      00
CurCylinder DB     00

ParmLen    EQU     75                 ;Bytes in parm buffers
OrigParms  EQU     THIS BYTE
SFOrig     DB      00
           DB      74 DUP(0)          ;Bulk storage for current settings
```

```
NewParms       EQU    THIS BYTE
SpecFuncNew DB        00
DeviceType  DB        00
DeviceAttr  DW        0000
Cylinders   DW        0000
MediaType   DB        00


DiskBPB        EQU    THIS BYTE
BytesSect   DW        0000
SectClust   DB        00
ResvSect    DW        0000
NumFATs     DB        00
RootDir     DW        0000
NumSect     DW        0000
MediaID     DB        00
SectFAT     DW        0000
SectTrack   DW        0000
NumHeads    DW        0000
NumHidden   DD        00000000
NumHuge     DD        00000000
Unused      DB        6 DUP (0)
TrackLayout DW        18*2+1 DUP (0)         ;Allow for as many as 18 sectors per track


FmtParms       EQU    THIS BYTE
FmtParmSF   DB        00
FmtParmHead DW        0000
FmtParmCyl  DW        0000


MIDStruct      EQU    THIS BYTE
InfoLevel   DW        0000
SerialNum   DD        00000000
VolLabel    DB        'Advanced    '
FileSys     DB        'FAT12   '


DiskIO         EQU    THIS BYTE
SectBegin   DW        0000,0000
SectCount   DW        0000
BuffStart   DW        0000,0000


DCTable        DW     OFFSET D360
               DW     OFFSET D120
               DW     OFFSET D720
               DW     OFFSET D144
```

continues

Listing 8.5. Continued

```
D360    DW      40              ;Number of cylinders (tracks)
        DW      512             ;Bytes per sector
        DB      2               ;Sectors per cluster
        DW      1               ;Reserved sectors
        DB      2               ;Number of FATs
        DW      112             ;Root directory entries
        DW      40*9*2          ;Total sectors
        DB      0FDh            ;Media descriptor
        DW      2               ;Sectors per FAT
        DW      9               ;Sectors per track
        DW      2               ;Number of heads
        DD      00000000        ;Hidden sectors
        DD      00000000        ;Large sector count

D120    DW      80              ;Number of cylinders (tracks)
        DW      512             ;Bytes per sector
        DB      1               ;Sectors per cluster
        DW      1               ;Reserved sectors
        DB      2               ;Number of FATs
        DW      224             ;Root directory entries
        DW      80*15*2         ;Total sectors
        DB      0F9h            ;Media descriptor
        DW      7               ;Sectors per FAT
        DW      15              ;Sectors per track
        DW      2               ;Number of heads
        DD      00000000        ;Hidden sectors
        DD      00000000        ;Large sector count

D720    DW      80              ;Number of cylinders (tracks)
        DW      512             ;Bytes per sector
        DB      2               ;Sectors per cluster
        DW      1               ;Reserved sectors
        DB      2               ;Number of FATs
        DW      112             ;Root directory entries
        DW      80*9*2          ;Total sectors
        DB      0F9h            ;Media descriptor
        DW      3               ;Sectors per FAT
        DW      9               ;Sectors per track
        DW      2               ;Number of heads
        DD      00000000        ;Hidden sectors
        DD      00000000        ;Large sector count
```

```
D144        DW      80                      ;Number of cylinders (tracks)
            DW      512                     ;Bytes per sector
            DB      1                       ;Sectors per cluster
            DW      1                       ;Reserved sectors
            DB      2                       ;Number of FATs
            DW      224                     ;Root directory entries
            DW      80*18*2                 ;Total sectors
            DB      0F0h                    ;Media descriptor
            DW      9                       ;Sectors per FAT
            DW      18                      ;Sectors per track
            DW      2                       ;Number of heads
            DD      00000000                ;Hidden sectors
            DD      00000000                ;Large sector count

DriveMsg    DB      'Format disk in drive A or B? ',0
DriveRdy    DB      'Ready to format'
DRMsg2      DB      ' disk in drive '
AscDrive    DB      'A:',13,10,0
Insert      DB      'Insert disk to be formatted and press a key',0
CRLF        DB      13,10,0

TypeTable   DW      OFFSET M525
            DW      OFFSET M350

M525        DB      '   1.   360K disk',13,10
            DB      '   2.   1.2M disk',13,10,0

M350        DB      '   1.   720K disk',13,10
            DB      '   2.   1.44M disk',13,10,0

TypeMsg     DB      13,10,'Select type 1 or 2: ',0

FmtMsg      DB      'Formatting ',0

FTTable     DW      OFFSET FT00
            DW      OFFSET FT01
            DW      OFFSET FT02
            DW      OFFSET FT03

FT00        DB      '360K 5.25"',0
FT01        DB      '1.2M 5.25"',0
FT02        DB      '720K 3.5"',0
FT03        DB      '1.44M 3.5"',0
```

continues

Listing 8.5. Continued

```
TrackMsg1    DB      13,'Formatting track ',0
TrackMsg2    DB      ' of ',0
FinishMsg    DB      13,'Format completed              ',13,10,0

EMsg1        DB      'Could not determine drive parameters',13,10,0
EMsg2        DB      'Could not work with this device type',13,10,0
EMsg3        DB      'Could not set proper parameters',13,10,0
EMsg4        DB      13,10,'Error formatting track',13,10,0

             .CODE
             .STARTUP
Fmt          PROC

; The following memory allocation code works because it is known that MASM
; sets DS and SS to the same segment address in the start-up code. Also, ES
; is set to the PSP for the program upon entry.

             MOV     BX,DS           ;Point to start of data segment
             MOV     AX,ES           ;Point to start of PSP
             SUB     BX,AX           ;Number of segments for code and data
             MOV     AX,SP           ;SP is pointing to top of stack area
             MOV     CL,4            ;Dividing by 16
             SHR     AX,CL
             ADD     BX,AX           ;BX=paragraphs needed
             MOV     AH,4Ah          ;Modify memory allocation
             INT     21h

; Check if running on system where A/B is one drive

             CALL    Cls

             MOV     AH,44h          ;IOCTL
             MOV     AL,0Eh          ;Get logical device map
             MOV     BL,1            ;Drive A:
             INT     21h
             JC      Error1
             CMP     AL,0
             JE      TwoDrives       ;Two drives present, continue
             CMP     AL,1            ;Already set to access as A:?
```

```
            JE      SetDrive            ;Yes, so continue
            MOV     AH,44h              ;IOCTL
            MOV     AL,0Fh              ;Set logical drive map
            MOV     BL,1                ;Make it drive A:
            INT     21h
            MOV     AL,1                ;Signal want drive A:
            JMP     SetDrive            ;No need to query on which drive

TwoDrives:  MOV     SI,OFFSET DriveMsg
            CALL    PrtString

TDLoop:     MOV     AH,0                ;Read keyboard character
            INT     16h
            CMP     AL,'a'              ;Into lowercase territory?
            JB      TD1                 ;No, continue
            SUB     AL,32               ;Make it uppercase
TD1:        CMP     AL,'A'              ;Less than minimum choice?
            JB      TDLoop              ;Yes, so keep asking
            CMP     AL,'B'              ;Greater than maximum?
            JA      TDLoop              ;Yes, so keep asking

            PUSH    AX                  ;Store keypress for a moment
            MOV     DL,AL               ;Print character
            MOV     AH,02h              ;Output a character
            INT     21h
            MOV     SI,OFFSET CRLF
            CALL    PrtString
            CALL    PrtString           ;Print it a second time
            POP     AX                  ;Get back keypress
            SUB     AL,64               ;Change to drive code

SetDrive:   MOV     Drive,AL            ;Store drive number
            ADD     AL,64               ;Make it into an ASCII character
            MOV     AscDrive,AL         ;Store it in message

            MOV     AL,0                ;Special function desired
            CALL    GetParms            ;Go find out about drive
            JC      Error1              ;Didn't work, so exit
            CALL    XferParms           ;Transfer to real work area

            MOV     SI,OFFSET DriveRdy
            CALL    PrtString
```

continues

Listing 8.5. Continued

```
                MOV     SI,OFFSET Insert     ;Prompt to put in disk
                CALL    KeyMsg
                MOV     SI,OFFSET CRLF
                CALL    PrtString
                CALL    PrtString

                MOV     AL,DeviceType
                CMP     AL,3                 ;Valid device types?
                JB      DeviceOK
                CMP     AL,7                 ;Still valid?
                JNE     Error2               ;Nope, so exit
                MOV     AL,3                 ;Force 7=3 for format type

DeviceOK:       MOV     FormatType,AL        ;Assume 0 or 2
                CMP     AL,0
                JE      Ready
                CMP     AL,2
                JE      Ready
                DEC     AL
                MOV     AH,0
                MOV     BX,OFFSET TypeTable  ;Start of type table
                ADD     BX,AX                ;Adjust to proper message
                MOV     SI,[BX]              ;Get address
                CALL    PrtString
                MOV     SI,OFFSET TypeMsg
                CALL    PrtString

GTLoop:         MOV     AH,0                 ;Read keyboard character
                INT     16h
                CMP     AL,'1'               ;Less than minimum choice?
                JB      GTLoop               ;Yes, so keep asking
                CMP     AL,'2'               ;Greater than maximum?
                JA      GTLoop               ;Yes, so keep asking

                PUSH    AX                   ;Store keypress for a moment
                MOV     DL,AL                ;Print character
                MOV     AH,02h               ;Output a character
                INT     21h
                MOV     SI,OFFSET CRLF
                CALL    PrtString
```

```
            CALL    PrtString               ;Print it a second time
            POP     AX                      ;Get back keypress
            CMP     AL,'2'                  ;Was default OK?
            JE      Ready                   ;Yes, so continue
            DEC     FormatType              ;No, so adjust

Ready:      MOV     SI,OFFSET FmtMsg
            CALL    PrtString
            MOV     AL,FormatType
            SHL     AL,1                    ;Multiply by 2
            MOV     AH,0
            MOV     BX,OFFSET FTTable
            ADD     BX,AX                   ;Adjust for proper message
            MOV     SI,[BX]                 ;Get address from table
            CALL    PrtString
            MOV     SI,OFFSET DRMsg2
            CALL    PrtString

            CALL    DoParms                 ;Set up parameters for format
            MOV     AL,5                    ;Special code desired
            CALL    SetParms                ;Send them to IOCTL
            JC      Error3

            MOV     CurHead,0
            MOV     CX,Cylinders            ;This is number of tracks to format
            MOV     CurCylinder,-1          ;First increment will be for track 0
FmtLoop:    INC     CurCylinder
            CALL    Status                  ;Display status
            CALL    FormatTrack             ;Go format the track
            JC      Error4
            LOOP    FmtLoop

            CALL    WriteBoot               ;Write the boot sector
            CALL    SetMID
            CALL    WriteFAT                ;Write the FAT
            CALL    WriteDir                ;Write the directory
            CALL    RestParms               ;Set the IOCTL stuff back right

            MOV     SI,OFFSET FinishMsg
            CALL    PrtString
            JMP     AllDone
```

continues

Listing 8.5. Continued

```
Error1:      MOV      SI,OFFSET EMsg1
             JMP      ErrCommon
Error2:      MOV      SI,OFFSET EMsg2
             JMP      ErrCommon
Error3:      CALL     RestParms              ;Restore parameters
             MOV      SI,OFFSET EMsg3
             JMP      ErrCommon
Error4:      CALL     RestParms              ;Restore parameters
             MOV      SI,OFFSET EMsg4
ErrCommon:   CALL     PrtString
AllDone:     .EXIT
Fmt          ENDP



; Get current parms for desired drive. Enter with AL equal to special function.

GetParms     PROC     USES AX BX CX DX
             MOV      SFOrig,AL             ;Want for current BPB
             MOV      AH,44h                ;IOCTL
             MOV      AL,0Dh                ;Generic block I/O
             MOV      BL,Drive
             MOV      CH,08h                ;Disk drive
             MOV      CL,60h                ;Get device parameters
             MOV      DX,OFFSET OrigParms
             INT      21h
             RET
GetParms     ENDP



; Transfer from retrieved parameter area into one that will be used
; for the real work in the program

XferParms    PROC     USES CX SI DI ES
             CLD
             PUSH     DS
             POP      ES
             MOV      SI,OFFSET OrigParms
             MOV      DI,OFFSET NewParms
             MOV      CX,ParmLen
             REP      MOVSB
```

```
            CLC                             ;Exit with no error
            RET
XferParms   ENDP



; Set parameters. Enter with AL equal to special function desired.

SetParms    PROC    USES AX BX CX DX
            MOV     SpecFuncNew,AL
            MOV     AH,44h                  ;IOCTL
            MOV     AL,0Dh                  ;Generic block I/O
            MOV     BL,Drive
            MOV     CH,08h                  ;Disk drive
            MOV     CL,40h                  ;Set device parameters
            MOV     DX,OFFSET NewParms
            INT     21h
            RET
SetParms    ENDP



; Restore parms to their old condition

RestParms   PROC    USES AX BX CX DX
            MOV     SFOrig,00000100b
            MOV     AH,44h                  ;IOCTL
            MOV     AL,0Dh                  ;Generic block I/O
            MOV     BL,Drive
            MOV     CH,08h                  ;Disk drive
            MOV     CL,40h                  ;Set device parameters
            MOV     DX,OFFSET OrigParms
            INT     21h
            RET
RestParms   ENDP



; Set up parameters (including BPB) for selected format type. Also
; transfer information into the BPB in the boot sector.

DoParms     PROC    USES AX BX CX SI DI ES
            MOV     AH,0
```

continues

Listing 8.5. Continued

```
               MOV      AL,FormatType
               SHL      AX,1                    ;Multiply by 2
               MOV      BX,OFFSET DCTable
               ADD      BX,AX                   ;Adjust for format type
               MOV      SI,[BX]                 ;Get proper address
               MOV      AX,[SI]                 ;Get number of cylinders
               INC      SI                      ;Point to next parameter
               INC      SI
               CMP      Cylinders,AX            ;Default capacity for drive?
               JE       DP1
               MOV      MediaType,1             ;Set for low format
               MOV      Cylinders,AX
DP1:           PUSH     SI                      ;Store for a moment
               MOV      CX,25                   ;Bytes to transfer
               MOV      DI,OFFSET DiskBPB
               PUSH     DS
               POP      ES
               CLD
               REP      MOVSB                   ;Transfer parms
               CALL     DoLayout

               POP      SI                      ;Get start of BPB back
               MOV      AX,SEG BootBPB
               MOV      ES,AX
               MOV      DI,OFFSET ES:BootBPB
               MOV      CX,25
               REP      MOVSB                   ;Transfer to boot sector
               RET
DoParms        ENDP


; Set the track layout field

DoLayout       PROC     USES AX BX CX SI DI ES
               CLD
               MOV      DI,OFFSET TrackLayout
               MOV      AX,SectTrack
               PUSH     DS
               POP      ES
```

```
            STOSW
            MOV     BX,1                  ;First sector number
            MOV     CX,AX                 ;Number of sectors per track
            MOV     DX,BytesSect          ;Bytes per sector
TrkLoop:    MOV     AX,BX                 ;Sector number
            STOSW
            INC     BX                    ;Point to next sector
            MOV     AX,DX                 ;Bytes per sector
            STOSW
            LOOP    TrkLoop               ;Do it all again
            RET
DoLayout    ENDP



; Set the media ID

SetMID      PROC    USES AX BX CX DX
            MOV     AH,44h                ;IOCTL
            MOV     AL,0Dh                ;Generic block I/O
            MOV     BL,Drive
            MOV     CH,08h                ;Disk drive
            MOV     CL,46h                ;Set media ID
            MOV     DX,OFFSET MIDStruct
            INT     21h
            RET
SetMID      ENDP



; Handle formatting a single track. Return with carry set if error.

FormatTrack PROC    USES CX
            MOV     CX,NumHeads
            DEC     CX                    ;Make zero-based
FTLoop:     MOV     CurHead,CL
            CALL    FormatSide
            JC      FTDone
            LOOP    FTLoop
            CLC                           ;Return with no errors
FTDone:     RET
FormatTrack ENDP
```

continues

Listing 8.5. Continued

```
; Format one head of a track. Return with carry set if error.

FormatSide  PROC    USES AX BX CX DX
            MOV     FmtParmSF,0
            MOV     AH,0
            MOV     AL,CurHead
            MOV     FmtParmHead,AX
            MOV     AL,CurCylinder
            MOV     FmtParmCyl,AX

            MOV     AH,44h               ;IOCTL
            MOV     AL,0Dh               ;Generic block I/O
            MOV     BH,0
            MOV     BL,Drive
            MOV     CH,08h               ;Disk drive
            MOV     CL,42h               ;Format/verify track
            MOV     DX,OFFSET FmtParms
            INT     21h
            RET
FormatSide  ENDP


; The following routine clears the screen and homes the cursor

Cls         PROC    USES AX BX CX DX
            MOV     AH,6                 ;Scroll window up
            MOV     AL,0                 ;Scroll full screen
            MOV     BH,7                 ;Normal white on black
            MOV     CX,0                 ;Upper left corner of screen
            MOV     DH,24                ;Bottom right
            MOV     DL,79
            INT     10h

            MOV     DX,0                 ;Upper left corner of screen
            MOV     BH,0                 ;Assume page 0
            MOV     AH,2                 ;Set cursor position
            INT     10h
            RET
Cls         ENDP
```

```
; Display the status message during formatting

Status       PROC    USES AX SI
             MOV     SI,OFFSET TrackMsg1
             CALL    PrtString
             MOV     AH,0
             MOV     AL,CurCylinder
             INC     AX                    ;Normalize number
             CALL    PrtDec
             MOV     SI,OFFSET TrackMsg2
             CALL    PrtString
             MOV     AX,Cylinders
             CALL    PrtDec
             RET
Status       ENDP



; The following routine prints the ASCIIZ string pointed to by DS:SI.
; DOS routines for character output are used.

PrtString    PROC    USES AX DX SI
PS1:         MOV     DL,[SI]               ;Get character
             INC     SI                    ;Point to next one
             CMP     DL,0                  ;End of string?
             JE      PS2                   ;Yes, so exit
             MOV     AH,02h                ;Output a character
             INT     21h
             JMP     PS1                   ;Keep doing it
PS2:         RET
PrtString    ENDP



; The following routine prints the message pointed to by SI and then
; waits for a keypress

KeyMsg       PROC    USES AX
             CALL    PrtString             ;Message pointed to by SI
             MOV     AH,0                  ;Read keyboard character
             INT     16h
             RET
KeyMsg       ENDP
```

continues

Listing 8.5. Continued

```
; The following routine prints the value in AX as a decimal number

PrtDec      PROC    USES AX CX DX
            MOV     CX,0FFFFh               ;Ending flag
            PUSH    CX
            MOV     CX,10
PD1:        MOV     DX,0
            DIV     CX                      ;Divide by 10
            ADD     DL,30h                  ;Convert to ASCII
            PUSH    DX                      ;Store remainder
            CMP     AX,0                    ;Are we done?
            JNE     PD1                     ;No, so continue

PD2:        POP     DX                      ;Character is now in DL
            CMP     DX,0FFFFh               ;Is it the ending flag?
            JE      PD3                     ;Yes, so continue
            MOV     AH,02h                  ;Output a character
            INT     21h
            JMP     PD2                     ;Keep doing it

PD3:        RET
PrtDec      ENDP



; Write the boot sector to the disk

WriteBoot   PROC    USES AX BX CX ES
            MOV     AX,SEG BootSector       ;Point to boot sector
            MOV     ES,AX
            MOV     BX,OFFSET ES:BootSector
            MOV     BuffStart[0],BX
            MOV     BuffStart[2],ES
            MOV     SectBegin,0
            MOV     SectCount,1
            MOV     AL,Drive
            DEC     AL                      ;Make it zero-based
            MOV     BX,OFFSET DiskIO        ;Point to buffer
            MOV     CX,-1
            INT     26h
            POP     AX                      ;Get rid of flags
```

```
            RET
WriteBoot   ENDP


; Write the FAT to the disk

WriteFAT    PROC    USES AX BX CX DX DI ES DS
            MOV     AX,SectFAT
            MOV     BL,32               ;Paragraphs per 512 bytes
            MUL     BL                  ;AX now contains paragraphs needed
            MOV     BX,AX               ;   for one FAT image
            MOV     AH,48h              ;Allocate memory
            INT     21h                 ;DOS services
            MOV     ES,AX               ;Put in proper place

            MOV     AX,SectFAT
            MOV     CL,8                ;2^8 power (256)
            SHL     AX,CL               ;Number of words in memory area
            MOV     CX,AX               ;Iteration count
            MOV     DI,0                ;Point to start of memory block
            MOV     AX,0                ;Want to clear memory area
            CLD                         ;Go in proper direction
            REP     STOSW               ;Store 0s in memory

            MOV     AX,0FFFFh
            MOV     BL,MediaID
            MOV     ES:[0],BL           ;Store FAT ID
            MOV     ES:[1],AX           ;Store filler

            MOV     AX,1
            MOV     CH,0
            MOV     CL,NumFATs
FATLoop:    CALL    PutFAT
            ADD     AX,SectFAT
            LOOP    FATLoop

            MOV     AH,49h              ;Release memory block
            INT     21h                 ;DOS services

            RET
WriteFAT    ENDP
```

continues

Listing 8.5. Continued

```
; Put one copy of the FAT on disk. Enter with AX=beginning sector number

PutFAT      PROC    USES AX BX CX ES
            MOV     BuffStart[0],0
            MOV     BuffStart[2],ES
            MOV     SectBegin,AX
            MOV     AX,SectFAT
            MOV     SectCount,AX
            MOV     AL,Drive
            DEC     AL                      ;Make it zero-based
            MOV     BX,OFFSET DiskIO        ;Point to buffer
            MOV     CX,-1
            INT     26h
            POP     AX                      ;Get rid of flags
            RET
PutFAT      ENDP



; Write the directory to the disk

WriteDIR    PROC    USES AX BX CX DX DI ES DS
            MOV     AX,RootDir              ;Maximum root directory entries
            MOV     CL,4                    ;2^4 power (16)
            SHR     AX,CL                   ;Divide by 16, now AX = sectors needed
            PUSH    AX                      ;Store for later

            MOV     BL,32                   ;Paragraphs per 512 bytes
            MUL     BL                      ;AX now contains paragraphs needed
            MOV     BX,AX
            MOV     AH,48h                  ;Allocate memory
            INT     21h                     ;DOS services
            MOV     ES,AX                   ;Put in proper place

            POP     AX                      ;Get back number of directory sectors
            PUSH    AX                      ;And store for later
            MOV     CL,8                    ;2^8 power (256)
            SHL     AX,CL                   ;AX now has number of words in data area
```

```
          MOV     CX,AX            ;Put into loop counter
          MOV     DI,0             ;Start at beginning of block
          MOV     AX,0             ;Want to clear memory area
          CLD                      ;Go in proper direction
          REP     STOSW            ;Store 0s in memory

          MOV     AX,SectFAT       ;Number of sectors in one FAT
          MOV     BL,NumFATs       ;Get number of FATs
          MUL     BL               ;AX now has number of sectors
          INC     AX               ;Point to sector past FAT

          MOV     BuffStart[0],0
          MOV     BuffStart[2],ES
          MOV     SectBegin,AX
          POP     AX               ;Get back directory sectors
          MOV     SectCount,AX
          MOV     AL,Drive
          DEC     AL               ;Make it zero-based
          MOV     BX,OFFSET DiskIO ;Point to buffer
          MOV     CX,-1
          INT     26h
          POP     AX               ;Get rid of flags

          MOV     AH,49h           ;Release memory block
          INT     21h              ;DOS services

          RET
WriteDIR  ENDP


; The following routine is the code that will be written
; to disk for the boot sector

BSect       SEGMENT PARA PRIVATE 'CODE'
            ASSUME CS:BSect, DS:BSect
            ORG     0                    ;Boot sector will be here

BootSector  DB      0EBh,03Ch,090h
;           JMP     SHORT BootCode
;           NOP
```

continues

Listing 8.5. Continued

```
; Note that the following information, between here and BootCode, is the BPB
; used by DOS. This info is compatible with DOS 5, but works also with
; earlier DOS versions.


            DB      'Assembly'
BootBPB     DB      25 DUP (0)
            DB      00                  ;Drive number, if a hard disk
            DB      00                  ;Reserved
            DB      29h                 ;Extended boot signature
            DD      00000000            ;Volume serial number
            DB      'Advanced    '      ;Volume label
            DB      'FAT12   '          ;File type

BootCode:   MOV     AX,7C0h             ;Standard loading place for
            MOV     DS,AX               ;    boot sector
            MOV     ES,AX

            MOV     AH,0Fh              ;Get current display mode
            INT     10h                 ;BIOS services

            MOV     SI,OFFSET BootMsg
MsgLoop:    MOV     AL,[SI]             ;Get next character
            CMP     AL,0                ;End of string?
            JE      MsgDone             ;Yes, so end
            MOV     AH,0Eh              ;Write text in teletype mode
            INT     10h                 ;BIOS services
            INC     SI
            JMP     SHORT MsgLoop

MsgDone:    MOV     AH,0                ;Read keyboard character
            INT     16h                 ;BIOS services
            MOV     AL,13               ;Process a carriage return
            MOV     AH,0Eh
            INT     10h
            MOV     AL,10               ;Process a line feed
            MOV     AH,0Eh
            INT     10h
            INT     19h                 ;Do a warm boot
```

```
BootMsg     DB      13,10,13,10
            DB      '                             This disk was formatted with a program from',13,10
            DB      '                             Advanced Assembly Language, by Allen L.
Wyatt.',13,10
            DB      13,10
            DB      '                             This is a non-system disk. Remove this disk',13,10
            DB      '                                 and press any key to reboot your system.',13,10
            DB      13,10, 43 DUP (' '), 0

            ORG     510
            DB      55h                 ;Boot sector has to end with
            DB      0AAh                ;    these bytes, in this order

BSect       ENDS

            END
```

To use this program, you just enter FMT at the DOS prompt. If you have a dual floppy system, you are asked which disk drive you want to use. If the drive you specify supports multiple media types (for instance, 360K and 1.2M), you are asked which type of disk you want to format.

That's it. Two questions, maximum, and the disk begins formatting. The program is not fancy, but it doesn't take much space either. The DOS FORMAT utility occupies more than 32,000 bytes; FMT.EXE occupies less than 3,000.

Because FMT.EXE is a bare-bones formatting program, there are many enhancements you can make to the program—for instance, improved error handling or support for nonstandard storage media. Such improvements can make for a great (yet small) utility program. I suspect that many other readers will want to take the subroutines from this program and link them to programs written in higher-level languages to increase their utility value.

This program has one feature you should be sure to notice. The segment at BSect is the boot sector written to the formatted disk. This type of boot sector displays a custom message when the user tries to boot the disk. The user then has the opportunity to remove the disk and reboot. The custom message can be changed easily and provides more context for novice users who may not understand what Non-system disk or disk error means.

Summary

This chapter explained how to use many of the IOCTL functions for both character and block devices. The IOCTL functions provide a generalized group of interfaces to a wide range of devices. The subject of this chapter leads directly into Chapter 9, which discusses how to write device drivers.

Device Drivers

I n Chapter 8, "Using IOCTL," you learned about the IOCTL functions supplied by DOS. This chapter discusses how those functions are supported by device drivers. If you are unclear about devices and their general categories, read Chapter 8 before reading this chapter.

Device drivers originally were borrowed from the UNIX environment as a way to make the operating system extensible—to make it something that could easily grow as the needs of computer users grew. Over the years, the vast majority of supporting routines for common devices have been built directly into DOS. You rarely see specialized device drivers, therefore, for items such as disk drives and keyboards. You do, however, find drivers for other peripherals such as mice or CD-ROM drives. Also, most of the basic internal components of DOS are treated as device drivers by the kernel. For instance, Table 9.1 shows the device drivers that are integral to DOS. These drivers are built into the system, but are still treated as device drivers by the other portions of the operating system.

Table 9.1. Predefined system devices.

Name	Meaning	Type
AUX	Auxiliary device	Character
CLOCK$	Real-time system clock	Character
COM*n*	Communications port	Character

continues

Name	Meaning	Type
CON	System console (keyboard and monitor)	Character
LPT*n*	Line printer	Character
NUL	Nonexistent input or output	Character
PRN	Printer device	Character
x:	Disk drive	Block

With device drivers, you have the opportunity to extend the operating system to recognize and use other devices. Many different device drivers are available, which control everything from the keyboard to RAM to scanners and tape drives. To illustrate some of the more common device drivers available, I searched my hard disk, along with the systems of a few friends. The results are shown in Table 9.2.

Table 9.2. Common device drivers.

File Name	Device Controlled	Vendor
ANSI.SYS	Keyboard and monitor	Microsoft
CACHE.EXE	Memory and disk drives	Digital Research
CDROM.SYS	CD-ROM	Always Technology
COUNTRY.SYS	Keyboard and monitor	Microsoft
DISPLAY.SYS	Monitor	Microsoft
DRIVER.SYS	Disk drive	Microsoft
EGA.SYS	Monitor	Microsoft
EMM386.SYS	Memory	Microsoft
EMMXMA.SYS	Memory	Digital Research
EMS.SYS	Memory	Quarterdeck
EMS2EXT.SYS	Memory	Quarterdeck
EXXTF210.SYS	CD-ROM	Dennon
HIDOS.SYS	Memory	Digital Research
HIMEM.SYS	Memory	Microsoft
HOOKROM.SYS	Memory	Quarterdeck
KEYBOARD.SYS	Keyboard	Microsoft

File Name	Device Controlled	Vendor
KEYSTACK.SYS	Keyboard	Symantec
LOADHI.SYS	Memory	Quarterdeck
LS300.SYS	Scanner	Princeton Graphics
MOUSE.SYS	Mouse	Microsoft
PRINTER.SYS	Printer	Microsoft
QEMM386.SYS	Memory	Quarterdeck
RAMBIOS.SYS	Video BIOS	ATI
RAMDRIVE.SYS	Virtual drive	Microsoft
RSTRCFG.SYS	Memory	Quarterdeck
SBPCD.SYS	CD-ROM	SoundBlaster
SMARTDRV.SYS	Virtual drive	Microsoft
V7ANSI.SYS	Keyboard and monitor	Video 7
VANSI.SYS	Keyboard and monitor	ATI
VDEFEND.SYS	Disk and memory	Central Point
VDISK.SYS	Virtual drive	Various vendors
XIS380GS.SYS	Scanner	Ventura

Each device driver is added to DOS when the computer boots. You do this by adding another DEVICE= line to the CONFIG.SYS file. How are these device drivers put together, though, and how can you develop your own?

Device Driver Construction

When you write a device driver, you can follow a simple formula that ensures success, at least as far as DOS is concerned. Getting your device driver to work with the external device can be tricky, and is related directly to the complexity of the device and your understanding of it. I don't say this to scare you away; you just need to understand that writing device drivers can be simple and straightforward for simple devices, and very complex for more exotic devices.

Conceptually, the DOS interface required for a device driver is simple to understand. Every device driver is made up of three distinct parts:

- The header
- The strategy routine
- The interrupt routine

These parts typically are combined in a binary (COM) file with the SYS extension, origination at offset 00h, and no stack. Beginning with DOS V3, however, you can program your driver in a standard EXE format. This chapter uses examples of device drivers in the straight binary format because they work on the widest range of machines, are the easiest to program, and result in the most compact files. This section looks at each part of a device driver in more detail.

The Header Section

Every device driver has a header that is 18 bytes long. The following structure is for this header:

```
Chain       DD      -1                  ;Link to next driver
Attribute   DW      0000                ;Driver attribute
StratOff    DW      OFFSET Strategy     ;Offset to strategy routine
IntOff      DW      OFFSET Interrupt    ;Offset to interrupt routine
DevName     DB      8 DUP (' ')         ;Driver name
```

The header structure contains pointers and identification information that enable DOS to effectively use the driver. Device drivers are loaded as one of the last steps in booting DOS. Immediately after the internal device drivers are initialized, DOS examines the CONFIG.SYS file to see whether additional device drivers should be loaded. If so, they are added to the front of a *device driver chain*, a linked list of device drivers that DOS can search when a function requests input or output from a device. In the example header structure, the Chain field provides the segment:offset address of the next driver in the driver chain. Figure 9.1 illustrates this linking process.

Because any device driver you may develop is added to the front of an existing device driver list, it always contains a pointer to the next driver. The last driver in a driver list, however, contains a –1 in the offset portion of the Chain field. When you are writing your own device driver, you should set the Chain field to –1; DOS resets this field when it finally loads the driver.

The driver attribute word, Attribute in the example structure, indicates what type of driver this header is for. The composition of the attribute word depends on whether the device is a character or block device. Table 9.3 shows the attribute word bit meanings for a character device; Table 9.4 details the same information for a block device.

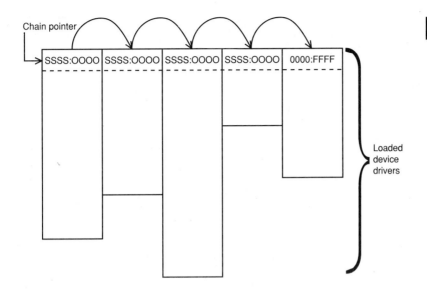

Chain pointer

| SSSS:0000 | SSSS:0000 | SSSS:0000 | SSSS:0000 | 0000:FFFF |

Loaded device drivers

Figure 9.1.

Device drivers are linked in memory through a series of pointers in the device driver header.

Table 9.3. Bit meanings for the attribute word of a character device.

Bit settings FEDCBA98 76543210	Meaning
1	Standard input device
0	Not a standard input device
1	Standard output device
0	Not a standard output device
0	Used to specify NUL device driver; because the resident NUL driver cannot be replaced, this bit must be set to 0 in your driver
1	Clock device
0	Not the clock device
1	Int 29h fast-character output supported
0	Int 29h fast-character output not supported
0	Reserved (set to 0)
1	Generic IOCTL functions supported
0	Generic IOCTL functions not supported
1	IOCTL queries supported

continues

Table 9.3. Continued

Bit settings FEDCBA98 76543210	Meaning
0	IOCTL queries not supported
xxx	Reserved
1	Open and close functions supported
0	Open and close functions not supported
0	Reserved (should be 0)
1	Output until busy supported
0	Output until busy not supported
1	IOCTL functions 02h and 03h are supported
0	IOCTL functions 02h and 03h are not supported
1	Character device

Table 9.4. Bit meanings for the attribute word of a block device.

Bit settings FEDCBA98 76543210	Meaning
0	Unused (set to 0)
1	32-bit sector addresses supported
0	32-bit sector addresses not supported
0000	Unused (set to 0)
1	Generic IOCTL functions supported
0	Generic IOCTL functions not supported
1	IOCTL queries supported
0	IOCTL queries not supported
000	Reserved (set to 0)
1	Open, close, and removable media functions supported
0	Open, close, and removable media functions not supported
0	Reserved (should be 0)

Bit settings FEDCBA98 76543210	Meaning
1	Media descriptor byte of the first FAT sector is required in order to determine media characteristics
0	Media characteristics not determined from FAT information
1	IOCTL functions 02h and 03h are supported
0	IOCTL functions 02h and 03h are not supported
0	Block device

Much of the information stored in the device attribute word may look familiar to you. In Chapter 8, "Using IOCTL," you learned that much of this information is returned by IOCTL function 00h.

Notice that the bit indicating whether the device driver indicates a block device or a character device is bit 15 (0Fh). This bit is set if it is a character device, and is clear if it is a block device.

The next two fields in the header, StratOff and IntOff, respectively indicate the offset from the start of the device driver to the strategy and interrupt routines. The makeup of these two routines is discussed in the following two sections.

The final part of the header is an 8-byte ASCII name. If the device name is less than eight characters, the remaining characters must be filled with spaces. The following are valid, correctly formatted device name fields from different headers:

```
DevName     DB      'CON     '
DevName     DB      'PRN     '
DevName     DB      'MYDRIVER'
DevName     DB      'WIDGET  '
DevName     DB      'MARK3   '
```

The first two example device driver names match preexisting system driver names. Because device drivers are added to the front of the device driver chain, devices with names that match existing devices effectively replace those devices because the search for a device stops when a matching name is found. Note that device names must be left-justified in the 8-character field.

This chapter has discussed only the naming of character device drivers. What about use of the DevName field for block devices? In this case, the majority of the field is unused. The first byte is the count of the number of physical devices controlled by the driver, and the other seven bytes are unused.

The Strategy Routine

The strategy routine is aptly misnamed, because it does no real strategy planning or implementation. The routine is called whenever the device driver is first loaded by DOS, and again whenever any I/O requests are issued. At minimum, only three lines of code need to be executed by this routine:

```
Strategy    PROC    FAR
            MOV     CS:ReqHdr[0],BX     ;Offset of request header
            MOV     CS:ReqHdr[2],ES     ;Segment of request header
            RET
Strategy    ENDP
```

You can do other things in the strategy routine, if required by your interrupt handler (see the following section, "The Interrupt Routine"), but they are not necessary. In any event, never issue any DOS function calls in the strategy routine. Remember that this routine is first called as the device driver is loaded, and the DOS functions have not been fully implemented. Also, DOS is not reentrant, and calling a DOS function in the strategy routine may corrupt internal pointers. The result is an unstable system with undependable operation (translation: probable system crash).

When the strategy routine is called by DOS, the address of a structure known as a *request header* is in the ES:BX registers. The request header is used by DOS to pass information to a device driver. Table 9.5 shows the layout of the request header.

Table 9.5. Request header layout.

Offset	Length	Meaning
00h	1 byte	Request header length
01h	1 byte	Unit number
02h	1 byte	Command code
03h	2 bytes	Return status word
05h	8 bytes	Reserved
0Dh	Varies	Depends on nature of I/O request

You should understand that even though the layout of the request header is discussed in this section, you cannot examine the request header until your interrupt routine is called. The primary purpose of the strategy routine is to save the request header address so that your interrupt routine knows where to look for information being passed by DOS.

The first byte of the request header indicates its total length, and its use should be self-explanatory. The unit number byte is used to indicate which block unit the I/O request is for. This value is applicable only for device drivers that control more than one physical device.

The command code is the way that DOS makes a request of the device driver. Table 9.6 lists the 21 possible values of this command code. Each of these commands is described in detail in the following section.

Table 9.6. Command code values in a request header.

Value	Meaning
00h	Init
01h	Media Check
02h	Build BPB
03h	Control Info Read
04h	Read
05h	Nondestructive Read
06h	Input Status
07h	Input Flush
08h	Write
09h	Write with Verify
0Ah	Output Status
0Bh	Output Flush
0Ch	Control Info Write
0Dh	Open Device
0Eh	Close Device
0Fh	Removeable Media
10h	Output Until Busy
13h	Generic IOCTL
17h	Get Logical Device
18h	Set Logical Device
19h	IOCTL Query

The return status word portion of the request header is the way in which your driver communicates status information to DOS. This word is best examined as individual bytes. Possible bit settings for the high-order portion are shown in Table 9.7.

Table 9.7. Bit meanings for the high-order byte of the return status word in the request header.

Bit settings 76543210	Meaning
1	Done
0	Not done
1	Busy
0	Not busy
xxxxx	Reserved
1	Error has occurred
0	No error

If bit 7 of the high-order byte is set, the low-order byte of the return status word is used to indicate the error code that occurred. If no error occurred, bit 7 of the high-order bit is clear, and the contents of the low-order byte do not matter. Table 9.8 lists the possible error codes that can be returned in the low-order byte.

Table 9.8. Error-code values for the low-order byte of the return status word in the request header.

Value	Meaning
00h	Write-protect error
01h	Unknown unit
02h	Drive not ready
03h	Unknown command
04h	CRC error
05h	Bad request structure length
06h	Seek error
07h	Unknown media

Value	Meaning
08h	Sector not found
09h	Out of paper
0Ah	Write fault
0Bh	Read fault
0Ch	General failure
0Fh	Invalid disk change

The Interrupt Routine

This portion of the device driver handles any commands passed through the request header at the address saved in the strategy routine. The interrupt routine should not be confused with an interrupt handler. It does not handle interrupts in the classical sense of the term; it is only a routine called by DOS immediately after the strategy routine is called during an I/O request.

The first task the interrupt routine must perform (in addition to saving the state of the registers and flags on entry) is to examine the command code at offset 02h of the request header, and then handle the command. When the command is completed, the values in the request header are updated, and control is returned to DOS.

Let's look again at the commands your interrupt routines are called on to do. Table 9.9 lists the 21 commands, but this time with their device driver classification and DOS version applicability.

Table 9.9. Commands that must be handled by an interrupt handler based on the type of driver and DOS version.

Command Code	Command Name	Character Driver	Block Driver	DOS Version
00h	Init	✓	✓	2.0
01h	Media Check		✓	2.0
02h	Build BPB		✓	2.0
03h	Control Info Read	✓	✓	2.0
04h	Read	✓	✓	2.0

continues

Table 9.9. Continued

Command Code	Command Name	Character Driver	Block Driver	DOS Version
05h	Nondestructive Read	✓		2.0
06h	Input Status	✓		2.0
07h	Input Flush	✓		2.0
08h	Write	✓	✓	2.0
09h	Write with Verify		✓	2.0
0Ah	Output Status	✓		2.0
0Bh	Output Flush	✓		2.0
0Ch	Control Info Write	✓	✓	2.0
0Dh	Open Device	✓	✓	3.0
0Eh	Close Device	✓	✓	3.0
0Fh	Removeable Media		✓	3.0
10h	Output Until Busy	✓		3.0
13h	Generic IOCTL	✓	✓	3.2
17h	Get Logical Device		✓	3.2
18h	Set Logical Device		✓	3.2
19h	IOCTL Query	✓	✓	5.0

By using Table 9.9, you can determine which functions you must support for your driver based on type and who your users will be. Remember that if you choose not to implement some command codes, you can load the return status word of the request header with 8003, which indicates an unknown command error. DOS then generates the appropriate error to the application that initiated the I/O request.

The following section looks at each possible command your driver may need to support.

Init

The Init command code is applicable to both character and block devices, and is the only command that absolutely must be included in your driver. Init must be included because it is issued only when DOS first loads the device driver, and DOS expects information back from the routine that it uses to fully install the driver. If the information is not returned, the driver cannot be loaded.

Because this command is used only once, in this portion of the device driver you set up interrupt vectors, initialize any hardware, and display any initialization messages. This part of the device driver is the only place where you can call any DOS functions. You can call the DOS I/O functions, 00h through 0Ch, as well as function 30h (Get DOS Version).

Regardless of the type of driver you are writing, DOS expects this command to return the amount of memory required by the driver. If no memory requirement is returned, the driver cannot be loaded. In addition, if you are writing a block device driver, this command must indicate the number of units this driver controls, and provide a pointer to a BPB (BIOS parameter block) array for the device. This array is a series of word offsets to the BPBs within the device driver. There should be in this array one entry for each unit the driver will control. If you need a refresher on BPBs, refer to Chapter 8, "Using IOCTL," particularly Table 8.10.

Table 9.10 summarizes the flow of information through the request header for this command.

Table 9.10. Request header settings for the Init command.

Offset	Bytes	Contents on Entry	Contents on Exit
00h	1	19h	19h
01h	1		
02h	1	0	
03h	2		Return status word
05h	8	Reserved	Reserved
0Dh	1		Number of units
0Eh	4		End-of-driver address
12h	4		BPB pointer array address
16h	1	Next drive unit available (0=A, and so on)	
17h	2		Error message flagged

If you attempt to initialize a device controlled by your driver and find that it is not available or cannot be initialized for some other reason, you can instruct

DOS to abort the driver installation by setting the end-of-driver address pointer to CS:0000, clearing bit 15 of the attribute word (driver then appears to be for a block device), and setting the number of units to 0.

Media Check

The Media Check command is applicable only to block devices. Character devices should return with the return status word set to 0100h, indicating that the command is finished.

This command is issued before DOS accesses the disk. The purpose is to give your driver a chance to indicate whether the disk has been changed. DOS passes the media ID of the media it believes is in the drive, and you can check this ID to determine whether a change has occurred. You can return one of the three values shown in Table 9.11.

Table 9.11. Media check return values.

Value	Meaning
−1	Disk has been changed
0	Cannot determine whether disk has been changed
1	Disk has not been changed

Unless you have a fairly sophisticated device driver and have figured out a way to always tell when a disk has changed, the best way to handle this command depends on the type of block device the driver is for. If the driver is for a hard disk or RAM drive, you can always return a change code of 1, indicating that there has been no change. Any other type of drive should return a 0, indicating that you are unsure about whether a change has occurred.

If the disk has been changed and bit 0Bh of the attribute word in the device header is set, you also must return a pointer to the previous ASCIIZ volume label.

Table 9.12 summarizes the flow of information through the request header for this command.

Table 9.12. Request header settings for the Media Check command.

Offset	Bytes	Contents on Entry	Contents on Exit
00h	1	13h	13h
01h	1	Unit code	
02h	1	1	
03h	2		Return status word
05h	8	Reserved	Reserved
0Dh	1	Media ID byte	
0Eh	1		Change code (–1, 0, or 1)
0Fh	4		Volume label address

Build BPB

The Build BPB command applies to block devices; character devices should return with the return status word set to 0100h, indicating that the command is finished.

This command is called by DOS when it suspects that the disk has changed (based on the return code from the Media Check command), or when it needs to refresh the BPB pointer.

When this command is issued, DOS provides the address of a sector-sized buffer in the request header. If bit 0Dh in the device attribute word of the device header is set, this buffer contains the first sector of the FAT so that you can get the media ID byte. In this case, this buffer area should not be disturbed. If bit 0Dh is not set, the buffer does not contain the FAT sector and it does not matter if you disturb the buffer.

Table 9.13 summarizes the flow of information through the request header for the Build BPB command.

Table 9.13. Request header settings for the Build BPB command.

Offset	Bytes	Contents on Entry	Contents on Exit
00h	1	16h	16h
01h	1	Unit code	
02h	1	2	
03h	2		Return status word

continues

Table 9.13. Continued

Offset	Bytes	Contents on Entry	Contents on Exit
05h	8	Reserved	Reserved
0Dh	1	Media ID byte	
0Eh	4	Buffer address	
12h	4		BPB address

If you are operating under at least DOS 3.0, you may want to have this command read and save the new volume label from the disk. This step is necessary only if you have instituted code in the Media Check command that compares volume labels to determine whether disks have been changed.

Control Info Read

The Control Info Read command applies to both block and character devices. It provides a way for a device driver to send control information directly to an application. The opposite of this command is the Control Info Write command, which enables the application to communicate directly with the driver.

DOS does no checking on the information passed with this command; it simply passes the information on. You cannot use this command, therefore, unless your application has detailed information about how the driver works. For this reason, the use of this command is limited for many drivers.

You should note that this command is valid only if bit 0Eh of the device attribute word in the device header is set. Table 9.14 summarizes the flow of information through the request header for this command.

Table 9.14. Request header settings for the Control Info Read command.

Offset	Bytes	Contents on Entry	Contents on Exit
00h	1	14h	14h
01h	1	Unit code	
02h	1	3	
03h	2		Return status word
05h	8	Reserved	Reserved
0Dh	1	Media ID byte	
0Eh	4	Buffer address	
12h	2	Byte count	Actual number of bytes transferred

Read

The Read command applies to both block and character devices. It causes the driver to transfer information from the device into a memory buffer specified by DOS. Even if an error occurs during the data transfer, all return values in the request header must be updated. Table 9.15 summarizes the flow of information through the request header for this command.

Table 9.15. Request header settings for the Read command.

Offset	Bytes	Contents on Entry	Contents on Exit
00h	1	1Eh	1Eh
01h	1	Unit code	
02h	1	4	
03h	2		Return status word
05h	8	Reserved	Reserved
0Dh	1	Media ID byte	
0Eh	4	Buffer address	
12h	2	Byte or sector count	Actual number of bytes or sectors transferred
14h	2	Starting sector number	
16h	4		Volume identifier
1Ah	4	32-bit sector number	Volume label address if error 0Fh is being returned

The 32-bit starting sector number at offset 16h is present only if the following conditions are met:

- The device is a block device.
- The logical drive is larger than 32M.
- Bit 1 of the device attribute word in the device header is set.
- The starting sector number at offset 14h is set to –1.

Nondestructive Read

The Nondestructive Read command applies to only character devices; block devices should return with the return status word set to 0100h, indicating that the command is finished.

This command enables devices, such as keyboards, modems, or serial ports, to fetch a character from the device before it is needed. Even though the character is returned in the request header, it is left in the input buffer so that it is available for the next Read command. The primary use of this command is for DOS to see what is available at the console pending completion of a current task. Table 9.16 summarizes the flow of information through the request header for this command.

Table 9.16. Request header settings for the Nondestructive Read command.

Offset	Bytes	Contents on Entry	Contents on Exit
00h	1	0Eh	0Eh
01h	1		
02h	1	5	
03h	2	Return status word	
05h	8	Reserved	Reserved
0Dh	1	Character	

Input Status

The Input Status command applies to only character devices; block devices should return with the return status word set to 0100h, indicating that the command is finished.

DOS uses this command to test whether characters are available in a buffer that may be maintained by the device. If they are available, the busy bit of the return status word is cleared, and the command returns to DOS. If no characters are available in the buffer, the busy bit is set and control returns. The return status word is the only information returned by this command. Table 9.17 summarizes the flow of information through the request header for this command.

Table 9.17. Request header settings for the Input Status command.

Offset	Bytes	Contents on Entry	Contents on Exit
00h	1	0Dh	0Dh
01h	1		

Offset	Bytes	Contents on Entry	Contents on Exit
02h	1	6	
03h	2	Return status word	
05h	8	Reserved	Reserved

Input Flush

The Input Flush command applies to only character devices; block devices should return with the return status word set to 0100h, indicating that the command is finished.

If the device or driver has an input buffer available, this command clears the buffer. All information previously in the buffer is lost. Table 9.18 summarizes the flow of information through the request header for this command.

Table 9.18. Request header settings for the Input Flush command.

Offset	Bytes	Contents on Entry	Contents on Exit
00h	1	0Dh	0Dh
01h	1		
02h	1	7	
03h	2		Return status word
05h	8	Reserved	Reserved

Write

The Write command applies to both block and character devices. It causes the driver to transfer information from a memory buffer to the device. If an error occurs during the data transfer, all return values in the request header must be updated. Table 9.19 summarizes the flow of information through the request header for this command.

Table 9.19. Request header settings for the Write command.

Offset	Bytes	Contents on Entry	Contents on Exit
00h	1	1Eh	1Eh
01h	1	Unit code	
02h	1	8	
03h	2		Return status word
05h	8	Reserved	Reserved
0Dh	1	Media ID byte	
0Eh	4	Buffer address	
12h	2	Byte or sector count	Actual number of bytes or sectors transferred
14h	2	Starting sector number	
16h	4		Volume identifier
1Ah	4	32-bit sector number	Volume label address if error 0Fh is being returned

The 32-bit starting sector number at offset 16h is present only if the following conditions are met:

- The device is a block device.

- The logical drive is larger than 32M.

- Bit 1 of the device attribute word in the device header is set.

- The starting sector number at offset 14h is set to –1.

Write with Verify

The Write with Verify command applies only to block devices and is similar to the Write command. The difference is that this command is supposed to double-check the data transfer to make sure that it occurred correctly.

For information on how the request header should be used, refer to Table 9.19. The only difference is the command field at offset 02h, which is set to 9 when the command is entered.

Output Status

The Output Status command applies only to character devices; block devices should return with the return status word set to 0100h, indicating that the command is finished.

DOS uses this command to test whether a device is ready to receive characters. If the device is ready, the busy bit of the return status word is cleared and the command returns to DOS. If the device is not available to receive output, the busy bit is set and control returns. The return status word is the only information returned by this command. Table 9.20 summarizes the flow of information through the request header for this command.

Table 9.20. Request header settings for the Output Status command.

Offset	Bytes	Contents on Entry	Contents on Exit
00h	1	0Dh	0Dh
01h	1		
02h	1	0Ah	
03h	2		Return status word
05h	8	Reserved	Reserved

Output Flush

The Output Flush command applies only to character devices; block devices should return with the return status word set to 0100h, indicating that the command is finished.

If the device or driver has an output buffer available, this command clears the buffer. All information previously in the buffer is lost, and it is not sent to or used by the device. Table 9.21 summarizes the flow of information through the request header for this command.

Table 9.21. Request header settings for the Output Flush command.

Offset	Bytes	Contents on Entry	Contents on Exit
00h	1	0Dh	0Dh
01h	1		
02h	1	0Bh	
03h	2		Return status word
05h	8	Reserved	Reserved

Control Info Write

The Control Info Write command applies to both block and character devices. This command provides a way for an application to send control information directly to a device driver. The opposite of this command is the Control Info Read command, which enables the driver to communicate directly with the application.

DOS does no checking on the information passed with this command; it simply passes the information on. You cannot use this command, therefore, unless your application has a detailed understanding of how the device driver works. For this reason, the use of this command is limited among many drivers.

This command is valid only if bit 0Eh of the device attribute word in the device header is set. Table 9.22 summarizes the flow of information through the request header for this command.

Table 9.22. Request header settings for the Control Info Write command.			
Offset	Bytes	Contents on Entry	Contents on Exit
00h	1	14h	14h
01h	1	Unit code	
02h	1	0Ch	
03h	2		Return status word
05h	8	Reserved	Reserved
0Dh	1	Media ID byte	
0Eh	4	Buffer address	
12h	2	Byte count	Actual number of bytes transferred

Open Device

The Open Device command applies to both character and block devices and became available with DOS 3.0. Bit 0Bh of the device attribute word in the device header indicates whether your driver supports this command.

The Open Device command is called by DOS whenever it uses a function that results in a file being opened. If your driver supports removable media, you may want your driver to support this command by keeping count of the files currently open. In this way, you can indicate an error if you detect that the media has been changed while the file count is greater than 0.

For character devices, you may want to use this command to send an initialization string to the device being opened. Table 9.23 summarizes the flow of information through the request header for this command.

Table 9.23. Request header settings for the Open Device command.			
Offset	**Bytes**	**Contents on Entry**	**Contents on Exit**
00h	1	0Dh	0Dh
01h	1	Unit code	
02h	1	0Dh	
03h	2		Return status word
05h	8	Reserved	Reserved

Close Device

The Close Device command is the opposite of the Open Device command. It applies to both block and character devices and became available beginning with DOS 3.0. You should set bit 0Bh of the device attribute word in the device header if your driver supports this command.

The request header use is exactly the same for this command as it is for the Open Device command, except that the command field at offset 02h contains 0Eh when the command is entered.

Removable Media

The Removable Media command is applicable to block devices only, and only under DOS 3.0 or later. If you support this command in your driver, you should set bit 0Bh of the device attribute word in the device header.

On a character device, this command should set the return status word to 0100h (indicating that the command is finished) and return to DOS.

DOS typically calls this command only once to determine whether the device supports removable media. If it does, your driver should set the busy bit in the return status word; if not, the busy bit should be cleared. This information helps DOS optimize performance for dealing with your device. Table 9.24 summarizes the flow of information through the request header for this command.

Table 9.24. Request header settings for the Removable Media command.

Offset	Bytes	Contents on Entry	Contents on Exit
00h	1	0Dh	0Dh
01h	1	Unit code	
02h	1	0Fh	
03h	2		Return status word
05h	8	Reserved	Reserved

Output Until Busy

The Output Until Busy command applies only to character devices; block devices should return with the return status word set to 0100h, indicating that the command is finished. This command is supported beginning with DOS 3.0. If your device driver supports this command, you should set the 0Dh of the device attribute word in the device header.

This command should be used to send a steady stream of data to the device. Transfer ceases only when the device says to stop or when the entire transfer is completed. On return from this command, it is possible that the number of bytes actually transferred is less than the number requested. This is not an error; it means simply that the device accepted all that it could for now. Table 9.25 summarizes the flow of information through the request header for this command.

Table 9.25. Request header settings for the Output Until Busy command.

Offset	Bytes	Contents on Entry	Contents on Exit
00h	1	14h	14h
01h	1		
02h	1	10h	
03h	2		Return status word
05h	8	Reserved	Reserved
0Dh	1	Unused	
0Eh	4	Buffer address	
12h	2	Bytes to transfer	Actual number of bytes transferred

Generic IOCTL

The Generic IOCTL command applies to both character and block devices and became available with DOS 3.2. Bit 6 of the device attribute word in the device header indicates whether your driver supports this command.

The functions supported by this command should correspond closely to the command set for DOS function 44h, subfunctions 0Ch and 0Dh (see Chapter 8, "Using IOCTL"). The information passed to your driver in the request header indicates which subfunction is being requested; it is up to your driver to implement support for these commands. Table 9.26 summarizes the flow of information through the request header for this command.

Table 9.26. Request header settings for the Generic IOCTL command.

Offset	Bytes	Contents on Entry	Contents on Exit
00h	1	17h	17h
01h	1	Unit number	
02h	1	13h	
03h	2		Return status word
05h	8	Reserved	Reserved
0Dh	1	Major code	
0Eh	1	Minor code	
0Fh	2	Contents of SI	
11h	2	Contents of DI	
13h	4	Buffer address	

The buffer pointed to by the address at offset 13h is the IOCTL parameter block, which varies by subfunction.

Get Logical Device

The Get Logical Device command is applicable to only block devices, and only under DOS 3.2 or later. If you support this command in your driver, you should set bit 6 of the device attribute word in the device header.

On a character device, this command should set the return status word to 0100h (indicating that the command is finished) and return to DOS.

This command is issued by DOS when an application program uses DOS function 44h, subfunction 0Eh (Get Logical Device Map). This command has particular relevance to device drivers that support a single physical device, but refer to it as two separate drives. Perhaps the best-known example is a single-floppy computer system: The single floppy drive is referred to as both A and B. This command should return, in the unit code field of the request header, the unit number that was used when last referencing the device.

If a direct one-to-one correlation exists between physical and logical devices in your driver, a zero should be returned in the unit code field. Table 9.27 summarizes the flow of information through the request header for this command.

Table 9.27. Request header settings for the Get Logical Device command.

Offset	Bytes	Contents on Entry	Contents on Exit
00h	1	0Dh	0Dh
01h	1	Unit number	Unit number last referenced
02h	1	17h	
03h	2		Return status word
05h	8	Reserved	Reserved

For more information on how DOS function 44h, subfunction 0Eh (and by extension, this command) is used, refer to Chapter 8, "Using IOCTL."

Set Logical Device

The Set Logical Device command, the opposite of the Get Logical Device command, is applicable to only block devices, and only under DOS 3.2 or later. If you support this command in your driver, you should set bit 6 of the device attribute word in the device header.

On a character device, this command should set the return status word to 0100h (indicating that the command is finished) and return to DOS.

Because this command is so closely related to the Get Logical Device command, you should refer to the discussion there. This command is called whenever an application issues DOS function 44h, subfunction 0Fh (Set Logical Device Map).

The request header use is the same as for the Get Logical Device command (refer to Table 9.27) except that the command field at offset 02h is set to 18h, and the unit code field at offset 01h indicates the setting you want used to override the drive that your device was last referred to as.

IOCTL Query

The IOCTL Query command applies to both block and character devices, and became available beginning with DOS 5.0. You should set bit 7 of the device attribute word in the device header if your driver supports this command.

DOS issues this command when DOS function 44h, subfunction 10h or 11h is used. If your driver implements this command, you should indicate in the return status word whether you support the IOCTL function and (if present) minor code. If your driver does support it, it should return with the done bit in the return status word set. If it does not, an error code 3 (unknown function) should be signaled in the return status word. Table 9.28 summarizes the flow of information through the request header for this command.

Table 9.28. Request header settings for the IOCTL Query command.

Offset	Bytes	Contents on Entry	Contents on Exit
00h	1	17h	17h
01h	1	Unit number	Unit number last referenced
02h	1	19h	
03h	2		Return status word
05h	8	Reserved	Reserved
0Dh	1	Command in question	
0Eh	1	Minor code in question	
0Fh	4	Reserved	
13h	4	Buffer address	

Note that some entry fields for this request header are not fully explained or implemented in DOS 5.0. For example, the buffer address at offset 13h is included in the formal definition of the request header for this command but is not used and should not be modified by your driver.

Building Your Device Driver

Perhaps the best way to start writing device drivers is to practice with a do-nothing skeleton that will install and do nothing else. This action is permissible in DOS, but you should install only the driver if you boot from a floppy. In this way, you can always bring your system up from the hard disk normally if something goes awry.

The following program, EMPTYDRV.ASM, assembles and links into a character device driver. It does nothing except install so that you can at least see how installation works and ensure that the driver really will load.

To create a driver (assuming that you have the source code ready), follow these steps:

1. Assemble the program as a regular EXE file.

2. Link the program; do not be concerned about stack or entry point warning messages.

3. Use EXE2BIN to convert the EXE file to a binary image.

4. Rename the BIN file to a SYS file.

At this point, you are ready to install the driver and test it. Again, you should install the driver only on a bootable floppy disk, at least until you are sure that everything works the way it should. Listing 9.1 shows the source code for EMPTYDRV.ASM.

Listing 9.1. EMPTYDRV.ASM

```
Page 60,132

Comment ¦
******************************************************************

File:       EMPTYDRV.ASM
Author:     Allen L. Wyatt
Date:       7/28/92
Assembler:  MASM 6.0

Purpose:    Skeleton device driver. Simply displays a message at
            installation. All other commands simply return with
            the done bit in the return status word set.

Format:     DEVICE = EMPTYDRV.SYS


******************************************************************¦
                                                                 ¦

; The following are equates used in this file

RHLength    TEXTEQU <SI>
UnitCode    TEXTEQU <SI+1>
Command     TEXTEQU <SI+2>
```

```
ReturnStat   TEXTEQU <SI+3>

; Error code equates

WPErr         EQU     00h
UnUnit        EQU     01h
NotReady      EQU     02h
BadCmd        EQU     03h
CRCErr        EQU     04h
BadRSLength   EQU     05h
SeekErr       EQU     06h
UnMedia       EQU     07h
SecNotFound   EQU     08h
OutOfPaper    EQU     09h
WriteFault    EQU     0Ah
ReadFault     EQU     0Bh
GeneralFail   EQU     0Ch
BadChange     EQU     0Fh


; Start of real program

_TEXT         SEGMENT WORD PUBLIC 'CODE'
              ASSUME CS:_TEXT, DS:_TEXT, ES:NOTHING
              ORG     0                     ;Boot sector will be here

; Start of device driver header

              DD      -1                    ;Next-driver link set by DOS
              DW      0C840h                ;Device attribute
              DW      OFFSET Strategy       ;Point to strategy routine
              DW      OFFSET Interrupt      ;Point to interrupt routine
              DB      'EMPTYDRV'            ;Device name

; Other data used by the driver

RHaddress     DW      0000,0000             ;Request header address storage

CmdTable      DW      OFFSET Init           ;Init
              DW      OFFSET MediaChk       ;Media Check
              DW      OFFSET BuildBPB       ;Build BPB
```

continues

Listing 9.1. Continued

```
        DW      OFFSET ReadInfo     ;Control Info Read
        DW      OFFSET Read         ;Read
        DW      OFFSET NDRead       ;Nondestructive Read
        DW      OFFSET InStat       ;Input Status
        DW      OFFSET InFlush      ;Input Flush
        DW      OFFSET Write        ;Write
        DW      OFFSET WriteVfy     ;Write with Verify
        DW      OFFSET OutStat      ;Output Status
        DW      OFFSET OutFlush     ;Output Flush
        DW      OFFSET WriteInfo    ;Control Info Write
        DW      OFFSET Open         ;Open Device
        DW      OFFSET Close        ;Close Device
        DW      OFFSET Removeable   ;Removeable Media
        DW      OFFSET OutTilBusy   ;Output Until Busy
        DW      OFFSET BadCommand   ;BadCommand
        DW      OFFSET BadCommand   ;BadCommand
        DW      OFFSET Generic      ;Generic IOCTL
        DW      OFFSET BadCommand   ;BadCommand
        DW      OFFSET BadCommand   ;BadCommand
        DW      OFFSET BadCommand   ;BadCommand
        DW      OFFSET GetDevice    ;Get Logical Device
        DW      OFFSET SetDevice    ;Set Logical Device
        DW      OFFSET Query        ;IOCTL Query

; Start of device driver strategy routine

Strategy    PROC    FAR
            MOV     CS:RHaddress[0],BX  ;Offset of request header
            MOV     CS:RHaddress[2],ES  ;Segment of request header
            RET
Strategy    ENDP

; Start of device driver interrupt routine

Interrupt   PROC    FAR
            PUSHF                       ;Save all the registers
            PUSH    AX
            PUSH    BX
            PUSH    CX
            PUSH    DX
```

```
        PUSH    SI
        PUSH    DI
        PUSH    DS
        PUSH    ES
        PUSH    BP

        PUSH    CS                      ;Set up addressing
        POP     DS

        MOV     SI,RHaddress[0]         ;Offset of request header
        MOV     ES,RHaddress[2]         ;Segment of request header
        MOV     BL,ES:[Command]         ;Get command from request header
        CMP     BL,25                   ;Is command out of range?
        JBE     CmdOK
        CALL    BadCommand
        JMP     AllDone

CmdOK:  MOV     BH,0
        SHL     BX,1                    ;Set up addressing for CmdTable
        CALL    WORD PTR [BX+CmdTable]

; When entering the command handlers, ES:SI is set to the address of
; the request header.

; When returning from the command handler, AX should be set with the
; return code. Following code determines whether AL has an error code
; in it, and sets the error bit accordingly. In any case, the done bit
; is set prior to return.

AllDone:  CMP   AL,0                    ;Is there an error code?
          JE    NoError                 ;No, so continue
          OR    AH,10000000b            ;Turn on error bit
NoError:  OR    AH,00000001b            ;Turn on done bit
          MOV   ES:[ReturnStat],AX      ;Store for return

          POP   BP                      ;Restore all registers
          POP   ES
          POP   DS
          POP   DI
          POP   SI
          POP   DX
          POP   CX
```

continues

Listing 9.1. Continued

```
                POP     BX
                POP     AX
                POPF
                RET
Interrupt       ENDP


; The following are the command handlers called from
; the interrupt routine

MediaChk        PROC    NEAR            ;Command 01h - Media Check

                MOV     AX,0            ;Set return code
                RET
MediaChk        ENDP


BuildBPB        PROC    NEAR            ;Command 02h - Build BPB

                MOV     AX,0            ;Set return code
                RET
BuildBPB        ENDP


ReadInfo        PROC    NEAR            ;Command 03h - Control Info Read

                MOV     AX,0            ;Set return code
                RET
ReadInfo        ENDP


Read            PROC    NEAR            ;Command 04h - Read

                MOV     AX,0            ;Set return code
                RET
Read            ENDP


NDRead          PROC    NEAR            ;Command 05h - Nondestructive Read

                MOV     AX,0            ;Set return code
                RET
NDRead          ENDP
```

```
InStat        PROC    NEAR            ;Command 06h - Input Status

              MOV     AX,0            ;Set return code
              RET
InStat        ENDP


InFlush       PROC    NEAR            ;Command 07h - Input Flush

              MOV     AX,0            ;Set return code
              RET
InFlush       ENDP


Write         PROC    NEAR            ;Command 08h - Write

              MOV     AX,0            ;Set return code
              RET
Write         ENDP


WriteVfy      PROC    NEAR            ;Command 09h - Write with Verify

              MOV     AX,0            ;Set return code
              RET
WriteVfy      ENDP


OutStat       PROC    NEAR            ;Command 0Ah - Output Status

              MOV     AX,0            ;Set return code
              RET
OutStat       ENDP


OutFlush      PROC    NEAR            ;Command 0Bh - Output Flush

              MOV     AX,0            ;Set return code
              RET
OutFlush      ENDP


WriteInfo     PROC    NEAR            ;Command 0Ch - Control Info Write

              MOV     AX,0            ;Set return code
              RET
WriteInfo     ENDP
```

continues

Listing 9.1. Continued

```
Open         PROC    NEAR                    ;Command 0Dh - Open Device

             MOV     AX,0                    ;Set return code
             RET
Open         ENDP


Close        PROC    NEAR                    ;Command 0Eh - Close Device

             MOV     AX,0                    ;Set return code
             RET
Close        ENDP


Removeable   PROC    NEAR                    ;Command 0Fh - Removeable Media

             MOV     AX,0                    ;Set return code
             RET
Removeable   ENDP


OutTilBusy   PROC    NEAR                    ;Command 10h - Output Until Busy

             MOV     AX,0                    ;Set return code
             RET
OutTilBusy   ENDP


Generic      PROC    NEAR                    ;Command 13h - Generic IOCTL

             MOV     AX,0                    ;Set return code
             RET
Generic      ENDP


GetDevice    PROC    NEAR                    ;Command 17h - Get Logical Device

             MOV     AX,0                    ;Set return code
             RET
GetDevice    ENDP


SetDevice    PROC    NEAR                    ;Command 18h - Set Logical Device

             MOV     AX,0                    ;Set return code
             RET
SetDevice    ENDP
```

```
Query       PROC    NEAR                    ;Command 19h - IOCTL Query

            MOV     AX,0                    ;Set return code
            RET
Query       ENDP


BadCommand  PROC    NEAR                    ;BadCommand
            MOV     AX,BadCmd               ;Set return code
            RET
BadCommand  ENDP


Init        PROC    NEAR                    ;Command 00h - Init
            PUSH    SI
            MOV     SI,OFFSET Welcome
            CALL    PrtString
            POP     SI
            MOV     ES:[SI+0Eh],OFFSET Init
            MOV     ES:[SI+10h],CS
            MOV     AX,0                    ;Set return code
            RET
Init        ENDP


; The following routine prints the ASCIIZ string pointed to by DS:SI

PrtString   PROC    NEAR USES AX DX SI
PS1:        MOV     DL,[SI]                 ;Get character
            INC     SI                      ;Point to next one
            CMP     DL,0                    ;End of string?
            JE      PS2                     ;Yes, so exit
            MOV     AH,02h                  ;Output a character
            INT     21h
            JMP     PS1                     ;Keep doing it
PS2:        RET
PrtString   ENDP


Welcome     DB      13,10,13,10
            DB      '         --- EMPTYDRV now loaded ---',13,10
            DB      ' Source code from Advanced Assembly Language',13,10
            DB      '                 by Allen L. Wyatt',13,10,10,10,0


_TEXT       ENDS
            END
```

Notice that command 0, Init, is physically situated at the end of the file so that the routine can be truncated after installation and initialization are complete. DOS takes care of this procedure automatically because of the end-of-program address loaded into the request header when initialization is completed.

A Practical Character Device Driver

In the preceding sections you learned how to make a bare-bones character device driver. This section expands on that template and creates a device driver that provides a useful system enhancement.

I'm sure that most readers are familiar with the MORE command. That program enables you to pipe input into it and have it paged to the screen. This capability is handy, but why not make the capability part of the system? The following device driver, presented in SCREEN.ASM, provides that capability. After it is installed in your system as a device, you can access the SCREEN device in any way you normally access a device, including the following:

- As the recipient of the copy command, that is,
  COPY FILENAME.EXT SCREEN

- As the recipient of redirected output, that is,
  TYPE FILENAME.EXT >SCREEN

- In an application program in which you open the device for output and write information to it

Whatever information you send to the SCREEN device is displayed on your monitor one screen at a time. When the screen is full, you are prompted to press a key for the next screen. Listing 9.2 shows the source code for SCREEN.SYS.

Listing 9.2. SCREEN.ASM

```
Page 60,132

Comment ¦
******************************************************************


File:      SCREEN.ASM
Author:    Allen L. Wyatt
Date:      7/28/92
Assembler: MASM 6.0
```

```
Purpose:    Installable character device driver. Can be used in
            programs or from the command line to display a screen
            of information at a time, and then pause for the user
            to press a key.

Format:     Installation:  DEVICE = SCREEN.SYS
            Use:  COPY FILENAME.EXT SCREEN
                  TYPE FILENAME.EXE >SCREEN
                  or, open the device for output


********************************************************************!
                                                                   ¦

; The following are equates used in this file

RHLength     TEXTEQU <SI>
UnitCode     TEXTEQU <SI+1>
Command      TEXTEQU <SI+2>
ReturnStat   TEXTEQU <SI+3>


LinesPer     EQU     23                 ;Number of lines to display per screen

; Error code equates

WPErr        EQU     00h
UnUnit       EQU     01h
NotReady     EQU     02h
BadCmd       EQU     03h
CRCErr       EQU     04h
BadRSLength  EQU     05h
SeekErr      EQU     06h
UnMedia      EQU     07h
SecNotFound  EQU     08h
OutOfPaper   EQU     09h
WriteFault   EQU     0Ah
ReadFault    EQU     0Bh
GeneralFail  EQU     0Ch
BadChange    EQU     0Fh



; Start of real program
```

continues

Listing 9.2. Continued

```
_TEXT         SEGMENT WORD PUBLIC 'CODE'
              ASSUME CS:_TEXT, DS:_TEXT, ES:NOTHING
              ORG     0                       ;Boot sector will be here

; Start of device driver header

              DD      -1                      ;Next-driver link set by DOS
              DW      0A800h                  ;Device attribute
              DW      OFFSET Strategy         ;Point to strategy routine
              DW      OFFSET Interrupt        ;Point to interrupt routine
              DB      'SCREEN  '              ;Device name

; Other data used by the driver

RHaddress     DW      0000,0000               ;Request header address storage

CharWanted    DW      0000                    ;Number of characters to transfer
CharDone      DW      0000                    ;Number done
CharCol       DB      00                      ;Character per line
VidPage       DB      -1                      ;Current video page
PauseMsg      DB      'Press any key to continue...',0
CRLF          DB      13,10,0

CmdTable      DW      OFFSET Init             ;Init
              DW      OFFSET MediaChk         ;Media Check
              DW      OFFSET BuildBPB         ;Build BPB
              DW      OFFSET ReadInfo         ;Control Info Read
              DW      OFFSET Read             ;Read
              DW      OFFSET NDRead           ;Nondestructive Read
              DW      OFFSET InStat           ;Input Status
              DW      OFFSET InFlush          ;Input Flush
              DW      OFFSET Write            ;Write
              DW      OFFSET WriteVfy         ;Write with Verify
              DW      OFFSET OutStat          ;Output Status
              DW      OFFSET OutFlush         ;Output Flush
              DW      OFFSET WriteInfo        ;Control Info Write
              DW      OFFSET Open             ;Open Device
              DW      OFFSET Close            ;Close Device
              DW      OFFSET Removeable       ;Removeable Media
              DW      OFFSET OutTilBusy       ;Output Until Busy
```

```
            DW      OFFSET BadCommand    ;BadCommand
            DW      OFFSET BadCommand    ;BadCommand
            DW      OFFSET Generic       ;Generic IOCTL
            DW      OFFSET BadCommand    ;BadCommand
            DW      OFFSET BadCommand    ;BadCommand
            DW      OFFSET BadCommand    ;BadCommand
            DW      OFFSET GetDevice     ;Get Logical Device
            DW      OFFSET SetDevice     ;Set Logical Device
            DW      OFFSET Query         ;IOCTL Query

; Start of device driver strategy routine

Strategy    PROC    FAR
            MOV     CS:RHaddress[0],BX   ;Offset of request header
            MOV     CS:RHaddress[2],ES   ;Segment of request header
            RET
Strategy    ENDP

; Start of device driver interrupt routine

Interrupt   PROC    FAR
            PUSHF                        ;Save all the registers
            PUSH    AX
            PUSH    BX
            PUSH    CX
            PUSH    DX
            PUSH    SI
            PUSH    DI
            PUSH    DS
            PUSH    ES
            PUSH    BP

            PUSH    CS                   ;Set up addressing
            POP     DS

            MOV     SI,RHaddress[0]      ;Offset of request header
            MOV     ES,RHaddress[2]      ;Segment of request header
            MOV     BL,ES:[Command]      ;Get command from request header
            CMP     BL,25                ;Is command out of range?
            JBE     CmdOK
            CALL    BadCommand
            JMP     AllDone
```

continues

Listing 9.2. Continued

```
CmdOK:      MOV    BH,0
            SHL    BX,1                        ;Set up addressing for CmdTable
            CALL   WORD PTR [BX+CmdTable]

; When entering the command handlers, ES:SI is set to the address of
; the request header.

; When returning from the command handler, AX should be set with the
; return code. Following code determines whether AL has an error code
; in it, and sets the error bit accordingly. In any case, the done bit
; is set prior to return.

AllDone:    CMP    AL,0                 ;Is there an error code?
            JE     NoError              ;No, so continue
            OR     AH,10000000b         ;Turn on error bit
NoError:    OR     AH,00000001b         ;Turn on done bit
            MOV    ES:[ReturnStat],AX   ;Store for return

            POP    BP                   ;Restore all registers
            POP    ES
            POP    DS
            POP    DI
            POP    SI
            POP    DX
            POP    CX
            POP    BX
            POP    AX
            POPF
            RET
Interrupt   ENDP


; The following are the command handlers called from
; the interrupt routine

MediaChk    PROC   NEAR                 ;Command 01h - Media Check

            MOV    AX,0                 ;Set return code
            RET
MediaChk    ENDP
```

```
BuildBPB    PROC    NEAR                ;Command 02h - Build BPB

            MOV     AX,0                ;Set return code
            RET
BuildBPB    ENDP

ReadInfo    PROC    NEAR                ;Command 03h - Control Info Read

            MOV     AX,0                ;Set return code
            RET
ReadInfo    ENDP

Read        PROC    NEAR                ;Command 04h - Read

            MOV     AX,0                ;Set return code
            RET
Read        ENDP

NDRead      PROC    NEAR                ;Command 05h - Nondestructive Read

            MOV     AX,0200h            ;Set busy bit in return code
            RET                         ; (no characters waiting in buffer)
NDRead      ENDP

InStat      PROC    NEAR                ;Command 06h - Input Status

            MOV     AX,0                ;Set return code
            RET
InStat      ENDP

InFlush     PROC    NEAR                ;Command 07h - Input Flush

            MOV     AX,0                ;Set return code
            RET
InFlush     ENDP

Write       PROC    NEAR USES BX CX     ;Command 08h - Write
            PUSH    ES
            PUSH    SI
            CALL    SetParms
```

continues

Listing 9.2. Continued

```
                MOV     AX,ES:[SI+0Eh]          ;Get offset
                MOV     BX,ES:[SI+10h]          ;Get segment
                MOV     CX,ES:[SI+12h]          ;Character count
                MOV     CharWanted,CX           ;Characters wanted
                MOV     CharDone,0              ;Actually done
                JCXZ    WriteDone               ;Nothing to transfer

                MOV     ES,BX                   ;Set up addressing
                MOV     SI,AX                   ;Now ES:SI points to transfer buffer
                CALL    DoScreen

WriteDone:      POP     SI
                POP     ES
                MOV     AX,0                    ;Assume no errors
                MOV     CX,CharDone
                MOV     ES:[SI+12h],CX          ;Number transferred
                CMP     CX,CharWanted
                JE      WriteEnd
                MOV     AL,WriteFault           ;Set for error
WriteEnd:       RET
Write           ENDP

WriteVfy        PROC    NEAR                    ;Command 09h - Write with Verify

                MOV     AX,0                    ;Set return code
                RET
WriteVfy        ENDP

OutStat         PROC    NEAR                    ;Command 0Ah - Output Status

                MOV     AX,0                    ;Set return code
                RET
OutStat         ENDP

OutFlush        PROC    NEAR                    ;Command 0Bh - Output Flush

                MOV     AX,0                    ;Set return code
                RET
OutFlush        ENDP
```

```
WriteInfo   PROC    NEAR                    ;Command 0Ch - Control Info Write

            MOV     AX,0                    ;Set return code
            RET
WriteInfo   ENDP


Open        PROC    NEAR                    ;Command 0Dh - Open Device
            CALL    SetParms
            CALL    Cls
            MOV     AX,0                    ;Set return code
            RET
Open        ENDP


Close       PROC    NEAR                    ;Command 0Eh - Close Device

            MOV     AX,0                    ;Set return code
            RET
Close       ENDP


Removeable  PROC    NEAR                    ;Command 0Fh - Removeable Media

            MOV     AX,0                    ;Set return code
            RET
Removeable  ENDP


OutTilBusy  PROC    NEAR                    ;Command 10h - Output Until Busy
            CALL    Write                   ;Handled by same routines
            AND     AX,7F00h                ;Turn off any errors
            RET
OutTilBusy  ENDP


Generic     PROC    NEAR                    ;Command 13h - Generic IOCTL

            MOV     AX,0                    ;Set return code
            RET
Generic     ENDP


GetDevice   PROC    NEAR                    ;Command 17h - Get Logical Device

            MOV     AX,0                    ;Set return code
            RET
```

continues

Listing 9.2. Continued

```
GetDevice   ENDP

SetDevice   PROC    NEAR                    ;Command 18h - Set Logical Device

            MOV     AX,0                    ;Set return code
            RET
SetDevice   ENDP

Query       PROC    NEAR                    ;Command 19h - IOCTL Query

            MOV     AX,0                    ;Set return code
            RET
Query       ENDP

BadCommand  PROC    NEAR                    ;BadCommand
            MOV     AX,BadCmd               ;Set return code
            RET
BadCommand  ENDP


; From here down through the rest of the driver are routines used
; in the command handlers

; Set parameters for video page and screen width

SetParms    PROC    NEAR USES AX BX
            MOV     AH,0Fh                  ;Get display mode
            INT     10h
            MOV     VidPage,BH              ;Display page
            MOV     CharCol,AH              ;Store character per line
            RET
SetParms    ENDP

; Display a screen of information. Enter with CX set to the number
; of characters to be displayed.

DoScreen    PROC    NEAR USES AX BX CX DX SI
            MOV     BH,VidPage              ;Grab video page
DSLoop:     PUSH    CX                      ;Store loop counter
            MOV     AL,ES:[SI]              ;Grab character
```

```
            INC     SI                  ;Point to next character
            MOV     AH,0Eh              ;BIOS output in teletype mode
            INT     10h
            INC     CharDone            ;Number of characters transferred

            MOV     AH,03h              ;Get cursor position
            INT     10h
            CMP     DH,LinesPer         ;Reached full screen?
            JB      DS2                 ;No, continue
            CALL    PagePause
            CALL    Cls
DS2:        POP     CX                  ;Get back loop counter
            LOOP    DSLoop

            RET
DoScreen    ENDP
```

; The following routine clears the screen and homes the cursor

```
Cls         PROC    USES AX BX CX DX
            MOV     AH,6                ;Scroll window up
            MOV     AL,0                ;Scroll full screen
            MOV     BH,7                ;Normal white on black
            MOV     CX,0                ;Upper left corner of screen
            MOV     DH,24               ;Bottom right
            MOV     DL,CharCol
            INT     10h

            MOV     DX,0                ;Upper left corner of screen
            MOV     BH,VidPage          ;Video page
            MOV     AH,2                ;Set cursor position
            INT     10h
            RET
Cls         ENDP
```

; The following routine pauses at the bottom of a page

```
PagePause   PROC    USES AX BX DX SI
            MOV     DH,24               ;Set up to print pause message
            MOV     DL,0
            MOV     BH,VidPage          ;Video page
            MOV     AH,2                ;Set cursor position
```

continues

Listing 9.2. Continued

```
            INT     10h
            MOV     SI,OFFSET PauseMsg   ;Point to start of pause message
            CALL    PrtString            ;Display the string
            MOV     AH,0                 ;Read keyboard character
            INT     16h
            RET
PagePause   ENDP


; The following routine prints the ASCIIZ string pointed to by DS:SI

PrtString   PROC    NEAR USES AX BX SI
            MOV     BH,VidPage
PS1:        MOV     AL,[SI]              ;Get character
            INC     SI                   ;Point to next one
            CMP     AL,0                 ;End of string?
            JE      PS2                  ;Yes, so exit
            MOV     AH,0Eh               ;Output a character
            INT     10h
            JMP     PS1                  ;Keep doing it
PS2:        RET
PrtString   ENDP



; Init command. This part of the driver is stripped after installation

Init        PROC    NEAR                 ;Command 00h - Init
            PUSH    SI
            MOV     SI,OFFSET Welcome
            CALL    PrtString
            POP     SI
            MOV     ES:[SI+0Eh],OFFSET Init
            MOV     ES:[SI+10h],CS
            MOV     AX,0                 ;Set return code
            RET
Init        ENDP

Welcome     DB      13,10,13,10
```

```
          DB          '--- SCREEN now loaded ---',13,10,13,10,0

_TEXT       ENDS
            END
```

The only IOCTL commands necessary to implement in this driver are the Init, Write, Open, and Output Until Busy commands. You may want to take a moment to examine how these commands are implemented.

Note that if you are using a display that has more than 25 lines of text on the screen, you can adjust the driver for this display by changing the LinesPer equate near the beginning of the program. This equate indicates how many lines of text you want displayed at a time.

A Practical Block Device Driver

Earlier in this chapter, you learned the basics of what is necessary to make a device driver. In this section, you learn how to create a block device driver.

Perhaps the classic example of a block device driver is a RAM disk. The program presented in this section, EMSDISK.ASM, creates a 720K RAM disk in expanded memory by using the EMS functions described in Chapter 6, "Expanded and Extended Memory."

To install a RAM disk in expanded memory, you must make sure that the EMM is installed before loading this device driver (because this driver relies on functions provided by the EMM). During the load process, the Init function of the driver does the following:

1. Determines whether the EMM is present and compatible with at least EMS 3.0

2. Determines the page frame used by the EMM

3. Determines whether enough pages are available to implement the RAM disk (45 16K-pages are needed for a 720K disk)

4. Allocates the necessary pages and initializes them to 0

5. "Formats" the RAM disk by creating a boot sector, FAT, and directory

When these steps are completed, the RAM disk is treated just like another disk drive by DOS. The only major logic you need to provide is for the Read and Write commands. Listing 9.3 shows the source code for EMSDRIVE.ASM.

Listing 9.3. EMSDISK.ASM

```
Page 60,132

Comment |
*********************************************************************


File:       EMSDISK.ASM
Author:     Allen L. Wyatt
Date:       8/1/92
Assembler:  MASM 6.0

Purpose:    Simple RAM drive that uses EMS memory. Installs a
            720K disk that uses the next available drive name.

Format:     Installation:  DEVICE = EMSDISK.SYS


*********************************************************************|
                                                                    |

; The following are equates used in this file

RHLength    TEXTEQU <SI>
UnitCode    TEXTEQU <SI+1>
Command     TEXTEQU <SI+2>
ReturnStat  TEXTEQU <SI+3>


; Equates used in program

SectSize    EQU     512                 ;Bytes per sector on RAM disk
RootDE      EQU     112                 ;Root directory entries
TtlSect     EQU     32*45               ;Modified 720K 3 1/2-inch disk
MediaID     EQU     0F9h                ;Use media ID for 720K 3 1/2-inch disk
NumFATs     EQU     1                   ;Number of FATs in disk (need only 1)
FATSect     EQU     3                   ;Number of sectors per FAT
RDStart     EQU     NumFATs*FATSect+1   ;Where the root directory starts


; Error code equates

WPErr       EQU     00h
UnUnit      EQU     01h
NotReady    EQU     02h
BadCmd      EQU     03h
CRCErr      EQU     04h
```

```
BadRSLength EQU      05h
SeekErr     EQU      06h
UnMedia     EQU      07h
SecNotFound EQU      08h
OutOfPaper  EQU      09h
WriteFault  EQU      0Ah
ReadFault   EQU      0Bh
GeneralFail EQU      0Ch
BadChange   EQU      0Fh


; Start of real program

_TEXT       SEGMENT WORD PUBLIC 'CODE'
            ASSUME CS:_TEXT, DS:_TEXT, ES:NOTHING
            ORG     0                    ;Boot sector will be here

; Start of device driver header

            DD      -1                   ;Next-driver link set by DOS
            DW      0800h                ;Device attribute
            DW      OFFSET Strategy      ;Point to strategy routine
            DW      OFFSET Interrupt     ;Point to interrupt routine
            DB      1                    ;Number of units controlled
            DB      7 DUP(0)             ;Device name

; Other data used by the driver

RHaddress   DW      0000,0000            ;Request header address storage

; This RAM disk is set up to have 45 32-sector tracks. That is because
; 32 512-byte sectors will fit in one 16K EMS page. Makes life easier later.

BootRec     EQU     THIS BYTE
            NOP                          ;Three bytes normally for jump statement
            NOP
            NOP
            DB      'MSDOS5.0'
BPB         DW      SectSize             ;Bytes per sector
            DB      02                   ;Sectors per cluster
            DW      0001                 ;Reserved sectors
```

continues

Listing 9.3. Continued

```
              DB      NumFATs             ;Number of FATs
              DW      RootDE              ;Number of root directory entries
              DW      TtlSect             ;Numer of sectors on disk
              DB      MediaID             ;Media ID
              DW      FATSect             ;Sectors per FAT
              DW      32                  ;Sectors per track
              DW      0001                ;Number of heads
              DD      00000000            ;Unused in our disk
              DD      00000000
              DB      6 DUP (0)
BRLen         EQU     $-OFFSET BootRec

SaveSS        DW      0000                ;Used to store DOS's stack pointers
SaveSP        DW      0000
Drive         DB      00                  ;Store drive assigned to this device
MemHandle     DW      0000                ;EMS memory block handle
PageFrame     DW      0000                ;EMS page frame
SectOff       DW      0000                ;Offset of sector in page frame
BuffOff       DW      0000
BuffSeg       DW      0000
SectCount     DW      0000
SectStart     DW      0000
SectDone      DW      0000                ;Sectors actually transferred

              EVEN                        ;Set up driver's stack area
              DW      128 DUP(0)
StackTop      EQU     $

CmdTable      DW      OFFSET Init         ;00 - Init
              DW      OFFSET MediaChk     ;01 - Media Check
              DW      OFFSET BuildBPB     ;02 - Build BPB
              DW      OFFSET MarkAsDone   ;03 - Control Info Read
              DW      OFFSET Read         ;04 - Read
              DW      OFFSET MarkAsDone   ;05 - Nondestructive Read
              DW      OFFSET MarkAsDone   ;06 - Input Status
              DW      OFFSET MarkAsDone   ;07 - Input Flush
              DW      OFFSET Write        ;08 - Write
              DW      OFFSET Write        ;09 - Write with Verify
              DW      OFFSET MarkAsDone   ;0A - Output Status
              DW      OFFSET MarkAsDone   ;0B - Output Flush
```

```
        DW      OFFSET MarkAsDone    ;0C - Control Info Write
        DW      OFFSET MarkAsDone    ;0D - Open Device
        DW      OFFSET MarkAsDone    ;0E - Close Device
        DW      OFFSET Removeable    ;0F - Removeable Media
        DW      OFFSET MarkAsDone    ;10 - Output Until Busy
        DW      OFFSET BadCommand    ;11 - BadCommand
        DW      OFFSET BadCommand    ;12 - BadCommand
        DW      OFFSET MarkAsDone    ;13 - Generic IOCTL
        DW      OFFSET BadCommand    ;14 - BadCommand
        DW      OFFSET BadCommand    ;15 - BadCommand
        DW      OFFSET BadCommand    ;16 - BadCommand
        DW      OFFSET MarkAsDone    ;17 - Get Logical Device
        DW      OFFSET MarkAsDone    ;18 - Set Logical Device
        DW      OFFSET MarkAsDone    ;19 - IOCTL Query

; Start of device driver strategy routine

Strategy    PROC    FAR
            MOV     CS:RHaddress[0],BX    ;Offset of request header
            MOV     CS:RHaddress[2],ES    ;Segment of request header
            RET
Strategy    ENDP

; Start of device driver interrupt routine

Interrupt   PROC    FAR
            PUSHF                         ;Save all the registers
            PUSH    AX
            PUSH    BX
            PUSH    CX
            PUSH    DX
            PUSH    SI
            PUSH    DI
            PUSH    DS
            PUSH    ES
            PUSH    BP

            MOV     AX,CS                 ;Set up addressing and stack
            MOV     DS,AX
            MOV     SaveSS,SS             ;Save DOS stack context
            MOV     SaveSP,SP
            MOV     SS,AX
```

continues

Listing 9.3. Continued

```
            MOV     SP,OFFSET StackTop

            MOV     SI,RHaddress[0]     ;Offset of request header
            MOV     ES,RHaddress[2]     ;Segment of request header
            MOV     BL,ES:[Command]     ;Get command from request header
            CMP     BL,25               ;Is command out of range?
            JBE     CmdOK
            CALL    BadCommand
            JMP     AllDone             ;Bypass context save and exit with error

CmdOK:      CMP     BL,0                ;Are we doing Init?
            JE      DoJump              ;Yes, skip EMS context call
            CALL    PutContext          ;Save current context
            JNC     DoJump              ;No error, continue
            MOV     AL,GeneralFail      ;Mark for general failure
            JMP     AllDone             ;And exit

DoJump:     MOV     BH,0
            SHL     BX,1                ;Set up addressing for CmdTable
            CALL    WORD PTR [BX+CmdTable]

; When entering the command handlers, ES:SI is set to the address of
; the request header.

; When returning from the command handler, AX should be set with the
; return code. Following code saves new EMS context, determines whether
; AL has an error code in it, and sets the error bit accordingly.
; In any case, the done bit is set prior to return.

            MOV     SI,RHaddress[0]     ;Offset of request header
            MOV     ES,RHaddress[2]     ;Segment of request header
            CMP     BYTE PTR ES:[Command],0 ;Are you finishing an Init?
            JE      AllDone             ;Yes, so don't restore context
            CALL    GetContext          ;Get back context
            JNC     AllDone             ;No error in this routine
            CMP     AL,0                ;Preexisting error?
            JNE     AllDone             ;Yes, so continue
            MOV     AL,GeneralFail      ;Mark for general failure and proceed
```

```
AllDone:    CMP     AL,0                    ;Is there an error code?
            JE      NoError                 ;No, so continue
            OR      AH,10000000b            ;Turn on error bit
NoError:    OR      AH,00000001b            ;Turn on done bit
            MOV     ES:[ReturnStat],AX      ;Store for return

            MOV     SS,SaveSS               ;Restore DOS stack context
            MOV     SP,SaveSP
            POP     BP                      ;Restore all registers
            POP     ES
            POP     DS
            POP     DI
            POP     SI
            POP     DX
            POP     CX
            POP     BX
            POP     AX
            POPF
            RET
Interrupt   ENDP



; The following are the command handlers called from
; the interrupt routine

MediaChk    PROC    NEAR                    ;Command 01h - Media Check
            MOV     BYTE PTR ES:[SI+0Eh],1  ;Disk not changed (couldn't be)
            MOV     AX,0                    ;Set return code
            RET
MediaChk    ENDP

BuildBPB    PROC    NEAR                    ;Command 02h - Build BPB
            MOV     ES:[SI+12h],OFFSET BPB  ;Point to BPB
            MOV     ES:[SI+14h],DS
            MOV     AX,0                    ;Set return code
            RET
BuildBPB    ENDP


; Command 04h - Read
```

continues

Listing 9.3. Continued

```
Read        PROC    NEAR USES BX CX DX SI DI ES
            CALL    XferSetup               ;Set up variables
            MOV     CX,SectCount            ;Number of sectors to transfer
            MOV     AX,SectStart            ;Starting sector number
            MOV     ES,BuffSeg
            MOV     DI,BuffOff

ReadLoop:   CALL    FindSect
            JC      ReadErr
            PUSH    CX                      ;Save exterior loop
            MOV     CX,SectSize
            MOV     SI,SectOff
            MOV     BX,PageFrame
            PUSH    DS                      ;Store temporarily
            MOV     DS,BX
            CLD                             ;Go proper direction
            REP     MOVSB
            POP     DS                      ;Get back addressing
            INC     AX                      ;Point to next sector
            POP     CX                      ;Get exterior loop back
            INC     SectDone                ;Finished another one
            LOOP    ReadLoop
            MOV     AX,0                    ;Set return code
            JMP     ReadDone

ReadErr:    MOV     AX,SecNotFound          ;Sector not found
ReadDone:   MOV     SI,RHaddress[0]         ;Offset of request header
            MOV     ES,RHaddress[2]         ;Segment of request header
            MOV     BX,SectDone
            MOV     ES:[SI+12h],BX
            RET
Read        ENDP


; Command 08h - Write

Write       PROC    NEAR USES BX CX DX  ;Command 08h - Write
            CALL    XferSetup           ;Set up variables
            MOV     CX,SectCount        ;Number of sectors to transfer
            MOV     AX,SectStart        ;Starting sector number
```

```
            MOV      SI,BuffOff
            MOV      ES,PageFrame

WriteLoop:  CALL     FindSect
            JC       WriteErr
            PUSH     CX                    ;Save exterior loop
            MOV      DI,SectOff            ;Proper place in page frame
            MOV      CX,SectSize           ;Bytes to transfer
            MOV      BX,BuffSeg
            PUSH     DS                    ;Set up for transfer
            MOV      DS,BX                 ;DS:SI points to buffer
            CLD                            ;Proper direction
            REP      MOVSB                 ;Transfer to EMS area
            POP      DS                    ;Get back proper data segment
            INC      AX                    ;Point to next sector
            POP      CX                    ;Get exterior loop back
            INC      SectDone              ;Finished another one
            LOOP     WriteLoop
            MOV      AX,0                  ;Set return code
            JMP      WriteDone

WriteErr:   MOV      AX,SecNotFound        ;Sector not found
WriteDone:  MOV      SI,RHaddress[0]       ;Offset of request header
            MOV      ES,RHaddress[2]       ;Segment of request header
            MOV      BX,SectDone
            MOV      ES:[SI+12h],BX
            RET
Write       ENDP


; Command 0Fh - Removeable Media

Removeable  PROC     NEAR
            MOV      AX,0200h              ;Set busy bit--indicates media is
            RET                            ;    not removeable
Removeable  ENDP


; The following command handler is used to simply mark a command as
; done. It does nothing else, and commands that are not implemented
; or supported are sent here.
```

continues

Listing 9.3. Continued

```
MarkAsDone  PROC    NEAR
            MOV     AX,0                    ;Set return code
            RET
MarkAsDone  ENDP


BadCommand  PROC    NEAR                    ;BadCommand
            MOV     AX,BadCmd               ;Set return code
            RET
BadCommand  ENDP



; From here down through the rest of the driver are routines used
; in the command handlers.

; Get sector specified in AX. Converts sector number to EMS page and
; offset. Sets SectOff variable to offset within page frame for start
; of sector. No registers affected. Carry clear on return if no error.
; Carry set on return if error dectected.

FindSect    PROC    NEAR USES AX BX CX DX
            MOV     DX,0                    ;Set high word to zero
            MOV     BX,32                   ;Dividing by 32 (sectors per EMS page)
            DIV     BX                      ;AX=EMS page, DX=sector in page
            MOV     BX,AX                   ;Put in place for mapping

            MOV     AX,DX                   ;Sector in page now in AX
            MOV     CX,SectSize
            MUL     CX                      ;AX=offset into EMS page
            MOV     SectOff,AX              ;Put offset in proper place

            CALL    GetPage                 ;Go get the EMS page
            RET
FindSect    ENDP


; Get an EMS page into physical page 0. Enter with BX set to logical
; page wanted. All registers return unchanged. Carry set if error.

GetPage     PROC    USES AX BX DX
            MOV     AH,44h                  ;No, so map page
```

```
                MOV     AL,0              ;Start of page frame
                MOV     DX,MemHandle
                INT     67h
                CMP     AL,0              ;Was there an error?
                JNE     BadGet            ;Yes, so exit
                CLC
                JNC     GPExit
BadGet:         STC
GPExit:         RET
GetPage         ENDP



; Transfer information to local variables from the request header.
; This routine is called before any read or write operation.
; ES:SI should be set to start of request header.

XferSetup       PROC    NEAR USES AX
                MOV     AX,ES:[SI+0Eh]    ;Get offset
                MOV     BuffOff,AX
                MOV     AX,ES:[SI+10h]    ;Get segment
                MOV     BuffSeg,AX
                MOV     AX,ES:[SI+12h]    ;Get sector count
                MOV     SectCount,AX
                MOV     AX,ES:[SI+14h]    ;Get starting sector
                MOV     SectStart,AX
                MOV     SectDone,0        ;Number of sectors transferred
                RET
XferSetup       ENDP



; Saves the page mapping info for MemHandle

PutContext      PROC    NEAR
                MOV     AH,47h            ;Save page map
                MOV     DX,MemHandle
                INT     67h
                CMP     AH,0              ;Any error?
                JNE     PCErr             ;Yes, exit
                CLC
                JNC     PCExit
```

continues

Listing 9.3. Continued

```
PCErr:      STC
PCExit:     RET
PutContext  ENDP


; Restores the page mapping info for MemHandle

GetContext  PROC    NEAR
            MOV     AH,48h              ;Restore page map
            MOV     DX,MemHandle
            INT     67h
            CMP     AH,0                ;Any error?
            JNE     GCErr               ;Yes, exit
            CLC
            JNC     GCExit
GCErr:      STC
GCExit:     RET
GetContext  ENDP


; Init command. This part of the driver is stripped after installation.

Init        PROC    NEAR                ;Command 00h - Init
            MOV     AL,ES:[SI+16h]      ;Drive number for this drive
            MOV     Drive,AL
            ADD     AL,'@'              ;Make printable ASCII
            MOV     DriveMsg,AL         ;Store for welcome message

            MOV     SI,OFFSET CRLF
            CALL    PrtString

            CALL    ChkEMS              ;See whether EMM is present
            JC      NoEMS               ;Not there, so go handle
            MOV     AH,41h              ;Get page frame
            INT     67h
            CMP     AH,0                ;Was there an error?
            JNE     NoPF                ;Yes, couldn't get page frame
            MOV     PageFrame,BX        ;And store for later
            MOV     AH,42h              ;Get pages available
            INT     67h
```

```
        CMP     AH,0                ;Was there an error?
        JNE     NoPA                ;Yes, couldn't determine pages available
        CMP     BX,45               ;You need 45 pages--is there enough?
        JB      NotEnough           ;Nope, go for error

; Everything is going great until now. EMM is installed, version number is
; right, and enough memory is available. Now need to allocate the memory.

        MOV     AH,43h              ;Allocate EMS memory
        MOV     BX,45               ;Want 720K
        INT     67h
        CMP     AH,0                ;Was there an error?
        JNE     BadAlloc            ;Yes, couldn't allocate
        MOV     MemHandle,DX        ;Save the handle for the block

; Ready to zero-out 45 pages of EMS memory just successfully requested

        MOV     ES,PageFrame
        MOV     CX,45               ;Number of pages to zero
        MOV     AX,0                ;Filling with this
        MOV     BX,0
FillLoop:  CALL  GetPage            ;Go get page
        JC      GetErr              ;Exit if error
        PUSH    CX                  ;Store loop counter
        MOV     CX,2000h            ;Zero this many words
        MOV     DI,0                ;ES:DI to physical page 0
        CLD                         ;Proper direction
        REP     STOSW               ;And store it all
        POP     CX                  ;Get back loop counter
        INC     BX                  ;Point to next page
        LOOP    FillLoop

        MOV     AX,0                ;Want to get sector 0
        CALL    FindSect
        JC      GetErr              ;Exit if error
        MOV     ES,PageFrame        ;Make ES:DI point to sector
        MOV     DI,SectOff
        MOV     SI,OFFSET BootRec
        MOV     CX,BRLen            ;Length of boot record
```

continues

Listing 9.3. Continued

```
            CLD                                 ;Proper direction
            REP     MOVSB

            MOV     AX,1                        ;Want first FAT sector
            CALL    FindSect
            JC      GetErr                      ;Exit if error
            MOV     ES,PageFrame                ;Make ES:DI point to sector
            MOV     DI,SectOff
            MOV     BYTE PTR ES:[DI],MediaID
            INC     DI
            MOV     WORD PTR ES:[DI],0FFFFh

            MOV     AX,RDStart                  ;Put a volume label in directory
            CALL    FindSect
            JC      GetErr
            MOV     ES,PageFrame
            MOV     DI,SectOff
            MOV     SI,OFFSET VolName
            MOV     CX,VNLen
            CLD
            REP     MOVSB
```

```
; Boot record and FAT are complete; all done setting up RAM disk.
; Ready to display all-OK message.
```

```
            MOV     SI,OFFSET Welcome
            CALL    PrtString

            MOV     SI,RHaddress[0]     ;Offset of request header
            MOV     ES,RHaddress[2]     ;Segment of request header
            MOV     BYTE PTR ES:[SI+0Dh],1 ;Number of block devices
            MOV     ES:[SI+0Eh],OFFSET Init
            MOV     ES:[SI+10h],CS
            MOV     ES:[SI+12h],OFFSET BPBarray ;Point to BPB array
            MOV     ES:[SI+14h],DS
            MOV     AX,0                ;Set return code
            JMP     InitDone            ;Exit with everything great
```

```
; Routines between here and InitDone receive control if there was an
; error during initialization and the driver installation must be aborted.
```

```
NoEMS:       MOV     SI,OFFSET EMSMsg     ;Point to error message
             JMP     ErrCommon
NoPF:        MOV     SI,OFFSET NoPFMsg
             JMP     ErrCommon
NoPA:        MOV     SI,OFFSET NoPAMsg
             JMP     ErrCommon
NotEnough:   MOV     SI,OFFSET NEMemMsg
             JMP     ErrCommon
BadAlloc:    MOV     SI,OFFSET BAMsg
             JMP     ErrCommon
GetErr:      MOV     SI,OFFSET GetMsg
ErrCommon:   CALL    PrtString

Abort:       MOV     SI,OFFSET AbortMsg   ;Generic abort message
             CALL    PrtString
             MOV     SI,RHaddress[0]      ;Offset of request header
             MOV     ES,RHaddress[2]      ;Segment of request header
             MOV     BYTE PTR ES:[SI+0Dh],0 ;No block devices
             MOV     WORD PTR ES:[SI+0Eh],0 ;Point to nowhere
             MOV     ES:[SI+10h],CS
             MOV     AX,0                 ;No error noted

InitDone:    MOV     SI,OFFSET CRLF
             CALL    PrtString
             RET
Init         ENDP


; The following routine checks to see whether an EMM is installed.
; If one is not, the carry flag is set on return.
; If one is, the carry flag is cleared on return.

ChkEMS       PROC    USES AX BX DX ES
             MOV     AX,0
             MOV     ES,AX
             MOV     BX,67h*4             ;Vector table position for EMS vector
             MOV     ES,ES:[BX+2]         ;Get offset
             MOV     DI,0Ah               ;Point to device driver header name
             MOV     SI,OFFSET EMSName    ;Point to name to check
```

continues

Listing 9.3. Continued

```
                MOV     CX,8                    ;Check eight characters
                CLD                             ;Go in right direction
                REPE    CMPSB                   ;Is it equal?
                JNE     NotThere                ;Nope, so exit

                MOV     AH,40h                  ;Check manager status
                INT     67h
                CMP     AH,0                    ;Error?
                JNE     NotThere                ;Yes, so exit

                MOV     AH,46h                  ;Get EMS version
                INT     67h
                CMP     AL,30h                  ;Running at least EMS 3.0?
                JB      NotThere                ;No, so can't use

                CLC                             ;Set for no error
                JNC     Done
NotThere:       STC
Done:           RET
ChkEMS          ENDP


; The following routine prints the ASCIIZ string pointed to by DS:SI

PrtString       PROC    NEAR USES AX BX SI
                MOV     BH,0                    ;Assume page 0
PS1:            MOV     AL,[SI]                 ;Get character
                INC     SI                      ;Point to next one
                CMP     AL,0                    ;End of string?
                JE      PS2                     ;Yes, so exit
                MOV     AH,0Eh                  ;Output a character
                INT     10h
                JMP     PS1                     ;Keep doing it
PS2:            RET
PrtString       ENDP


; Data area used by the init portion of the driver. Contains information not
; needed after device driver is loaded.
```

```
EMSName      DB       'EMMXXXX0'
BPBarray     DW       OFFSET BPB            ;Array for initialization
CRLF         DB       13,10,0
Welcome      DB       55 DUP('-'),13,10
             DB       ' EMSDisk -- A 720K disk emulator using expanded memory',13,10
             DB       '      Source code from Advanced Assembly Language',13,10
             DB       '                    by Allen L. Wyatt',13,10,13,10
             DB       '               EMSDisk is drive '
DriveMsg     DB       '?:',13,10
             DB       55 DUP('-'),13,10,0
EMSMsg       DB       'Could not locate a functional EMS driver'
             DB       'EMSdisk needs a driver compatible with at least EMS 3.0',13,10,0
NoPFMsg      DB       'Could not determine EMS page frame',13,10,0
NoPAMsg      DB       'Could not determine available EMS memory',13,10,0
NEMemMsg     DB       'Not enough EMS memory available for installation',13,10,0
BAMsg        DB       'Could not allocate 720K of EMS memory',13,10,0
GetMsg       DB       'Could not initialize the EMS memory',13,10,0
AbortMsg     DB       'EMSDisk was not loaded',13,10,0

; The following is a directory entry for the volume name

VolName      DB       'Advanced   '          ;Volume name
             DB       00001000b              ;File attributes (volume label)
             DB       10 DUP(0)              ;Unused area
             DW       0000100000000000b      ;Time stamp
             DW       0001101100000001b      ;Date stamp
             DW       0000                   ;Beginning cluster (N/A on volume)
             DD       00000000               ;File size (N/A on volume)
VNLen        EQU      $-VolName


_TEXT        ENDS
             END
```

Notice in this driver that it is necessary to save the EMS context every time a driver command is issued. This context then is restored after the command is completed. This action enables EMSDISK.SYS to work with other programs that use expanded memory.

If you worked with the character device driver presented in the preceding section, perhaps you noticed immediately that there were few device driver commands you had to allow for in implementing the RAM drive. The reason is that, in theory, a RAM drive is a simple device. You don't have to worry about many of the "large-ticket" coding problems associated with creating a device driver for a physical device. For instance, you don't have to worry about the generic IOCTL support routines, which can take a large percentage of your coding time. You don't have to worry about these because allowing the user to format a RAM disk is not necessary. (You can make the format functions zero out everything on the RAM drive; this command would be relatively simple to implement.)

If you want to try your hand at modification, you might try changing EMSDISK.ASM so that it accepts and interprets a size parameter from the command line. In this way, you can make your RAM drive as big as you want. If you choose to do this, you may want to refer to the information contained in Chapter 6, "Expanded and Extended Memory," and Chapter 7, "Working with Disk Files and Directories,"—it is helpful.

Summary

This chapter has explained quite a bit about both character and block device drivers. You learned how they are created, how they work with DOS, and how they handle IOCTL requests. Combined with the information in Chapter 8, "Using IOCTL," you have learned much about the marvelously complex and flexible system implemented through device drivers.

Chapter 10 describes how to program for one of the most common devices installed with a device driver: the mouse.

Programming for the Mouse

E arlier, this book discussed the keyboard and how it works. This chapter discusses an alternative input device, the mouse, and how you can use it in your programs.

Use of the mouse is common in today's programs. Adding the functionality of a mouse to your programs is easy, as you will learn. After the mouse driver software is loaded, you can allow for mouse control and input with just a few additional lines of code.

Before getting into coding, let's look at the mouse from the vantage point of the hardware and the software.

The Mouse: A Hardware View

Mechanically, the mouse is even simpler than the keyboard. It consists of a set of two or more sensors that detect movement, and one or more buttons. When the sensors detect movement, or one or more of the buttons is pressed, the mouse sends this information to the computer across a serial communication channel.

The exact method used by the mouse to detect motion is decided by the manufacturer of that particular mouse. The Microsoft mouse uses a hard rubber ball that is free to rotate in a holding cup. Three rollers in the sides of the holding cup move as the ball rotates. Two of the rollers are used to detect movement along the X and Y axes; the third roller is for stability.

The Mouse: A Driver View

It would be a misnomer to refer to the BIOS view of the mouse, because the BIOS does not know or care whether the mouse exists. The BIOS allows keyboard input (as explained in Chapter 2, "Controlling the Keyboard"), but, beyond that, recognition and control of the mouse are up to additional control programs called *software drivers*.

When you purchased your mouse, you should have received with it at least one disk of software that contains the driver used to interface the mouse to your computer. If a mouse was included in your computer purchase, chances are that the company from which you purchased the machine installed the mouse drivers already.

You can use the software that came with the mouse to install and modify the way the mouse functions. After the mouse driver is installed, it is loaded in one of two ways every time you start your computer. It can be loaded as a device in the CONFIG.SYS file or as a TSR program in the AUTOEXEC.BAT file. Which one is better? It doesn't make much difference.

The driver controls the way the mouse's movement and control are presented to your program through the mouse functions, which are described later in this chapter, in the section "The Mouse Functions." Before reading about them, however, you should understand a few underlying concepts about the mouse.

Virtual Coordinates

The major function of the mouse driver is to translate the movement of the mouse into coordinates that can be presented to your program so that you can determine the exact location of the mouse cursor. Everything else the driver does is secondary to this function. The range of these coordinates is determined by the video mode in use when the mouse is activated.

The mouse uses a set of virtual coordinates, maintained internally, to determine the location of the mouse cursor. When your program switches video modes, the mouse driver switches the set of virtual coordinates it uses. The virtual coordinates reflect the resolution used by the mouse driver for the particular video mode. For some video modes, the resolution used by the mouse driver is synonymous with the resolution of the video card for that mode. In others, the mouse driver uses a higher resolution. Table 10.1 shows common video modes and how the resolution compares to the mouse driver's resolution.

Table 10.1. A comparison of actual and virtual coordinate resolution for different video modes.

Mode (Hex)	Video Adapter	Display Type	Actual Resolution	Mouse Resolution
00	C/E/V/MC	Text	320×200	640×200
01	C/E/V/MC	Text	320×200	640×200
02	C/E/V/MC	Text	640×200	640×200
03	C/E/V/MC	Text	640×200	640×200
04	C/E/V/MC	Graphics	320×200	640×200
05	C/E/V/MC	Graphics	320×200	640×200
06	C/E/V/MC	Graphics	640×200	640×200
07	M/C/E/V/MC	Text	720×350	640×200
0D	E/V	Graphics	320×200	640×200
0E	E/V	Graphics	640×200	640×200
0F	M/E/V	Graphics	640×350	640×350
10	E/V	Graphics	640×350	640×350
11	V/MC	Graphics	640×480	640×480
12	V	Graphics	640×480	640×480
13	V/MC	Graphics	320×200	640×200
21	H	Graphics	720×348	720×348
22	H	Graphics	720×348	720×348
25	X	Graphics	1024×768	1024×768

Video adapter codes:

M	*Monochrome Display Adapter*
C	*Color Graphics Adapter*
E	*Enhanced Graphics Adapter*
V	*Virtual Graphics Array*
MC	*MultiColor Graphics Array*
H	*Hercules Graphics Adapter*
X	*Extended (Super) VGA*

Notice in Table 10.1 that in no instance is the mouse resolution lower than the actual resolution. In many cases, the mouse resolution is higher. As you work with the mouse functions, keep in mind how the virtual coordinates used by the mouse driver correspond to actual screen coordinates.

Mickeys

The mouse driver controls also how physical, linear movement of the mouse translates to the virtual movement of the mouse cursor. For instance, when the mouse is moved one inch in any direction, how should that translate to how far the mouse cursor moves?

Your mouse is designed with a certain resolution, which defines how sensitive it is. For instance, many mice have a sensitivity of 1/200 of an inch, sometimes expressed as 200 ppi (points per inch). Newer mice have a sensitivity of 400 ppi. As you move your mouse over a specific actual distance (one inch, for example), the distance is translated by the mouse into a unit of measure called a *mickey* (guess who that term was named after). The length of a mickey is determined by the resolution of the mouse. Mice with a resolution of 200 ppi translate one inch of movement into 200 mickeys. Likewise, 400 ppi mice translate one inch of movement into 400 mickeys.

The mouse hardware passes mickey counts to the mouse driver. This count represents the relative motion, vertical and horizontal, of the mouse on your desktop. The mouse driver uses this information to recalculate the new virtual coordinates of the mouse cursor.

The Mouse Functions

Similar to other DOS and BIOS functions, the mouse functions are accessible through the use of software interrupts. All mouse functions use interrupt 33h. Parameters are set and values returned through the use of registers. Although the DOS and BIOS functions use the AH register to specify the desired function, the desired mouse function is specified in the AL register. AH usually is set to 0 because it typically is not used.

The number of mouse functions available depends on your mouse driver. It depends also on the version of mouse driver you are using. Because virtually all mouse drivers emulate the function set provided by the Microsoft mouse, this book focuses on the mouse functions provided with the Microsoft mouse drivers.

Table 10.1 provides a quick overview of the mouse functions available.

Table 10.1. The mouse functions.

Function	Driver	Purpose
0		Reset/initialize mouse
1		Show mouse cursor
2		Hide mouse cursor

Function	Driver	Purpose
3		Get mouse status
4		Set cursor position
5		Get button press info
6		Get button release info
7		Set horizontal boundaries
8		Set vertical boundaries
9		Set graphics cursor block
10		Set text cursor
11		Read motion counters
12		Set interrupt subroutine
13		Enable light-pen emulation
14		Disable light-pen emulation
15		Set mickey-to-pixel ratio
16		Conditional off
19		Set double-speed threshold
20		Swap interrupt subroutines
21		Get mouse driver state storage needs
22		Save mouse driver state
23		Restore mouse driver state
24		Set alternate subroutine
25		Get alternate interrupt address
26		Set mouse sensitivity
27		Get mouse sensitivity
28		Set interrupt rate
29		Set CRT page number
30		Get CRT page number
31		Disable mouse driver
32		Enable mouse driver
33		Software reset
34		Set language for messages (international version only)

continues

Table 10.1. Continued

Function	Driver	Purpose
35		Get language (international version only)
36		Get driver version info
37	6.26	Get general driver info
38	6.26	Get maximum virtual coordinates
39	7.01	Get cursor masks and mickey counts
40	7.0	Set video mode
41	7.0	Get supported video modes
42	7.02	Get cursor hot spot
43	7.0	Set acceleration curves
44	7.0	Get acceleration curves
45	7.0	Set or get active acceleration curve
47	7.02	Mouse hardware reset
48	7.04	Set or get BallPoint information
49	7.05	Get virtual coordinates
50	7.05	Get active advanced functions
51	7.05	Get switch settings
52	8.0	Get MOUSE.INI

Fifty mouse functions are listed in Table 10.1; the number available to you depends on your specific mouse driver. If you are using the Microsoft drivers, you should always use the latest driver, distributed with various Microsoft products.

Even though there are many different mouse functions, only a few of them are used regularly. The programs in this chapter discuss and use the most common mouse functions. For specific details about individual mouse functions, see Appendix B, "The Mouse Functions."

Determining Whether a Mouse Is Available

To take advantage of the mouse, one of the first tasks you must do in your programs is determine whether a mouse is present in your system. Because all mouse functions are accessed through Int 33h, you can determine easily whether a mouse driver is loaded by seeing whether an interrupt handler is associated with Int 33h. To do this, you must determine first whether there is a vector address for Int 33h. This is easy to do using Int 21h, function 35h. If the address returned by this function is 0000:0000, no driver is loaded.

You must perform a second step at this point, however. On some computer systems, it is possible that a valid address is returned but the only programming code at that address is an IRET. In this case, the mouse driver is not loaded, and any INT 33h that is executed returns immediately. Understanding that this situation is a possibility, it is easy to make allowances and check for it. You just look at the value of the memory byte pointed to by the address returned by Int 21h, function 35h. If it is CFh (the op-code for IRET), then the mouse driver is not loaded.

After you have determined that the mouse driver is loaded, you must see whether a mouse is attached to the computer. You do this through mouse function 0, which enables you to reset the mouse. If no mouse is present, the function returns 0 in the AX register. Any other value returned means that the mouse has been initialized and is ready for use.

The following subroutine can be used to determine whether a mouse is available and ready for use in your system. If a mouse is there, the carry flag is clear on return. If a mouse is not there, the carry flag is set. The routine also displays error messages, using the DOS functions, if the driver or mouse is not found.

```
; The following routine checks to see whether a mouse is installed.
; If one is not, then the appropriate message is displayed and the
;    carry flag is set on return.
; If one is, then the mouse is reset and the carry flag is cleared.


          .DATA
NoDriver  DB      13,10,'Sorry, the mouse driver was not loaded$'
NoMouse   DB      13,10,'A mouse is not attached to the system$'

          .CODE
ChkMouse  PROC    USES AX BX DX ES
```

```
            MOV     AH,35h              ;Get interrupt vector
            MOV     AL,33h              ;Mouse interrupt
            INT     21h

            OR      AX,BX              ;Was an address returned?
            JZ      CM1                ;No, so give error
            CMP     BYTE PTR ES:[BX],0CFh ;Is it simply IRET at address?
            JNE     CM2                ;No, so driver is installed
CM1:        MOV     DX,OFFSET NoDriver ;Point to error message
            JMP     CM3                ;Go print it

CM2:        MOV     AX,0               ;Initialize mouse
            INT     33h
            CMP     AX,0               ;0 returned if no mouse
            JNE     CM4                ;Mouse is there
            MOV     DX,OFFSET NoMouse  ;Point to error message
CM3:        MOV     AH,9               ;Display a string using DOS
            INT     21h
            STC                        ;Set error indication
            JC      CMDone

CM4:        CLC
CMDone:     RET
ChkMouse    ENDP
```

You can use this routine as a basis for a similar routine in your programs, particularly to change the way the error messages are displayed. This routine (as is) is used throughout the other examples in this chapter.

The Mouse and Driver

Several mouse functions can be used to determine information about the mouse or driver. This information is important because if you decide to use several of the advanced mouse functions, you can do so for only certain versions of the mouse driver. The examples in this chapter use the functions provided with various versions of the Microsoft mouse driver; those provided with different versions of your mouse driver may vary.

The program in Listing 10.1, MINFO.ASM, uses different mouse functions to detail information about the mouse. This program does not enable the mouse cursor—it only displays information derived from the mouse informational functions.

Listing 10.1. MINFO.ASM

```
Page 60,132

Comment ¦
*******************************************************************


File:       MINFO.ASM
Author:     Allen L. Wyatt
Date:       5/13/92
Assembler:  MASM 6.0


Purpose:    Display information about the mouse and driver


Format:     MINFO


*******************************************************************¦


            .MODEL  small
            .STACK                      ;Default 1K stack is OK
            .DATA

Installed   DB      13,10,13,10
            DB      'The mouse driver is installed, version $'
TypeTable   DW      OFFSET Type1
            DW      OFFSET Type2
            DW      OFFSET Type3
            DW      OFFSET Type4
            DW      OFFSET Type5

Type1       DB      13,10,'This is a bus mouse',13,10,'$'
Type2       DB      13,10,'This is a serial mouse',13,10,'$'
Type3       DB      13,10,'This is an InPort mouse',13,10,'$'
Type4       DB      13,10,'This is a PS/2 mouse',13,10,'$'
Type5       DB      13,10,'This is an HP mouse',13,10,'$'

FileType    DB      'The driver was loaded as a $'
SysType     DB      'SYS file in CONFIG.SYS',13,10,'$'
ComType     DB      'COM file',13,10,'$'
MDD         DB      'The driver is newer Mouse Display Driver (MDD)',13,10,'$'
NonInt      DB      'The driver is of the non-integrated variety',13,10,'$'
```

continues

Listing 10.1. Continued

```
Cur         DB      'The mouse is set to use the $'

CurTable    DW      OFFSET Cur1
            DW      OFFSET Cur2
            DW      OFFSET Cur3
            DW      OFFSET Cur3

Cur1        DB      'software text cursor',13,10,'$'
Cur2        DB      'hardware text cursor',13,10,'$'
Cur3        DB      'graphics text cursor',13,10,'$'

VidModes    DB      13,10
            DB      'The following video modes are supported by the driver:'
            DB      13,10,'$'

Mode        DB      'Mode $'
Spaces      DB      '    $'
NoVid       DB      '[no description provided]'
CRLF        DB      13,10,'$'

Pause       DB      13,10,'Press any key to continue...$'

VNum        DW      0000
Count       DB      00

            .CODE
            .STARTUP
Minfo       PROC

            CALL    ChkMouse            ;Go see whether mouse is there
            JC      AllDone             ;Error, so exit

            MOV     DX,OFFSET Installed ;Point to installed message
            MOV     AH,9                ;Display a string using DOS
            INT     21h

            MOV     AX,36               ;Get driver info
            INT     33h
            MOV     VNum,BX             ;Store the version

            MOV     AX,0                ;Reset value
```

```
        MOV     AL,BH               ;Major version number
        CALL    PrtDec              ;Go print it
        MOV     DL,'.'
        MOV     AH,02h              ;Output a character
        INT     21h
        MOV     AX,0                ;Reset value
        MOV     AL,BL               ;Minor version number
        CALL    PrtDec              ;Go print it
        MOV     BH,0                ;Reset high byte
        MOV     BL,CH               ;Mouse type
        DEC     BL                  ;Use as index
        SHL     BX,1                ;Multiply by 2
        MOV     DX,TypeTable[BX]    ;Get proper type
        MOV     AH,9                ;Display a string using DOS
        INT     21h

        CMP     VNum,061Ah          ;Is this version 6.26?
        JL      AllDone             ;Nope; earlier version, so exit

        MOV     DX,OFFSET FileType  ;Point to next message
        MOV     AH,9                ;Display a string using DOS
        INT     21h
        MOV     AX,37               ;Get mouse driver info
        INT     33h
        PUSH    AX                  ;Store flags for a moment
        MOV     DX,OFFSET ComType   ;Assume COM file
        AND     AX,8000h            ;Want only bit 15
        JZ      M1                  ;Not a SYS file
        MOV     DX,OFFSET SysType   ;Using SYS file
M1:     MOV     AH,9                ;Display a string using DOS
        INT     21h
        POP     AX                  ;Get flags back
        PUSH    AX                  ;Store flags again
        MOV     DX,OFFSET MDD       ;Assume MDD driver
        AND     AX,4000h            ;Want only bit 14
        JNZ     M2                  ;Not a COM file
        MOV     DX,OFFSET NonInt    ;Using non-integrated driver
M2:     MOV     AH,9                ;Display a string using DOS
        INT     21h
        MOV     DX,OFFSET Cur       ;Point to next message
        MOV     AH,9                ;Display a string using DOS
        INT     21h
        POP     AX                  ;Get flags back
```

continues

Listing 10.1. Continued

```
                AND     AX,3000h            ;Want only bits 13 and 12
                XCHG    AH,AL
                MOV     CL,3
                SHR     AX,CL               ;Right-justify bits/multiply by 2
                MOV     BX,AX
                MOV     DX,CurTable[BX]
                MOV     AH,9                ;Display a string using DOS
                INT     21h

                CMP     VNum,0700h          ;Is this version 6.26?
                JL      AllDone             ;Nope; earlier version, so exit

                MOV     DX,OFFSET VidModes  ;Message about video modes
                MOV     AH,9                ;Display a string using DOS
                INT     21h

                MOV     Count,16            ;Have already printed six lines
                MOV     CX,0                ;Start enumerating video modes
EnumLoop:       MOV     AX,41               ;Enumerate video modes
                INT     33h
                JCXZ    AllDone             ;Quit when no more modes
                PUSH    CX                  ;Save video mode
                PUSH    BX                  ;Save segment
                PUSH    DX                  ;Save offset
                MOV     DX,OFFSET Mode
                MOV     AH,9                ;Display a string using DOS
                INT     21h

                MOV     AX,CX
                CALL    PrtDec
                MOV     DX,OFFSET Spaces
                MOV     AH,9                ;Display a string using DOS
                INT     21h

                POP     DX                  ;Get offset back
                POP     AX                  ;Get segment back
                CMP     DX,0                ;Is offset 0?
                JNE     M3                  ;No, continue
                CMP     AX,0                ;Is segment 0?
                JE      M4                  ;Yes, so none there
```

```
M3:         PUSH    DS
            MOV     DS,AX
            MOV     AH,9                ;Display a string using DOS
            INT     21h
            POP     DS
            MOV     DX,OFFSET CRLF
            MOV     AH,9                ;Display a string using DOS
            INT     21h
            JMP     M5


M4:         MOV     DX,OFFSET NoVid
            MOV     AH,9                ;Display a string using DOS
            INT     21h


M5:         DEC     Count               ;At end of page?
            JNZ     M6
            CALL    PagePause           ;Go pause
            MOV     Count,23            ;Allow for full page


M6:         POP     CX                  ;Get video mode back
            JMP     EnumLoop


AllDone:
            .EXIT
Minfo       ENDP



; The following routine checks to see whether a mouse is installed.
; If one is not, then the appropriate message is displayed, and the
;    carry flag is set on return
; If one is, then the mouse is reset, and the carry flag is cleared


            .DATA
NoDriver    DB      13,10,'Sorry, the mouse driver was not loaded$'
NoMouse     DB      13,10,'A mouse is not attached to the system$'


            .CODE
ChkMouse    PROC    USES AX BX DX ES

            MOV     AH,35h              ;Get interrupt vector
            MOV     AL,33h              ;Mouse interrupt
            INT     21h
```

Listing 10.1. Continued

```
            OR      AX,BX                   ;Was an address returned?
            JZ      CM1                     ;No, so give error
            CMP     BYTE PTR ES:[BX],0CFh   ;Is it simply IRET at address?
            JNE     CM2                     ;No, so driver is installed
CM1:        MOV     DX,OFFSET NoDriver      ;Point to error message
            JMP     CM3                     ;Go print it

CM2:        MOV     AX,0                    ;Initialize mouse
            INT     33h
            CMP     AX,0                    ;0 returned if no mouse
            JNE     CM4                     ;Mouse is there
            MOV     DX,OFFSET NoMouse       ;Point to error message
CM3:        MOV     AH,9                    ;Display a string using DOS
            INT     21h
            STC                             ;Set error indication
            JC      CMDone

CM4:        CLC
CMDone:     RET
ChkMouse    ENDP


; The following routine clears the screen

Cls         PROC    USES AX BX CX DX
            MOV     AH,6                    ;Scroll window up
            MOV     AL,0                    ;Scroll full screen
            MOV     BH,7                    ;Normal white on black
            MOV     CX,0                    ;Upper left corner of screen
            MOV     DH,24                   ;Bottom right
            MOV     DL,79
            INT     10h
            RET
Cls         ENDP


; The following routine prints the value in AX as a decimal number

PrtDec      PROC    USES AX CX DX
            MOV     CX,0FFFFh               ;Ending flag
```

```
            PUSH    CX
            MOV     CX,10
PD1:        MOV     DX,0
            DIV     CX              ;Divide by 10
            ADD     DL,30h          ;Convert to ASCII
            PUSH    DX              ;Store remainder
            CMP     AX,0            ;Are we done?
            JNE     PD1             ;No, so continue

PD2:        POP     DX              ;Character is now in DL
            CMP     DX,0FFFFh       ;Is it the ending flag?
            JE      PD3             ;Yes, so continue
            MOV     AH,02h          ;Output a character
            INT     21h
            JMP     PD2             ;Keep doing it

PD3:        RET
PrtDec      ENDP


; The following routine pauses at the bottom of a page

PagePause   PROC    USES AX BX DX
            MOV     DX,OFFSET Pause ;Point to start of pause message
            MOV     AH,9            ;Display a string using DOS
            INT     21h
            MOV     AH,0            ;Read keyboard character
            INT     16h
            MOV     DX,OFFSET CRLF
            MOV     AH,9            ;Display a string using DOS
            INT     21h
            RET
PagePause   ENDP

            END
```

Basically, only a couple of mouse functions are used in this program. The main body of the program uses functions 36, 37, and 41 to provide the information that is displayed. Before using functions 37 and 41, however, the version of the mouse driver is double-checked to make sure that the functions are supported.

This program uses also several subroutines, which you will see used throughout the remainder of the programs in this chapter. The ChkMouse subroutine is described earlier in this chapter. Cls is a simple subroutine to clear the screen, and PrtDec is used to convert a hex number to a printable decimal number and then to display it.

The PagePause subroutine is called after displaying 23 lines of information on the screen. The point at which PagePause is called is controlled by monitoring the Count variable. When PagePause is called, it displays a message and waits for the user to press a key before continuing.

When you run MINFO.EXE, your output appears similar to the following:

```
The mouse driver is installed, version 7.3
This is a serial mouse
The driver was loaded as a SYS file in CONFIG.SYS
The driver is of the non-integrated variety
The mouse is set to use the software text cursor

The following video modes are supported by the driver:
Mode 1     [no description provided]
Mode 2     [no description provided]
Mode 3     [no description provided]
Mode 4     [no description provided]
Mode 5     [no description provided]
Mode 6     [no description provided]
Mode 7     [no description provided]
Mode 8     [no description provided]
Mode 9     [no description provided]
Mode 10    [no description provided]
Mode 13    [no description provided]
Mode 14    [no description provided]
Mode 15    [no description provided]
Mode 16    [no description provided]
Mode 17    [no description provided]
Mode 18    [no description provided]

Press any key to continue...
Mode 19    [no description provided]
Mode 32    [no description provided]
Mode 33    [no description provided]
Mode 34    [no description provided]
Mode 35    [no description provided]
Mode 36    [no description provided]
Mode 38    [no description provided]
Mode 48    [no description provided]
```

```
Mode 64      [no description provided]
Mode 116     [no description provided]
Mode 126     [no description provided]
Mode 64      [no description provided]
Mode 65      [no description provided]
Mode 66      [no description provided]
Mode 67      [no description provided]
Mode 68      [no description provided]
Mode 69      [no description provided]
Mode 96      [no description provided]
Mode 97      [no description provided]
Mode 98      [no description provided]
Mode 96      [no description provided]
Mode 97      [no description provided]
Mode 110     [no description provided]

Press any key to continue...
Mode 111     [no description provided]
Mode 112     [no description provided]
Mode 113     [no description provided]
Mode 114     [no description provided]
Mode 120     [no description provided]
Mode 121     [no description provided]
Mode 122     [no description provided]
Mode 123     [no description provided]
```

Mouse function 41 is used to display the supported video modes. This function became available only with version 7 of the mouse driver, and has not been implemented fully. This function allows for the mouse driver to return a pointer to the name of the video mode, but—as is obvious from the output of this program—the names have not been included in the driver.

Notice that function 41 does not necessarily return video modes in ascending order, nor is there any guarantee that they will not be repeated, apparently because different mode numbers can be used by different video adapters in different ways. There would be a need, therefore, for the mouse driver to allow support for multiple occurrences of the same video mode, depending on the video adapter in use.

Using the Mouse in Text Mode

To use the mouse in text mode, your program has only to reset the mouse (function 0) and turn it on (function 1). Then you can use other mouse functions to determine the position of the mouse cursor and the state of the buttons. What you do with that information then is up to you. The program in Listing 10.2, MOUSE1.ASM, enables the mouse in text mode:

Listing 10.2. MOUSE1.ASM

```
Page 60,132

Comment |
********************************************************************

File:       MOUSE1.ASM
Author:     Allen L. Wyatt
Date:       5/7/92
Assembler:  MASM 6.0

Purpose:    Enable the text mouse cursor and display status info

Format:     MOUSE1


********************************************************************|

            .MODEL  small
            .STACK                          ;Default 1K stack is OK
            .DATA
XPos        DB      'X Position: $'
YPos        DB      '    Y Position: $'
Blank       DB      '    $'

Msg         DB      'Click on the right mouse button to exit program$'

OldX        DW      0000
OldY        DW      0000

            .CODE
            .STARTUP
Mouse1      PROC

            CALL    ChkMouse            ;Go see whether mouse is there
            JC      AllDone             ;Error, so exit

            CALL    Cls                 ;Clear the screen
            MOV     DH,24               ;Row 24
```

```
            MOV     DL,0              ;To the left
            MOV     BH,0              ;Assume page 0
            MOV     AH,2              ;Set cursor position
            INT     10h
            MOV     DX,OFFSET Msg     ;Point to exit message
            MOV     AH,9              ;Display a string using DOS
            INT     21h

            CALL    ShowMouse         ;Go show mouse cursor

Mloop:      MOV     AX,3              ;Read mouse status
            INT     33h

            CMP     BX,2              ;Was right button pressed?
            JE      Exit              ;Yes, so exit

            CMP     CX,OldX           ;Did X position change?
            JNE     Change            ;Yes, so handle
            CMP     DX,OldY           ;Did Y position change?
            JE      Mloop             ;No, so continue loop

Change:     MOV     OldX,CX           ;Store X position
            MOV     OldY,DX           ;Store Y position
            CALL    Coords            ;Display changes
            JMP     Mloop             ;Do it all again

Exit:       MOV     AX,0              ;Reset mouse
            INT     33h
            CALL    Cls               ;Clear the screen

AllDone:
            .EXIT
Mouse1      ENDP


; The following routine checks to see whether a mouse is installed.
; If one is not, then the appropriate message is displayed, and the
;    carry flag is set on return
; If one is, then the mouse is reset and the carry flag is cleared

            .DATA
NoDriver    DB      13,10,'Sorry, the mouse driver was not loaded$'
```

continues

Listing 10.2. Continued

```
NoMouse      DB      13,10,'A mouse is not attached to the system$'

             .CODE
ChkMouse     PROC    USES AX BX DX ES

             MOV     AH,35h              ;Get interrupt vector
             MOV     AL,33h              ;Mouse interrupt
             INT     21h

             OR      AX,BX              ;Was an address returned?
             JZ      CM1                ;No, so give error
             CMP     BYTE PTR ES:[BX],0CFh ;Is it simply IRET at address?
             JNE     CM2                ;No, so driver is installed
CM1:         MOV     DX,OFFSET NoDriver ;Point to error message
             JMP     CM3                ;Go print it

CM2:         MOV     AX,0               ;Initialize mouse
             INT     33h
             CMP     AX,0               ;0 returned if no mouse
             JNE     CM4                ;Mouse is there
             MOV     DX,OFFSET NoMouse  ;Point to error message
CM3:         MOV     AH,9               ;Display a string using DOS
             INT     21h
             STC                        ;Set error indication
             JC      CMDone

CM4:         CLC
CMDone:      RET
ChkMouse     ENDP


; The following routine hides the mouse cursor

HideMouse    PROC    USES    AX
             MOV     AX,2
             INT     33h
             RET
HideMouse    ENDP
```

```
; The following routine displays the mouse cursor

ShowMouse   PROC    USES    AX
            MOV     AX,1
            INT     33h
            RET
ShowMouse   ENDP



; The following routine clears the screen

Cls         PROC    USES AX BX CX DX
            MOV     AH,6            ;Scroll window up
            MOV     AL,0            ;Scroll full screen
            MOV     BH,7            ;Normal white on black
            MOV     CX,0            ;Upper left corner of screen
            MOV     DH,24           ;Bottom right
            MOV     DL,79
            INT     10h
            RET
Cls         ENDP



; The following routine updates the coordinate information on the screen
; Pass X position in CX, and Y position in DX

Coords      PROC    USES AX BX CX DX

            CALL    HideMouse       ;Hide the mouse cursor
            PUSH    DX              ;Store Y position
            PUSH    CX              ;Store X position

            MOV     DH,22           ;Row 22
            MOV     DL,0            ;To the left
            MOV     BH,0            ;Assume page 0
            MOV     AH,2            ;Set cursor position
            INT     10h

            MOV     DX,OFFSET XPos  ;Point to positioning message
            MOV     AH,9            ;Display a string using DOS
            INT     21h
            POP     AX              ;Get back X position
```

continues

Listing 10.2. Continued

```
            CALL    PrtDec                  ;Go print it

            MOV     DX,OFFSET YPos          ;Point to positioning message
            MOV     AH,9                    ;Display a string using DOS
            INT     21h
            POP     AX                      ;Get back Y position
            CALL    PrtDec                  ;Go print it

            MOV     DX,OFFSET Blank         ;Blank string
            MOV     AH,9                    ;Display a string using DOS
            INT     21h

            CALL    ShowMouse               ;OK to redisplay mouse cursor
            RET
Coords      ENDP


; The following routine prints the value in AX as a decimal number

PrtDec      PROC    USES AX CX DX
            MOV     CX,0FFFFh               ;Ending flag
            PUSH    CX
            MOV     CX,10
PD1:        MOV     DX,0
            DIV     CX                      ;Divide by 10
            ADD     DL,30h                  ;Convert to ASCII
            PUSH    DX                      ;Store remainder
            CMP     AX,0                    ;Are we done?
            JNE     PD1                     ;No, so continue

PD2:        POP     DX                      ;Character is now in DL
            CMP     DX,0FFFFh               ;Is it the ending flag?
            JE      PD3                     ;Yes, so continue
            MOV     AH,02h                  ;Output a character
            INT     21h
            JMP     PD2                     ;Keep doing it

PD3:        RET
PrtDec      ENDP

            END
```

When you run this program, the mouse cursor appears as a solid block that overlies the character underneath it. You can move the cursor anywhere on the screen, and the position of the mouse cursor is displayed at the bottom of the screen. This information is determined through the use of mouse function 3.

Coordinates displayed at the bottom of the screen do not correspond to the rows and columns of character positions. Rather, these coordinates reflect the virtual coordinates described earlier in this chapter.

When you finish using the program, you can press the right mouse button to exit.

Look at the program listing for MOUSE1.ASM. Many of the subroutines were discussed earlier in this chapter, but pay particular attention to Coords. This subroutine displays, at the bottom of the screen, the coordinate position of the mouse cursor. Notice what is done by this routine before actually updating the screen: The mouse is turned off (by calling HideMouse) and turned back on only when screen updating is done (by calling ShowMouse). This sequence is important because the mouse driver accesses the screen many times per second, which results in actual characters and the characters used for the mouse cursor flipping back and forth. The only way, therefore, to make sure that the screen is stable enough for updates is to turn off the mouse cursor before updating and turn it on after the update is finished. This process should present no problems, however, because updating is done so quickly that a user never notices that the mouse cursor was turned off.

Using the Mouse in Graphics Mode

Using the mouse in graphics mode is similar to using it in text mode. The only difference is in the appearance of the mouse cursor. The mouse cursor appears as a solid block in text mode, and appears as an arrow in graphics mode. The program in Listing 10.3, MOUSE2.ASM, performs the same functions as MOUSE1.ASM, and accomplishes the same purpose.

Listing 10.3. MOUSE2.ASM

```
Page 60,132


Comment ¦
******************************************************************


File:      MOUSE2.ASM
Author:    Allen L. Wyatt
```

continues

Listing 10.3. Continued

```
Date:          5/13/92
Assembler:     MASM 6.0

Purpose:       Enable the graphics mouse cursor and display status info
               This program assumes that you have an EGA or VGA monitor

Format:        MOUSE2


*********************************************************************!
                                                                    !

               .MODEL  small
               .STACK                          ;Default 1K stack is OK
               .DATA
XPos           DB      'X Position: $'
YPos           DB      '    Y Position: $'
Blank          DB      '   $'

Msg            DB      'Click on the right mouse button to exit program$'

VidMode        DB      00
OldX           DW      0000
OldY           DW      0000

               .CODE
               .STARTUP
Mouse2         PROC

               CALL    ChkMouse         ;Go see whether mouse is there
               JC      AllDone          ;Error, so exit

               MOV     AH,0Fh           ;Get video mode
               INT     10h
               MOV     VidMode,AL       ;Store for later

               MOV     AH,0             ;BIOS set video mode
               MOV     AL,10h
               INT     10h

               CALL    Cls              ;Clear the screen
               MOV     DH,24            ;Row 24
```

```
             MOV     DL,0                ;To the left
             MOV     BH,0                ;Assume page 0
             MOV     AH,2                ;Set cursor position
             INT     10h
             MOV     DX,OFFSET Msg       ;Point to exit message
             MOV     AH,9                ;Display a string using DOS
             INT     21h

             CALL    ShowMouse           ;Go show mouse cursor

Mloop:       MOV     AX,3                ;Read mouse status
             INT     33h

             CMP     BX,2                ;Was right button pressed?
             JE      Exit                ;Yes, so exit

             CMP     CX,OldX             ;Did X position change?
             JNE     Change              ;Yes, so handle
             CMP     DX,OldY             ;Did Y position change?
             JE      Mloop               ;No, so continue loop

Change:      MOV     OldX,CX             ;Store X position
             MOV     OldY,DX             ;Store Y position
             CALL    Coords              ;Display changes
             JMP     Mloop               ;Do it all again

Exit:        MOV     AX,0                ;Reset mouse
             INT     33h
             MOV     AH,0                ;BIOS set video mode
             MOV     AL,VidMode
             INT     10h
             CALL    Cls                 ;Clear the screen

AllDone:
             .EXIT
Mouse2       ENDP


; The following routine checks to see whether a mouse is installed.
; If one is not, then the appropriate message is displayed and the
;    carry flag is set on return
; If one is, then the mouse is reset and the carry flag is cleared
```

continues

Listing 10.3. Continued

```
                .DATA
NoDriver        DB      13,10,'Sorry, the mouse driver was not loaded$'
NoMouse         DB      13,10,'A mouse is not attached to the system$'

                .CODE
ChkMouse        PROC    USES AX BX DX ES

                MOV     AH,35h                  ;Get interrupt vector
                MOV     AL,33h                  ;Mouse interrupt
                INT     21h

                OR      AX,BX                   ;Was an address returned?
                JZ      CM1                     ;No, so give error
                CMP     BYTE PTR ES:[BX],0CFh   ;Is it simply IRET at address?
                JNE     CM2                     ;No, so driver is installed
CM1:            MOV     DX,OFFSET NoDriver      ;Point to error message
                JMP     CM3                     ;Go print it

CM2:            MOV     AX,0                    ;Initialize mouse
                INT     33h
                CMP     AX,0                    ;0 returned if no mouse
                JNE     CM4                     ;Mouse is there
                MOV     DX,OFFSET NoMouse       ;Point to error message
CM3:            MOV     AH,9                    ;Display a string using DOS
                INT     21h
                STC                             ;Set error indication
                JC      CMDone

CM4:            CLC
CMDone:         RET
ChkMouse        ENDP


; The following routine hides the mouse cursor

HideMouse       PROC    USES    AX
                MOV     AX,2
                INT     33h
                RET
HideMouse       ENDP
```

```
; The following routine displays the mouse cursor

ShowMouse   PROC     USES    AX
            MOV      AX,1
            INT      33h
            RET
ShowMouse   ENDP


; The following routine clears the screen
; It uses the attribute of the character at the current cursor position
;      as the attribute for the cleared screen

Cls         PROC     USES AX BX CX DX
            MOV      AH,8              ;Read character and attribute
            MOV      BH,0              ;Assume page 0
            INT      10h
            MOV      BH,AH             ;Put attribute in right place

            MOV      AH,6              ;Scroll window up
            MOV      AL,0              ;Scroll full screen
            MOV      CX,0              ;Upper left corner of screen
            MOV      DH,24             ;Bottom right
            MOV      DL,79
            INT      10h
            RET
Cls         ENDP


; The following routine updates the coordinate information on the screen
; Pass X position in CX, and Y position in DX

Coords      PROC     USES AX BX CX DX

            CALL     HideMouse         ;Hide the mouse cursor
            PUSH     DX                ;Store Y position
            PUSH     CX                ;Store X position

            MOV      DH,22             ;Row 22
            MOV      DL,0              ;To the left
            MOV      BH,0              ;Assume page 0
            MOV      AH,2              ;Set cursor position
            INT      10h
```

continues

Listing 10.3. Continued

```
            MOV     DX,OFFSET XPos      ;Point to positioning message
            MOV     AH,9                ;Display a string using DOS
            INT     21h
            POP     AX                  ;Get back X position
            CALL    PrtDec              ;Go print it

            MOV     DX,OFFSET YPos      ;Point to positioning message
            MOV     AH,9                ;Display a string using DOS
            INT     21h
            POP     AX                  ;Get back Y position
            CALL    PrtDec              ;Go print it

            MOV     DX,OFFSET Blank     ;Blank string
            MOV     AH,9                ;Display a string using DOS
            INT     21h

            CALL    ShowMouse           ;OK to redisplay mouse cursor
            RET
Coords      ENDP


; The following routine prints the value in AX as a decimal number

PrtDec      PROC    USES AX CX DX
            MOV     CX,0FFFFh           ;Ending flag
            PUSH    CX
            MOV     CX,10
PD1:        MOV     DX,0
            DIV     CX                  ;Divide by 10
            ADD     DL,30h              ;Convert to ASCII
            PUSH    DX                  ;Store remainder
            CMP     AX,0                ;Are we done?
            JNE     PD1                 ;No, so continue

PD2:        POP     DX                  ;Character is now in DL
            CMP     DX,0FFFFh           ;Is it the ending flag?
            JE      PD3                 ;Yes, so continue
            MOV     AH,02h              ;Output a character
            INT     21h
```

```
          JMP      PD2                 ;Keep doing it

PD3:      RET
PrtDec    ENDP


          END
```

This program assumes that you have an EGA or VGA monitor. If you do not, you may want to change the video mode used by this program. The program does this early, in the following three code lines:

```
MOV    AH,0                 ;BIOS set video mode
MOV    AL,10h
INT    10h
```

Simply load AL with the video mode you want to use. MOUSE2.ASM resets the video mode back to the original mode before exiting the program.

When you run MOUSE2.EXE, notice that the information displayed by the Coords subroutine, which was derived from mouse function 3, corresponds to the actual screen coordinates of the upper left corner of the mouse cursor. This point, called the *hot spot*, can be changed through mouse function 9. For most purposes, however, the default hot spot is appropriate.

Using the Mouse to Get Screen Information

Now that you have learned how to use the mouse in both text and graphics modes, let's look at how you can use this information to extract information from the screen.

Suppose that you want to enable the program user to select a word from the screen by pointing and clicking. This capability is not uncommon in many programs. The program in Listing 10.4, MOUSE3.ASM, illustrates how this is done.

Listing 10.4. MOUSE3.ASM

```
Page 60,132


Comment ¦
*********************************************************************
```

continues

Listing 10.4. Continued

```
File:        MOUSE3.ASM
Author:      Allen L. Wyatt
Date:        5/13/92
Assembler:   MASM 6.0

Purpose:     In graphics mode, enable the user to select a word by
             pointing and clicking on the left mouse button.
             This program assumes that you have an EGA or VGA monitor.


Format:      MOUSE3


****************************************************************!

             .MODEL  small
             .STACK                          ;Default 1K stack is OK
             .DATA
XPos         DB      'X Position: $'
YPos         DB      '    Y Position: $'

XCPos        DB      'Column: $'
YCPos        DB      '    Row: $'
NoWord       DB      'There is no word where you clicked$'
WordMsg      DB      'Word last clicked on:  '
BufLen       EQU     40
Buffer       DB      BufLen DUP(' ')
             DB      ' $'
Blank        DB      '          $'

Msg          DB      'Click on the right mouse button to exit program$'
Text         DB      'These are random words on a line.  $'

VidMode      DB      00
VidPage      DB      00
OldX         DW      0000
OldY         DW      0000
ClickX       DB      00
ClickY       DB      00
CurX         DB      00
CurY         DB      00
FirstChar    DB      00
```

```
            .CODE
            .STARTUP
Mouse3      PROC

            CALL    ChkMouse            ;Go see whether mouse is there
            JC      AllDone             ;Error, so exit

            MOV     AH,0Fh              ;Get video mode
            INT     10h
            MOV     VidMode,AL          ;Store for later

            MOV     AH,0                ;BIOS set video mode
            MOV     AL,10h
            INT     10h

            MOV     AH,0Fh              ;Get video mode (want display page)
            INT     10h
            MOV     VidPage,BH          ;Will use this later

            CALL    Cls                 ;Clear the screen
            MOV     DH,24               ;Row 24
            MOV     DL,0                ;To the left
            MOV     BH,VidPage
            MOV     AH,2                ;Set cursor position
            INT     10h
            MOV     DX,OFFSET Msg       ;Point to exit message
            MOV     AH,9                ;Display a string using DOS
            INT     21h

            MOV     DX,0                ;Upper left corner
            MOV     BH,VidPage
            MOV     AH,2                ;Set cursor position
            INT     10h

            MOV     CX,32
FillScrn:   MOV     DX,OFFSET Text      ;Text for screen top
            MOV     AH,9                ;Display a string using DOS
            INT     21h
            LOOP    FillScrn

            CALL    ShowMouse           ;Go show mouse cursor
```

continues

Listing 10.4. Continued

```
Mloop:      MOV     AX,3            ;Read mouse status
            INT     33h

            CMP     BX,2            ;Was right button pressed?
            JE      Exit            ;Yes, so exit

            CMP     BX,1            ;Was left button pressed?
            JNE     M1              ;No, so do position
            PUSH    DX              ;Store Y
            PUSH    CX              ;Store X

            MOV     AX,DX           ;Set up for division
            MOV     CL,14
            DIV     CL              ;AL now contains Y character position
            MOV     ClickY,AL
            POP     AX              ;Get back X position
            PUSH    AX              ;And store again
            MOV     CL,3            ;Divide by 8
            SHR     AX,CL           ;AL contains X character position
            MOV     ClickX,AL       ;Store for a while

            CALL    Position        ;Print position of click
            CALL    Xfer            ;Go move word
            CALL    DispWord        ;Display word

            POP     CX              ;Restore X
            POP     DX              ;Restore Y

M1:         CMP     CX,OldX         ;Did X position change?
            JNE     Change          ;Yes, so handle
            CMP     DX,OldY         ;Did Y position change?
            JE      Mloop           ;No, so continue loop

Change:     MOV     OldX,CX         ;Store X position
            MOV     OldY,DX         ;Store Y position
            CALL    Coords          ;Display changes
            JMP     Mloop           ;Do it all again

Exit:       MOV     AX,0            ;Reset mouse
            INT     33h
            MOV     AH,0            ;BIOS set video mode
```

```
          MOV     AL,VidMode
          INT     10h
          CALL    Cls                     ;Clear the screen

AllDone:
          .EXIT
Mouse3    ENDP



; The following routine checks to see whether a mouse is installed.
; If one is not, then the appropriate message is displayed and the
;   carry flag is set on return
; If one is, then the mouse is reset and the carry flag is cleared

          .DATA
NoDriver  DB      13,10,'Sorry, the mouse driver was not loaded$'
NoMouse   DB      13,10,'A mouse is not attached to the system$'

          .CODE
ChkMouse  PROC    USES AX BX DX ES

          MOV     AH,35h                  ;Get interrupt vector
          MOV     AL,33h                  ;Mouse interrupt
          INT     21h

          OR      AX,BX                   ;Was an address returned?
          JZ      CM1                     ;No, so give error
          CMP     BYTE PTR ES:[BX],0CFh   ;Is it simply IRET at address?
          JNE     CM2                     ;No, so driver is installed
CM1:      MOV     DX,OFFSET NoDriver      ;Point to error message
          JMP     CM3                     ;Go print it

CM2:      MOV     AX,0                    ;Initialize mouse
          INT     33h
          CMP     AX,0                    ;0 returned if no mouse
          JNE     CM4                     ;Mouse is there
          MOV     DX,OFFSET NoMouse       ;Point to error message
CM3:      MOV     AH,9                    ;Display a string using DOS
          INT     21h
          STC                             ;Set error indication
          JC      CMDone
```

continues

Listing 10.4. Continued

```
CM4:        CLC
CMDone:     RET
ChkMouse    ENDP


; The following routine hides the mouse cursor

HideMouse   PROC    USES    AX
            MOV     AX,2
            INT     33h
            RET
HideMouse   ENDP


; The following routine displays the mouse cursor

ShowMouse   PROC    USES    AX
            MOV     AX,1
            INT     33h
            RET
ShowMouse   ENDP


; The following routine clears the screen
; Uses the attribute of the character at the current cursor position
;     as the attribute for the cleared screen

Cls         PROC    USES AX BX CX DX
            MOV     AH,8                ;Read character and attribute
            MOV     BH,VidPage
            INT     10h
            MOV     BH,AH               ;Put attribute in right place

            MOV     AH,6                ;Scroll window up
            MOV     AL,0                ;Scroll full screen
            MOV     CX,0                ;Upper left corner of screen
            MOV     DH,24               ;Bottom right
            MOV     DL,79
            INT     10h
            RET
Cls         ENDP
```

```
; The following routine updates the coordinate information on the screen.
; Pass X position in CX, and Y position in DX

Coords      PROC    USES AX BX CX DX

            CALL    HideMouse               ;Hide the mouse cursor
            PUSH    DX                      ;Store Y position
            PUSH    CX                      ;Store X position

            MOV     DH,21                   ;Row 21
            MOV     DL,0                    ;To the left
            MOV     BH,VidPage
            MOV     AH,2                    ;Set cursor position
            INT     10h

            MOV     DX,OFFSET XPos          ;Point to positioning message
            MOV     AH,9                    ;Display a string using DOS
            INT     21h
            POP     AX                      ;Get back X position
            CALL    PrtDec                  ;Go print it

            MOV     DX,OFFSET YPos          ;Point to positioning message
            MOV     AH,9                    ;Display a string using DOS
            INT     21h
            POP     AX                      ;Get back Y position
            CALL    PrtDec                  ;Go print it

            MOV     DX,OFFSET Blank         ;Blank string
            MOV     AH,9                    ;Display a string using DOS
            INT     21h

            CALL    ShowMouse               ;OK to redisplay mouse cursor
            RET
Coords      ENDP


; The following routine prints the value in AX as a decimal number

PrtDec      PROC    USES AX CX DX
            MOV     CX,0FFFFh               ;Ending flag
            PUSH    CX
            MOV     CX,10
```

continues

Listing 10.4. Continued

```
PD1:        MOV     DX,0
            DIV     CX              ;Divide by 10
            ADD     DL,30h          ;Convert to ASCII
            PUSH    DX              ;Store remainder
            CMP     AX,0            ;Are we done?
            JNE     PD1             ;No, so continue

PD2:        POP     DX              ;Character is now in DL
            CMP     DX,0FFFFh       ;Is it the ending flag?
            JE      PD3             ;Yes, so continue
            MOV     AH,02h          ;Output a character
            INT     21h
            JMP     PD2             ;Keep doing it

PD3:        RET
PrtDec      ENDP


; The following routine displays the word last clicked on by the mouse.
; Word is assumed to be in BUFFER.
; If there is no word (starts with a space), then a message is displayed.

DispWord    PROC    USES AX BX DX
            CALL    HideMouse       ;Hide the mouse cursor
            MOV     DH,22           ;Row 22
            MOV     DL,0            ;To the left
            MOV     BH,VidPage
            MOV     AH,2            ;Set cursor position
            INT     10h

            MOV     DX,OFFSET NoWord   ;Assume no word there
            MOV     AL,Buffer          ;Get character
            CMP     AL,' '             ;Is it a space?
            JE      DW1                ;Yes, so don't display

            MOV     DX,OFFSET WordMsg  ;Point to display string
DW1:        MOV     AH,9               ;Display a string using DOS
            INT     21h
```

```
                CALL      ShowMouse              ;Display the cursor again
                RET
DispWord        ENDP


; The following routine displays the character coordinates when the left
;    mouse button is pressed. Assume that ClickX and ClickY are set.

Position        PROC      USES AX BX CX DX

                CALL      HideMouse              ;Hide the mouse cursor
                MOV       DH,23                  ;Row 23
                MOV       DL,0                   ;To the left
                MOV       BH,VidPage
                MOV       AH,2                   ;Set cursor position
                INT       10h

                MOV       DX,OFFSET XCPos        ;Point to positioning message
                MOV       AH,9                   ;Display a string using DOS
                INT       21h
                MOV       AH,0
                MOV       AL,ClickX              ;Get X position
                CALL      PrtDec                 ;Go print it

                MOV       DX,OFFSET YCPos        ;Point to positioning message
                MOV       AH,9                   ;Display a string using DOS
                INT       21h
                MOV       AH,0
                MOV       AL,ClickY              ;Get Y position
                CALL      PrtDec                 ;Go print it

                MOV       DX,OFFSET Blank        ;Blank string
                MOV       AH,9                   ;Display a string using DOS
                INT       21h

                CALL      ShowMouse              ;Display mouse cursor
                RET
Position        ENDP


; The following clears the buffer area

ZapBuf          PROC      USES CX ES DI
```

continues

Listing 10.4. Continued

```
              PUSH     DS
              POP      ES
              MOV      DI,OFFSET Buffer
              MOV      CX,BufLen
ZB1:          MOV      BYTE PTR [DI],' '
              INC      DI
              LOOP     ZB1
              RET
ZapBuf        ENDP


; The following transfers the word at the current cursor location
; to the buffer area

Xfer          PROC     USES AX BX CX DX

              CALL     ZapBuf
              MOV      FirstChar,1          ;Set flag for first character
              MOV      AL,ClickX
              MOV      CurX,AL
              MOV      AL,ClickY
              MOV      CurY,AL
              CALL     HideMouse            ;Hide the mouse cursor

XF1:          MOV      AH,2                 ;Make sure set to CurX/CurY
              MOV      BH,VidPage
              MOV      DH,CurY
              MOV      DL,CurX
              INT      10h

              MOV      AH,8                 ;Read character at cursor
              MOV      BH,VidPage
              INT      10h
              CMP      AL,0                 ;Was it a space?
              JE       XF5                  ;Yes, found beginning
              CMP      AL,'.'               ;Was it punctuation?
              JE       XF5                  ;Yes, found beginning

              CMP      CurX,0               ;Are we at position 0?
              JNE      XF2                  ;No, so continue
```

```
            CMP    CurY,0              ;Are we at upper left?
            JE     XF7                 ;Yes, assume found word start
            DEC    CurY                ;No, so previous row
            MOV    CurX,80             ;Point to right side of screen
XF2:        DEC    CurX
            MOV    FirstChar,0         ;No longer on first character
            JMP    XF1                 ;Continue looking

XF5:        CMP    FirstChar,0         ;On first character?
            JNE    XF7                 ;Yes, no need to increment
            INC    CurX                ;Point to space after separator
            CMP    CurX,80             ;Past right side?
            JNE    XF6
            MOV    CurX,0              ;Point to left side
            INC    CurY
XF6:        MOV    AH,2                ;Set cursor position
            MOV    BH,VidPage
            MOV    DH,CurY
            MOV    DL,CurX
            INT    10h

XF7:        MOV    BX,OFFSET Buffer    ;Point to start of buffer
            MOV    CX,BufLen           ;Length of buffer

XF8:        PUSH   BX                  ;Save position in buffer
            MOV    AH,8                ;Read character at cursor
            MOV    BH,0                ;Assume page 0
            INT    10h
            POP    BX                  ;Get back buffer position
            CMP    AL,0                ;Was it a space?
            JE     XFDone              ;Yes, found end
            CMP    AL,'.'              ;Was it punctuation?
            JE     XFDone              ;Yes, found end
            MOV    [BX],AL             ;Store character
            INC    BX                  ;Point to next one

            INC    CurX                ;Point to next screen location
            CMP    CurX,80             ;Past right side?
            JNE    XF9
            MOV    CurX,0              ;Point to left side
            INC    CurY
XF9:        PUSH   BX                  ;Save position in buffer
            MOV    AH,2                ;Set cursor position
```

continues

Listing 10.4. Continued

```
            MOV     BH,0                ;Assume page 0
            MOV     DH,CurY
            MOV     DL,CurX
            INT     10h

            POP     BX                  ;Get back buffer position
            DEC     CX                  ;Counter adjustment
            JNZ     XF8                 ;Keep going as far as we can

XFDone:     MOV     AH,2                ;Set cursor position
            MOV     BH,0                ;Assume page 0
            MOV     DH,ClickY
            MOV     DL,ClickX
            INT     10h
            CALL    ShowMouse           ;OK to show mouse cursor again
            RET
Xfer        ENDP

            END
```

Several new subroutines are in this program. DispWord is used to display the word on which the user clicked the left button. Position is used to display the character row and column on which the left button was clicked. ZapBuff clears out the temporary buffer used by both DispWord and Xfer. Finally, Xfer is used to transfer information from the screen to a temporary buffer.

The Position subroutine performs a similar function to Coords. It displays the row and column on which the mouse cursor resided when the left button was clicked. This position is determined by dividing the virtual mouse coordinates by the character cell size. For the video mode used in this program, cell size is 8×14. You therefore must divide the horizontal coordinate by 8 and the vertical coordinate by 14 to get the character column and row.

The algorithm used in MOUSE3.ASM to perform this coordinate-to-position translation works only because the virtual coordinates used by the mouse driver correspond directly to the actual coordinates used by the video card for this video mode. Both are 640×350. If you code similar functions in your own programs, you should make sure that your algorithm reflects the correct relationship of virtual coordinates to actual resolution to character cell size.

Xfer uses the BIOS character-reading functions to extract a word from the screen. Simplistic in nature, Xfer recognizes only spaces or periods as delimiters between words. If you were using this routine in a full-blown program, you obviously would need to allow for different delimiters.

DispWord displays the word that Xfer deposits in the temporary buffer. If the first character of Buffer is a space, a different message is displayed—one which indicates that there is no word where the mouse was clicked.

Like other subroutines that read or write the screen, both Xfer and DispWord turn off the mouse cursor before doing their work. They do so because accurate reading and writing of the screen is not possible, within the vicinity of the mouse cursor, while the mouse cursor is displayed.

When you use MOUSE3.EXE, you can point the mouse anywhere on the screen and click it. The word on which you click is displayed at the bottom of the screen. To exit from the program, click the right button.

Controlling Mouse Sensitivity

As a final exercise for this chapter, let's look at how you can change the sensitivity of the mouse. The simplest way is by using mouse function 26.

This function lets you control three factors of mouse movement:

- Horizontal sensitivity
- Vertical sensitivity
- Double-speed threshold sensitivity

All three factors can be set to any value between 1 and 100. One represents the slowest movement possible, and 100 represents the fastest. Fifty is an average, normal movement.

The values set by this function are used as offsets into a table maintained by the mouse driver. This table contains values that are multiplied by the mickey count (discussed earlier in this chapter) before it is returned to the mouse driver. A value of 50, therefore, means that the multiplication factor in the table is simply 1: The mickey count is passed through as is.

The *double-speed threshold* is the mickey count at which the apparent speed of the mouse cursor will double. For instance, the default double-speed threshold is 64. If you move the mouse faster than 64 mickeys per second, the apparent speed of the mouse doubles.

The program in Listing 10.5, MOUSE4.ASM, displays a simple control panel on the screen and enables you to modify horizontal, vertical, and double-speed threshold sensitivity. This sensitivity is controlled through mouse function 26, as described earlier.

Listing 10.5. MOUSE4.ASM

```
Page 60,132

Comment ¦
*********************************************************************

File:      MOUSE4.ASM
Author:    Allen L. Wyatt
Date:      5/14/92
Assembler: MASM 6.0

Purpose:   Illustrate differing mouse speeds.
           This program assumes that you have an EGA or VGA monitor.

Format:    MOUSE4

*********************************************************************¦

           .MODEL  small
           .STACK                              ;Default 1K stack is OK
           .DATA
XPos       DB      'X Position: $'
YPos       DB      '    Y Position: $'
Blank      DB      '    $'

Msg        DB      'Click on the controls to affect sensitivity',13,10
           DB      'Click on the right mouse button to exit program$'
Controls   DB      '┌─────────────────────────────────────────────────┐',13,10
           DB      '│   Horizontal   │    Vertical    │  Double Speed   │',13,10
           DB      '│                │                │                 │',13,10
           DB      '│   ',24,'            ',25,'    │    ',24
           DB      '        ',25,'   │    ',24,'        ',25,'   ║ ',13,10
           DB      '└─────────────────────────────────────────────────┘',13,10
           DB      '$'

VidMode    DB      00
Horiz      DW      0000
Vert       DW      0000
DSThresh   DW      0000
```

```
THoriz      DW      0000
TVert       DW      0000
TDSThresh   DW      0000
OldX        DW      0000
OldY        DW      0000
ClickX      DB      00
ClickY      DB      00


            .CODE
            .STARTUP
Mouse4      PROC

            CALL    ChkMouse            ;Go see whether mouse is there
            JC      AllDone             ;Error, so exit

            MOV     AH,0Fh              ;Get video mode
            INT     10h
            MOV     VidMode,AL          ;Store for later

            MOV     AH,0                ;BIOS set video mode
            MOV     AL,10h
            INT     10h

            CALL    Cls                 ;Clear the screen
            MOV     DX,0                ;Top left corner
            MOV     BH,0                ;Assume page 0
            MOV     AH,2                ;Set cursor position
            INT     10h
            MOV     DX,OFFSET Controls  ;Want to display controls
            MOV     AH,9                ;Display a string using DOS
            INT     21h

            MOV     DH,23               ;Row 23
            MOV     DL,0                ;To the left
            MOV     BH,0                ;Assume page 0
            MOV     AH,2                ;Set cursor position
            INT     10h
            MOV     DX,OFFSET Msg       ;Point to exit message
            MOV     AH,9                ;Display a string using DOS
```

Listing 10.5. Continued

```
              INT     21h

              MOV     AX,27              ;Get mouse sensitivity
              INT     33h
              MOV     Horiz,BX           ;And store the parameters
              MOV     Vert,CX            ;  for later reset
              MOV     DSThresh,DX

              MOV     THoriz,BX          ;Store them again in work area
              MOV     TVert,CX
              MOV     TDSThresh,DX

              CALL    DispParms          ;Display initial values
              CALL    ShowMouse          ;Go show mouse cursor

Mloop:        MOV     AX,3               ;Read mouse status
              INT     33h

              CMP     BX,2               ;Was right button pressed?
              JE      Exit               ;Yes, so exit

              CMP     BX,1               ;Was left button pressed?
              JNE     M5                 ;No, so do positioning
              CALL    LeftButton         ;Go handle left button press

M5:           CMP     CX,OldX            ;Did X position change?
              JNE     Change             ;Yes, so handle
              CMP     DX,OldY            ;Did Y position change?
              JE      Mloop              ;No, so continue loop

Change:       MOV     OldX,CX            ;Store X position
              MOV     OldY,DX            ;Store Y position
              CALL    Coords             ;Display changes
              JMP     Mloop              ;Do it all again

Exit:         MOV     BX,Horiz           ;Get sensitivity parameters
              MOV     CX,Vert
              MOV     DX,DSThresh
              MOV     AX,26              ;Set mouse sensitivity
              INT     33h
```

```
            MOV     AX,0                    ;Reset mouse
            INT     33h
            MOV     AH,0                    ;BIOS set video mode
            MOV     AL,VidMode
            INT     10h
            CALL    Cls                     ;Clear the screen

AllDone:
            .EXIT
Mouse4      ENDP



; The following routine checks to see whether a mouse is installed
; If one is not, then the appropriate message is displayed and the
;    carry flag is set on return
; If one is, then the mouse is reset and the carry flag is cleared

            .DATA
NoDriver    DB      13,10,'Sorry, the mouse driver was not loaded$'
NoMouse     DB      13,10,'A mouse is not attached to the system$'

            .CODE
ChkMouse    PROC    USES AX BX DX ES

            MOV     AH,35h                  ;Get interrupt vector
            MOV     AL,33h                  ;Mouse interrupt
            INT     21h

            OR      AX,BX                   ;Was an address returned?
            JZ      CM1                     ;No, so give error
            CMP     BYTE PTR ES:[BX],0CFh   ;Is it simply IRET at address?
            JNE     CM2                     ;No, so driver is installed
CM1:        MOV     DX,OFFSET NoDriver      ;Point to error message
            JMP     CM3                     ;Go print it

CM2:        MOV     AX,0                    ;Initialize mouse
            INT     33h
            CMP     AX,0                    ;0 returned if no mouse
            JNE     CM4                     ;Mouse is there
            MOV     DX,OFFSET NoMouse       ;Point to error message
CM3:        MOV     AH,9                    ;Display a string using DOS
            INT     21h
```

continues

Listing 10.5. Continued

```
                STC                         ;Set error indication
                JC       CMDone

CM4:            CLC
CMDone:         RET
ChkMouse        ENDP



; The following routine hides the mouse cursor

HideMouse       PROC     USES    AX
                MOV      AX,2
                INT      33h
                RET
HideMouse       ENDP



; The following routine displays the mouse cursor

ShowMouse       PROC     USES    AX
                MOV      AX,1
                INT      33h
                RET
ShowMouse       ENDP



; The following routine handles what goes on when the left mouse
;    button is pressed. All registers undisturbed on return.

LeftButton      PROC     USES AX BX CX DX

                PUSH     CX                 ;Store X position
                MOV      AX,DX              ;Set up for division
                MOV      CL,14
                DIV      CL                 ;AL now contains Y character position
                MOV      ClickY,AL
                POP      AX                 ;Get back X position
                MOV      CL,3               ;Divide by 8
```

```
        SHR     AX,CL               ;AL contains X character position
        MOV     ClickX,AL           ;Store for a while

        CMP     ClickY,3            ;Are we on the right row?
        JNE     LBError             ;No, so go handle error

        CMP     ClickX,3            ;Horizontal Up?
        JNE     LB1                 ;No, continue
        CMP     THoriz,100          ;Already at limit?
        JE      LBError             ;Yes, so exit
        INC     THoriz
        JMP     LBSet

LB1:    CMP     ClickX,11           ;Horizontal Down?
        JNE     LB2                 ;No, continue
        CMP     THoriz,5            ;Already at meaningful bottom limit?
        JE      LBError             ;Yes, so exit
        DEC     THoriz
        JMP     LBSet

LB2:    CMP     ClickX,18           ;Vertical Up?
        JNE     LB3                 ;No, continue
        CMP     TVert,100           ;Already at limit?
        JE      LBError             ;Yes, so exit
        INC     TVert
        JMP     LBSet

LB3:    CMP     ClickX,26           ;Vertical Down?
        JNE     LB4                 ;No, continue
        CMP     TVert,5             ;Already at meaningful bottom limit?
        JE      LBError             ;Yes, so exit
        DEC     TVert
        JMP     LBSet

LB4:    CMP     ClickX,33           ;DS Up?
        JNE     LB5                 ;No, continue
        CMP     TDSThresh,100       ;Already at limit?
        JE      LBError             ;Yes, so exit
        INC     TDSThresh
        JMP     LBSet
```

continues

Listing 10.5. Continued

```
LB5:        CMP     ClickX,41        ;DS Down?
            JNE     LBError          ;No, so must be an error
            CMP     TDSThresh,5      ;Already at meaningful bottom limit?
            JE      LBError          ;Yes, so exit
            DEC     TDSThresh

LBSet:      MOV     BX,THoriz        ;Get sensitivity parameters
            MOV     CX,TVert
            MOV     DX,TDSThresh
            MOV     AX,26            ;Set mouse sensitivity
            INT     33h

            CALL    DispParms        ;Go display values
            JMP     LBDone

LBError:    MOV     AH,02            ;Output a character
            MOV     DL,07            ;Bell character
            INT     21h

LBDone:     RET
LeftButton  ENDP


; The following routine clears the screen
; It uses the attribute of the character at the current cursor position
;       as the attribute for the cleared screen

Cls         PROC    USES AX BX CX DX
            MOV     AH,8             ;Read character and attribute
            MOV     BH,0             ;Assume page 0
            INT     10h
            MOV     BH,AH            ;Put attribute in right place

            MOV     AH,6             ;Scroll window up
            MOV     AL,0             ;Scroll full screen
            MOV     CX,0             ;Upper left corner of screen
            MOV     DH,24            ;Bottom right
            MOV     DL,79
            INT     10h
```

```
          RET
Cls       ENDP


; The following routine updates the coordinate information on the screen
; Pass X position in CX, and Y position in DX

Coords    PROC      USES AX BX CX DX

          CALL      HideMouse              ;Hide the mouse cursor
          PUSH      DX                     ;Store Y position
          PUSH      CX                     ;Store X position

          MOV       DH,21                  ;Row 21
          MOV       DL,0                   ;To the left
          MOV       BH,0                   ;Assume page 0
          MOV       AH,2                   ;Set cursor position
          INT       10h

          MOV       DX,OFFSET XPos         ;Point to positioning message
          MOV       AH,9                   ;Display a string using DOS
          INT       21h
          POP       AX                     ;Get back X position
          MOV       BL,0                   ;Print as is
          CALL      PadDec                 ;Go print it

          MOV       DX,OFFSET YPos         ;Point to positioning message
          MOV       AH,9                   ;Display a string using DOS
          INT       21h
          POP       AX                     ;Get back Y position
          MOV       BL,0                   ;Print as is
          CALL      PadDec                 ;Go print it

          MOV       DX,OFFSET Blank        ;Blank string
          MOV       AH,9                   ;Display a string using DOS
          INT       21h

          CALL      ShowMouse              ;OK to redisplay mouse cursor
          RET
Coords    ENDP
```

continues

Listing 10.5. Continued

```
; The following routine displays the mouse parameters

DispParms   PROC    USES    AX BX DX

            CALL    HideMouse               ;Hide the mouse cursor
            MOV     DH,3                    ;Row 3
            MOV     DL,6                    ;Column 6
            MOV     BH,0                    ;Assume page 0
            MOV     AH,2                    ;Set cursor position
            INT     10h
            MOV     AX,THoriz
            MOV     BL,3                    ;Take 3 spaces
            CALL    PadDec                  ;Go print it

            MOV     DH,3                    ;Row 3
            MOV     DL,21                   ;Column 21
            MOV     BH,0                    ;Assume page 0
            MOV     AH,2                    ;Set cursor position
            INT     10h
            MOV     AX,TVert
            MOV     BL,3                    ;Take 3 spaces
            CALL    PadDec                  ;Go print it

            MOV     DH,3                    ;Row 3
            MOV     DL,36                   ;Column 36
            MOV     BH,0                    ;Assume page 0
            MOV     AH,2                    ;Set cursor position
            INT     10h
            MOV     AX,TDSThresh
            MOV     BL,3                    ;Take 3 spaces
            CALL    PadDec                  ;Go print it

            CALL    ShowMouse               ;OK to redisplay mouse cursor
            RET
DispParms   ENDP


; The following routine prints the value in AX as a decimal number.
; The number is right-justified in a field defined by the contents
;    of BL. If BL is 0 or is a value too small for the width of
```

```
;     the number being printed, then the number is printed as is.

PadDec      PROC    USES AX BX CX DX
            MOV     BH,0                    ;Counter for number of digits
            MOV     CX,0FFFFh               ;Ending flag
            PUSH    CX
            MOV     CX,10
PD1:        MOV     DX,0
            DIV     CX                      ;Divide by 10
            ADD     DL,30h                  ;Convert to ASCII
            PUSH    DX                      ;Store remainder
            INC     BH                      ;One more digit
            CMP     AX,0                    ;Are we done?
            JNE     PD1                     ;No, so continue

            SUB     BL,BH                   ;BL now contains spaces to print
            CMP     BL,0                    ;No space or below 0?
            JLE     PD3                     ;Yes, so don't do spaces
            MOV     CH,0
            MOV     CL,BL
PD2:        MOV     AH,02h                  ;Output a character
            MOV     DL,' '
            INT     21h
            LOOP    PD2

PD3:        POP     DX                      ;Character is now in DL
            CMP     DX,0FFFFh               ;Is it the ending flag?
            JE      PD4                     ;Yes, so continue
            MOV     AH,02h                  ;Output a character
            INT     21h
            JMP     PD3                     ;Keep doing it

PD4:        RET
PadDec      ENDP

            END
```

The only new subroutines in this program are LeftButton, DispParms, and
PadDec. LeftButton is used to determine what happens when the left button
is pressed. First, it checks whether the mouse cursor is on the up or down
controls, as determined by the character positions of the six controls. Then
the settings for the horizontal, vertical, or double-speed threshold values are
changed.

DispParms displays the three settings for the horizontal, vertical, or double-speed threshold values. PadDec is an adaptation of the PrtDec subroutine used in other programs in this chapter. PadDec right-justifies a number within a field, and is suited particularly to the needs of DispParms.

When you run MOUSE4.EXE, you can change any of the sensitivity parameters. The changes you make take effect immediately. You therefore can see what happens when you use different settings. MOUSE4.EXE accomplishes essentially the same task as the control panel program that comes with the Microsoft mouse.

When you finish with the program, you can click the right mouse button to exit from the program.

Summary

The mouse is becoming more common as an input device on today's computers. You easily can add the functionality of the mouse to your programs. You need to understand just a few underlying concepts, and the rest is a matter of determining position and the actions that can or cannot be taken at that position.

This chapter introduced the mouse functions and illustrated how they can be used in your programs. You learned how to discern information about your mouse, how to display the mouse cursor in text and graphics modes, how to read information from the screen with the mouse, and, finally, how to control mouse sensitivity.

You can control and use the mouse in your programs in many ways. The mouse functions enable you to control every aspect of how your mouse is used. If you want more information about the mouse functions, see Appendix B, "The Mouse Functions."

Chapter 11 discusses another applied assembly language topic: using the EXEC function.

Using the EXEC Function

One popular feature of many full-function programs on the market is the capability to execute an operating system command from within the program. In many programs, you can even "shell out" of the program to execute several DOS commands and then return to the program when you finish.

The feature of DOS that makes this possible is the EXEC function. With this function, you can perform any of the following tasks:

- Load and execute another program
- Load another program without executing it
- Load a file as a program overlay

The first of these three options, the most common use of the EXEC function, is discussed in this chapter.

Basic EXEC Concepts

Any program, while it is executing, has the capability to run another program while the original program remains in memory. The original program is called the *parent*, the program being loaded is called the *child* or *child process*, and the process of creating a child program is called *spawning*.

While the child process is running, the parent process remains dormant. Because DOS is not a multitasking environment, it is not possible to execute multiple programs simultaneously. The parent program also occupies memory that is not available to the child process.

Several conditions must occur before you can successfully spawn a program, however. The most important of these conditions is that you must have sufficient memory to load and execute the child process. It is possible to continue spawning programs until you simply run out of memory.

To utilize the EXEC function, you use interrupt 21h, function 4Bh. This function requires the register settings shown in Table 11.1 before invoking the interrupt. Notice that the value of the AL register controls what the EXEC function does with the program being loaded. As mentioned, the most common use of the EXEC function is for loading and executing a child process. All the examples in this chapter, therefore, use only this capability.

Table 11.1. Register settings for the EXEC function.

Register	Value	Meaning
AH	4Bh	The EXEC function
AL	00h	Load and execute a child process
	01h	Load a child process
	03h	Load a program overlay
	05h	Enter the EXEC state
DS:DX		Pointer to child process name (when AL=00h, 01h, or 03h)
		Pointer to EXEC state structure (when AL=05h)
ES:BX		Pointer to parameter block

The Child Process File Name

When you are specifying a program name to load, use the DS:DX register pair as a pointer to the program name. The program name is nothing but an ASCIIZ string that indicates the full path name of the file to be loaded.

Because only one file is loaded at a time by the EXEC function, you cannot use wild-card characters in the file name. Although this restriction may be obvious, a few other restrictions on the file name may not be as obvious and should not be taken for granted. For instance, the file name must be explicit, which means that you must supply the full path name, from the current path, in order for the file to be loaded. You can use relative or absolute path names, however. Therefore, if you are working in the \ASSEMBLY\SOURCE

subdirectory, and the file to be spawned (EXAMPLE.EXE) is in the
\ASSEMBLY\EXE subdirectory, either of the following path specifications is
valid:

> \ASSEMBLY\EXE\EXAMPLE.EXE

> ..\EXE\EXAMPLE.EXE

The first example is an absolute path name, and the second is a relative path
name. Notice that you must supply the extension for the file name. You can
use the EXEC function only to directly load and execute EXE or COM files; BAT
files cannot be directly executed. When you enter a program name at the DOS
prompt, it is not necessary to use the COM or EXE extensions, and you can
specify batch files for execution. All these shortcuts are features of
COMMAND.COM, the DOS command processor.

Notice that because COMMAND.COM itself is a COM file, you can spawn
COMMAND.COM as a child process and use it to execute batch files. Both of
these possibilities are discussed later in this chapter.

The Child Process Parameter Block

When you are calling the EXEC function, the register pair ES:BX points to a 14-
byte parameter block used by EXEC to build the environment and PSP for the
child process. Table 11.2 shows the layout of this parameter block. The
doubleword pointer values are stored in typical Intel fashion: offset first, and
then segment.

Table 11.2. EXEC function parameter block pointed to by ES:BX.

Offset	Length	Use
00h	Word	Segment of environment block
02h	Doubleword	Pointer to command tail
06h	Doubleword	Pointer to first FCB
0Ah	Doubleword	Pointer to second FCB

The following section discusses each element of this parameter block.

The Environment Block Segment Pointer

The environment block is maintained by DOS to indicate system parameters that DOS or programs use in executing. The contents of the parameter block originally are set in the CONFIG.SYS file or by using the SET, PROMPT, or PATH commands. Entries within this block are stored in memory as a series of ASCIIZ strings, with each one taking the form NAME=VALUE. The end of the block is denoted by a NUL (0) value where the first character of the next entry normally would be expected. Figure 11.1 shows a memory dump of an environment block. This environment block starts at 0A04:0000 and ends at 0A04:0148.

```
0A04:0000  43 4F 4D 53 50 45 43 3D-43 3A 5C 44 4F 53 5C 43   COMSPEC=C:\DOS\C
0A04:0010  4F 4D 4D 41 4E 44 2E 43-4F 4D 00 50 41 54 48 3D   OMMAND.COM.PATH=
0A04:0020  43 3A 5C 3B 43 3A 5C 44-4F 53 3B 43 3A 5C 42 49   C:\;C:\DOS;C:\BI
0A04:0030  4E 3B 43 3A 5C 4D 45 4E-55 3B 43 3A 5C 4C 41 4E   N;C:\MENU;C:\LAN
0A04:0040  47 3B 43 3A 5C 4D 45 4E-55 42 41 54 3B 43 3A 5C   G;C:\MENUBAT;C:\
0A04:0050  55 54 49 4C 49 54 59 5C-42 55 46 46 41 4C 4F 3B   UTILITY\BUFFALO;
0A04:0060  43 3A 5C 55 54 49 4C 49-54 59 5C 4E 4F 52 54 4F   C:\UTILITY\NORTO
0A04:0070  4E 3B 43 3A 5C 55 54 49-4C 49 54 59 5C 50 4B 5A   N;C:\UTILITY\PKZ
0A04:0080  49 50 3B 44 3A 5C 4F 52-41 43 4C 45 36 5C 50 42   IP;D:\ORACLE6\PB
0A04:0090  49 4E 3B 44 3A 5C 4F 52-41 43 00 50 52 4F 4D 50   IN;D:\ORAC.PROMP
0A04:00A0  54 3D 24 70 24 67 00 54-45 4D 50 3D 63 3A 5C 74   T=$p$g.TEMP=c:\t
0A04:00B0  65 6D 70 00 4D 45 4E 55-3D 63 3A 5C 6D 65 6E 75   emp.MENU=c:\menu
0A04:00C0  00 4D 54 4F 43 3D 63 3A-5C 62 69 6E 00 42 4C 41   .MTOC=c:\bin.BLA
0A04:00D0  53 54 45 52 3D 61 32 32-30 20 69 37 20 64 31 20   STER=a220 i7 d1
0A04:00E0  74 32 00 53 4F 55 4E 44-3D 63 3A 5C 75 74 69 6C   t2.SOUND=c:\util
0A04:00F0  69 74 79 5C 73 62 70 72-6F 00 49 51 3D 2F 68 44   ity\sbpro.IQ=/hD
0A04:0100  3A 5C 49 4E 46 4F 51 55-45 20 2F 73 44 3A 5C 00   :\INFOQUE /sD:\.
0A04:0110  4D 47 52 50 41 54 48 3D-43 3A 5C 55 54 49 4C 49   MGRPATH=C:\UTILI
0A04:0120  54 59 5C 42 55 46 46 41-4C 4F 00 43 4F 4E 46 49   TY\BUFFALO.CONFI
0A04:0130  47 3D 64 3A 5C 6F 72 61-63 6C 65 36 5C 63 6F 6E   G=d:\oracle6\con
0A04:0140  66 69 67 2E 6F 72 61 00-00 6F 72 79 20 62 6C      fig.ora..ory bl
```

Because environment blocks always start on paragraph boundaries, the absolute address at which the block begins is evenly divisible by 16. You can specify the start of an environment block with a single address pointer, which represents the segment address. The offset address must be 0.

Every child process executed with the EXEC function inherits an environment block from its parent. This block typically is a copy of the parent's environment block, but you can build your own environment block.

To indicate that you want EXEC to use a copy of the existing environment block, set the environment block segment pointer to 0. If you want to construct your own environment block, start it at a paragraph boundary, and set the value of the pointer to the beginning of your newly constructed block. You can pattern your environment block after the memory dump shown in Figure 11.1.

The Command Tail Pointer

The command tail is nothing more than an ASCII string which indicates the string that should be tacked on to the end of the program name when the program is executed. The command tail can include parameters and switches for the proper functioning of the program pointed to by the child process file name.

The structure of the string pointed to by the command tail pointer is simple. The first byte is a count of the characters in the command tail, including spaces, followed by the actual command tail, and then a carriage return (ASCII 13).

As an example, assume that you want the child process to run the FORMAT command to format a 720K disk in drive B:. If you type the command at the DOS prompt, it appears as follows:

FORMAT B: /F:720

The command FORMAT is the program name you are going to run. The command tail is everything after it. The structure of the command tail for the EXEC function is

```
DB      9                      ;Length of command tail
DB      'B: /F:720'            ;Actual command tail
DB      13                     ;Trailing carriage return
```

Notice that the trailing carriage return is not counted in the length of the command tail.

The FCB Pointers

Finally, two pointers point toward file control blocks (FCBs). These pointers are part of the PSP that the EXEC function creates for the child process. They are constructed as normal FCBs. If the child process will not use any FCB functions, then what you set these pointers to does not matter.

For more information on the structure of file control blocks, refer to *Using Assembly Language*, 3rd Edition (published by Que Corporation). FCBs are discussed in the DOS functions reference section.

EXEC and Register Use

When you invoke the EXEC function, it is possible for all your registers to change, except for CS and IP. These registers are the only ones guaranteed to remain unchanged. Your stack segment (SS) and stack pointer (SP) registers therefore can get trashed.

The only way to guard against the potentially devastating effects of these registers changing is to store the contents of SS and SP in memory locations you can access after returning from the EXEC function. You can store the contents of any other registers on the stack before you store SS and SP. When you return from EXEC, restore SS and SP, and then POP the contents of the other registers you stored.

Using EXEC to Spawn an EXE or COM File

Earlier, this chapter mentioned that you can use the EXEC function to spawn a child process that runs an EXE or COM file. This process is relatively straight-forward, as you can see in Listing 11.1. This program spawns a child process that runs TREE.COM, a DOS utility that displays the directory structure for your drive.

Listing 11.1. EXEC1.ASM

```
Page 60,132

Comment ¦
*********************************************************************


File:       EXEC1.ASM
Author:     Allen L. Wyatt
Date:       6/6/92
Assembler:  MASM 6.0

Purpose:    Demonstrate how to use the EXEC function to spawn a COM
            or EXE child. Program uses EXEC to run TREE.COM, a DOS
            utility.

Format:     EXEC1


*********************************************************************¦
```

```
        .MODEL  small
        .STACK                      ;Default 1K stack is OK
        .DATA

Path    DB      'C:\DOS\TREE.COM',0

Parms   DW      0                   ;Parent environment block is OK
        DW      OFFSET CmdTail      ;Command tail address
        DW      SEG CmdTail
        DW      0,0                 ;FCB pointers don't matter
        DW      0,0                 ;    for this example

CmdTail DB      3                   ;Length of command tail
        DB      'C:\',13            ;Actual command tail

SaveSS  DW      0                   ;Temporary storage areas
SaveSP  DW      0
Error   DW      0

Message1 DB     'Press any key to enter child program...$'
Message2 DB     13,10,'Back from child program',13,10,'$'
Message3 DB     'Ending parent program'
CRLF     DB     13,10,'$'
ErrMsg   DB     'Error during EXEC function: $'

ErrorTable DW   OFFSET ErrorX
        DW      OFFSET Error1
        DW      OFFSET Error2
        DW      OFFSET Error3
        DW      OFFSET Error4
        DW      OFFSET Error5
        DW      OFFSET ErrorX
        DW      OFFSET ErrorX
        DW      OFFSET Error8
        DW      OFFSET ErrorX
        DW      OFFSET ErrorA
        DW      OFFSET ErrorB

Error1  DB      ' (invalid function)$'
Error2  DB      ' (file not found)$'
Error3  DB      ' (path not found)$'
```

continues

Listing 11.1. Continued

```
Error4     DB      ' (too many open files)$'
Error5     DB      ' (access denied)$'
Error8     DB      ' (not enough memory)$'
ErrorA     DB      ' (bad environment)$'
ErrorB     DB      ' (bad format)$'
ErrorX     DB      ' (unknown error value)$'

           .CODE
           .STARTUP
Exec1      PROC

; The following memory allocation code works because it is known that MASM
; sets DS and SS to the same segment address in the start-up code. Also, ES
; is set to the PSP for the program upon entry.

           MOV     BX,DS               ;Point to start of data segment
           MOV     AX,ES               ;Point to start of PSP
           SUB     BX,AX               ;Number of segments for code and data
           MOV     AX,SP               ;SP is pointing to top of stack area
           MOV     CL,4                ;Dividing by 16
           SHR     AX,CL
           ADD     BX,AX               ;BX=paragraphs needed
           MOV     AH,4Ah              ;Modify memory allocation
           INT     21h

           CALL    Cls                 ;Clear the screen
           MOV     DX,0                ;Set up to print message
           MOV     BH,0                ;Assume page 0
           MOV     AH,2                ;Set cursor position
           INT     10h
           MOV     DX,OFFSET Message1  ;Point to starting message
           MOV     AH,9                ;Display a string using DOS
           INT     21h
           MOV     AH,0                ;Read keyboard character
           INT     16h
           MOV     DX,OFFSET CRLF      ;Go to next line
           MOV     AH,9                ;Display a string using DOS
           INT     21h
```

```
            MOV     Error,0              ;Assume that no error will occur
            MOV     AH,4Bh               ;EXEC function
            MOV     AL,0                 ;Load and execute
            MOV     DX,OFFSET Path       ;Path name to file to execute
            PUSH    DS
            POP     ES                   ;ES:BX must point to
            MOV     BX,OFFSET Parms      ;   parameter block
            MOV     SaveSS,SS            ;Don't want to lose SP:SS during
            MOV     SaveSP,SP            ;   EXEC call
            INT     21h
            JNC     Back                 ;No error, so continue
            MOV     Error,AX             ;Put error value in its place

Back:       MOV     SS,SaveSS            ;Restore SP:SS from saved values
            MOV     SP,SaveSP
            MOV     DX,OFFSET Message2   ;Point to return message
            MOV     AH,9                 ;Display a string using DOS
            INT     21h

            CMP     Error,0              ;Was there an error?
            JE      Done                 ;No, so exit
            MOV     DX,OFFSET ErrMsg     ;Point to error message
            MOV     AH,9                 ;Display a string using DOS
            INT     21h
            MOV     AX,Error             ;Get the value
            CALL    PrtDec               ;Go print it
            MOV     BX,Error             ;Get error value
            SHL     BX,1                 ;Multiply by 2
            MOV     DX,ErrorTable[BX]    ;Get the error message
            MOV     AH,9                 ;Display a string using DOS
            INT     21h

            MOV     DX,OFFSET CRLF       ;Go to next line
            MOV     AH,9                 ;Display a string using DOS
            INT     21h

Done:       MOV     DX,OFFSET Message3   ;Point to exit message
            MOV     AH,9                 ;Display a string using DOS
            INT     21h
```

continues

Listing 11.1. Continued

```
                .EXIT
Exec1           ENDP


; The following routine clears the screen

Cls             PROC    USES AX BX CX DX
                MOV     AH,6            ;Scroll window up
                MOV     AL,0            ;Scroll full screen
                MOV     BH,7            ;Normal white on black
                MOV     CX,0            ;Upper left corner of screen
                MOV     DH,24           ;Bottom right
                MOV     DL,79
                INT     10h
                RET
Cls             ENDP


; The following routine prints the value in AX as a decimal number

PrtDec          PROC    USES AX CX DX
                MOV     CX,0FFFFh       ;Ending flag
                PUSH    CX
                MOV     CX,10
PD1:            MOV     DX,0
                DIV     CX              ;Divide by 10
                ADD     DL,30h          ;Convert to ASCII
                PUSH    DX              ;Store remainder
                CMP     AX,0            ;Are we done?
                JNE     PD1             ;No, so continue

PD2:            POP     DX              ;Character is now in DL
                CMP     DX,0FFFFh       ;Is it the ending flag?
                JE      PD3             ;Yes, so continue
                MOV     AH,02h          ;Output a character
                INT     21h
                JMP     PD2             ;Keep doing it

PD3:            RET
PrtDec          ENDP

                END
```

Notice the first executable lines in the program. These lines are included to release memory back to the available memory pool. When MASM creates an EXE file, it stores information in the EXE header that instructs DOS to reserve all of the memory for the program, if possible. In this sense, the EXE file is like a COM file: They both grab all the memory they can, even though they don't need it.

To solve this problem, the program calculates the number of paragraphs needed by the program, data, and stack. Then the memory allocation function is called to shrink the amount of memory reserved for the program. If this action were not taken, spawning a child process would be impossible because DOS would always return an out-of-memory error.

The program then displays a message and waits for a keypress before spawning the child process. The values of SS and SP also are stored before invoking EXEC, as discussed earlier.

On returning from the EXEC function, the carry flag is set if there was an error and an appropriate error message is displayed by the program. Then the parent program ends.

You can use this same program to run any COM or EXE file. You just change the variables `Path` and `CmdTail`.

Using EXEC to Spawn a Copy of COMMAND.COM

Many commercial programs enable you to "shell out" of the main program to DOS, where you can run commands or other programs. As mentioned, COMMAND.COM is nothing more than another program you can spawn with the EXEC function. There is, however, one hitch in doing this easily: You never can be sure where COMMAND.COM resides. Sometimes it's in the root directory of the hard drive, and sometimes it's in a subdirectory. In either case, you should be able to examine the environment area and discover where COMMAND.COM is located by using the COMSPEC system variable.

The program in Listing 11.2 uses the COMSPEC system variable in order to locate COMMAND.COM. Then COMMAND.COM is spawned. To return to the parent program, the EXIT command is used.

Listing 11.2. EXEC2.ASM

```
Page 60,132

Comment |
******************************************************************


File:       EXEC2.ASM
Author:     Allen L. Wyatt
Date:       6/6/92
Assembler:  MASM 6.0

Purpose:    Demonstrate how to use the EXEC function to spawn
            COMMAND.COM.

Format:     EXEC2


******************************************************************!


            .MODEL  small
            .STACK                      ;Default 1K stack is OK
            .DATA

ComSpec     DB      'COMSPEC=',0

Path        DB      80 DUP(0)
Parms       DW      0                   ;Parent environment block is OK
            DW      OFFSET CmdTail      ;Command tail address
            DW      SEG CmdTail
            DW      0,0                 ;FCB pointers don't matter
            DW      0,0                 ;    for this example

CmdTail     DB      0                   ;Length of command tail
            DB      13                  ;Actual command tail

SaveEnv     DW      0                   ;Temporary storage areas
SaveSS      DW      0
SaveSP      DW      0
Error       DW      0

Message1    DB      'Press any key to enter child program...$'
Message2    DB      13,10,13,10
```

```
            DB        'To return to parent program, use the EXIT command'
            DB        13,10,'$'
Message3    DB        'Back from child program',13,10,'$'
Message4    DB        'Ending parent program',13,10,'$'
CSLong      DB        'The COMSPEC environment variable was too long',13,10,'$'
NoComSpec   DB        'A COMSPEC environment variable could not be located'
CRLF        DB        13,10,'$'
ErrMsg      DB        'Error during EXEC function: $'

ErrorTable  DW        OFFSET ErrorX
            DW        OFFSET Error1
            DW        OFFSET Error2
            DW        OFFSET Error3
            DW        OFFSET Error4
            DW        OFFSET Error5
            DW        OFFSET ErrorX
            DW        OFFSET ErrorX
            DW        OFFSET Error8
            DW        OFFSET ErrorX
            DW        OFFSET ErrorA
            DW        OFFSET ErrorB

Error1      DB        ' (invalid function)$'
Error2      DB        ' (file not found)$'
Error3      DB        ' (path not found)$'
Error4      DB        ' (too many open files)$'
Error5      DB        ' (access denied)$'
Error8      DB        ' (not enough memory)$'
ErrorA      DB        ' (bad environment)$'
ErrorB      DB        ' (bad format)$'
ErrorX      DB        ' (unknown error value)$'

            .CODE
            .STARTUP
Exec2       PROC

            MOV       AX,ES:[2Ch]        ;Get environment segment
            MOV       SaveEnv,AX         ;And, save it for later use

; The following memory allocation code works because it is known that MASM
; sets DS and SS to the same segment address in the start-up code. Also, ES
; is set to the PSP for the program upon entry.
```

continues

Listing 11.2. Continued

```
                MOV     BX,DS              ;Point to start of data segment
                MOV     AX,ES              ;Point to start of PSP
                SUB     BX,AX              ;Number of segments for code and data
                MOV     AX,SP              ;SP is pointing to top of stack area
                MOV     CL,4               ;Dividing by 16
                SHR     AX,CL
                ADD     BX,AX              ;BX=paragraphs needed
                MOV     AH,4Ah             ;Modify memory allocation
                INT     21h

                MOV     SI,OFFSET ComSpec  ;Search for this
                CALL    SrchEnv            ;And find it
                JNC     GotComSpec         ;Found it, so continue
                MOV     DX,OFFSET NoComSpec ;Point to error message
                MOV     AH,9               ;Display a string using DOS
                INT     21h
                JMP     Done

GotComSpec: MOV     BX,OFFSET Path     ;Point to path buffer
                MOV     CL,0
GCS1:           MOV     AL,BYTE PTR ES:[DI] ;Get character
                MOV     BYTE PTR [BX],AL   ;Store character
                INC     DI
                INC     BX
                INC     CL
                CMP     AL,0               ;End of transfer?
                JE      GCS2               ;Yes, so exit
                CMP     CL,80              ;Too many characters?
                JL      GCS1               ;No, so continue
                MOV     DX,OFFSET CSLong   ;Point to error message
                MOV     AH,9               ;Display a string using DOS
                INT     21h
                JMP     Done

GCS2:           CALL    Cls                ;Clear the screen
                MOV     DX,0               ;Set up to print message
                MOV     BH,0               ;Assume page 0
                MOV     AH,2               ;Set cursor position
                INT     10h
                MOV     DX,OFFSET Message1 ;Point to starting message
```

```
        MOV     AH,9                    ;Display a string using DOS
        INT     21h
        MOV     AH,0                    ;Read keyboard character
        INT     16h
        MOV     DX,OFFSET CRLF          ;Go to next line
        MOV     AH,9                    ;Display a string using DOS
        INT     21h
        MOV     DX,OFFSET Message2      ;Point to parent message
        MOV     AH,9                    ;Display a string using DOS
        INT     21h

        MOV     Error,0                 ;Assume that no error will occur
        MOV     AH,4Bh                  ;EXEC function
        MOV     AL,0                    ;Load and execute
        MOV     DX,OFFSET Path          ;Path name to file to execute
        PUSH    DS
        POP     ES                      ;ES:BX must point to
        MOV     BX,OFFSET Parms         ;   parameter block
        MOV     SaveSS,SS               ;Don't want to lose SP:SS during
        MOV     SaveSP,SP               ;   EXEC call
        INT     21h
        JNC     Back                    ;No error, so continue
        MOV     Error,AX                ;Put error value in its place

Back:   MOV     SS,SaveSS               ;Restore SP:SS from saved values
        MOV     SP,SaveSP
        MOV     DX,OFFSET Message3      ;Point to return message
        MOV     AH,9                    ;Display a string using DOS
        INT     21h

        CMP     Error,0                 ;Was there an error?
        JE      Done                    ;No, so exit
        MOV     DX,OFFSET ErrMsg        ;Point to error message
        MOV     AH,9                    ;Display a string using DOS
        INT     21h
        MOV     AX,Error                ;Get the value
        CALL    PrtDec                  ;Go print it
        MOV     BX,Error                ;Get error value
        SHL     BX,1                    ;Multiply by 2
        MOV     DX,ErrorTable[BX]       ;Get the error message
        MOV     AH,9                    ;Display a string using DOS
        INT     21h
```

continues

Listing 11.2. Continued

```
              MOV      DX,OFFSET CRLF         ;Go to next line
              MOV      AH,9                   ;Display a string using DOS
              INT      21h

Done:         MOV      DX,OFFSET Message4     ;Point to exit message
              MOV      AH,9                   ;Display a string using DOS
              INT      21h

              .EXIT
Exec2         ENDP


; The following routine clears the screen

Cls           PROC     USES AX BX CX DX
              MOV      AH,6                   ;Scroll window up
              MOV      AL,0                   ;Scroll full screen
              MOV      BH,7                   ;Normal white on black
              MOV      CX,0                   ;Upper left corner of screen
              MOV      DH,24                  ;Bottom right
              MOV      DL,79
              INT      10h
              RET
Cls           ENDP


; The following routine prints the value in AX as a decimal number

PrtDec        PROC     USES AX CX DX
              MOV      CX,0FFFFh              ;Ending flag
              PUSH     CX
              MOV      CX,10
PD1:          MOV      DX,0
              DIV      CX                     ;Divide by 10
              ADD      DL,30h                 ;Convert to ASCII
              PUSH     DX                     ;Store remainder
              CMP      AX,0                   ;Are we done?
              JNE      PD1                    ;No, so continue

PD2:          POP      DX                     ;Character is now in DL
              CMP      DX,0FFFFh              ;Is it the ending flag?
              JE       PD3                    ;Yes, so continue
```

```
              MOV     AH,02h              ;Output a character
              INT     21h
              JMP     PD2                 ;Keep doing it


PD3:          RET
PrtDec        ENDP


; The following routine searches the environment area for a string
; pointed to by DS:SI. Returns with ES:DI pointing to the variable.
; Carry is set if not found.


SrchEnv       PROC    USES AX BX SI
              MOV     ES,SaveEnv          ;Get original environment
              MOV     DI,0                ;ES:DI points to start of environment
              MOV     BX,SI               ;Point to start of variable name


SE1:          MOV     AX,ES:[DI]          ;Get character word at pointer
              CMP     AX,0                ;Is this the end of environment block?
              JE      NotFound            ;Yes, so exit with error


SE2:          MOV     AL,[BX]             ;Get character from variable name
              INC     BX                  ;Point to next character
              CMP     AL,0                ;End of variable?
              JE      Found               ;Yes, so we found it

              CMP     AL,ES:[DI]          ;Same as in the environment block?
              JNE     SE3                 ;No, so ignore this entry
              INC     DI                  ;Point to next environment character
              JMP     SE2                 ;Keep comparing


SE3:          INC     DI                  ;Point to next environment character
              CMP     BYTE PTR ES:[DI],0  ;At end of entry?
              JNE     SE3                 ;No, continue scanning
              JMP     SE1                 ;Go back to beginning


Found:        CLC
              JNC     SEDone
NotFound:     STC
SEDone:       RET
SrchEnv       ENDP


              END
```

Notice that many things in this program are similar to the program shown in the preceding section. The major changes are in searching the environment block (the SrchEnv routine) and the messages displayed. Note also that the command tail has been eliminated. The length byte and the carriage return are still necessary, however, for the successful completion of the EXEC function.

When you are using the spawned version of COMMAND.COM, you can change any environment variables you want. For instance, you can use the PROMPT or PATH commands to make changes necessary for any commands you want to run. These changes, however, have no effect on the parent program; when you use the EXIT command to return to the parent, the environment reverts to the way it was before COMMAND.COM was spawned. This is not the case, however, if you change directories. You can change subdirectories (using the CD command), and the parent program does not remember what directory it was in when COMMAND.COM was spawned. This may not be a problem for you, but you should be aware of it when you are planning what your users will be allowed to do.

Using EXEC to Run an Internal DOS Command or Batch File

In the preceding program, you learned how to use EXEC to spawn another copy of COMMAND.COM. How should you code the same program, however, if you want simply to execute one internal command and then return to the parent program? The program in Listing 11.3 does that—it spawns COMMAND.COM to run the DIR command. When DIR is run, it is used with the /O and /P options to modify the way the directory is displayed.

Listing 11.3. EXEC3.ASM

```
Page 60,132

Comment |
************************************************************************

File:     EXEC3.ASM
Author:   Allen L. Wyatt
Date:     6/6/92
Assembler: MASM 6.0
```

```
Purpose:     Demonstrate how to use the EXEC function to spawn
             COMMAND.COM.

Format:      EXEC3


*******************************************************************|

             .MODEL  small
             .STACK                        ;Default 1K stack is OK
             .DATA

ComSpec      DB      'COMSPEC=',0

Path         DB      80 DUP(0)
Parms        DW      0                     ;Parent environment block is OK
             DW      OFFSET CmdTail        ;Command tail address
             DW      SEG CmdTail
             DW      0,0                   ;FCB pointers don't matter
             DW      0,0                   ;  for this example

CmdTail      DB      14                    ;Length of command tail
             DB      '/C DIR /OEN /P'      ;Actual command tail
             DB      13                    ;Trailing carriage return

SaveEnv      DW      0                     ;Temporary storage areas
SaveSS       DW      0
SaveSP       DW      0
Error        DW      0

Message1     DB      'Press any key to enter child program...$'
Message2     DB      13,10,13,10
             DB      'To return to parent program, use the EXIT command'
             DB      13,10,'$'
Message3     DB      'Back from child program',13,10,'$'
Message4     DB      'Ending parent program',13,10,'$'
CSLong       DB      'The COMSPEC environment variable was too long',13,10,'$'
NoComSpec    DB      'A COMSPEC environment variable could not be located'
CRLF         DB      13,10,'$'
ErrMsg       DB      'Error during EXEC function: $'
```

continues

Listing 11.3. Continued

```
ErrorTable  DW      OFFSET ErrorX
            DW      OFFSET Error1
            DW      OFFSET Error2
            DW      OFFSET Error3
            DW      OFFSET Error4
            DW      OFFSET Error5
            DW      OFFSET ErrorX
            DW      OFFSET ErrorX
            DW      OFFSET Error8
            DW      OFFSET ErrorX
            DW      OFFSET ErrorA
            DW      OFFSET ErrorB

Error1      DB      ' (invalid function)$'
Error2      DB      ' (file not found)$'
Error3      DB      ' (path not found)$'
Error4      DB      ' (too many open files)$'
Error5      DB      ' (access denied)$'
Error8      DB      ' (not enough memory)$'
ErrorA      DB      ' (bad environment)$'
ErrorB      DB      ' (bad format)$'
ErrorX      DB      ' (unknown error value)$'

            .CODE
            .STARTUP
Exec3       PROC

            MOV     AX,ES:[2Ch]         ;Get environment segment
            MOV     SaveEnv,AX          ;And save it for later use

; The following memory allocation code works because it is known that MASM
; sets DS and SS to the same segment address in the start-up code. Also, ES
; is set to the PSP for the program upon entry.

            MOV     BX,DS               ;Point to start of data segment
            MOV     AX,ES               ;Point to start of PSP
            SUB     BX,AX               ;Number of segments for code and data
            MOV     AX,SP               ;SP is pointing to top of stack area
            MOV     CL,4                ;Dividing by 16
            SHR     AX,CL
```

```
                ADD      BX,AX                  ;BX=paragraphs needed
                MOV      AH,4Ah                 ;Modify memory allocation
                INT      21h

                MOV      SI,OFFSET ComSpec       ;Search for this
                CALL     SrchEnv                 ;And find it
                JNC      GotComSpec              ;Found it, so continue
                MOV      DX,OFFSET NoComSpec     ;Point to error message
                MOV      AH,9                    ;Display a string using DOS
                INT      21h
                JMP      Done

GotComSpec:     MOV      BX,OFFSET Path          ;Point to path buffer
                MOV      CL,0
GCS1:           MOV      AL,BYTE PTR ES:[DI]     ;Get character
                MOV      BYTE PTR [BX],AL        ;Store character
                INC      DI
                INC      BX
                INC      CL
                CMP      AL,0                    ;End of transfer?
                JE       GCS2                    ;Yes, so exit
                CMP      CL,80                   ;Too many characters?
                JL       GCS1                    ;No, so continue
                MOV      DX,OFFSET CSLong        ;Point to error message
                MOV      AH,9                    ;Display a string using DOS
                INT      21h
                JMP      Done

GCS2:           CALL     Cls                     ;Clear the screen
                MOV      DX,0                    ;Set up to print message
                MOV      BH,0                    ;Assume page 0
                MOV      AH,2                    ;Set cursor position
                INT      10h
                MOV      DX,OFFSET Message1      ;Point to starting message
                MOV      AH,9                    ;Display a string using DOS
                INT      21h
                MOV      AH,0                    ;Read keyboard character
                INT      16h
                MOV      DX,OFFSET CRLF          ;Go to next line
                MOV      AH,9                    ;Display a string using DOS
                INT      21h
```

continues

Listing 11.3. Continued

```
        MOV     DX,OFFSET Message2    ;Point to parent message
        MOV     AH,9                  ;Display a string using DOS
        INT     21h

        MOV     Error,0               ;Assume that no error will occur
        MOV     AH,4Bh                ;EXEC function
        MOV     AL,0                  ;Load and execute
        MOV     DX,OFFSET Path        ;Path name to file to execute
        PUSH    DS
        POP     ES                    ;ES:BX must point to
        MOV     BX,OFFSET Parms       ;  parameter block
        MOV     SaveSS,SS             ;Don't want to lose SP:SS during
        MOV     SaveSP,SP             ;  EXEC call
        INT     21h
        JNC     Back                  ;No error, so continue
        MOV     Error,AX              ;Put error value in its place

Back:   MOV     SS,SaveSS             ;Restore SP:SS from saved values
        MOV     SP,SaveSP
        MOV     DX,OFFSET Message3    ;Point to return message
        MOV     AH,9                  ;Display a string using DOS
        INT     21h

        CMP     Error,0               ;Was there an error?
        JE      Done                  ;No, so exit
        MOV     DX,OFFSET ErrMsg      ;Point to error message
        MOV     AH,9                  ;Display a string using DOS
        INT     21h
        MOV     AX,Error              ;Get the value
        CALL    PrtDec                ;Go print it
        MOV     BX,Error              ;Get error value
        SHL     BX,1                  ;Multiply by 2
        MOV     DX,ErrorTable[BX]     ;Get the error message
        MOV     AH,9                  ;Display a string using DOS
        INT     21h

        MOV     DX,OFFSET CRLF        ;Go to next line
        MOV     AH,9                  ;Display a string using DOS
        INT     21h
```

```
Done:       MOV     DX,OFFSET Message4  ;Point to exit message
            MOV     AH,9               ;Display a string using DOS
            INT     21h


            .EXIT
Exec3       ENDP



; The following routine clears the screen

Cls         PROC    USES AX BX CX DX
            MOV     AH,6               ;Scroll window up
            MOV     AL,0               ;Scroll full screen
            MOV     BH,7               ;Normal white on black
            MOV     CX,0               ;Upper left corner of screen
            MOV     DH,24              ;Bottom right
            MOV     DL,79
            INT     10h
            RET
Cls         ENDP

; The following routine prints the value in AX as a decimal number

PrtDec      PROC    USES AX CX DX
            MOV     CX,0FFFFh          ;Ending flag
            PUSH    CX
            MOV     CX,10
PD1:        MOV     DX,0
            DIV     CX                 ;Divide by 10
            ADD     DL,30h             ;Convert to ASCII
            PUSH    DX                 ;Store remainder
            CMP     AX,0               ;Are we done?
            JNE     PD1                ;No, so continue

PD2:        POP     DX                 ;Character is now in DL
            CMP     DX,0FFFFh          ;Is it the ending flag?
            JE      PD3                ;Yes, so continue
            MOV     AH,02h             ;Output a character
            INT     21h
            JMP     PD2                ;Keep doing it
```

continues

Listing 11.3. Continued

```
PD3:        RET
PrtDec      ENDP

; The following routine searches the environment area for a string
; pointed to by DS:SI. Returns with ES:DI pointing to the variable.
; Carry is set if not found.

SrchEnv     PROC    USES AX BX SI
            MOV     ES,SaveEnv          ;Get original environment
            MOV     DI,0                ;ES:DI points to start of environment
            MOV     BX,SI               ;Point to start of variable name

SE1:        MOV     AX,ES:[DI]          ;Get character word at pointer
            CMP     AX,0                ;Is this the end of environment block?
            JE      NotFound            ;Yes, so exit with error

SE2:        MOV     AL,[BX]             ;Get character from variable name
            INC     BX                  ;Point to next character
            CMP     AL,0                ;End of variable?
            JE      Found               ;Yes, so we found it

            CMP     AL,ES:[DI]          ;Same as in the environment block?
            JNE     SE3                 ;No, so ignore this entry
            INC     DI                  ;Point to next environment character
            JMP     SE2                 ;Keep comparing

SE3:        INC     DI                  ;Point to next environment character
            CMP     BYTE PTR ES:[DI],0  ;At end of entry?
            JNE     SE3                 ;No, continue scanning
            JMP     SE1                 ;Go back to beginning

Found:      CLC
            JNC     SEDone
NotFound:   STC
SEDone:     RET
SrchEnv     ENDP

            END
```

The key to how this program works is in the command tail. Notice the /C switch, which instructs COMMAND.COM to execute a single command and then terminate. After the DIR command is done, therefore, control returns to the parent process.

You can use this same technique to run batch files or to run other programs when you are not sure where they reside on the hard disk (but are relatively sure that they can be found in the search path). COMMAND.COM takes care of running the batch file or searching for the COM or EXE file to run.

Remember that if you change the subdirectory, it remains changed when control returns to the parent process.

The Effect of EXEC on Memory

To see what effect the EXEC function has on memory, you may find the program in this section interesting. By using the MEM command from DOS, you can see what memory use looks like. For instance, I invoked MEM, with the /C switch, on my computer and produced the following report:

```
Conventional Memory :

    Name            Size in Decimal        Size in Hex
    -----------     --------------------   ------------

    MSDOS           13008    ( 12.7K)         32D0
    QEMM386          2416    (  2.4K)          970
    LOADHI            160    (  0.2K)           A0
    LOADHI            160    (  0.2K)           A0
    MOUSE           22464    ( 21.9K)         57C0
    LOADHI            160    (  0.2K)           A0
    COMMAND          3392    (  3.3K)          D40
    MODE              464    (  0.5K)          1D0
    MGR             13024    ( 12.7K)         32E0
    FREE               64    (  0.1K)           40
    FREE              352    (  0.3K)          160
    FREE           599392    (585.3K)        92560

Total  FREE :      599808    (585.8K)


Total bytes available to programs :            599808    (585.8K)
Largest executable program size :              598912    (584.9K)
```

```
8110080 bytes total EMS memory
7421952 bytes free EMS memory

7340032 bytes total contiguous extended memory
      0 bytes available contiguous extended memory
7421952 bytes available XMS memory
        MS-DOS resident in High Memory Area
```

Next, because I wanted to see what memory use looked like when a child process is spawned, I modified EXEC1.ASM (from earlier in this chapter) to create the program in Listing 11.4.

Listing 11.4. EXEC4.ASM

```
Page 60,132

Comment |
*********************************************************************


File:       EXEC4.ASM
Author:     Allen L. Wyatt
Date:       6/6/92
Assembler:  MASM 6.0

Purpose:    Demonstrate the effect of EXEC on memory use. Spawns
            a child process that runs MEM.EXE, a DOS utility.

Format:     EXEC4


*********************************************************************|


            .MODEL  small
            .STACK                      ;Default 1K stack is OK
            .DATA

Path        DB      'C:\DOS\MEM.EXE',0

Parms       DW      0                   ;Parent environment block is OK
            DW      OFFSET CmdTail      ;Command tail address
            DW      SEG CmdTail
            DW      0,0                 ;FCB pointers don't matter
            DW      0,0                 ;  for this example
```

```
CmdTail     DB      2                       ;Length of command tail
            DB      '/C',13                 ;Actual command tail

SaveSS      DW      0                       ;Temporary storage areas
SaveSP      DW      0
Error       DW      0

Message1    DB      'Press any key to enter child program...$'
Message2    DB      13,10,'Back from child program',13,10,'$'
Message3    DB      'Ending parent program'
CRLF        DB      13,10,'$'
ErrMsg      DB      'Error during EXEC function: $'

ErrorTable  DW      OFFSET ErrorX
            DW      OFFSET Error1
            DW      OFFSET Error2
            DW      OFFSET Error3
            DW      OFFSET Error4
            DW      OFFSET Error5
            DW      OFFSET ErrorX
            DW      OFFSET ErrorX
            DW      OFFSET Error8
            DW      OFFSET ErrorX
            DW      OFFSET ErrorA
            DW      OFFSET ErrorB

Error1      DB      ' (invalid function)$'
Error2      DB      ' (file not found)$'
Error3      DB      ' (path not found)$'
Error4      DB      ' (too many open files)$'
Error5      DB      ' (access denied)$'
Error8      DB      ' (not enough memory)$'
ErrorA      DB      ' (bad environment)$'
ErrorB      DB      ' (bad format)$'
ErrorX      DB      ' (unknown error value)$'

            .CODE
            .STARTUP
Exec4       PROC
```

continues

Listing 11.4. Continued

```
; The following memory allocation code works because it is known that MASM
; sets DS and SS to the same segment address in the start-up code. Also, ES
; is set to the PSP for the program upon entry.

        MOV     BX,DS               ;Point to start of data segment
        MOV     AX,ES               ;Point to start of PSP
        SUB     BX,AX               ;Number of segments for code and data
        MOV     AX,SP               ;SP is pointing to top of stack area
        MOV     CL,4                ;Dividing by 16
        SHR     AX,CL
        ADD     BX,AX               ;BX=paragraphs needed
        MOV     AH,4Ah              ;Modify memory allocation
        INT     21h

        CALL    Cls                 ;Clear the screen
        MOV     DX,0                ;Set up to print message
        MOV     BH,0                ;Assume page 0
        MOV     AH,2                ;Set cursor position
        INT     10h
        MOV     DX,OFFSET Message1  ;Point to starting message
        MOV     AH,9                ;Display a string using DOS
        INT     21h
        MOV     AH,0                ;Read keyboard character
        INT     16h
        MOV     DX,OFFSET CRLF      ;Go to next line
        MOV     AH,9                ;Display a string using DOS
        INT     21h

        MOV     Error,0             ;Assume that no error will occur
        MOV     AH,4Bh              ;EXEC function
        MOV     AL,0                ;Load and execute
        MOV     DX,OFFSET Path      ;Path name to file to execute
        PUSH    DS
        POP     ES                  ;ES:BX must point to
        MOV     BX,OFFSET Parms     ;   parameter block
        MOV     SaveSS,SS           ;Don't want to lose SP:SS during
        MOV     SaveSP,SP           ;   EXEC call
        INT     21h
        JNC     Back                ;No error, so continue
        MOV     Error,AX            ;Put error value in its place
```

```
Back:       MOV     SS,SaveSS           ;Restore SP:SS from saved values
            MOV     SP,SaveSP
            MOV     DX,OFFSET Message2  ;Point to return message
            MOV     AH,9                ;Display a string using DOS
            INT     21h

            CMP     Error,0             ;Was there an error?
            JE      Done                ;No, so exit
            MOV     DX,OFFSET ErrMsg    ;Point to error message
            MOV     AH,9                ;Display a string using DOS
            INT     21h
            MOV     AX,Error            ;Get the value
            CALL    PrtDec              ;Go print it
            MOV     BX,Error            ;Get error value
            SHL     BX,1                ;Multiply by 2
            MOV     DX,ErrorTable[BX]   ;Get the error message
            MOV     AH,9                ;Display a string using DOS
            INT     21h

            MOV     DX,OFFSET CRLF      ;Go to next line
            MOV     AH,9                ;Display a string using DOS
            INT     21h

Done:       MOV     DX,OFFSET Message3  ;Point to exit message
            MOV     AH,9                ;Display a string using DOS
            INT     21h

            .EXIT
Exec4       ENDP


; The following routine clears the screen

Cls         PROC    USES AX BX CX DX
            MOV     AH,6                ;Scroll window up
            MOV     AL,0                ;Scroll full screen
            MOV     BH,7                ;Normal white on black
            MOV     CX,0                ;Upper left corner of screen
            MOV     DH,24               ;Bottom right
            MOV     DL,79
            INT     10h
            RET
Cls         ENDP
```

continues

Listing 11.4. Continued

```
; The following routine prints the value in AX as a decimal number

PrtDec      PROC    USES AX CX DX
            MOV     CX,0FFFFh           ;Ending flag
            PUSH    CX
            MOV     CX,10
PD1:        MOV     DX,0
            DIV     CX                  ;Divide by 10
            ADD     DL,30h              ;Convert to ASCII
            PUSH    DX                  ;Store remainder
            CMP     AX,0                ;Are we done?
            JNE     PD1                 ;No, so continue

PD2:        POP     DX                  ;Character is now in DL
            CMP     DX,0FFFFh           ;Is it the ending flag?
            JE      PD3                 ;Yes, so continue
            MOV     AH,02h              ;Output a character
            INT     21h
            JMP     PD2                 ;Keep doing it

PD3:        RET
PrtDec      ENDP

            END
```

When I assembled and ran the program, the following was the resulting output:
Press any key to enter child program...

Conventional Memory :

Name	Size in Decimal		Size in Hex
MSDOS	13008	(12.7K)	32D0
QEMM386	2416	(2.4K)	970
LOADHI	160	(0.2K)	A0
LOADHI	160	(0.2K)	A0
MOUSE	22464	(21.9K)	57C0
LOADHI	160	(0.2K)	A0
COMMAND	3392	(3.3K)	D40
MODE	464	(0.5K)	1D0
MGR	13024	(12.7K)	32E0

```
EXEC4           2368      (  2.3K)      940
FREE              64      (  0.1K)       40
FREE             352      (  0.3K)      160
FREE          596992      (583.0K)    91C00

Total  FREE :  597408      (583.4K)

Total bytes available to programs :         597408    (583.4K)
Largest executable program size :           596512    (582.5K)

  8110080 bytes total EMS memory
  7421952 bytes free EMS memory

  7340032 bytes total contiguous extended memory
        0 bytes available contiguous extended memory
  7421952 bytes available XMS memory
          MS-DOS resident in High Memory Area

Back from child program
Ending parent program
```

Notice that another program, EXEC4, has been added to the list of those consuming memory. It occupies only 2,368 bytes, and available memory has been reduced by a similar amount.

Based on how much memory each child process consumes, you could keep spawning processes until you ran completely out of memory. Although the temptation to do so can be great, in real-world situations you probably will have to spawn processes to only one or two levels.

Summary

The EXEC function is a powerful tool that enables you to suspend the current program and begin other processes. When that process is done, control is returned to the parent program. The application of the EXEC function depends on the purpose and design of your program, but it can add a level of flexibility that you may find helpful in your programs.

Chapter 12 discusses another topic of memory and program management: protected mode programming.

Protected Mode Programming

To some people, the term *protected mode programming* conjures up the same scary demons that the thought of programming in assembly language does for those limited to programming in high-level languages. Yet protected mode programming, in and of itself, is not that different from real-mode assembly language programming. The concepts of how you do things remain the same—it is only some of the ways those concepts are implemented that must change.

Before reading this chapter, make sure that you have read and understood the concepts presented in Chapter 6, "Expanded and Extended Memory." The memory concepts presented there, particularly those dealing with extended memory, are vital to understanding the concepts in this chapter.

The information presented in this chapter deals primarily with the protected modes of the 80386 and 80486 computers. The first couple of sections in this chapter briefly discuss concepts that are applicable to the 80286; the majority of the discussion and the programming examples, however, concern the 80386 and 80486 systems.

Few, if any, native protected mode programming tools are available because no widely accepted operating environment is available that takes full advantage of protected mode. Perhaps this situation will change in a few years; for now, however, DOS assembly language programmers are left with only a few options:

■ Work only in real mode, using tools with which you are familiar and comfortable

■ Write your own DOS protected mode interface in line with current standards (such as VCPI or DPMI, presented in Chapter 6, "Expanded and Extended Memory"

■ Do the majority of your work in real mode, and switch to protected mode only as necessary to accomplish well-defined tasks that can be done best in protected mode

The first option, the most conservative, may be the correct solution for many programmers. Despite the limitations that many people point out in the DOS environment, you still can do a lot without resorting to protected mode programming. You are forced to accept this option if you are programming strictly for the 8086/8088 CPU set. Protected mode is available on only 80286 computers or later.

The second option is the most radical. If you pursue this option, you are in effect building your own DOS extender. Commercial DOS extenders are available, but they don't yet offer much of an option for assembly language programmers because the extenders are oriented primarily toward programs developed in higher-level languages such as C.

The third option is perhaps the most feasible for the majority of people considering protected mode programming from assembly language. This chapter focuses on this option. It offers the best of both worlds with a minimum of environment-related hassle.

The Family Tree Revisited

Before getting into the programming, you should understand a few things about the CPUs in the 8086/8088 family from Intel. The first member of this family, the 8086/8088, operates only in real mode. You are limited to working with 1 megabyte of memory, as described in detail in Chapter 6.

The 80286 operates, by default, in real mode. You can switch to 16-bit protected mode if you want, but it is extremely difficult and tricky to switch back to real mode. Some people believe that the people at Intel were so enamored with the positive side of protected mode that they assumed that no one would *want* to return to real mode after they were operating in protected mode. The people at Microsoft made sure that this desire to return was a no-brainer because they failed to deliver an operating system that would work in protected mode.

The 80386 and 80486 also operate by default in real mode. Unlike the 80286, however, you can switch between real mode and protected mode (16-bit or 32-bit) and back again, with relatively little problem. Also, these CPUs provide a third operating mode, virtual 8086, or V86, mode, which allowed multiple encapsulated real mode environments within a single machine. This book does not discuss the technical details of real mode and V86 mode, but the examples presented here work equally well in either environment.

Talk about fun! The possibilities presented by the 80386 and 80486 chips are enough to make your teeth ache. The limitation imposed by the operating system still exists, however. You cannot access a real mode operating system from protected mode, because when you enter protected mode, similar to entering the twilight zone, reality as we have come to know it takes a shift.

Life in the P-Zone

After you "throw the switch" and enter protected mode, you must look at the world around you with a different perspective. All the registers you learned to understand and trust in real mode are still available. What has changed the most is how the CPU treats memory. Suddenly you must deal with heretofore unknown elements such as selectors and descriptors.

In real mode, an address is composed of a segment and an offset. (You know this!) To calculate a physical address, you shift the segment four places to the left (multiply by 16) and add the offset. The segment registers, shown in Table 12.1, are used specifically to indicate the region of memory to be accessed.

Table 12.1. Segment registers and their use.

Register	Use
CS	Code segment
DS	Data segment
ES	Extra segment
FS	Additional segment
GS	Additional segment

In the protected mode environment, the segment registers do not function as they do in real mode. To avoid confusion, then, they are called *selector registers*. As in real mode, they are 16 bits long, but the bits have special meanings (see Table 12.2).

Table 12.2. Layout of a selector.

Bit settings FEDCBA98 76543210	Meaning
xx	Requested privilege level
x	Table indicator
xxxxxxxx xxxxx	Index

The requested privilege level concerns system security. There are four privilege levels, 0 through 3. Privilege level 0 has global access to everything in the computer, and levels 1 through 3 have decreasing access to resources. Privilege levels are used to keep low-level tasks from mucking up the works in other portions of the computer. This sort of an arrangement is vital to successful and secure multitasking.

The index value, which can range from 0 to 8,191, is used as a pointer into a look-up table called a *descriptor table*. The three types of descriptor tables are shown in Table 12.3.

Table 12.3. Types of descriptor tables.

Initials	Name	Register
GDT	Global descriptor table	GDTR
LDT	Local descriptor table	LDTR
IDT	Interrupt descriptor table	IDTR

The table indicator bit in a selector indicates whether the index value is a pointer into the global descriptor table (indicator bit is 0) or a local descriptor table (indicator bit is 1).

Generally, the global descriptor table, or GDT, contains descriptors used to describe the environment of the entire computer. The local descriptor table, or LDT, contains descriptors applicable to a localized program's environment. The third type of table, the interrupt descriptor table, or IDT, is used for management of interrupts and cannot be accessed through a selector. The interrupt descriptor table is analogous to the interrupt vector table maintained in low memory in real mode.

A system can have only one GDT and one IDT, but it can have many different LDTs. These descriptor tables can reside virtually anywhere in memory; the starting address of each table (along with its size) is contained in special CPU registers (refer to Table 12.3). Because there is one GDT that describes the entire environment accessible by the CPU, the GDT must be initialized before entering protected mode.

Each descriptor table is made up of individual *descriptors*. Each descriptor is 8 bytes long, and different bits in the descriptors have different meanings. There can be as many as 8,192 descriptors in either a GDT or LDT, although the first descriptor in the GDT cannot be accessed by the CPU. (Remember that the selector index value can range from 0 to 8,191.) Either descriptor table, therefore, can be as much as 64 kilobytes in length. Realistically, these tables are much shorter—approximately 100 bytes is probably larger than most descriptor tables. There are several different types of descriptors which, are shown in this list:

- Segment descriptors
- System segment descriptors
- System gate descriptors

The following two sections describe each type of descriptor.

Segment Descriptors

Segment descriptors are used as a "master key" to control an entire portion of memory. The 8 bytes that make up the segment descriptor are laid out differently, depending on whether you are using the 80286 or the 80386/80486. The layout for a segment descriptor on the 80286 is shown in Figure 12.1.

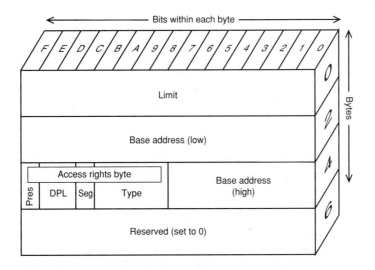

Figure 12.1.

The segment descriptor for the 80286 in protected mode.

For the 80286, the segment descriptor contains the following fields:

- *Base address*—bytes 2 through 4 (24 bits)
- *Limit*—bytes 0 and 1 (16 bits)
- *Access rights*—byte 5 (8 bits)

The base address is where, in the 16-megabytes address space of the 80286, the segment begins. The limit field is the effective length of the segment; this offset is the last valid one for the segment.

The access rights byte, as shown in Figure 12.1, is made up of several fields. The four bits comprising the type field indicate a few attributes of the segment, as shown in Table 12.4.

Table 12.4. Bit meanings for the type field of an access rights byte in a segment descriptor on the 80286.

Bit settings 3210	Meaning
1	Segment has been accessed
0	Segment has not been accessed
000	Normal, read-only data segment
001	Normal, read/write data segment
010	Expand-down, read-only data segment
011	Expand-down, read/write data segment
100	Execute-only, nonconforming code segment
101	Readable, nonconforming code segment
110	Execute-only, conforming code segment
111	Readable, conforming code segment

Any attempt to write to a segment that shows as read-only, or to write to a code segment, or to read an execute-only code segment, results in a fault condition.

For segment descriptors, bit 4 of the access rights byte (marked as *Seg* in Figure 12.1) must be set to 1. The DPL field, bits 5 and 6, is the descriptor privilege level. It is used to indicate the privilege level necessary to access the descriptor's segment. If you attempt to access a segment that has a higher privilege level than you, a fault occurs.

Finally, bit 7 of the access rights byte (marked as *Pres* in Figure 12.1) indicates whether the data for this descriptor's segment is currently in memory. If the bit is set, the data is in memory; if it is clear, the data has been spooled to disk. If you access a segment descriptor whose data is on disk, a fault occurs, and the operating system is supposed to fetch the data from disk so that you can access it normally.

If you are using an 80386 or 80486, the segment descriptor is a little different from the 80286. Figure 12.2 shows the layout of the 80386/80486 segment descriptor.

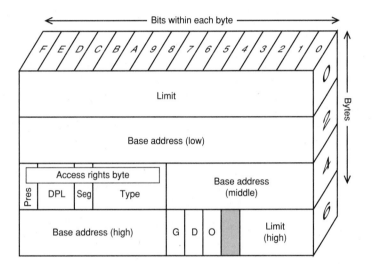

Figure 12.2.

The segment descriptor for the 80386/80486 in protected mode.

The only differences between the segment descriptor for the 80386/80486 and the 80286 are that the base address size for the 80386/80486 is increased to 32 bytes (byte 6 is used as bits 24 through 31 of the address), the limit field has been increased to 20 bits (the first 4 bits of byte 5 are used as bits 16 through 19 of the limit field), and a few new flags have been added.

The flag marked as *G* in Figure 12.2 (bit 7 of byte 5) indicates the granularity of the limit field. If this bit is clear, the limit indicates the number of actual bytes to be used as a limit. If the bit is set, the limit indicates the number of pages (not bytes) for the limit, with each page being 4 kilobytes. The maximum limit, therefore, for a 20-bit limit field with byte granularity is 1,048,575 bytes (1 megabyte). With page granularity, it increases to 4,294,963,200 bytes.

Bit 6 of byte 5, marked as *D* in Figure 12.2, determines the default operand and addressing modes. In the Intel documentation, this bit is marked as *B*, meaning "big." If the bit is clear, addresses are limited to 16 bits, as in the 80286. If the bit is set, the full 32-bit addressing power of the 80386/80486 can be utilized.

System Segment and System Gate Descriptors

Notice in the preceding section that the segment bit (bit 4) of the access rights byte in the segment descriptors was set to 1. If this bit is set to 0, the descriptor takes on special meaning to the system. With this bit cleared, the type field indicates the type of segment the descriptor controls (see Table 12.5).

Table 12.5. Bit meanings for the type field of the access rights byte in a system segment descriptor.

Bit settings 3210	Meaning
0001	Task state segment
0010	Local descriptor table (LDT)
0011	Busy task state segment
0100	Call gate
0101	Task gate
0110	Interrupt gate
0111	Trap gate

All other fields in the descriptor remain the same, based on the CPU type.

System segment descriptors (type values 1 through 3) are used to indicate segment addresses for various system tables used in memory and task management. For instance, if the type value is 2, the descriptor points to an LDT for the current program. In this way, programs can control their own memory environments in a distinct manner from other programs that may be running on the system.

System gate descriptors (type values 4 through 7) are used to facilitate the transfer of control between processes (including processes executing at differing privilege levels).

How Does All This Make Sense?

It should be obvious from the previous sections that the view of the world is, indeed, much different in protected mode than in real mode. No individual program can assume that it owns all the resources in the computer. Rather, it is possible for an operating system that takes advantage of the protection mechanisms in protected mode to force good behavior on the part of applications.

You should be able now to understand a portion of what the brave souls who jumped on the Windows bandwagon early had to contend with. Windows takes advantage of the protection features of these chips, and forces applications programs to behave. Many of the crashes that occurred in Windows 386 and Windows 3.0 occurred because applications programmers still were adjusting to the world view imposed by protected mode programming and the protection schemes enforced by the operating system. Since those early days of Windows as a protected mode operating system, however, even Windows itself has improved at error detection, correction, and compensation.

Why, then, would programmers willingly submit to shackling their programs (make them follow stringent protection rules)? The answer is simple: They want orderly access to the full power of the 80386 and 80486, and they want to create programs that can coexist peacefully and even have communication with other programs running at the same time. With this in mind, prepare to try your hand at a few programs in the following sections that dabble in protected mode.

A First Try at Protected Mode

The easiest way to dip into protected mode is to conform to one of the interface standards presented in Chapter 6, "Expanded and Extended Memory." VCPI and DPMI were developed to allow uniform access to protected mode and extended memory from DOS. The extended memory portion was discussed in Chapter 6. Let's look at the protected mode access portion.

The examples in this chapter require the presence of a DPMI server. For most people, this means Windows. You can run these sample programs from the DOS prompt within Windows. The program in listing 12.1, POSTCARD.ASM, is virtually the simplest program you can devise using protected mode programming. It does the following:

- Ensures the presence of a DPMI server
- Displays a nontraditional, not-so-boring "hello world" message
- Exits to real mode; exits from the program

Listing 12.1. POSTCARD.ASM

```
Page 60,132

Comment ¦
********************************************************************


File:      POSTCARD.ASM
Author:    Allen L. Wyatt
Date:      8/2/92
Assembler: MASM 6.0

Purpose:   Example of operating in protected mode.
           This program just switches modes, displays a
           message, and then terminates.

           Program must be run with a DPMI host (such as Windows)
           present.

Format:    POSTCARD


********************************************************************¦


           .MODEL  small
           .STACK                      ;Default 1K stack is OK
           .386                        ;Instructions require 80386
           .DATA

ReadyMsg   DB      13,10,10,'Switching to protected mode.',13,10,10,0
MadeIt     DB      '     Hello to the folks at home from the p-zone!',13,10
           DB      '     Hugs and kisses to the kids; will write soon...',13,10,10,0
EndMsg     DB      'Back home again after a successful jaunt beyond the edge',13,10
           DB      'Program completed.',13,10,10,0

Flag32     DB      00
ProcType   DB      00
VerNum     DW      0000
MemNeeded  DW      0000
DPMIentry  DW      0000,0000

; Register storage areas for cross-mode interrupt handling.
; This structure is defined by the DPMI specifications for
; use with function 0300h.
```

```
RegSet      EQU     THIS BYTE
SaveDI      EQU     THIS WORD
SaveEDI     DD      00000000
SaveSI      EQU     THIS WORD
SaveESI     DD      00000000
SaveBP      EQU     THIS WORD
SaveEBP     DD      00000000
            DD      00000000            ;Reserved area--set to 0
SaveBX      EQU     THIS WORD
SaveEBX     DD      00000000
SaveDX      EQU     THIS WORD
SaveEDX     DD      00000000
SaveCX      EQU     THIS WORD
SaveECX     DD      00000000
SaveAX      EQU     THIS WORD
SaveEAX     DD      00000000
SaveFlags   DW      0000
SaveES      DW      0000
SaveDS      DW      0000
SaveFS      DW      0000
SaveGS      DW      0000
SaveIP      DW      0000
SaveCS      DW      0000
SaveSP      DW      0000
SaveSS      DW      0000


; Error messages

EMsg1       DB      'No DPMI host detected',13,10,0
EMsg2       DB      'Could not allocate real-mode memory requested',13,10,0
EMsg3       DB      'The switch to protected mode did not work',13,10,0


            .CODE
            .STARTUP
PostCard    PROC
; The following memory allocation code works because it is known that MASM
; sets DS and SS to the same segment address in the start-up code. Also, ES
; is set to the PSP for the program upon entry.

            MOV     BX,DS               ;Point to start of data segment
            MOV     AX,ES               ;Point to start of PSP
```

continues

Listing 12.1. Continued

```
                SUB     BX,AX               ;Number of segments for code and data
                MOV     AX,SP               ;SP is pointing to top of stack area
                MOV     CL,4                ;Dividing by 16
                SHR     AX,CL
                ADD     BX,AX               ;BX=paragraphs needed
                MOV     AH,4Ah              ;Modify memory allocation
                INT     21h

; Check to see whether DPMI is available, and make the switch if it is
                CALL    ChkDPMI             ;See whether host is present
                JC      Error1              ;Not there

                MOV     SI,OFFSET ReadyMsg  ;Ready to switch
                CALL    PrtString
                MOV     AX,0                ;In case no memory needed
                MOV     BX,MemNeeded        ;Get number of paragraphs needed by host
                CMP     BX,0                ;Any allocation needed?
                JE      Plunge              ;No, so continue
                MOV     AH,48h              ;Allocate memory
                INT     21h
                JC      Error2              ;Could not allocate

Plunge:         MOV     ES,AX
                MOV     AX,0                ;Indicate 16-bit application
                CALL    DWORD PTR DPMIentry ;Switch to protected mode
                JC      Error3              ;Error--still in real mode

; If you reach this point, you are operating in protected mode

                MOV     SI,OFFSET MadeIt    ;Message to folks back home
                CALL    PMPrtString         ;Print from protected mode
                MOV     SI,OFFSET EndMsg
                CALL    PMPrtString
                JMP     AllDone

Error1:         MOV     SI,OFFSET EMsg1
                JMP     ErrCommon
Error2:         MOV     SI,OFFSET EMsg2
                JMP     ErrCommon
Error3:         MOV     SI,OFFSET EMsg3
```

```
ErrCommon:  CALL      PrtString

AllDone:
            .EXIT
PostCard    ENDP


; The following routine checks to see whether a DPMI master program is installed.
; If one is not, the carry flag is set on return.
; If one is, the stat info is stored and the carry flag is cleared on return.

ChkDPMI     PROC      USES AX BX CX DX SI DI ES
            MOV       AX,1687h            ;Get DPMI host address
            INT       2Fh                 ;Multiplex interrupt
            CMP       AX,0                ;Was it there?
            JNE       NotThere            ;Nope, so exit

            AND       BL,00000001b        ;Test bit 1 (32-bit OK?)
            SETNE     AL
            MOV       Flag32,AL
            MOV       ProcType,CL
            MOV       VerNum,DX
            MOV       MemNeeded,SI
            MOV       DPMIentry[0],DI
            MOV       DPMIentry[2],ES
            CLC                           ;Set for no error
            JNC       Done

NotThere:   STC
Done:       RET
ChkDPMI     ENDP


; Save registers

SaveRegs    PROC      NEAR USES AX
            MOV       SaveAX,AX
            MOV       SaveBX,BX
            MOV       SaveCX,CX
            MOV       SaveDX,DX
            MOV       SaveSI,SI
            MOV       SaveDI,DI
```

continues

Listing 12.1. Continued

```
                MOV     SaveBP,BP
                PUSHF
                POP     AX
                MOV     SaveFlags,AX
                RET
SaveRegs        ENDP

GetRegs         PROC    NEAR
                MOV     AX,SaveFlags
                PUSH    AX
                POPF
                MOV     AX,SaveAX
                MOV     BX,SaveBX
                MOV     CX,SaveCX
                MOV     DX,SaveDX
                MOV     SI,SaveSI
                MOV     DI,SaveDI
                MOV     BP,SaveBP
                RET
GetRegs         ENDP


DOSfunc         PROC    NEAR USES AX BX CX ES
                MOV     AX,0300h            ;Simulate real-mode interrupt
                MOV     BL,21h              ;Want the DOS interrupt
                MOV     BH,0                ;Should be 0
                MOV     CX,0                ;Copy nothing from stack
                PUSH    DS                  ;ES:DI must point to data structure
                POP     ES
                MOV     DI,OFFSET RegSet
                INT     31h
                RET
DOSfunc         ENDP

; The following routine prints the ASCIIZ string pointed to by DS:SI.
; Works from protected mode by switching to real mode to do DOS function.

PMPrtString PROC    USES AX DX SI
PS1:            MOV     DL,[SI]             ;Get character
```

```
            INC     SI                  ;Point to next one
            CMP     DL,0                ;End of string?
            JE      PS2                 ;Yes, so exit
            MOV     AH,02h              ;Output a character
            CALL    SaveRegs
            CALL    DOSfunc
            CALL    GetRegs
            JMP     PS1                 ;Keep doing it
PS2:        RET
PMPrtString ENDP



; The following routine prints the ASCIIZ string pointed to by DS:SI

PrtString   PROC    FAR USES AX DX SI
PS1:        MOV     DL,[SI]             ;Get character
            INC     SI                  ;Point to next one
            CMP     DL,0                ;End of string?
            JE      PS2                 ;Yes, so exit
            MOV     AH,02h              ;Output a character
            INT     21h
            JMP     PS1                 ;Keep doing it
PS2:        RET
PrtString   ENDP


            END
```

This program uses the DPMI interface to switch to protected mode. This is done through the entry point returned from interrupt 2Fh, function 1687h. The address returned by this function is called as a far routine, and on return the processor is running in protected mode. The following code does this in the program:

```
Plunge:     MOV     ES,AX
            MOV     AX,0                ;Indicate 16-bit application
            CALL    DWORD PTR DPMIentry ;Switch to protected mode
            JC      Error3              ;Error--still in real mode
```

The value required in ES is the segment address of a memory block that the DPMI host uses for real-mode housekeeping. The size of this block is indicated by the host when you call interrupt 2Fh, function 1687h.

The value in AX indicates the type of protected mode program you will be running. If AX is 0, the host expects a 16-bit application; if AX is 1, the host expects 32 bits.

On return from the far call (to DPMIentry in this example), the environment is set up as follows:

- CS contains a selector with a base address equivalent to the real-mode CS, and a limit of 64K

- SS contains a selector with a base address equivalent to the real-mode SS, and a limit of 64K

- DS contains a selector with a base address equivalent to the real-mode DS, and a limit of 64K

- ES contains a selector with a base address equivalent to the original program's PSP with a limit of 256 bytes

- FS is set to 0

- GS is set to 0

Now you are ready to try your hand in the protected mode environment. Remember that DOS and other system functions are not as readily available as you probably take for granted. Notice the way that DOS interrupts are handled from the protected mode side of the DPMI interface in this program: First, all the registers must be saved in a rigid register structure in memory; then DPMI function 0300h is invoked; and then the registers are reloaded on return from the function. This process may seem cumbersome, but it works well. In fact, notice that in equivalent routines (one real mode and one protected mode), many times the only difference is that this line:

```
INT     21h
```

changes to these lines:

```
CALL    SaveRegs
CALL    DOSfunc
CALL    GetRegs
```

The remainder of the coding for the routines may be able to stay the same.

When the program is complete, you use a regular interrupt 21h, function 4Ch to end the program. The DPMI host intercepts this function call, cleans up the protected mode side of the fence, switches to real mode, and issues the same termination interrupt again. This time, however, DOS does the housekeeping and then neatly returns to the DOS prompt.

A Somewhat Larger Foray

You must remember that there is no real applications development environment for protected mode—*none*. Therefore, any examples here are for the sake of experimentation. It is doubtful that you could easily or cheaply (time-wise) develop, with the tools available today, a protected mode application of any major significance, at least not in assembly language. Perhaps a couple of years down the road, things might be different.

Let's look at the final example program for this chapter. This example does a little more than POSTCARD.ASM, and takes advantage of the prime benefit of working in protected mode—large masses of memory. The program in listing 12.2, PMTEST.ASM, does the following:

- Ensures the presence of a DPMI server
- Switches to protected mode
- Allocates a large buffer in extended memory
- Makes the buffer addressable through manipulation of the LDT descriptor for the buffer
- Fills a portion of the buffer with text
- Reads the text and displays it on-screen
- Releases all previously allocated memory
- Releases the LDT descriptor previously allocated
- Exits to real mode; exits from the program

This list sounds like a lot, and it does take a little more work than an equivalent program in real mode. Listing 12.2 shows the listing for PMTEST.ASM.

Listing 12.2. PMTEST.ASM

```
Page 60,132


Comment ¦
*******************************************************************


File:      PMTEST.ASM
Author:    Allen L. Wyatt
Date:      8/2/92
Assembler: MASM 6.0
```

continues

Listing 12.2. Continued

```
Purpose:     Example of operating in protected mode to accomplish
             a task

Format:      PMTEST


******************************************************************!
                                                                 '

             .MODEL   small
             .STACK   2048
             .386                        ;Instructions require 80386
             .DATA

ReadyMsg     DB        'Switching to protected mode...'
CRLF         DB        13,10,0

BufSelector  DW        0000
BufHandleH   DW        0000
BufHandleL   DW        0000
BufLAddrH    DW        0000
BufLAddrL    DW        0000
DOSBufSel    DW        0000
DOSBufSeg    DW        0000

Flag32       DB        00
ProcType     DB        00
VerNum       DW        0000
MemNeeded    DW        0000
DPMIentry    DD        00000000

FillMsg      DB        'Filling a portion of the buffer...',13,10,0
ReadMsg      DB        'Reading the buffer...',13,10,0
TestMsg      DB        13,'Reading from protected mode, message ',0

; Register storage areas for cross-mode interrupt handling.
; This structure is defined by the DPMI specifications for
; use with function 0300h.

RegSet       EQU       THIS BYTE
SaveDI       EQU       THIS WORD
SaveEDI      DD        00000000
```

```
SaveSI      EQU     THIS WORD
SaveESI     DD      00000000
SaveBP      EQU     THIS WORD
SaveEBP     DD      00000000
            DD      00000000         ;Reserved area--set to 0
SaveBX      EQU     THIS WORD
SaveEBX     DD      00000000
SaveDX      EQU     THIS WORD
SaveEDX     DD      00000000
SaveCX      EQU     THIS WORD
SaveECX     DD      00000000
SaveAX      EQU     THIS WORD
SaveEAX     DD      00000000
SaveFlags   DW      0000
SaveES      DW      0000
SaveDS      DW      0000
SaveFS      DW      0000
SaveGS      DW      0000
SaveIP      DW      0000
SaveCS      DW      0000
SaveSP      DW      0000
SaveSS      DW      0000


; Error messages

ErrMsg      DB      'Error - '
ErrNum      DW      0000,0000
            DB      '    ',0
EMsg1       DB      'No DPMI host detected',13,10,0
EMsg2       DB      'Could not allocate memory for mode switch',13,10,0
EMsg3       DB      'Could not switch to protected mode',13,10,0
EMsg4       DB      'Could not allocate LDT',13,10,0
EMsg5       DB      'Could not set up 1Mb buffer',13,10,0
EMsg6       DB      'Could not set descriptor base address',13,10,0
EMsg7       DB      'Could not set descriptor limit',13,10,0


            .CODE
            .STARTUP
PMTest      PROC
```

continues

Listing 12.2. Continued

```
; The following memory allocation code works because it is known that MASM
; sets DS and SS to the same segment address in the start-up code. Also, ES
; is set to the PSP for the program upon entry.

            MOV     BX,DS               ;Point to start of data segment
            MOV     AX,ES               ;Point to start of PSP
            SUB     BX,AX               ;Number of segments for code and data
            MOV     AX,SP               ;SP is pointing to top of stack area
            MOV     CL,4                ;Dividing by 16
            SHR     AX,CL
            ADD     BX,AX               ;BX=paragraphs needed
            MOV     AH,4Ah              ;Modify memory allocation
            INT     21h

; Check to see whether DPMI is available (makes no sense to go on if not)
            CALL    ChkDPMI             ;See whether host is present
            JC      Error1              ;Not there

            MOV     SI,OFFSET ReadyMsg  ;Ready to switch
            CALL    PrtString
            MOV     AX,0                ;In case no memory needed
            MOV     BX,MemNeeded        ;Get number of paragraphs needed by host
            CMP     BX,0                ;Any allocation needed?
            JE      PM1                 ;No, so continue
            MOV     AH,48h              ;Allocate memory
            INT     21h
            JC      Error2              ;Could not allocate

PM1:        MOV     ES,AX               ;Segment of allocated memory
            MOV     AX,0                ;Indicate 16-bit application
            CALL    DPMIentry           ;Switch to protected mode
            JC      Error3              ;Error--still in real mode

; If you reach this point, you are operating in protected mode

            PUSH    DS
            POP     GS                  ;Save the data selector in secure place

            MOV     AX,0000h            ;Allocate LDT descriptor
            MOV     CX,1                ;Need only one descriptor
```

```
        INT     31h
        JC      Error4              ;Could not allocate descriptor
        MOV     BufSelector,AX

        MOV     AX,0501h            ;Allocate memory block
        MOV     BX,10h              ;BX:CX = 100000h (1M) bytes wanted
        MOV     CX,0000h
        INT     31h
        JC      Error5
        MOV     BufHandleH,SI       ;Store handle
        MOV     BufHandleL,DI
        MOV     BufLAddrH,BX
        MOV     BufLAddrL,CX

        MOV     AX,0007h            ;Set base address to address
        MOV     BX,BufSelector      ;Move selector to proper place
        MOV     CX,BufLAddrH        ;Get linear address in CX:DX
        MOV     DX,BufLAddrL
        INT     31h
        JC      Error6              ;Could not set base address

        MOV     AX,0008h            ;Set limit
        MOV     BX,BufSelector
        MOV     CX,0h               ;Buffer size in CX:DX
        MOV     DX,0FFFFh
        INT     31h
        JC      Error7              ;Could not set limit

; Ready to fill buffer with string.

        MOV     SI,OFFSET FillMsg
        CALL    PMPrtString
        MOV     CX,1680             ;39-character message fits this
        CLD                         ;   many times in buffer
        MOV     ES,BufSelector
        MOV     DI,0                ;Start of page buffer
InLoop: PUSH    CX
        MOV     SI,OFFSET TestMsg
        MOV     CX,39               ;Length of message
        REP     MOVSB
        POP     CX
```

continues

Listing 12.2. Continued

```
              LOOP    InLoop
              MOV     AL,0FFh
              STOSB

              MOV     SI,OFFSET ReadMsg
              CALL    PMPrtString
              MOV     DS,BufSelector
              MOV     SI,0
              MOV     AX,1              ;Reading message 1
              MOV     DX,0
OutLoop:      CALL    PMPrtString
              CALL    PMPrtDec
              INC     AX
              CMP     BYTE PTR [SI],0FFh
              JNE     OutLoop
              PUSH    GS
              POP     DS                ;Default data selector

              JMP     CleanUp

Error1:       MOV     SI,OFFSET EMsg1
              CALL    PrtString
              JMP     AllDone
Error2:       MOV     SI,OFFSET EMsg2
              CALL    PrtString
              JMP     AllDone
Error3:       MOV     SI,OFFSET EMsg3
              CALL    PrtString
              JMP     AllDone
Error4:       MOV     SI,OFFSET EMsg4
              CALL    PMAlert
              JMP     AllDone
Error5:       MOV     SI,OFFSET EMsg5
              CALL    PMAlert
              JMP     AllDone
Error6:       MOV     SI,OFFSET EMsg6
              CALL    PMAlert
              JMP     CleanUp
Error7:       MOV     SI,OFFSET EMsg7
              CALL    PMAlert
```

```
CleanUp:     MOV     AX,0001h              ;Release descriptor
             MOV     BX,BufSelector
             INT     31h
             MOV     AX,0502h              ;Release memory block
             MOV     SI,BufHandleH         ;Store handle
             MOV     DI,BufHandleL
             INT     31h


AllDone:
             .EXIT
PMTest       ENDP



; The following routine checks to see whether a DPMI master program is installed.
; If one is not, the carry flag is set on return.
; If one is, the stat info is stored and the carry flag is cleared on return.

ChkDPMI      PROC    NEAR USES AX BX CX DX SI DI ES
             MOV     AX,1687h              ;Get DPMI host address
             INT     2Fh                   ;Multiplex interrupt
             CMP     AX,0                  ;Was it there?
             JNE     NotThere              ;Nope, so exit

             AND     BL,00000001b          ;Test bit 1 (32-bit OK?)
             SETNE   AL
             MOV     Flag32,AL
             MOV     ProcType,CL
             MOV     VerNum,DX
             MOV     MemNeeded,SI
             MOV     WORD PTR DPMIentry,DI
             MOV     WORD PTR DPMIentry+2,ES
             CLC                           ;Set for no error
             JNC     Done

NotThere:    STC
Done:        RET
ChkDPMI      ENDP



; Save registers
```

continues

Listing 12.2. Continued

```
SaveRegs    PROC    NEAR USES AX DS
            PUSH    GS
            POP     DS                  ;Default data selector
            MOV     SaveAX,AX
            MOV     SaveBX,BX
            MOV     SaveCX,CX
            MOV     SaveDX,DX
            MOV     SaveSI,SI
            MOV     SaveDI,DI
            MOV     SaveBP,BP
            PUSHF
            POP     AX
            MOV     SaveFlags,AX
            RET
SaveRegs    ENDP


GetRegs     PROC    NEAR USES DS
            PUSH    GS
            POP     DS                  ;Default data selector
            MOV     AX,SaveFlags
            PUSH    AX
            POPF
            MOV     AX,SaveAX
            MOV     BX,SaveBX
            MOV     CX,SaveCX
            MOV     DX,SaveDX
            MOV     SI,SaveSI
            MOV     DI,SaveDI
            MOV     BP,SaveBP
            RET
GetRegs     ENDP


DOSfunc     PROC    NEAR USES AX BX CX ES
            MOV     AX,0300h            ;Simulate real-mode interrupt
            MOV     BL,21h              ;Want the DOS interrupt
            MOV     BH,0                ;Should be 0
            MOV     CX,0                ;Copy nothing from stack
            PUSH    GS
            POP     ES                  ;ES:DI must point to data structure
```

```
            MOV     DI,OFFSET ES:RegSet
            INT     31h
            RET
DOSfunc     ENDP
```

; The following routine prints the ASCIIZ string pointed to by DS:SI.
; Works from protected mode by switching to real mode to do DOS function.

```
PMPrtString PROC    NEAR USES AX DX
PS1:        MOV     DL,[SI]         ;Get character
            INC     SI              ;Point to next one
            CMP     DL,0            ;End of string?
            JE      PS2             ;Yes, so exit
            MOV     AH,02h          ;Output a character
            CALL    SaveRegs
            CALL    DOSfunc
            CALL    GetRegs
            JMP     PS1             ;Keep doing it
PS2:        RET
PMPrtString ENDP
```

; The following routine prints the ASCIIZ string pointed to by DS:SI

```
PrtString   PROC    NEAR USES AX DX SI
PS1:        MOV     DL,[SI]         ;Get character
            INC     SI              ;Point to next one
            CMP     DL,0            ;End of string?
            JE      PS2             ;Yes, so exit
            MOV     AH,02h          ;Output a character
            INT     21h
            JMP     PS1             ;Keep doing it
PS2:        RET
PrtString   ENDP
```

; The following routine prints the value in AX as a decimal number.
; Will accept numbers up to 655,359,999. Anything larger will not print.

continues

Listing 12.2. Continued

```
            .DATA
Temp        DW      0000

            .CODE
PMPrtDec    PROC    NEAR USES AX BX CX DX DS

            PUSH    GS
            POP     DS              ;Default data selector
            MOV     CX,0FFFFh       ;Ending flag
            PUSH    CX

PD0:        MOV     CX,10000        ;Divide by 10,000
            DIV     CX
            MOV     Temp,AX         ;Store whole portion
            MOV     BX,0            ;Count for this iteration

            MOV     AX,DX
            MOV     CX,10
PD1:        MOV     DX,0
            DIV     CX              ;Divide by 10
            ADD     DL,30h          ;Convert to ASCII
            PUSH    DX              ;Store remainder
            INC     BX              ;Cycle count
            CMP     AX,0            ;Are we done?
            JNE     PD1             ;No, so continue
            MOV     DX,0
            MOV     AX,Temp         ;Get back part above 10,000
            CMP     AX,0
            JE      PD3
            MOV     CX,'0'
PD2:        CMP     BX,4            ;Did we push 4 numbers?
            JE      PD0             ;Yes, continue
            PUSH    CX              ;No, so push it
            INC     BX              ;Push counter
            JMP     PD2

PD3:        POP     DX              ;Character is now in DL
            CMP     DX,0FFFFh       ;Is it the ending flag?
            JE      PD4             ;Yes, so continue
            MOV     AH,02h          ;Output a character
            CALL    SaveRegs
```

```
            CALL    DOSfunc
            CALL    GetRegs
            JMP     PD3                 ;Keep doing it

PD4:        RET
PMPrtDec    ENDP



; Print error number and message in protected mode

PMAlert     PROC
            CMP     VerNum,5Ah          ;Running under version .9?
            JE      NoErrNum            ;Yes, so there are no error numbers
            CALL    ConHexLong
            MOV     ErrNum[0],AX
            MOV     ErrNum[2],DX
            PUSH    SI
            MOV     SI,OFFSET ErrMsg
            CALL    PMPrtString
            POP     SI
NoErrNum:   CALL    PMPrtString
            RET
PMAlert     ENDP



; The following routine converts the number in AL into an ASCII
; representation of the hex value, with a leading zero. Value
; is returned in AX as well.

ConHex      PROC    USES CX
            MOV     CL,10h              ;What you will be dividing by
            MOV     AH,0
            DIV     CL                  ;Divide by 16
            OR      AX,3030h            ;Convert to ASCII
            CMP     AL,'9'              ;Is it greater than 9?
            JBE     CA4                 ;No, so continue
            ADD     AL,7                ;Make into hex digit
CA4:        CMP     AH,'9'              ;Is it greater than 9?
            JBE     CA5                 ;No, so continue
            ADD     AH,7                ;Make into hex digit
CA5:        RET
ConHex      ENDP
```

continues

Listing 12.2. Continued

```
; The following uses ConHex to convert a long number (AX) into its ASCII
; equivalent in DX:AX

ConHexLong    PROC
              PUSH    AX
              CALL    ConHex
              MOV     DX,AX
              POP     AX
              MOV     AL,AH
              CALL    ConHex
              RET
ConHexLong    ENDP

              END
```

Some of the routines in this program may look familiar if you have worked through POSTCARD.ASM; the concepts are the same. A few points, however, are worth noting.

First, look at the entire process of allocating memory and manipulating the LDT. The memory allocation is pretty straightforward. You use DPMI function 0501h, and specify in BX:CX how much memory you want. In this example, I requested 100000h bytes, or 1M. On return, you are provided with two pieces of information. The first, the memory block handle in SI:DI, must be saved so that you can release the memory block at the end of the program. The other piece of information is the linear address of the memory block, returned in BX:CX.

Next, you have to assign the base address (BX:CX) to the LDT descriptor. You do this with DPMI function 0007h, but the address must be transferred to CX:DX. When this function is complete, you must set the limit for the descriptor with DPMI function 0008h. The problem is that, if you are using a 16-bit application (as this one is), the largest limit you can have is a 16-bit limit. This limit means that you can directly address 64K only in any one segment described by a descriptor. You don't have that limitation if you are developing a 32-bit application, but mixing 16-bit and 32-bit code in even a short example program is beyond the scope of this book. In this program, therefore, even though the allocated memory block is 1M, only a portion of that amount (64K) is accessed directly.

After the LDT descriptor is straightened out, you can write to the segment and read from it normally. I made one change here that may need some clarification. When the information is being read from the buffer, the selector in DS has to point to the buffer in order for PMPrtString to display the information in the buffer. The problem is that the SaveRegs, GetRegs, and DOSfunc routines all have to access data elements in the default data segment. Rather than cause a major program rewrite (and to keep the example as simple as possible), I used the GS register, which is not used anywhere else in the program, as a "keeper of the keys." Immediately after the switch to protected mode, GS was loaded with a copy of the selector in DS. Then it was an easy task to point back to the proper segment area in the subroutines.

Finally, look at the PMAlert routine near the end of the program. This routine prints an error code and the error message. The problem is that DPMI version 0.9 did not specify error codes to be returned when an error occurs. This oversight was corrected in version 1.0, but that means that printing the value of AX in case of an error has meaning only if you are working with DPMI version 1.0. This routine checks the DPMI version number and acts accordingly.

Summary

Protected mode programming is a brave new world for most programmers. As time goes by, we all undoubtedly will program more for this environment. For assembly language programmers, that day will be hastened only when decent tools (assemblers and debuggers) are available that work in both real and protected mode. In the meantime, you are left with the tried-and-true ancient methods of debugging (for example, put a print statement here or there to see what's going on).

Keyboard Interpretation Tables

This appendix contains tables to aid in programming for the keyboard. The appendix is divided into three sections. The first section presents the original 83-key keyboard from IBM; the second, the modified 84-key keyboard; and the third section, the 101/102-key enhanced keyboard.

The 83-Key Keyboard

The 83-key keyboard, available on the original IBM PC computers, was used to develop the original PC scan codes. Figure A.1 illustrates this keyboard; Figure A.2 shows the key numbers assigned to each key. Table A.1 provides the interpretation of each key, along with the scan code (AH) and ASCII values (AL) returned by Int 16/00 and Int 16/01. If you are using Int 16/10 or Int 16/11, the same codes are returned.

The original IBM PC
83-key keyboard.

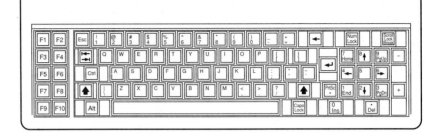

Key code numbers
assigned to the original
IBM PC 83-key keyboard.

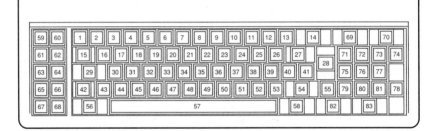

Table A.1. Key interpretation table for the 83-key keyboard.

Key Dec	Code Hex	Key Cap	Scan/ASCII Code			
			Normal	Shift	Ctrl	Alt
1	01h	Esc	01h/1Bh	01h/1Bh	01h/1Bh	
2	02h	1 !	02h/31h	02h/21h		78h/00h
3	03h	2 @	03h/32h	03h/40h	03h/00h	79h/00h
4	04h	3 #	04h/33h	04h/23h		7Ah/00h
5	05h	4 $	05h/34h	05h/24h		7Bh/00h
6	06h	5 %	06h/35h	06h/25h		7Ch/00h
7	07h	6 ^	07h/36h	07h/5Eh	07h/1Eh	7Dh/00h
8	08h	7 &	08h/37h	08h/26h		7Eh/00h
9	09h	8 *	09h/38h	09h/2Ah		7Fh/00h
10	0Ah	9 (	0Ah/39h	0Ah/28h		80h/00h
11	0Bh	0)	0Bh/30h	0Bh/29h		81h/00h
12	0Ch	- _	0Ch/2Dh	0Ch/5Fh	0Ch/1Fh	82h/00h
13	0Dh	= +	0Dh/3Dh	0Dh/2Bh		83h/00h

Key Dec	Code Hex	Key Cap	Scan/ASCII Code			
			Normal	**Shift**	**Ctrl**	**Alt**
14	0Eh	Backspace	0Eh/08h	0Eh/08h	0Eh/7Fh	
15	0Fh	Tab	0Fh/09h	0Fh/00h		
16	10h	Q	10h/71h	10h/51h	10h/11h	10h/00h
17	11h	W	11h/77h	11h/57h	11h/17h	11h/00h
18	12h	E	12h/65h	12h/45h	12h/05h	12h/00h
19	13h	R	13h/72h	13h/52h	13h/12h	13h/00h
20	14h	T	14h/74h	14h/54h	14h/14h	14h/00h
21	15h	Y	15h/79h	15h/59h	15h/19h	15h/00h
22	16h	U	16h/75h	16h/55h	16h/15h	16h/00h
23	17h	I	17h/69h	17h/49h	17h/09h	17h/00h
24	18h	O	18h/6Fh	18h/4Fh	18h/0Fh	18h/00h
25	19h	P	19h/70h	19h/50h	19h/10h	19h/00h
26	1Ah	[{	1Ah/5Bh	1Ah/7Bh	1Ah/1Bh	
27	1Bh	] }	1Bh/5Dh	1Bh/7Dh	1Bh/1Dh	
28	1Ch	Enter	1Ch/0Dh	1Ch/0Dh	1Ch/0Ah	
29	1Dh	Ctrl	1Dh			
30	1Eh	A	1Eh/61h	1Eh/41h	1Eh/01h	1Eh/00h
31	1Fh	S	1Fh/73h	1Fh/53h	1Fh/13h	1Fh/00h
32	20h	D	20h/64h	20h/44h	20h/04h	20h/00h
33	21h	F	21h/66h	21h/46h	21h/06h	21h/00h
34	22h	G	22h/67h	22h/47h	22h/07h	22h/00h
35	23h	H	23h/68h	23h/48h	23h/08h	23h/00h
36	24h	J	24h/6Ah	24h/4Ah	24h/0Ah	24h/00h
37	25h	K	25h/6Bh	25h/4Bh	25h/0Bh	25h/00h
38	26h	L	26h/6Ch	26h/4Ch	26h/0Ch	26h/00h
39	27h	; :	27h/3Bh	27h/3Ah		
40	28h	' "	28h/27h	28h/22h		
41	29h	` ~	29h/60h	29h/7Eh		

continues

Table A.1. Continued

Key Dec	Code Hex	Key Cap	Normal	Shift	Ctrl	Alt
				—Scan/ASCII Code—		
42	2Ah	Left Shift	2Ah			
43	2Bh	\ |	2Bh/5Ch	2Bh/7Ch	2Bh/1Ch	
44	2Ch	Z	2Ch/7Ah	2Ch/5Ah	2Ch/1Ah	2Ch/00h
45	2Dh	X	2Dh/78h	2Dh/58h	2Dh/18h	2Dh/00h
46	2Eh	C	2Eh/63h	2Eh/43h	2Eh/03h	2Eh/00h
47	2Fh	V	2Fh/76h	2Fh/56h	2Fh/16h	2Fh/00h
48	30h	B	30h/62h	30h/42h	30h/02h	30h/00h
49	31h	N	31h/6Eh	31h/4Eh	31h/0Eh	31h/00h
50	32h	M	32h/6Dh	32h/4Dh	32h/0Dh	32h/00h
51	33h	, <	33h/2Ch	33h/3Ch		
52	34h	. >	34h/2Eh	34h/3Eh		
53	35h	/ ?	35h/2Fh	35h/3Fh		
54	36h	Right Shift	36h			
55	37h	* PrtSc	37h/2Ah			
56	38h	Alt	38h			
57	39h	Space	39h/20h	39h/20h	39h/20h	39h/20h
58	3Ah	Caps Lock	3Ah			
59	3Bh	F1	3Bh/00h	54h/00h	5Eh/00h	68h/00h
60	3Ch	F2	3Ch/00h	55h/00h	5Fh/00h	69h/00h
61	3Dh	F3	3Dh/00h	56h/00h	60h/00h	6Ah/00h
62	3Eh	F4	3Eh/00h	57h/00h	61h/00h	6Bh/00h
63	3Fh	F5	3Fh/00h	58h/00h	62h/00h	6Ch/00h
64	40h	F6	40h/00h	59h/00h	63h/00h	6Dh/00h
65	41h	F7	41h/00h	5Ah/00h	64h/00h	6Eh/00h
66	42h	F8	42h/00h	5Bh/00h	65h/00h	6Fh/00h
67	43h	F9	43h/00h	5Ch/00h	66h/00h	70h/00h
68	44h	F10	44h/00h	5Dh/00h	67h/00h	71h/00h
69	45h	Num Lock	45h			

Key Dec	Code Hex	Key Cap	Scan/ASCII Code			
			Normal	Shift	Ctrl	Alt
70	46h	Scroll Lock	46h			
71	47h	7 Home	47h/00h	47h/37h	77h/00h	
72	48h	8 Up arrow	48h/00h	48h/38h		
73	49h	9 PgUp	49h/00h	49h/39h	84h/00h	
74	4Ah	-	4Ah/2Dh	4Ah/2Dh		
75	4Bh	4 Left arrow	4Bh/00h	4Bh/34h	73h/00h	
76	4Ch	5	4Ch/00h	4Ch/35h		
77	4Dh	6 Right arrow	4Dh/00h	4Dh/36h	74h/00h	
78	4Eh	+	4Eh/2Bh	4Eh/2Bh		
79	4Fh	1 End	4Fh/00h	4Fh/31h	75h/00h	
80	50h	2 Down arrow	50h/00h	50h/32h		
81	51h	3 PgDn	51h/00h	51h/33h	76h/00h	
82	52h	0 Ins	52h/00h	52h/30h		
83	53h	. Del	53h/00h	53h/2Eh		

The 84-Key Keyboard

The 84-key keyboard was available beginning with the IBM AT computers. Figure A.3 illustrates this keyboard; Figure A.4 shows the key numbers assigned to each key.

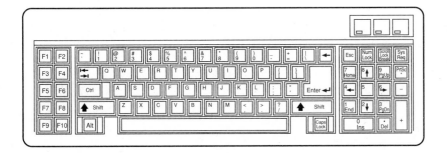

Figure A.3.

The 84-key keyboard.

Key code numbers
assigned to the 84-key
keyboard.

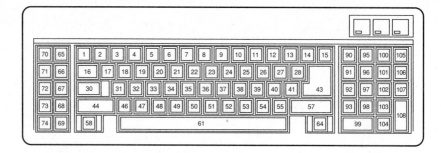

Notice in Figure A.4 that, unlike the original IBM PC keyboard, this keyboard
does not number keys sequentially. In fact, no keys correspond to key codes
29, 42, 45, 56, 59, 60, 62, 63, 75 through 89, or 94. Several keys were shifted
around, an additional key was added (the Sys Req key), and all the keys were
renumbered.

To maintain compatibility with the original IBM PC keyboard, the keyboard
microprocessor and system BIOS had to undergo additional translations to
convert the new key codes to scan codes that were backward-compatible.
Table A.2 provides the interpretation of each key, along with the scan code
(AH) and ASCII values (AL) returned by Int 16/00 and Int 16/01. If you are using
Int 16/10 or Int 16/11, the same codes are returned.

Table A.2. Key interpretation table for the 84-key keyboard.

Key Dec	Code Hex	Key Cap	Scan/ASCII Code			
			Normal	Shift	Ctrl	Alt
1	01h	` ~	29h/60h	29h/7Eh		
2	02h	1 !	02h/31h	02h/21h		78h/00h
3	03h	2 @	03h/32h	03h/40h	03h/00h	79h/00h
4	04h	3 #	04h/33h	04h/23h		7Ah/00h
5	05h	4 $	05h/34h	05h/24h		7Bh/00h
6	06h	5 %	06h/35h	06h/25h		7Ch/00h
7	07h	6 ^	07h/36h	07h/5Eh	07h/1Eh	7Dh/00h
8	08h	7 &	08h/37h	08h/26h		7Eh/00h
9	09h	8 *	09h/38h	09h/2Ah		7Fh/00h
10	0Ah	9 (	0Ah/39h	0Ah/28h		80h/00h
11	0Bh	0)	0Bh/30h	0Bh/29h		81h/00h

Key Dec	Code Hex	Key Cap	Scan/ASCII Code			
			Normal	Shift	Ctrl	Alt
12	0Ch	- _	0Ch/2Dh	0Ch/5Fh	0Ch/1Fh	82h/00h
13	0Dh	= +	0Dh/3Dh	0Dh/2Bh		83h/00h
14	0Eh	\ |	2Bh/5Ch	2Bh/7Ch	2Bh/1Ch	
15	0Fh	Backspace	0Eh/08h	0Eh/08h	0Eh/7Fh	
16	10h	Tab	0Fh/09h	0Fh/00h		
17	11h	Q	10h/71h	10h/51h	10h/11h	10h/00h
18	12h	W	11h/77h	11h/57h	11h/17h	11h/00h
19	13h	E	12h/65h	12h/45h	12h/05h	12h/00h
20	14h	R	13h/72h	13h/52h	13h/12h	13h/00h
21	15h	T	14h/74h	14h/54h	14h/14h	14h/00h
22	16h	Y	15h/79h	15h/59h	15h/19h	15h/00h
23	17h	U	16h/75h	16h/55h	16h/15h	16h/00h
24	18h	I	17h/69h	17h/49h	17h/09h	17h/00h
25	19h	O	18h/6Fh	18h/4Fh	18h/0Fh	18h/00h
26	1Ah	P	19h/70h	19h/50h	19h/10h	19h/00h
27	1Bh	[{	1Ah/5Bh	1Ah/7Bh	1Ah/1Bh	
28	1Ch	] }	1Bh/5Dh	1Bh/7Dh	1Bh/1Dh	
30	1Eh	Ctrl	1Dh			
31	1Fh	A	1Eh/61h	1Eh/41h	1Eh/01h	1Eh/00h
32	20h	S	1Fh/73h	1Fh/53h	1Fh/13h	1Fh/00h
33	21h	D	20h/64h	20h/44h	20h/04h	20h/00h
34	22h	F	21h/66h	21h/46h	21h/06h	21h/00h
35	23h	G	22h/67h	22h/47h	22h/07h	22h/00h
36	24h	H	23h/68h	23h/48h	23h/08h	23h/00h
37	25h	J	24h/6Ah	24h/4Ah	24h/0Ah	24h/00h
38	26h	K	25h/6Bh	25h/4Bh	25h/0Bh	25h/00h
39	27h	L	26h/6Ch	26h/4Ch	26h/0Ch	26h/00h
40	28h	; :	27h/3Bh	27h/3Ah		
41	29h	' "	28h/27h	28h/22h		

continues

Table A.2. Continued

Key Dec	Code Hex	Key Cap	Scan/ASCII Code Normal	Shift	Ctrl	Alt
43	2Bh	Enter	1Ch/0Dh	1Ch/0Dh	1Ch/0Ah	
44	2Ch	Left Shift	2Ah			
46	2Eh	Z	2Ch/7Ah	2Ch/5Ah	2Ch/1Ah	2Ch/00h
47	2Fh	X	2Dh/78h	2Dh/58h	2Dh/18h	2Dh/00h
48	30h	C	2Eh/63h	2Eh/43h	2Eh/03h	2Eh/00h
49	31h	V	2Fh/76h	2Fh/56h	2Fh/16h	2Fh/00h
50	32h	B	30h/62h	30h/42h	30h/02h	30h/00h
51	33h	N	31h/6Eh	31h/4Eh	31h/0Eh	31h/00h
52	34h	M	32h/6Dh	32h/4Dh	32h/0Dh	32h/00h
53	35h	, <	33h/2Ch	33h/3Ch		
54	36h	. >	34h/2Eh	34h/3Eh		
55	37h	/ ?	35h/2Fh	35h/3Fh		
57	39h	Right Shift	36h			
58	3Ah	Alt	38h			
61	3Dh	Space	39h/20h	39h/20h	39h/20h	39h/20h
64	40h	Caps Lock	3Ah			
65	41h	F2	3Ch/00h	55h/00h	5Fh/00h	69h/00h
66	42h	F4	3Eh/00h	57h/00h	61h/00h	6Bh/00h
67	43h	F6	40h/00h	59h/00h	63h/00h	6Dh/00h
68	44h	F8	42h/00h	5Bh/00h	65h/00h	6Fh/00h
69	45h	F10	44h/00h	5Dh/00h	67h/00h	71h/00h
70	46h	F1	3Bh/00h	54h/00h	5Eh/00h	68h/00h
71	47h	F3	3Dh/00h	56h/00h	60h/00h	6Ah/00h
72	48h	F5	3Fh/00h	58h/00h	62h/00h	6Ch/00h
73	49h	F7	41h/00h	5Ah/00h	64h/00h	6Eh/00h
74	4Ah	F9	43h/00h	5Ch/00h	66h/00h	70h/00h
90	5Ah	Esc	01h/1Bh	01h/1Bh	01h/1Bh	
91	5Bh	7 Home	47h/00h	47h/37h	77h/00h	

Key Dec	Code Hex	Key Cap	Scan/ASCII Code			
			Normal	Shift	Ctrl	Alt
92	5Ch	4 Left arrow	4Bh/00h	4Bh/34h	73h/00h	
93	5Dh	1 End	4Fh/00h	4Fh/31h	75h/00h	
95	5Fh	Num Lock	45h			
96	60h	8 Up arrow	48h/00h	48h/38h		
97	61h	5	4Ch/00h	4Ch/35h		
98	62h	2 Down arrow	50h/00h	50h/32h		
99	63h	0 Ins	52h/00h	52h/30h		
100	64h	Scroll Lock/Break	46h			
101	65h	9 PgUp	49h/00h	49h/39h	84h/00h	
102	66h	6 Right arrow	4Dh/00h	4Dh/36h	74h/00h	
103	67h	3 PgDn	51h/00h	51h/33h	76h/00h	
104	68h	. Del	53h/00h	53h/2Eh		
105	69h	Sys Req				
106	6Ah	* PrtSc	37h/2Ah			
107	6Bh	-	4Ah/2Dh	4Ah/2Dh		
108	6Ch	+	4Eh/2Bh	4Eh/2Bh		

The Enhanced Keyboard

The enhanced keyboard became available some time after the introduction of the IBM AT computers. It is distinguished from its predecessors by the inclusion of the function keys across the top of the keyboard rather than on the left side. This keyboard comes in several different configurations; it is referred to collectively as "enhanced." The differences between the configurations are in the placement of the backslash key; these differences, however, are minor. Figure A.5 illustrates a typical enhanced keyboard; Figure A.6 shows the key numbers assigned to each key.

Notice in Figure A.6 that the keys on the enhanced keyboard are not numbered sequentially. The key codes are similar to those on the 84-key keyboard, with the addition of several new keys. These new keys are primarily for cursor control.

Figure A.5.

Figure A.5.

The enhanced keyboard.

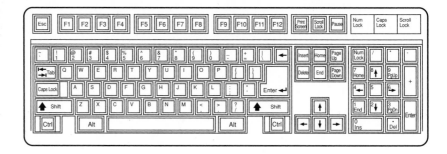

Figure A.6.

Key code numbers
assigned to the enhanced
keyboard.

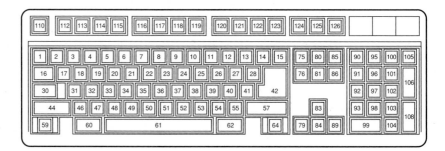

To maintain compatibility with previous keyboards, the keyboard microprocessor and system BIOS have to undergo additional translations to convert the
new key codes to scan codes that are backward-compatible. Table A.3 gives
the interpretation of each key, along with the scan code (AH) and ASCII values
(AL) returned by Int 16/00 and Int 16/01.

Table A.3. Key interpretation table for the enhanced keyboard.

Key Dec	Code Hex	Key Cap	Normal	Shift	Ctrl	Alt
1	01h	` ~	29h/60h	29h/7Eh		29h/00h*
2	02h	1 !	02h/31h	02h/21h		78h/00h
3	03h	2 @	03h/32h	03h/40h	03h/00h	79h/00h
4	04h	3 #	04h/33h	04h/23h		7Ah/00h
5	05h	4 $	05h/34h	05h/24h		7Bh/00h
6	06h	5 %	06h/35h	06h/25h		7Ch/00h
7	07h	6 ^	07h/36h	07h/5Eh	07h/1Eh	7Dh/00h
8	08h	7 &	08h/37h	08h/26h		7Eh/00h

Key Dec	Code Hex	Key Cap	Scan/ASCII Code			
			Normal	**Shift**	**Ctrl**	**Alt**
9	09h	8 *	09h/38h	09h/2Ah		7Fh/00h
10	0Ah	9 (	0Ah/39h	0Ah/28h		80h/00h
11	0Bh	0)	0Bh/30h	0Bh/29h		81h/00h
12	0Ch	- _	0Ch/2Dh	0Ch/5Fh	0Ch/1Fh	82h/00h
13	0Dh	= +	0Dh/3Dh	0Dh/2Bh		83h/00h
14	0Eh	\		2Bh/5Ch	2Bh/7Ch	2Bh/1Ch	
15	0Fh	Backspace	0Eh/08h	0Eh/08h	0Eh/7Fh	0Eh/00h*
16	10h	Tab	0Fh/09h	0Fh/00h	94h/00h*	A5h/00h*
17	11h	Q	10h/71h	10h/51h	10h/11h	10h/00h
18	12h	W	11h/77h	11h/57h	11h/17h	11h/00h
19	13h	E	12h/65h	12h/45h	12h/05h	12h/00h
20	14h	R	13h/72h	13h/52h	13h/12h	13h/00h
21	15h	T	14h/74h	14h/54h	14h/14h	14h/00h
22	16h	Y	15h/79h	15h/59h	15h/19h	15h/00h
23	17h	U	16h/75h	16h/55h	16h/15h	16h/00h
24	18h	I	17h/69h	17h/49h	17h/09h	17h/00h
25	19h	O	18h/6Fh	18h/4Fh	18h/0Fh	18h/00h
26	1Ah	P	19h/70h	19h/50h	19h/10h	19h/00h
27	1Bh	[{	1Ah/5Bh	1Ah/7Bh	1Ah/1Bh	1Ah/00h*
28	1Ch	] }	1Bh/5Dh	1Bh/7Dh	1Bh/1Dh	1Bh/00h*
29	1Dh	\		2Bh/5Ch	2Bh/7Ch	2Bh/1Ch	2Bh/00h*
30	1Eh	Caps Lock	3Ah			
31	1Fh	A	1Eh/61h	1Eh/41h	1Eh/01h	1Eh/00h
32	20h	S	1Fh/73h	1Fh/53h	1Fh/13h	1Fh/00h
33	21h	D	20h/64h	20h/44h	20h/04h	20h/00h
34	22h	F	21h/66h	21h/46h	21h/06h	21h/00h
35	23h	G	22h/67h	22h/47h	22h/07h	22h/00h
36	24h	H	23h/68h	23h/48h	23h/08h	23h/00h
37	25h	J	24h/6Ah	24h/4Ah	24h/0Ah	24h/00h

continues

ADVANCED ASSEMBLY LANGUAGE

Table A.3. Continued

Key Dec	Code Hex	Key Cap	Scan/ASCII Code Normal	Shift	Ctrl	Alt
38	26h	K	25h/6Bh	25h/4Bh	25h/0Bh	25h/00h
39	27h	L	26h/6Ch	26h/4Ch	26h/0Ch	26h/00h
40	28h	; :	27h/3Bh	27h/3Ah		27h/00h*
41	29h	' "	28h/27h	28h/22h		28h/00h*
42	2Ah	Enter	1Ch/0Dh	1Ch/0Dh	1Ch/0Ah	1Ch/00h*
44	2Ch	Left Shift	2Ah			
46	2Eh	Z	2Ch/7Ah	2Ch/5Ah	2Ch/1Ah	2Ch/00h
47	2Fh	X	2Dh/78h	2Dh/58h	2Dh/18h	2Dh/00h
48	30h	C	2Eh/63h	2Eh/43h	2Eh/03h	2Eh/00h
49	31h	V	2Fh/76h	2Fh/56h	2Fh/16h	2Fh/00h
50	32h	B	30h/62h	30h/42h	30h/02h	30h/00h
51	33h	N	31h/6Eh	31h/4Eh	31h/0Eh	31h/00h
52	34h	M	32h/6Dh	32h/4Dh	32h/0Dh	32h/00h
53	35h	, <	33h/2Ch	33h/3Ch		33h/00h*
54	36h	. >	34h/2Eh	34h/3Eh		34h/00h*
55	37h	/ ?	35h/2Fh	35h/3Fh		35h/00h*
57	39h	Right Shift	36h			
58	3Ah	Left Ctrl	1Dh			
60	3Ch	Left Alt	38h			
61	3Dh	Space	39h/20h	39h/20h	39h/20h	39h/20h
62	3Eh	Right Alt	38h			
64	40h	Right Ctrl	1Dh			
75	4Bh	Insert	52h/00h	52h/00h		
			52h/E0h*	52h/E0h*	92h/E0h*	A2h/00h*
76	4Ch	Delete	53h/00h	53h/00h		
			53h/E0h*	53h/E0h*	93h/E0h*	A3h/00h*
79	4Fh	Left arrow	4Bh/00h	4Bh/00h	73h/00h	
			4Bh/E0h*	4Bh/E0h*	73h/E0h*	9Bh/00h*

Key Dec	Code Hex	Key Cap	Scan/ASCII Code			
			Normal	Shift	Ctrl	Alt
80	50h	Home	47h/00h	47h/00h	77h/00h	
			47h/E0h*	47h/E0h*	77h/E0h*	97h/00h*
81	51h	End	4Fh/00h	4Fh/00h	75h/00h	
			4Fh/E0h*	4Fh/E0h*	75h/E0h*	9Fh/00h*
83	53h	Up arrow	48h/00h	48h/00h		
			48h/E0h*	48h/E0h*	8Dh/E0h*	98h/00h*
84	54h	Down arrow	50h/00h	50h/00h		
			50h/E0h*	50h/E0h*	91h/E0h*	A0h/00h*
85	55h	Page Up	49h/00h	49h/00h	84h/00h	
			49h/E0h*	49h/E0h*	84h/E0h*	99h/00h*
86	56h	Page Dn	51h/00h	51h/00h	76h/00h	
			51h/E0h*	51h/E0h*	76h/E0h*	A1h/00h*
89	59h	Right arrow	4Dh/00h	4Dh/00h	74h/00h	
			4Dh/E0h*	4Dh/E0h*	74h/E0h*	9Dh/00h*
90	5Ah	Num Lock	45h			
91	5Bh	7 Home	47h/00h	47h/37h	77h/00h	
92	5Ch	4 Left arrow	4Bh/00h	4Bh/34h	73h/00h	
93	5Dh	1 End	4Fh/00h	4Fh/31h	75h/00h	
95	5Fh	/	35h/2Fh	35h/2Fh		
			E0h/2Fh*	E0h/2Fh*	95h/00h*	A4h/00h*
96	60h	8 Up arrow	48h/00h	48h/38h	8Dh/00h*	
97	61h	5	4Ch/00h	4Ch/35h	8Fh/00h	
98	62h	2 Down arrow	50h/00h	50h/32h	91h/00h*	
99	63h	0 Ins	52h/00h	52h/30h	92h/00h*	
100	64h	*	37h/2Ah	37h/2Ah	96h/00h*	37h/00h*
101	65h	9 PgUp	49h/00h	49h/39h	84h/00h	
102	66h	6 Right arrow	4Dh/00h	4Dh/36h	74h/00h	
103	67h	3 PgDn	51h/00h	51h/33h	76h/00h	
104	68h	. Del	53h/00h	53h/2Eh	93h/00h*	

continues

Table A.3. Continued

Key Dec	Code Hex	Key Cap	Scan/ASCII Code			
			Normal	Shift	Ctrl	Alt
105	69h	-	4Ah/2Dh	4Ah/2Dh	8Eh/00h*	4Ah/00h*
106	6Ah	+	4Eh/2Bh	4Eh/2Bh	90h/00h*	4Eh/00h*
108	6Ch	Enter	1Ch/0Dh	1Ch/0Dh	1Ch/0Ah	
			E0h/0Dh*	E0h/0Dh*	E0h/0Ah*	A6h/00h*
110	6Eh	Esc	01h/1Bh	01h/1Bh	01h/1Bh	01h/00h*
112	70h	F1	3Bh/00h	54h/00h	5Eh/00h	68h/00h
113	71h	F2	3Ch/00h	55h/00h	5Fh/00h	69h/00h
114	72h	F3	3Dh/00h	56h/00h	60h/00h	6Ah/00h
115	73h	F4	3Eh/00h	57h/00h	61h/00h	6Bh/00h
116	74h	F5	3Fh/00h	58h/00h	62h/00h	6Ch/00h
117	75h	F6	40h/00h	59h/00h	63h/00h	6Dh/00h
118	76h	F7	41h/00h	5Ah/00h	64h/00h	6Eh/00h
119	77h	F8	42h/00h	5Bh/00h	65h/00h	6Fh/00h
120	78h	F9	43h/00h	5Ch/00h	66h/00h	70h/00h
121	79h	F10	44h/00h	5Dh/00h	67h/00h	71h/00h
122	7Ah	F11	85h/00h*	87h/00h*	89h/00h*	8Bh/00h*
123	7Bh	F12	86h/00h*	88h/00h*	8Ah/00h*	8Ch/00h*
124	7Ch	Print Screen/ Sys Rq				
125	7Dh	Scroll Lock	46h			
126	7Eh	Pause/Break				

Codes marked with an asterisk are returned only if you are using Int 16/10 or Int 16/11.

The Scan Codes

The scan codes assigned to each keystroke are consistent regardless of the keyboard you are using. Table A.4 lists the scan codes and the applicable keyboards that use them. The scan and ASCII codes listed in Table A.4 are returned by Int 16/00 and Int 16/01.

Table A.4. Scan and ASCII code combinations for the IBM PC family of computers.

Scan/ASCII Code	Keyboard 83	84	Enh	Keypress
01h/00h*			X	Alt-Esc
01h/1Bh	X	X	X	Esc
02h/21h	X	X	X	!
02h/31h	X	X	X	1
03h/00h	X	X	X	Ctrl-2
03h/32h	X	X	X	2
03h/40h	X	X	X	@
04h/23h	X	X	X	#
04h/33h	X	X	X	3
05h/24h	X	X	X	$
05h/34h	X	X	X	4
06h/25h	X	X	X	%
06h/35h	X	X	X	5
07h/1Eh	X	X	X	Ctrl-6
07h/36h	X	X	X	6
07h/5Eh	X	X	X	^
08h/26h	X	X	X	&
08h/37h	X	X	X	7
09h/2Ah	X	X	X	*
09h/38h	X	X	X	8
0Ah/28h	X	X	X	(
0Ah/39h	X	X	X	9
0Bh/29h	X	X	X	)
0Bh/30h	X	X	X	0
0Ch/1Fh	X	X	X	Ctrl--
0Ch/2Dh	X	X	X	-
0Ch/5Fh	X	X	X	_

continues

Table A.4. Continued

Scan/ASCII Code	83	84	Enh	Keypress
0Dh/2Bh	X	X	X	+
0Dh/3Dh	X	X	X	=
0Eh/00h*			X	Alt-Backspace
0Eh/08h	X	X	X	Backspace
0Eh/7Fh	X	X	X	Ctrl-Backspace
0Fh/00h	X	X	X	Shift-Tab
0Fh/09h	X	X	X	Tab
10h/00h	X	X	X	Alt-Q
10h/11h	X	X	X	Ctrl-Q
10h/51h	X	X	X	Q
10h/71h	X	X	X	q
11h/00h	X	X	X	Alt-W
11h/17h	X	X	X	Ctrl-W
11h/57h	X	X	X	W
11h/77h	X	X	X	w
12h/00h	X	X	X	Alt-E
12h/05h	X	X	X	Ctrl-E
12h/45h	X	X	X	E
12h/65h	X	X	X	e
13h/00h	X	X	X	Alt-R
13h/12h	X	X	X	Ctrl-R
13h/52h	X	X	X	R
13h/72h	X	X	X	r
14h/00h	X	X	X	Alt-T
14h/14h	X	X	X	Ctrl-T
14h/54h	X	X	X	T
14h/74h	X	X	X	t
15h/00h	X	X	X	Alt-Y
15h/19h	X	X	X	Ctrl-Y

Scan/ASCII Code	Keyboard			Keypress
	83	84	Enh	
15h/59h	X	X	X	Y
15h/79h	X	X	X	y
16h/00h	X	X	X	Alt-U
16h/15h	X	X	X	Ctrl-U
16h/55h	X	X	X	U
16h/75h	X	X	X	u
17h/00h	X	X	X	Alt-I
17h/09h	X	X	X	Ctrl-I
17h/49h	X	X	X	I
17h/69h	X	X	X	i
18h/00h	X	X	X	Alt-O
18h/0Fh	X	X	X	Ctrl-O
18h/4Fh	X	X	X	O
18h/6Fh	X	X	X	o
19h/00h	X	X	X	Alt-P
19h/10h	X	X	X	Ctrl-P
19h/50h	X	X	X	P
19h/70h	X	X	X	p
1Ah/00h*			X	Alt-[
1Ah/1Bh	X	X	X	Ctrl-[
1Ah/5Bh	X	X	X	[
1Ah/7Bh	X	X	X	{
1Bh/00h*			X	Alt-]
1Bh/1Dh	X	X	X	Ctrl-]
1Bh/5Dh	X	X	X	]
1Bh/7Dh	X	X	X	}
1Ch/00h*			X	Alt-Enter
1Ch/0Ah	X	X	X	Ctrl-Enter
1Ch/0Dh	X	X	X	Enter

continues

Table A.4. Continued

Scan/ASCII Code	Keyboard 83	84	Enh	Keypress
1Dh	X	X	X	Ctrl
1Eh/00h	X	X	X	Alt-A
1Eh/01h	X	X	X	Ctrl-A
1Eh/41h	X	X	X	A
1Eh/61h	X	X	X	a
1Fh/00h	X	X	X	Alt-S
1Fh/13h	X	X	X	Ctrl-S
1Fh/53h	X	X	X	S
1Fh/73h	X	X	X	s
20h/00h	X	X	X	Alt-D
20h/04h	X	X	X	Ctrl-D
20h/44h	X	X	X	D
20h/64h	X	X	X	d
21h/00h	X	X	X	Alt-F
21h/06h	X	X	X	Ctrl-F
21h/46h	X	X	X	F
21h/66h	X	X	X	f
22h/00h	X	X	X	Alt-G
22h/07h	X	X	X	Ctrl-G
22h/47h	X	X	X	G
22h/67h	X	X	X	g
23h/00h	X	X	X	Alt-H
23h/08h	X	X	X	Ctrl-H
23h/48h	X	X	X	H
23h/68h	X	X	X	h
24h/00h	X	X	X	Alt-J
24h/0Ah	X	X	X	Ctrl-J
24h/4Ah	X	X	X	J

Scan/ASCII Code	Keyboard 83	84	Enh	Keypress
24h/6Ah	X	X	X	j
25h/00h	X	X	X	Alt-K
25h/0Bh	X	X	X	Ctrl-K
25h/4Bh	X	X	X	K
25h/6Bh	X	X	X	k
26h/00h	X	X	X	Alt-L
26h/0Ch	X	X	X	Ctrl-L
26h/4Ch	X	X	X	L
26h/6Ch	X	X	X	l
27h/00h*			X	Alt-;
27h/3Ah	X	X	X	:
27h/3Bh	X	X	X	;
28h/00h*			X	Alt-'
28h/22h	X	X	X	"
28h/27h	X	X	X	'
29h/00h*			X	Alt-'
29h/60h	X	X	X	'
29h/7Eh	X	X	X	~
2Ah	X	X	X	Left Shift
2Bh/00h*			X	Alt-\
2Bh/1Ch	X	X	X	Ctrl-\
2Bh/5Ch	X	X	X	\
2Bh/7Ch	X	X	X	¦
2Ch/00h	X	X	X	Alt-Z
2Ch/1Ah	X	X	X	Ctrl-Z
2Ch/5Ah	X	X	X	Z
2Ch/7Ah	X	X	X	z
2Dh/00h	X	X	X	Alt-X
2Dh/18h	X	X	X	Ctrl-X

continues

Table A.4. Continued

Scan/ASCII Code	Keyboard 83	84	Enh	Keypress
2Dh/58h	X	X	X	X
2Dh/78h	X	X	X	x
2Eh/00h	X	X	X	Alt-C
2Eh/03h	X	X	X	Ctrl-C
2Eh/43h	X	X	X	C
2Eh/63h	X	X	X	c
2Fh/00h	X	X	X	Alt-V
2Fh/16h	X	X	X	Ctrl-V
2Fh/56h	X	X	X	V
2Fh/76h	X	X	X	v
30h/00h	X	X	X	Alt-B
30h/02h	X	X	X	Ctrl-B
30h/42h	X	X	X	B
30h/62h	X	X	X	b
31h/00h	X	X	X	Alt-N
31h/0Eh	X	X	X	Ctrl-N
31h/4Eh	X	X	X	N
31h/6Eh	X	X	X	n
32h/00h	X	X	X	Alt-M
32h/0Dh	X	X	X	Ctrl-M
32h/4Dh	X	X	X	M
32h/6Dh	X	X	X	m
33h/00h*			X	Ctrl-,
33h/2Ch	X	X	X	,
33h/3Ch	X	X	X	<
34h/00h*			X	Ctrl-.
34h/2Eh	X	X	X	.
34h/3Eh	X	X	X	>

Scan/ASCII Code	Keyboard 83	84	Enh	Keypress
35h/00h*			X	Ctrl-/
35h/2Fh	X	X	X	/
35h/3Fh	X	X	X	?
36h	X	X	X	Right Shift
37h/00h*			X	Alt-* (keypad)
37h/2Ah			X	* (keypad)
37h/2Ah	X	X		* (PrtSc)
38h	X	X	X	Alt
39h/20h	X	X	X	Space
3Ah	X	X	X	Caps Lock
3Bh/00h	X	X	X	F1
3Ch/00h	X	X	X	F2
3Dh/00h	X	X	X	F3
3Eh/00h	X	X	X	F4
3Fh/00h	X	X	X	F5
40h/00h	X	X	X	F6
41h/00h	X	X	X	F7
42h/00h	X	X	X	F8
43h/00h	X	X	X	F9
44h/00h	X	X	X	F10
45h	X	X	X	Num Lock
46h	X	X	X	Scroll Lock
47h/00h	X	X	X	Home
47h/37h	X	X	X	7 (keypad)
47h/E0h*			X	Home
48h/00h	X	X	X	Up arrow
48h/38h	X	X	X	8 (keypad)
48h/E0h*			X	Shift-Up arrow
48h/E0h*			X	Up arrow

continues

Table A.4. Continued

Scan/ASCII Code	Keyboard 83	84	Enh	Keypress
49h/00h	X	X	X	Page Up
49h/39h	X	X	X	9 (keypad)
49h/E0h*			X	Page Up
4Ah/00h*			X	Alt-- (keypad)
4Ah/2Dh	X	X	X	- (keypad)
4Bh/00h	X	X	X	Left arrow
4Bh/34h	X	X	X	4 (keypad)
4Bh/E0h*			X	Left arrow
4Ch/00h	X	X	X	5 (keypad)
4Ch/35h	X	X	X	Shift 5 (keypad)
4Dh/00h	X	X	X	Right arrow
4Dh/36h	X	X	X	6 (keypad)
4Dh/E0h*			X	Right arrow
4Eh/00h*			X	Alt-+ (keypad)
4Eh/2Bh	X	X	X	+ (keypad)
4Fh/00h	X	X	X	End
4Fh/31h	X	X	X	1 (keypad)
4Fh/E0h*			X	End
50h/00h	X	X	X	Down arrow
50h/32h	X	X	X	2 (keypad)
50h/E0h*			X	Down arrow
51h/00h	X	X	X	Page Dn
51h/33h	X	X	X	3 (keypad)
51h/E0h*			X	Page Dn
52h/00h	X	X	X	Insert
52h/30h	X	X	X	0 (keypad)
52h/E0h*			X	Insert
53h/00h	X	X	X	Delete

Scan/ASCII Code	Keyboard 83	84	Enh	Keypress
53h/2Eh	X	X	X	. (keypad)
53h/E0h*			X	Delete
54h/00h	X	X	X	Shift-F1
55h/00h	X	X	X	Shift-F2
56h/00h	X	X	X	Shift-F3
57h/00h	X	X	X	Shift-F4
58h/00h	X	X	X	Shift-F5
59h/00h	X	X	X	Shift-F6
5Ah/00h	X	X	X	Shift-F7
5Bh/00h	X	X	X	Shift-F8
5Ch/00h	X	X	X	Shift-F9
5Dh/00h	X	X	X	Shift-F10
5Eh/00h	X	X	X	Ctrl-F1
5Fh/00h	X	X	X	Ctrl-F2
60h/00h	X	X	X	Ctrl-F3
61h/00h	X	X	X	Ctrl-F4
62h/00h	X	X	X	Ctrl-F5
63h/00h	X	X	X	Ctrl-F6
64h/00h	X	X	X	Ctrl-F7
65h/00h	X	X	X	Ctrl-F8
66h/00h	X	X	X	Ctrl-F9
67h/00h	X	X	X	Ctrl-F10
68h/00h	X	X	X	Alt-F1
69h/00h	X	X	X	Alt-F2
6Ah/00h	X	X	X	Alt-F3
6Bh/00h	X	X	X	Alt-F4
6Ch/00h	X	X	X	Alt-F5
6Dh/00h	X	X	X	Alt-F6
6Eh/00h	X	X	X	Alt-F7

continues

Table A.4. Continued

Scan/ASCII Code	Keyboard 83	84	Enh	Keypress
6Fh/00h	X	X	X	Alt-F8
70h/00h	X	X	X	Alt-F9
71h/00h	X	X	X	Alt-F10
73h/00h	X	X	X	Ctrl-Left arrow
73h/E0h*			X	Ctrl-Left arrow
74h/00h	X	X	X	Ctrl-Right arrow
74h/E0h*			X	Ctrl-Right arrow
75h/00h	X	X	X	Ctrl-End
75h/E0h*			X	Ctrl-End
76h/00h	X	X	X	Ctrl-Page Dn
76h/E0h*			X	Ctrl-Page Dn
77h/00h	X	X	X	Ctrl-Home
77h/E0h*			X	Ctrl-Home
78h/00h	X	X	X	Alt-1
79h/00h	X	X	X	Alt-2
7Ah/00h	X	X	X	Alt-3
7Bh/00h	X	X	X	Alt-4
7Ch/00h	X	X	X	Alt-5
7Dh/00h	X	X	X	Alt-6
7Eh/00h	X	X	X	Alt-7
7Fh/00h	X	X	X	Alt-8
80h/00h	X	X	X	Alt-9
81h/00h	X	X	X	Alt-0
82h/00h	X	X	X	Alt--
83h/00h	X	X	X	Alt-=
84h/00h	X	X	X	Ctrl-Page Up
84h/E0h*			X	Ctrl-Page Up
85h/00h*			X	F11

Scan/ASCII Code	Keyboard 83	84	Enh	Keypress
86h/00h*			X	F12
87h/00h*			X	Shift-F11
88h/00h*			X	Shift-F12
89h/00h*			X	Ctrl-F11
8Ah/00h*			X	Ctrl-F12
8Bh/00h*			X	Alt-F11
8Ch/00h*			X	Alt-F12
8Dh/00h*			X	Ctrl-Up arrow (keypad)
8Dh/E0h*			X	Ctrl-Up arrow
8Eh/00h*			X	Ctrl-- (keypad)
8Fh/00h			X	Ctrl-5 (keypad)
90h/00h*			X	Ctrl-+ (keypad)
91h/00h*			X	Ctrl-Down arrow (keypad)
91h/E0h*			X	Ctrl-Down arrow
92h/00h*			X	Ctrl-Ins (keypad)
92h/E0h*			X	Ctrl-Insert
93h/00h*			X	Ctrl-Del (keypad)
93h/E0h*			X	Ctrl-Delete
94h/00h*			X	Ctrl-Tab
95h/00h*			X	Ctrl-/ (keypad)
96h/00h*			X	Ctrl-* (keypad)
97h/00h*			X	Alt-Home
98h/00h*			X	Alt-Up arrow
99h/00h*			X	Alt-Page Up
9Bh/00h*			X	Alt-Left arrow
9Dh/00h*			X	Alt-Right arrow
9Fh/00h*			X	Alt-End
A0h/00h*			X	Alt-Down arrow
A1h/00h*			X	Alt-Page Dn

continues

Table A.4. Continued

Scan/ASCII Code	83	Keyboard 84	Enh	Keypress
A2h/00h*			X	Alt-Insert
A3h/00h*			X	Alt-Delete
A4h/00h*			X	Alt-/ (keypad)
A5h/00h*			X	Alt-Tab
A6h/00h*			X	Alt-Enter (keypad)
E0h/0Ah*			X	CtrlEnter (keypad)
E0h/0Dh*			X	Enter (keypad)
E0h/2Fh*			X	/ (keypad)

* Codes marked with an asterisk are returned only if you are using Int 16/10 or Int 16/11.

The Mouse Functions

There are 50 mouse functions you can use to control the mouse driver or the information translated by the mouse driver. This appendix describes each mouse function and how it is used within the DOS environment. For more information on how to program for the mouse, see Chapter 10, "Programming for the Mouse."

Table B.1 shows the mouse functions in function number order. Table B.2 shows the mouse functions in function category order.

Table B.1. The mouse functions in function number order.		
Function	**Category**	**Purpose**
00h	Mouse and driver	Reset or initialize mouse
01h	Cursor control	Show mouse cursor
02h	Cursor control	Hide mouse cursor
03h	Button control	Get mouse status
04h	Cursor control	Set cursor position
05h	Button control	Get button press info
06h	Button control	Get button release info
07h	Cursor control	Set horizontal boundaries
08h	Cursor control	Set vertical boundaries
09h	Cursor control	Set graphics cursor block

continues

Table B.1. Continued

Function	Category	Purpose
0Ah	Cursor control	Set text cursor
0Bh	Motion control	Read motion counters
0Ch	Mouse and driver	Set interrupt subroutine
0Dh	Mouse and driver	Enable light-pen emulation
0Eh	Mouse and driver	Disable light-pen emulation
0Fh	Motion control	Set mickey-to-pixel ratio
10h	Cursor control	Conditional off
13h	Motion control	Set double-speed threshold
14h	Mouse and driver	Swap interrupt subroutines
15h	Mouse and driver	Get mouse driver state storage needs
16h	Mouse and driver	Save mouse driver state
17h	Mouse and driver	Restore mouse driver state
18h	Mouse and driver	Set alternate subroutine
19h	Mouse and driver	Get alternate interrupt address
1Ah	Motion control	Set mouse sensitivity
1Bh	Motion control	Get mouse sensitivity
1Ch	Mouse and driver	Set interrupt rate
1Dh	Video control	Set CRT page number
1Eh	Video control	Get CRT page number
1Fh	Mouse and driver	Disable mouse driver
20h	Mouse and driver	Enable mouse driver
21h	Mouse and driver	Software reset
22h	Mouse and driver	Set language for messages (international version only)
23h	Mouse and driver	Get language (international version only)
24h	Mouse and driver	Get driver version info
25h	Mouse and driver	Get general driver info
26h	Cursor control	Get maximum virtual coordinates
27h	Cursor control	Get cursor masks and mickey counts

Function	Category	Purpose
28h	Video control	Set video mode
29h	Video control	Get supported video modes
2Ah	Cursor control	Get cursor hot spot
2Bh	Motion control	Set acceleration curves
2Ch	Motion control	Get acceleration curves
2Dh	Motion control	Set or get active acceleration curve
2Fh	Mouse and driver	Mouse hardware reset
30h	Mouse and driver	Set or get `BallPoint` information
31h	Cursor control	Get virtual coordinates
32h	Mouse and driver	Get active advanced functions
33h	Mouse and driver	Get switch settings
34h	Mouse and driver	Get MOUSE.INI

Table B.2. The mouse functions in function category order.

Function	Category

Button Control

03h	Get mouse status
05h	Get button press info
06h	Get button release info

Cursor Control

01h	Show mouse cursor
02h	Hide mouse cursor
04h	Set cursor position
07h	Set horizontal boundaries
08h	Set vertical boundaries
09h	Set graphics cursor block
0Ah	Set text cursor
10h	Conditional off
26h	Get maximum virtual coordinates

continues

Table B.2. Continued

Function	Category
27h	Get cursor masks and mickey counts
2Ah	Get cursor hot spot
31h	Get virtual coordinates

Motion Control

Function	Category
0Bh	Read motion counters
0Fh	Set mickey-to-pixel ratio
13h	Set double-speed threshold
1Ah	Set mouse sensitivity
1Bh	Get mouse sensitivity
2Bh	Set acceleration curves
2Ch	Get acceleration curves
2Dh	Set or get active acceleration curve

Mouse and Driver Control

Function	Category
00h	Reset or initialize mouse
0Ch	Set interrupt subroutine
0Dh	Enable light-pen emulation
0Eh	Disable light-pen emulation
14h	Swap interrupt subroutines
15h	Get mouse driver state storage needs
16h	Save mouse driver state
17h	Restore mouse driver state
18h	Set alternate subroutine
19h	Get alternate interrupt address
1Ch	Set interrupt rate
1Fh	Disable mouse driver
20h	Enable mouse driver
21h	Software reset
22h	Set language for messages (international version only)

Function	Category
23h	Get language (international version only)
24h	Get driver version info
25h	Get general driver info
2Fh	Mouse hardware reset
30h	Set or get BallPoint information
32h	Get active advanced functions
33h	Get switch settings
34h	Get MOUSE.INI
Video Control	
1Dh	Set CRT page number
1Eh	Get CRT page number
28h	Set video mode
29h	Get supported video modes

Function 00h, Reset/Initialize Mouse

Category: Mouse and driver control

Register or Flag	On Entry	On Return
AX	00h	Mouse settings
BX		Number of buttons

Syntax:

```
MOV    AX,0              ;Reset/initialize mouse
INT    33h
CMP    AX,0              ;Is the mouse there?
JE     NotThere          ;Nope, continue
MOV    Buttons,BX        ;Yes, store number of buttons
```

Description: You use this function when you want to initialize the mouse and prepare it for first use. When the mouse is used, it is set to default values as defined in Table B.3.

Table B.3. Default mouse values.

Parameter	Default Value
CRT page number	0
Cursor visibility	Off
Minimum horizontal cursor position	0
Minimum vertical cursor position	0
Current cursor position	Center of screen
Maximum horizontal cursor position	Maximum for display mode
Maximum vertical cursor position	Maximum for display mode
Double-speed threshold	64 mickeys per second
Graphics cursor	Arrow
Text cursor	Reverse block
Horizontal mickey-to-pixel ratio	1 to 1
Vertical mickey-to-pixel ratio	2 to 1
Light-pen emulation	On
Interrupt call mask	0

Function 00h resets both the software and hardware mouse values. To reset only the software values, see function 21h; for a hardware-only reset, see function 2Fh.

Function 01h, Show Mouse Cursor

Category: Cursor control

Register or Flag	On Entry	On Return
AX	01h	

Syntax:

```
MOV    AX,01h          ;Show mouse cursor
INT    33h
```

Description: Sets the value of the internal cursor visibility flag so that the mouse cursor appears on the screen. The cursor used depends on the current video mode and the cursor mask that is defined.

To turn the mouse cursor off, use function 02h.

Function 02h, Hide Mouse Cursor

Category: Cursor control

Register or Flag	On Entry	On Return
AX	02h	

Syntax:

```
MOV    AX,02h          ;Hide mouse cursor
INT    33h
```

Description: The inverse of function 01h, this function sets the value of the internal cursor visibility flag so that the mouse cursor disappears from the screen—the only thing that is changed. The mouse driver continues to track the position of the mouse cursor as though it were visible.

If you are updating information on the screen, make sure that you use this function to turn off the cursor first. When the screen updates are finished, you can use function 01h to turn the cursor back on.

As an alternative to this function, you can use functions 00h or 21h also to turn off the cursor.

Function 03h, Get Mouse Status

Category: Button control

Register or Flag	On Entry	On Return
AX	03h	
BX		Button status
CX		Horizontal cursor position
DX		Vertical cursor position

Syntax:

```
MOV   AX,03h                ;Get mouse status
INT   33h
MOV   Horiz,CX              ;Save horizontal position
MOV   Vert,DX              ;Save vertical position
CMP   BL,00000011b         ;Were both buttons pressed?
JE    BothPressed          ;Yes, go handle
TEST  BL,00000001b         ;Was the left button pressed?
JNZ   LeftPressed          ;Yes, so go handle
TEST  BL,00000010b         ;Was the right button pressed?
JNZ   RightPressed         ;Yes, so go there
JZ    NonePressed          ;No, so none pressed
```

Description: With this function, one of the most-used mouse functions, you can determine both the position of the mouse on the screen and which button (if any) has been pressed.

The value returned in bits 0 and 1 of BX indicate the status of the buttons. Bit 0 corresponds to the left button; bit 1 to the right button. If the bit is set, the button is being depressed. If it is clear, the button is not depressed.

The cursor coordinates returned in CX and DX always are within the valid vertical and horizontal mouse ranges for the current screen mode, or within the limits set with mouse functions 07h and 08h.

Function 04h, Set Cursor Position

Category: Cursor control

Register or Flag	On Entry	On Return
AX	04h	
CX	Horizontal cursor position	
DX	Vertical cursor position	

Syntax:

```
MOV   AX,04h               ;Set cursor position
MOV   CX,Horiz             ;Horizontal position
MOV   DX,Vert              ;Vertical position
INT   33h
```

Description: Assuming that you have enabled the display of the mouse cursor, this function enables you to change the cursor position. The coordinates you specify in CX and DX must be within the valid range for the current display mode, or within the range limits set with mouse functions 07h and 08h.

Function 05, Get Button Press Info

Category: Button control

Register or Flag	On Entry	On Return
AX	05h	Button status
BX	Button desired	Number of presses
CX		Horizontal coordinate at last press
DX		Vertical coordinate at last press

Syntax:

```
MOV     AX,05h          ;Get button information
MOV     BX,0            ;Want left button
INT     33h
MOV     Horiz,CX        ;Save horizontal position
MOV     Vert,DX         ;Save vertical position
TEST    AL,00000001b    ;Is the left button pressed?
JNZ     LeftPressed     ;Yes, so continue
CMP     BX,0            ;Has it been pressed recently?
JNE     LeftPressed     ;Yes, so go handle
```

Description: This function returns two important pieces of information related to the status of the mouse buttons. You call the function with BX containing a value indicating the button you want to check on. If BX contains 0, the returned information is for the left button. If BX contains 1, the information is for the right button.

Similar to function 03h, the value returned in bits 0 and 1 of AX indicates the status of the buttons (function 03h returns this same information in BX). Bit 0 corresponds to the left button; bit 1 to the right button. If the bit is set, the button is being depressed. If it is clear, the button is not depressed.

This function goes beyond this capability, however, in that it returns in the BX register the number of times the button has been pressed since the last time you called this function. Because of this capability, this function is helpful when your program has been delayed doing other work and has not recently checked on the mouse activity.

The cursor coordinates returned in CX and DX reflect the mouse cursor position at the time of the last button click for the specified button. These coordinates always are within the valid vertical and horizontal mouse ranges for the current screen mode, or within the limits set with mouse functions 07h and 08h.

This function can be used in conjunction with function 06h to implement "dragging" operations, in which you have to know where a mouse button was pressed and where it was released.

Function 06h, Get Button Release Info

Category: Button control

Register or Flag	On Entry	On Return
AX	06h	Button status
BX	Button desired	Number of releases
CX		Horizontal coordinate at last release
DX		Vertical coordinate at last release

Syntax:

```
MOV     AX,06h          ;Get button release information
MOV     BX,0            ;Want left button
INT     33h
MOV     Horiz,CX        ;Save horizontal position
MOV     Vert,DX         ;Save vertical position
TEST    AL,00000001b    ;Is the left button currently pressed?
JNZ     LeftPressed     ;Yes, so continue
CMP     BX,0            ;Has it been released recently?
JNE     LeftRelease     ;Yes, so go handle
```

Description: This function is complementary to function 05h. As with function 05h, you call the function with BX containing a value indicating the button you want to check on. If BX contains 0, the returned information is for the left button. If BX contains 1, the information is for the right button.

Similar to function 03h, and the same as function 05h, the value returned in bits 0 and 1 of AX indicate the status of the buttons (function 03h returns this information in BX). Bit 0 corresponds to the left button; bit 1 to the right button. If the bit is set, the button is being depressed. If it is clear, the button is not depressed.

You can check the value returned in BX to see how many times the button has been released since the last call to this function. The cursor coordinates returned in CX and DX reflect the mouse cursor position at the time of the last button release for the specified button. These coordinates always are within the valid vertical and horizontal mouse ranges for the current screen mode, or within the limits set with mouse functions 07h and 08h.

This function is perhaps most helpful used in conjunction with function 05h, because you can determine where the mouse button was pressed and where it was released. With this information you can implement a "click and drag" function in your program.

Function 07h, Set Horizontal Boundaries

Category: Cursor control

Register or Flag	On Entry	On Return
AX	07h	
CX	Minimum horizontal position	
DX	Maximum horizontal position	

Syntax:

```
MOV     AX,07h              ;Limit horizontal motion
MOV     CX,LowerHBound
MOV     DX,UpperHBound
INT     33h
```

Description: You use this function to restrict the horizontal movement of the mouse cursor to a specific area of the screen. You specify in CX and DX the range of valid cursor positions. The value specified in CX should be less than what is specified in DX. If it is not, the mouse driver reverses the values. The lower value therefore always is considered the minimum, and the greater value is the maximum.

Position values should be within the valid range of horizontal values for the current screen mode.

Function 08h, Set Vertical Boundaries

Category: Cursor control

Register or Flag	On Entry	On Return
AX	08h	
CX	Minimum vertical position	
DX	Maximum vertical position	

Syntax:

```
MOV    AX,08h              ;Limit vertical motion
MOV    CX,LowerVBound
MOV    DX,UpperVBound
INT    33h
```

Description: Use this function to restrict the vertical movement of the mouse cursor to a specific area of the screen. You specify in CX and DX the range of valid cursor positions. The value specified in CX should be less than what is specified in DX. If it is not, the mouse driver reverses the values. The lower value therefore always is considered the minimum, and the greater value is the maximum.

Position values should be within the valid range of vertical values for the current screen mode.

Function 09h, Set Graphics Cursor Block

Category: Cursor control

Register or Flag	On Entry	On Return
AX	09h	
BX	Horizontal hot spot	
CX	Vertical hot spot	
DX	Offset address of mask	
ES	Segment address of mask	

Syntax:

```
            .DATA
HorizHS     DW      7
VertHS      DW      7

Mask7       DW      0011111111111000b       ;Start of screen mask
            DW      0001111111110000b
            DW      0000111111100001b
            DW      1000011111000011b
            DW      1100001110000111b
            DW      1110000100001111b
            DW      1111000000011111b
            DW      1111100000111111b
            DW      1111100000111111b
            DW      1111000000011111b
            DW      1110000100001111b
            DW      1100001110000111b
            DW      1000011111000011b
            DW      0000111111100001b
            DW      0001111111110000b
            DW      0011111111111000b

            DW      1000000000000011b       ;Start of cursor mask
            DW      1100000000000110b
            DW      0110000000001100b
            DW      0011000000011000b
            DW      0001100000110000b
            DW      0000110001100000b
            DW      0000011011000000b
            DW      0000001110000000b
            DW      0000001110000000b
            DW      0000011011000000b
            DW      0000110001100000b
            DW      0001100000110000b
            DW      0011000000011000b
            DW      0110000000001100b
            DW      1100000000000110b
            DW      1000000000000011b

            .CODE
            MOV     AX,09h                  ;Set graphics cursor block
            MOV     BX,HorizHS
```

```
MOV     CX,VertHS
PUSH    ES                      ;Store of later
PUSH    DS
POP     ES
MOV     DX,OFFSET Mask
INT     33h
POP     ES                      ;Get segment back
```

Description: You can use this function to redefine the appearance of the graphics mode mouse cursor. BX and CX are loaded with the offset, from the upper left corner of the cursor, of the pixel that will be considered the real pointer for the cursor. The position of this "hot spot" determines the values returned by any function that provide positioning coordinates. An offset of 0,0 is the top left corner of the cursor. The hot spot offsets can be any value –128 through +127; in the example code, the hot spot is defined as the center of the cursor mask.

ES:DX contains the address of the screen and cursor mask definitions. These masks are 16×16 pixel bit maps used by the mouse driver to create the graphics mode mouse cursor. Effectively, the screen mask is first ANDed with the area it overlays on the screen, and then this result is XORed with the value in the cursor mask. The preceding example code depicts a screen and cursor mask that result in an x appearing on the screen.

Function 0Ah, Set Text Cursor

Category: Cursor control

Register or Flag	On Entry	On Return
AX	0Ah	
BX	Cursor wanted	
CX	Screen mask or beginning scan line	
DX	Cursor mask or ending scan line	

Syntax:

```
MOV     AX,0Ah          ;Set text cursor block
MOV     BX,1            ;Want hardware cursor
MOV     CX,BegSL        ;Starting scan line
MOV     DX,EndSL        ;Ending scan line
INT     33h
```

Description: This function is used to define the appearance of the hardware or software text cursor. You specify which cursor you want by the value in BX. If BX is 0, the software cursor is used; if it is 1, the hardware cursor is selected.

If you are selecting the hardware cursor, the values in CX and DX indicate the beginning and ending scan lines for the cursor. If you are selecting the software cursor, these registers contain the screen and cursor masks. The screen mask is a 16-bit value that is ANDed with the 16 bits that make up the displayed character (remember that one byte is the ASCII character, and the other is the display attribute). Then the result is XORed with the 16-bit cursor mask, resulting in the cursor that is displayed.

Function 0Bh, Read Motion Counters

Category: Motion control

Register or Flag	On Entry	On Return
AX	0Bh	
CX		Horizontal change
DX		Vertical change

Syntax:

```
MOV     AX,0Bh          ;Get mouse position change
INT     33h
MOV     CX,HorizChange
MOV     DX,VertChange
```

Description: This function returns the relative change of the mouse position since the last time you called this function. The values returned in CX and DX are mickeys. The physical distance traveled by the mouse is translated by the mouse driver into a unit of measure called a mickey. The distance represented by one mickey depends on the resolution of the mouse.

Use of this function relieves you of having to perform math on "before" and "after" mouse coordinates to determine where the mouse has moved.

Function 0Ch, Set Interrupt Subroutine

Category: Mouse and driver control

Register or Flag	On Entry	On Return
AX	0Ch	
CX	Interrupt mask	
DX	Subroutine offset address	
ES	Subroutine segment address	

Syntax:

```
MOV     AX,0Ch              ;Set interrupt subroutine
MOV     CX,06h              ;Interrupt when left button changes
PUSH    ES                  ;Save segment register
PUSH    CS
POP     ES
MOV     DX,OFFSET CS:LHandle ;Point to handler
INT     33h
POP     ES                  ;Get back segment register
```

Description: The mouse driver is interrupt driven. Every time an action involving the mouse occurs, an interrupt occurs that is handled by the driver. Use of this function enables you to "tack on" your own routine after certain mouse actions, which effectively enables you to handle mouse events in an interrupt-driven manner.

You specify, in CX, the mouse actions on which you want your subroutine called. ES:DX contains the address of the far routine to be invoked when the action occurs. Table B.4 indicates the settings used in CX for the interrupt mask.

Table B.4. The interrupt mask bit settings for function 0Ch.

Bit settings FEDCBA98 76543210	Action Resulting in an Interrupt
`               1`	Change in cursor position
`              1 `	Left button is pressed
`             1  `	Left button is released
`            1   `	Right button is pressed
`           1    `	Right button is released
`xxxxxxxx xxx    `	Unused (ignored)

To enable an interrupt on a certain action, set the appropriate mask bit. To disable the interrupt on that action, clear the bit. If this function does not provide enough event-trapping conditions for your needs, see the descriptions for functions 18h and 19h.

When your interrupt routine is invoked, the mouse driver loads the registers as shown in Table B.5, and then transfers control to your routine.

Table B.5. Register settings after invocation of a mouse action interrupt subroutine.

Register	Contents
AX	Action indicator
BX	Button state
CX	Horizontal cursor position
DX	Vertical cursor position
SI	Horizontal change
DI	Vertical change

The action indicator (AX) uses the same bit settings as the interrupt mask does (refer to Table B.4). If a bit is set, that indicates what caused your routine to be called.

Bits 0 and 1 of the BX register indicate the button status. Bit 0 corresponds to the left button; bit 1 to the right button. If the bit is set, the button is being depressed. If it is clear, the button is not depressed.

The cursor coordinates in CX and DX always are within the valid vertical and horizontal mouse ranges for the current screen mode, or within the limits set with mouse functions 07h and 08h.

The values in SI and DI indicate the relative change of the mouse position since the last interrupt, in mickeys. The physical distance traveled by the mouse is translated by the mouse driver into a unit of measure called a mickey. The distance represented by one mickey depends on the resolution of the mouse.

You can call other mouse functions from within your routine. You do not have to maintain the register values before you return from your handler. For more information on writing interrupt handlers, refer to the first several chapters of this book, particularly Chapters 1, 3, 4, and 5.

It is important to remember to clear all interrupt mask bits before your program ends. If you do not, your computer may hang, because the mouse driver will attempt to jump to an interrupt handler that may no longer be in memory. You can use function 00h to easily reset the mouse interrupt mask, as well as most other mouse parameters.

Function 0Dh, Enable Light-Pen Emulation

Category: Mouse and driver control

Register or Flag	On Entry	On Return
AX	0Dh	

Syntax:

```
MOV    AX,0Dh              ;Enable light pen emulation
INT    33h
```

Description: This function causes the mouse to behave as though it were a light pen. Because this condition is the default for the system, this function has to be called only if you have turned off light-pen emulation (function 0Eh) and want to turn it back on.

After using this function, system calls to the light-pen functions are intercepted and responded to by the mouse driver. When you press both buttons, the pen is considered down. Releasing at least one button is analogous to lifting the pen.

Function 0Eh, Disable Light-Pen Emulation

Category: Mouse and driver control

Register or Flag	On Entry	On Return
AX	0Eh	

Syntax:

```
MOV    AX,0Eh              ;Disable light-pen emulation
INT    33h
```

Description: This function is the opposite of function 0Dh. This function disables the light-pen emulation functions of the mouse driver. See function 0Dh for more information.

Function 0Fh, Set Mickey-to-Pixel Ratio

Category: Motion control

Register or Flag	On Entry	On Return
AX	0Fh	
CX	Horizontal ratio	
DX	Vertical ratio	

Syntax:

```
MOV     AX,0Fh              ;Set mickey-to-pixel ratio
MOV     CX,HorizMPR
MOV     DX,VertMPR
INT     33h
```

Description: Using this function, you can change the speed of the mouse on the screen. You do this by changing how the mouse driver translates the movement of the mouse.

The physical distance traveled by the mouse is translated by the mouse driver into a unit of measure called a mickey. The distance represented by one mickey depends on the resolution of the mouse. This function enables you to indicate how many mickeys the mouse must move in order to move the screen cursor 8 pixels in either the horizontal or vertical direction. The default is a 1-to-1 ratio. Therefore, if you want to have to move the mouse twice as far to move the cursor on-screen, you should set the ratio to 16. (The ratio is then 16-to-8 rather than the regular 8-to-8.)

You can also use function 1Ah to set the mouse sensitivity.

Function 10h, Conditional Off

Category: Cursor control

Register or Flag	On Entry	On Return
AX	10h	
CX	Left coordinate	
DX	Top coordinate	
SI	Right coordinate	
DI	Bottom coordinate	

Syntax:

```
MOV     AX,10h              ;Conditional off
MOV     CX,10               ;Left
MOV     DX,10               ;Top
MOV     SI,20               ;Right
MOV     DI,20               ;Bottom
INT     33h
```

Description: Whenever you update information on the screen or read information from the screen, you must turn off the mouse cursor for the action to be reliable. Although you can use function 02h to turn off the cursor completely, this function provides a localized alternative.

Function 10h enables you to specify a rectangular area of the screen. If the mouse cursor moves into that area (or is in there already), it is hidden. Otherwise, the mouse cursor is visible. In the preceding example, the rectangular area is defined as 10,10 to 20,20.

Function 13h, Set Double-Speed Threshold

Category: Motion control

Register or Flag	On Entry	On Return
AX	13h	
DX	Threshold value	

Syntax:

```
MOV     AX,13h              ;Set double-speed threshold
MOV     DX,25               ;Mickeys per second
INT     33h
```

Description: The mouse driver has the capability of doubling the speed at which the mouse cursor moves, if the mouse is moved physically at a rate faster than a certain threshold. This function enables you to set that threshold. Such a capability is useful if your program requires the user to move the mouse often across the entire screen.

By default, the double-speed threshold is 64 mickeys per second. You can specify any value you want, however. If you assign a threshold value of 0, or if you use function 00h or 21h, the threshold reverts to the default value.

You can also use function 1Ah to adjust mouse sensitivity.

Function 14h, Swap Interrupt Subroutines

Category: Mouse and driver control

Register or Flag	On Entry	On Return
AX	14h	
CX	Interrupt mask	Old interrupt mask
DX	Subroutine offset address	Old offset address
ES	Subroutine segment address	Old segment address

Syntax:

```
MOV     AX,14h              ;Swap interrupt subroutine
MOV     CX,06h              ;Interrupt when left button changes
PUSH    ES                  ;Save segment register
PUSH    CS
POP     ES
MOV     DX,OFFSET CS:LHandle ;Point to handler
INT     33h
MOV     AX,ES               ;Save old address
MOV     OldSeg,AX
MOV     OldOff,DX
MOV     OldMask,CX
POP     ES                  ;Get back segment register
```

Description: The mouse driver is interrupt driven. Every time an action involving the mouse occurs, an interrupt occurs that is handled by the driver. Use of this function enables you to "tack on" your own routine after certain mouse actions, replacing an address and mask that were already there (see function 0Ch).

To use this function, you specify in CX the mouse actions on which you want your subroutine called. ES:DX contains the address of the far routine to be invoked when the action occurs. The description for function 0Ch includes detailed information on register settings and a couple of Tables that are applicable to this function also. If this function does not provide enough event-trapping conditions for your needs, see the descriptions for functions 18h and 19h.

Upon return, the address of the old interrupt subroutine and the preceding interrupt mask are in the ES:DX and CX registers and can be stored for future use.

You should remember to clear all interrupt mask bits before your program ends. If you do not, your computer may hang, because the mouse driver will attempt to jump to an interrupt handler that may no longer be in memory. You can use function 00h to easily reset the mouse interrupt mask and most other mouse parameters.

Function 15h, Get Mouse Driver State Storage Needs

Category: Mouse and driver control

Register or Flag	On Entry	On Return
AX	15h	
BX		Buffer size needed

Syntax:

```
MOV     AX,15h          ;Get storage needs
INT     33h
MOV     CX,4
SHR     BX,CL           ;Divide by 16 (need paragraphs)
MOV     AH,48h          ;Allocate memory
INT     21h
MOV     ES,AX           ;Point to memory block
MOV     MSBuff,AX       ;And store for later use
MOV     DX,0            :Offset is 0
MOV     AX,16h          ;Store mouse driver state
INT     33h
```

Description: This function, used in conjunction with functions 16h and 17h, enables you to save the condition of the mouse driver and restore it. In particular, this function returns the number of storage bytes necessary to save the mouse state.

You should use these three functions when you are executing a child program that also may use the mouse.

Function 16h, Save Mouse Driver State

Category: Mouse and driver control

Register or Flag	On Entry	On Return
AX	16h	
DX	Buffer offset	
ES	Buffer segment	

Syntax:

```
MOV     AX,15h              ;Get storage needs
INT     33h
MOV     CX,4
SHR     BX,CL               ;Divide by 16 (need paragraphs)
MOV     AH,48h              ;Allocate memory
INT     21h
MOV     ES,AX               ;Point to memory block
MOV     MSBuff,AX           ;And store for later use
MOV     DX,0                :Offset is 0
MOV     AX,16h              ;Store mouse driver state
INT     33h
```

Description: This function, used in conjunction with functions 15h and 17h, enables you to save the condition of the mouse driver and restore it. In particular, this function transfers the mouse condition to the buffer pointed to by ES:DX.

You should use these three functions when you are executing a child program that also may use the mouse.

Function 17h, Restore Mouse Driver State

Category: Mouse and driver control

Register or Flag	On Entry	On Return
AX	17h	
DX	Buffer offset	
ES	Buffer segment	

Syntax:

```
PUSH    ES
MOV     AX,MSBuff               ;Get stored offset
MOV     ES,AX                   ;Put in proper segment
MOV     DX,0                    :Offset is 0
MOV     AX,17h                  ;Restore mouse driver state
INT     33h
POP     ES
```

Description: This function, used in conjunction with functions 15h and 16h, enables you to save the condition of the mouse driver and restore it. In particular, this function transfers the mouse condition from the buffer pointed to by ES:DX to the internal mouse variables.

You should use these three functions when you are executing a child program that also may use the mouse.

Function 18h, Set Alternate Subroutine

Category: Mouse and driver control

Register or Flag	On Entry	On Return
AX	18h	
CX	Interrupt mask	
DX	Subroutine offset address	
ES	Subroutine segment address	
Carry	Clear	Set

Syntax:

```
MOV     AX,18h                  ;Set alternate interrupt subroutine
MOV     CX,20h                  ;Interrupt when Shift key pressed with button
PUSH    ES                      ;Save segment register
PUSH    CS
POP     ES
MOV     DX,OFFSET CS:ShiftPress ;Point to handler
INT     33h
POP     ES                      ;Get back segment register
```

Description: The mouse driver is interrupt driven. Every time an action involving the mouse occurs, an interrupt occurs that is handled by the driver. Use of this function enables you to "tack on" your own routine after certain mouse actions, which effectively enables you to handle mouse events in an interrupt-driven manner. This function's name refers to alternate subroutine addresses because functions 0Ch and 14h are used to set the primary interrupt subroutines.

You specify, in CX, the mouse actions on which you want your subroutine called. ES:DX contains the address of the far routine to be invoked when the action occurs. Table B.6 indicates the settings used in CX for the interrupt mask.

Table B.6. The interrupt mask bit settings for function 18h.

Bit settings FEDCBA98 76543210	Action Resulting in an Interrupt
1	Change in cursor position
1	Left button is pressed
1	Left button is released
1	Right button is pressed
1	Right button is released
1	Shift key depressed while button is pressed
1	Ctrl key depressed while button is pressed
1	Alt key depressed while button is pressed
xxxxxxx	Unused (ignored)

To enable an interrupt on a certain action, set the appropriate mask bit. To disable the interrupt on that action, clear the bit.

When your interrupt routine is invoked, the mouse driver loads the registers as shown in Table B.7 and then transfers control to your routine.

Table B.7. Register settings after invocation of a mouse action interrupt subroutine.

Register	Contents
AX	Action indicator
BX	Button state
CX	Horizontal cursor position

continues

Table B.7. Continued

Register	Contents
DX	Vertical cursor position
SI	Horizontal change
DI	Vertical change

The action indicator returned in AX uses the bit settings shown in Table B.8. If a bit is set, that indicates what caused your routine to be called.

Table B.8. The action indicator bit settings in the AX register.

Bit settings FEDCBA98 76543210	Action Causing the Interrupt
1	Cursor position changed
1	Left button was pressed
1	Left button was released
1	Right button was pressed
1	Right button was released
xxxxxxxx xxx	Unused (ignored)

Bits 0 and 1 of the BX register indicate the button status. Bit 0 corresponds to the left button; bit 1 to the right button. If the bit is set, the button is being depressed. If it is clear, the button is not depressed.

The cursor coordinates in CX and DX always are within the valid vertical and horizontal mouse ranges for the current screen mode, or within the limits set with mouse functions 07h and 08h.

The values in SI and DI indicate the relative change of the mouse position since the last interrupt, in mickeys. Mickeys are the resolution units for the mouse.

You can call other mouse functions from within your routine. You do not have to maintain the register values before you return from your handler. For more information on writing interrupt handlers, refer to the first several chapters of this book, particularly Chapters 1, 3, 4, and 5.

It is important to remember to clear all interrupt mask bits before your program ends. If you do not, your computer may hang, because the mouse driver will attempt to jump to an interrupt handler that may no longer be in memory. To clear the alternate call masks, you must use this function with CX set to 0.

Function 19h, Get Alternate Interrupt Address

Category: Mouse and driver control

Register or Flag	On Entry	On Return If Successful	If Unsuccessful
AX	19h	< > –1	–1
BX		Segment address	0
CX	Interrupt mask	Interrupt mask	0
DX		Offset address	0
ES		Old segment address	0

Syntax:

```
MOV    AX,19h          ;Get interrupt subroutine address
MOV    CX,06h          ;Interrupt mask
INT    33h
CMP    AX,-1           ;Value returned?
JE     NoSave          ;No, so don't save
MOV    OldSeg,BX
MOV    OldOff,DX
MOV    OldMask,CX
```

Description: The mouse driver is interrupt driven. Every time an action involving the mouse occurs, an interrupt occurs that is handled by the driver. Use of this function enables you to recover an interrupt subroutine address that you set previously with function 0Ch or function 18h.

To use this function, you specify an interrupt mask in CX, as detailed in Table B.6. Depending on the mask you use, this function returns the address of the interrupt subroutine last assigned to the interrupt mask. Upon return, the value in AX is –1 if there was no subroutine address to return. If AX does not contain –1, BX:DX contains the address of the interrupt subroutine, and CX contains the interrupt mask for the subroutine.

Function 1Ah, Set Mouse Sensitivity

Category: Motion control

Register or Flag	On Entry	On Return
AX	1Ah	
BX	Horizontal sensitivity	
CX	Vertical sensitivity	
DX	Double-speed threshold	

Syntax:

```
MOV    AX,1Ah        ;Set mouse sensitivity
MOV    BX,20         ;Horizontal sensitivity
MOV    CX,20         ;Vertical sensitivity
MOV    DX,50         ;Double-speed threshold
INT    33h
```

Description: The physical distance traveled by the mouse is translated, by the mouse driver, into a unit of measure called a mickey. The distance represented by one mickey depends on the resolution of the mouse. This function enables you to accomplish two tasks that affect how the mouse driver interprets the mickey count received from the mouse.

To use the function, you load BX and CX with values used by the mouse driver to scale the mickey count it receives. The values can be between 1 and 100, and represent ratios between about 33 percent and 350 percent. This ratio is applied to the mickey count returned by the physical mouse, before the ratio set by function 0Fh is applied. The default ratio value is 50.

The second part of this function enables you to set the double-speed threshold. The mouse driver has the capability of doubling the speed at which the mouse cursor moves, if the mouse is moved physically at a rate faster than a certain threshold. Similar to function 13h, this function enables you to set that threshold; unlike function 13h, however, this function uses a ratio rather than an absolute mickey count. As with the horizontal and vertical scaling, the double-speed threshold ratio varies between 1 and 100, with a default of 50.

To determine the current sensitivity, use function 1Bh.

Function 1Bh, Get Mouse Sensitivity

Category: Motion control

Register or Flag	On Entry	On Return
AX	1Bh	
BX		Horizontal sensitivity
CX		Vertical sensitivity
DX		Double-speed threshold

Syntax:

```
MOV     AX,1Bh          ;Get mouse sensitivity
INT     33h
MOV     Horiz,BX        ;And store the parameters
MOV     Vert,CX         ;    for later reset
MOV     DSThresh,DX
```

Description: This function, the opposite of function 1Ah, enables you to get the sensitivity ratios the mouse driver is using. You should use this function so that you can save the current settings and restore them when your program is complete.

For more information about the sensitivity ratios, see the description of function 1Ah.

Function 1Ch, Set Interrupt Rate

Category: Mouse and driver control

Register or Flag	On Entry	On Return
AX	1Ch	
BX	Interrupts per second	

Syntax:

```
MOV     AX,1Ch          ;Set interrupt rate
MOV     BX,2            ;50 interrupts per second
INT     33h
```

Description: This function, which applies to only the InPort mouse, enables you to set the number of interrupts per second that the mouse driver should execute. This number affects how often the driver checks to see whether an action or event has occurred with the mouse.

You use the function by specifying a value in BX that indicates the maximum number of interrupts wanted per second. The default value is 30 maximum interrupts per second. Table B.9 indicates possible rate settings for this function.

Table B.9. Function 1Ch interrupt value settings.

Value	Meaning
0	Turn off interrupts
1	30 interrupts per second
2	50 interrupts per second
3	100 interrupts per second
4	200 interrupts per second

If you use any other value than those shown in Table B.9, the results are unpredictable.

Function 1Dh, Set CRT Page Number

Category: Video control

Register or Flag	On Entry	On Return
AX	1Dh	
BX	CRT page	

Syntax:

```
MOV     AX,1Dh              ;Set CRT page
MOV     BX,0                ;Use page 0
INT     33h
```

Description: If you have been programming on the PC for any length of time, you probably already know about video pages. Different video cards support different numbers of video pages, depending on the mode in which they are operating. This function enables you to specify on which video page the mouse driver should display the cursor.

This function does not change the video page used by other system functions such as BIOS and DOS—only the video page used by the mouse driver.

Function 1Eh, Get CRT Page Number

Category: Video control

Register or Flag	On Entry	On Return
AX	1Eh	
BX		CRT page

Syntax:

```
MOV     AX,1Eh              ;Get CRT page
INT     33h
MOV     OldPage,BX          ;Save page number for later
```

Description: This function, the opposite of function 1Dh, enables you to determine on which video page the mouse driver is displaying the cursor. You should use this function to store the current video page if you will be using function 1Dh to modify the CRT page during your program. You then can restore the original CRT page before exiting from your program.

Function 1Fh, Disable Mouse Driver

Category: Mouse and driver control

Register or Flag	On Entry	On Return If Successful	If Unsuccessful
AX	1Fh	< > −1	−1
BX		Offset address	
ES		Segment address	

Syntax:

```
MOV     AX,1Fh              ;Disable mouse
INT     33h
CMP     AX,-1               ;Did an error occur?
```

```
JE      Error               ;Yes, go handle
MOV     AX,ES
MOV     I33VectSeg,AX        ;Store current address
MOV     I33VectOff,BX
```

Description: This function enables you to effectively turn off the mouse driver. This way of accomplishing the task is preferred because directly changing the vector addresses yourself or accessing the interrupt vector table can cause problems. The mouse driver intercepts several interrupt vectors, and this function enables you to instruct the mouse driver to disconnect itself. In this way you can be sure that all appropriate vectors are restored properly to their "unmoused" condition.

This function does not free any memory occupied by the mouse driver—it simply turns it off. Subsequently, you can use function 20h to enable the mouse driver again.

On return from this function, AX is set to –1 if the mouse driver cannot fully disable itself. In this case, the driver is left enabled.

Function 20h, Enable Mouse Driver

Category: Mouse and driver control

Register or Flag	On Entry	On Return
AX	20h	

Syntax:

```
MOV     AX,20h              ;Enable mouse
INT     33h
```

Description: This function, the opposite of function 1Fh, enables the mouse driver by rehooking all the interrupt vectors necessary for successful use of the mouse.

Function 21h, Software Reset

Category: Mouse and driver control

Register or Flag	On Entry	On Return If Successful	If Unsuccessful
AX	21h	0FFFFh	21h
BX		02h	

Syntax:

```
MOV     AX,21h          ;Software reset
INT     33h
CMP     AX,-1           ;Error?
JNE     Error           ;Yes, driver not installed
```

Description: This function operates in a manner similar to function 00h, except that only the software variables maintained by the mouse driver are reset. On return from the function, AX is set to −1 if the function was successful; otherwise it is unchanged. Table B.10 indicates the default software values set by this function.

Table B.10. Default mouse software values.

Parameter	Default Value
Cursor visibility	Off
Minimum horizontal cursor position	0
Minimum vertical cursor position	0
Current cursor position	Center of screen
Maximum horizontal cursor position	Maximum for display mode
Maximum vertical cursor position	Maximum for display mode
Double-speed threshold	64 mickeys per second
Graphics cursor	Arrow
Text cursor	Reverse block
Horizontal mickey/pixel ratio	1 to 1
Vertical mickey/pixel ration	2 to 1
Interrupt call mask	0

To reset only hardware values, see function 2Fh. To reset both software and hardware values, see function 00h.

Function 22h, Set Language for Messages

Category: Mouse and driver control

Register or Flag	On Entry	On Return
AX	22h	
BX	Language number	

Syntax:

```
MOV    AX,22h        ;Set language
MOV    BX,3          ;Want German
INT    33h
```

Description: This function works with only the international version of the mouse driver. It enables you to set the language the mouse driver will use to display messages. If you attempt to use this function on the domestic version of the mouse driver, it has no effect. Table B.11 indicates the valid language numbers.

Table B.11. Language numbers for functions 22h and 23h.

Number	Language
0	English
1	French
2	Dutch
3	German
4	Swedish
5	Finnish
6	Spanish
7	Portuguese
8	Italian

Function 23h, Get Language

Category: Mouse and driver control

Register or Flag	On Entry	On Return
AX	23h	
BX		Language number

Syntax:

```
MOV     AX,23h              ;Get language
INT     33h
MOV     Lang,BX
```

Description: The opposite of function 22h, this function enables you to determine which language the mouse driver is using to display messages. This function is available for use with only the international version of the mouse driver. The value returned in BX is one of the values shown in Table B.11. If you have the domestic version of the mouse driver, a 0 always is returned as the language number in BX.

Function 24h, Get Driver Version Info

Category: Mouse and driver control

Register or Flag	On Entry	On Return
AX	24h	
BH		Major version number
BL		Minor version number
CH		Mouse type
CL		IRQ number

Syntax:

```
MOV     AX,24h              ;Get driver info
INT     33h
MOV     Major,BH            ;Store version number
MOV     Minor,BL
MOV     MouseType,CH        ;Store mouse info
MOV     IRQNum,CL
```

Description: Using this function, you can determine basic information about the mouse environment in which your program is operating. Additional information is returned in function 25h.

The values returned in BH and BL are the major and minor version numbers for the mouse driver. The major version number is the number to the left of the decimal point, and the minor is to the right. The value returned in CH is the type of mouse being used (see Table B.12).

Table B.12. Mouse hardware types returned by function 24h.

Value	Mouse Type
1	Bus
2	Serial
3	InPort
4	PS/2
5	Hewlett-Packard

The IRQ number returned in CL indicates the interrupt request line used by the mouse.

Function 25h, Get General Driver Info

Category: Mouse and driver control

Register or Flag	On Entry	On Return
AX	25h	Driver information

Syntax:

```
MOV     AX,25h              ;Get driver info
INT     33h
MOV     InfoWord,AX         ;Store info for later
```

Description: This function can be used in conjunction with function 24h to provide a fuller picture of the mouse environment you are operating within.

Different bits of the value returned in AX have different meanings. Table B.13 indicates the specific bit meanings.

Table B.13. Bit meanings returned in AX by function 25h.

Bit settings FEDCBA98 76543210	Meaning
xxxxxxx	Currently active MDD count (used only if bit 14 is 1)
xxxx	Mouse driver interrupt rate
00	Software text cursor active

Bit settings FEDCBA98 76543210	Meaning
01	Hardware text cursor active
10	Graphics cursor active
11	Graphics cursor active
1	Integrated mouse display driver (MDD)
0	Non-integrated mouse driver
1	Driver was loaded as a SYS file
0	Driver was loaded as a COM file

Function 26h, Get Maximum Virtual Coordinates

Category: Cursor control

Register or Flag	On Entry	On Return
AX	26h	
BX		Mouse driver status
CX		Maximum horizontal coordinate
DX		Maximum vertical coordinate

Syntax:

```
MOV    AX,26h          ;Get maximum coordinates
INT    33h
CMP    BX,0            ;Is mouse driver disabled?
JNE    Disabled        ;Yes, so continue
MOV    MaxX,CX
MOV    MaxY,DX
```

Description: You can use this function to determine two pieces of information. First, the value returned in BX indicates whether the mouse driver has been disabled. If the value is 0, the driver is enabled; nonzero indicates that it has been disabled with function 1Fh.

The values returned in CX and DX indicate the maximum horizontal and vertical mouse coordinates, based on the current display mode. The minimum coordinates are assumed to be 0,0.

Function 27h, Get Cursor Masks And Mickey Counts

Category: Cursor control

Register or Flag	On Entry	On Return
AX	27h	Screen mask or beginning scan line
BX		Cursor mask or ending scan line
CX		Horizontal mickey count
DX		Vertical mickey count

Syntax:

```
MOV     AX,27h              ;Get masks and mickeys
INT     33h
MOV     SMask,AX            ;Store values for later
MOV     CMask,BX
MOV     HMickey,CX
MOV     VMickey,DX
```

Description: If you are operating the mouse in graphics mode, this function has only limited value. It returns the text cursor and screen masks, or the beginning and ending scan lines, depending on which type of cursor you are using.

If you are using the hardware text cursor, the values in AX and BX indicate the beginning and ending scan lines for the cursor. If you are using the software text cursor, these registers contain the screen and cursor masks currently in use. These scan lines or masks can be set with function 0Ah.

In addition to the cursor information, the values in CX and DX indicate the number of mickeys accumulated since the last time a function was used to access the mickey count.

Function 28h, Set Video Mode

Category: Video control

Register or Flag	On Entry	On Return If Successful	If Unsuccessful
AX	28h		
CX	Video mode	0	Unchanged
DX	Font size		

Syntax:

```
MOV     AX,28h          ;Set video mode
MOV     CX,UseMode      ;Video mode wanted
MOV     DH,HorFont      ;Horizontal font size
MOV     DL,VerFont      ;Vertical font size
INT     33h
CMP     CX,0            ;Was the mode valid?
JNE     Error           ;No, so handle error
```

Description: This function enables you to specify which video mode the mouse driver should use. The video mode you specify in CX should be one supported by your video card, because the actual video mode of your video card is changed by this function. Before using this function, you can use function 29h to determine which video modes are valid on your computer and for your mouse driver.

If your video card supports font definitions, you can specify a font size in DX. The value returned in CX is 0 if the mode switch worked; otherwise, CX is unchanged.

Function 29h, Get Supported Video Modes

Category: Video control

Register or Flag	On Entry	On Return If Successful	If Unsuccessful
AX	29h		
BX		Description segment	
CX	Search flag	Mode number	0
DX		Description offset	

Syntax:

```
          MOV     CX,0          ;Start enumerating video modes
EnumLoop: MOV     AX,29h        ;Enumerate video modes
          INT     33h
          JCXZ    AllDone       ;Quit when no more modes
          PUSH    CX            ;Save video mode
          CMP     DX,0          ;Is offset 0?
          JNE     M3            ;No, continue
          CMP     BX,0          ;Is segment 0?
```

```
            JE      NoDesc              ;Yes, so no description there
M3:         PUSH    DS
            MOV     DS,BX
            MOV     AH,9                ;Display a string using DOS
            INT     21h
            POP     DS
NoDesc:     POP     CX                  ;Get video mode back
            JMP     EnumLoop
```

Description: The mouse driver supports various video modes on many different video cards. This function lets you determine which modes are supported by the mouse driver for your video card. It searches the internal list of supported video modes maintained by the driver.

To use this function, load CX with a flag indicating which type of search you want to do. If CX is 0, the first video mode is returned from the list. If CX is nonzero, the next mode is returned.

The address returned in BX:DX indicates the ASCIIZ description of the video mode from the internal list. This description is optional; if BX and DX are 0, no ASCIIZ description string is available.

Function 2Ah, Get Cursor Hot Spot

Category: Cursor control

Register or Flag	On Entry	On Return
AX	2Ah	Display flag
BX		Horizontal hot spot
CX		Vertical hot spot
DX		Mouse type

Syntax:

```
MOV     AX,2Ah              ;Get hot spot
INT     33h
MOV     HHotSpot,BX
MOV     VHotSpot,CX
```

Description: This function enables you primarily to retrieve information you set originally with function 09h. The value returned in BX and CX represents the pixel offset from the upper left corner of the graphics cursor mask that is considered the "hot spot" for the cursor. When you click the mouse button, the cursor is considered positioned wherever the hot spot is located. The position of this hot spot also is returned when you use a function that indicates where the mouse cursor is located.

If you are not using the mouse in one of the graphics modes, this function is of limited value. You can, however, use this function also to return, in AX, the display flag. This internal flag indicates whether the mouse cursor is currently displayed. If the value in AX is 0, the cursor is turned on; if it is nonzero, the cursor is off.

The value returned in DX is the same as the value returned in the CH register by function 24h. This value indicates the type of mouse installed on the system. Refer to Table B.12 for possible settings for this register.

Function 2Bh, Set Acceleration Curves

Category: Motion control

Register or Flag	On Entry	On Return If Successful	On Return If Unsuccessful
AX	2Bh	0	< > 0
BX	Curve number		
SI	Buffer offset		
ES	Buffer segment		

Syntax:

```
        .DATA
ATable1 DB      13              ;Acceleration curve 1
        DB      00              ;Not using this curve
        DB      00              ;Or this curve
        DB      00              ;Or this one

        DB      1,6,11,16,21,26,31,36,41,51,61,71,91
        DB      19 DUP(0)       ;Filler

        DB      32 DUP(0)       ;Filler
        DB      32 DUP(0)       ;Filler
        DB      32 DUP(0)       ;Filler
```

```
        DB      8,16,19,22,25,28,31,34,37,40,43,46,48
        DB      19 DUP(0)           ;Filler

        DB      32 DUP(0)           ;Filler
        DB      32 DUP(0)           ;Filler
        DB      32 DUP(0)           ;Filler

        DB      'TESTING CURVE    '
        DB      16 DUP(' ')
        DB      16 DUP(' ')
        DB      16 DUP(' ')

        .CODE
        MOV     AX,2Bh              ;Set acceleration curve table
        MOV     BX,1                ;Use curve #1
        PUSH    ES                  ;Store for later
        PUSH    DS
        POP     ES
        MOV     SI,OFFSET ATable1
        INT     33h
        POP     ES                  ;Get segment back
```

Description: Use this function to define acceleration curves used by the mouse driver. Acceleration curves control how the raw mouse-movement data (accumulated in mickeys) should be translated into actual cursor movement. The use of acceleration tables enables you to exercise a greater degree of control over how the mouse moves than would be possible otherwise with regular sensitivity settings (see functions 0Fh, 13h, 1Ah, and 1Bh).

The value in ES:SI is the address of a 324-byte buffer containing the acceleration table. The value in BX indicates which curve to use after the acceleration table is loaded. Four possible curves are defined by the table (1 through 4), or you can set BX to –1 to leave the curve selector unchanged.

The acceleration table pointed to by ES:SI is shown in Table B.14.

Table B.14. Acceleration curve table layout.

Offset	Length	Meaning
00h	1 byte	Curve 1 counts and factors
01h	1 byte	Curve 2 counts and factors
02h	1 byte	Curve 3 counts and factors
03h	1 byte	Curve 4 counts and factors

Offset	Length	Meaning
04h	20h bytes	Curve 1 mouse-count threshold array
24h	20h bytes	Curve 2 mouse-count threshold array
44h	20h bytes	Curve 3 mouse-count threshold array
64h	20h bytes	Curve 4 mouse-count threshold array
84h	20h bytes	Curve 1 scale factor array
A4h	20h bytes	Curve 2 scale factor array
C4h	20h bytes	Curve 3 scale factor array
E4h	20h bytes	Curve 4 scale factor array
104h	10h bytes	Curve 1 name (right-padded ASCII)
114h	10h bytes	Curve 2 name (right-padded ASCII)
124h	10h bytes	Curve 3 name (right-padded ASCII)
134h	10h bytes	Curve 4 name (right-padded ASCII)

To explain how the acceleration curve table is used by the mouse driver, assume that you specify that curve 2 should be used. You already know that the mouse driver keeps track of mouse movement in units called mickeys. When it is time to position the cursor on-screen, the driver looks at the byte at offset 01h. This byte indicates how many entries are in the other two table arrays for acceleration curve 2. The driver then starts searching the array at offset 24h until it finds a value that is greater than the number of mickeys moved. The corresponding value is loaded from the array at offset A4h, and this value is multiplied by the raw movement data to determine where the cursor should be displayed.

To help you understand how this table information is used, look at Figure B.1, which represents the table for acceleration curve 2. The mouse driver looks down column 1 until it finds a value greater than the raw mickey count. It takes the corresponding value from column 2, which is the scaling factor applied to the mickey count. The value at offset 01h indicates the number of rows in this table.

The ASCII names beginning at offset 104h are the final element of the acceleration curve table. These names are left-justified, space-filled ASCII names. Each name can be as much as 16 (10h) bytes long.

Figure B.1.

An acceleration curve
table.

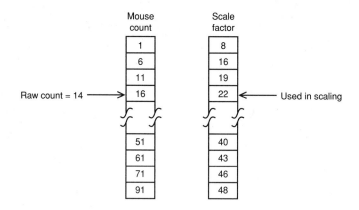

Function 2Ch, Get Acceleration Curves

Category: Motion control

| Register | | On Return | |
or Flag	On Entry	If Successful	If Unsuccessful
AX	2Ch	0	< > 0
BX		Current curve	
SI		Table offset	
ES		Table segment	

Syntax:

```
MOV     AX,2Ch              ;Get acceleration curve table
INT     33h
CMP     AX,0                ;Was function OK?
JNE     Error               ;No, go handle
MOV     Curve,BX            ;Curve in use
```

Description: With this function you can determine the acceleration curve
being used by the mouse driver. If you are going to change the acceleration
curve table (function 2Bh), you should use this function to find the address of
the current table and then transfer that information to a buffer area where you
can reset it when your program ends.

The acceleration curve table has the layout shown in Table B.14. See the
description for function 2Bh for more information about acceleration curves.

Function 2Dh, Set Or Get Active Acceleration Curve

Category: Motion control

Register or Flag	On Entry	On Return If Successful	If Unsuccessful
AX	2Dh	0	0FFFEh
BX	Action flag	Curve number	
SI		Curve name string offset	
ES		Curve name string segment	

Syntax:

```
MOV    AX,2Dh          ;Set/get curve number
MOV    BX,-1           ;Determine current curve
INT    33h
CMP    AX,0            ;Was function OK?
JNE    Error           ;No, go handle
MOV    Curve,BX        ;Curve in use
```

Description: If you want to know which acceleration curve is being used, or if you want to set which curve is used but do not want to redefine the entire acceleration curve table, you can use this function by specifying in BX the action you want to take. If you supply a number between 1 and 4, the curve is changed to the acceleration curve indicated by the number. If you load BX with –1, the function returns the current curve number in BX.

The value in AX indicates the success of the function. If AX is 0, the function was successful. If AX is nonzero, an error occurred.

The curve name pointed to by ES:SI is the 16-byte name contained in the acceleration curve table. For more information on this table, refer to the description of function 2Bh and to Table B.14.

Function 2Fh, Mouse Hardware Reset

Category: Mouse and driver control

Register or Flag	On Entry	On Return If Successful	If Unsuccessful
AX	2Fh	0FFFFh	0

Syntax:

```
MOV    AX,2Fh           ;Hardware reset
INT    33h
CMP    AX,-1            ;Error?
JNE    Error            ;Yes, could not reset
```

Description: This function operates in a similar manner to function 00h, except that only a few variables maintained by the mouse driver are reset, along with a reset of the physical mouse. On return from the function, AX is set to –1 if the function was successful; otherwise, it is unchanged. The only variables that are reset have to do with the CRT page number and the light-pen emulation. All other variables maintained by the mouse driver are considered software variables and can be reset by using function 21h.

Function 30h, Set Or Get BallPoint Information

Category: Mouse and driver control

Register or Flag	On Entry	On Return If Successful	If Unsuccessful
AX	30h	Button state	0FFFFh
BX	Rotation angle	Rotation angle	
CX	Command	Button masks	

Syntax:

```
MOV    AX,30h           ;Set BallPoint Info
MOV    CX,0             ;Get current settings
INT    33h
CMP    AX,-1            ;Error?
JNE    Error            ;Yes, could not reset
MOV    Angle,BX
MOV    Buttons,CX
```

Description: The most recent mouse available from Microsoft is the *BallPoint Mouse*. Used predominantly by laptop and portable computer users, it attaches to the left or right side of the computer case, next to the keyboard, and looks almost like an upside-down mouse. Users can manipulate the mouse cursor by moving the mouse ball with their thumb. Four buttons are on the BallPoint mouse, but only two can be active at a time.

This function enables you to either read the status of the BallPoint mouse or change the internal rotational pointer maintained by the mouse driver. You also can change which mouse buttons you will use.

On calling this function, if the value contained in CX is zero, the driver assumes that you want to read the mouse status. In this case, the value returned in BX is the rotation angle of the internal pointer. The value in CX is the button mask, which specifies which of the four buttons is mapped to the primary (left) and secondary (right) button positions.

If, on calling the function, CX is set to a nonzero value, this value is assumed to be the button masks you want set for the BallPoint mouse, and BX is assumed to be loaded with the desired rotational angle. This angle can range from –32,768 to +32,767 degrees.

The button masks set in CX are double masks: CH contains the bit settings for the primary mask (corresponding to the left mouse button), and CL contains the setting for the secondary mask (corresponding to the right button).

Function 31h, Get Virtual Coordinates

Category: Cursor control

Register or Flag	On Entry	On Return
AX	31h	Minimum horizontal coordinate
BX		Minimum vertical coordinate
CX		Maximum horizontal coordinate
DX		Maximum vertical coordinate

Syntax:

```
MOV     AX,31h              ;Get virtual coordinate ranges
INT     33h
MOV     MinX,AX
MOV     MinY,BX
MOV     MaxX,CX
MOV     MaxY,DX
```

Description: This function enables you to determine the minimum and maximum virtual coordinates that were set with functions 07h and 08h. See those functions for more information about virtual coordinates.

Function 32h, Get Active Advanced Functions

Category: Mouse and driver control

Register or Flag	On Entry	On Return
AX	32h	Function flags

Syntax:

```
MOV     AX,32h               ;Get advanced flags
INT     33h
```

Description: Using this function can help you determine which advanced functions are available with your mouse driver. Each bit of the value returned in AX indicates whether a specific function is available. Table B.15 lists the meaning of each bit.

Table B.15. Bit meanings for function 32h. (If the bit is set, the related function is available in the driver.)

Bit settings `FEDCBA98 76543210`	Meaning
`                x`	Is function 34h available?
`               x `	Is function 33h available?
`              x  `	Is function 32h available?
`             x   `	Is function 31h available?
`            x    `	Is function 30h available?
`           x     `	Is function 2Fh available?
`          x      `	Is function 2Eh available?
`         x       `	Is function 2Dh available?
`       x         `	Is function 2Ch available?
`      x          `	Is function 2Bh available?
`     x           `	Is function 2Ah available?
`    x            `	Is function 29h available?
`   x             `	Is function 28h available?
`  x              `	Is function 27h available?
` x               `	Is function 26h available?
`x                `	Is function 25h available?

If this function is not supported by your mouse driver, AX is unchanged upon return.

Function 33h, Get Switch Settings

Category: Mouse and driver control

Register or Flag	On Entry	On Return
AX	33h	0
CX	Buffer length	Bytes in buffer
DI	Buffer offset	Buffer offset
ES	Buffer segment	Buffer segment

Syntax:

```
MOV    AX,33h              ;Get switch settings
PUSH   ES                  ;Save for later
PUSH   DS
POP    ES
MOV    DI,OFFSET Buffer    ;Point to buffer
MOV    CX,340              ;Get full information
INT    33h
```

Description: When you start the mouse driver from the command line, you have the option of including command-line switches that affect the way the driver operates. This function enables you to inspect the settings of these switches. ES:DX should point to the address of a 340-byte buffer. You can use a smaller buffer, but not all switch values then are returned.

On return from this function, the buffer at ES:DX contains the information in Table B.16.

Table B.16. Switch settings information returned by function 33h.		
Offset	**Length**	**Meaning**
00h	1 byte	Mouse type and port
01h	1 byte	Language
02h	1 byte	Horizontal sensitivity
03h	1 byte	Vertical sensitivity

continues

Table B.16. Continued

Offset	Length	Meaning
04h	1 byte	Double-speed threshold
05h	1 byte	Ballistic curve
06h	1 byte	Interrupt rate
07h	1 byte	Cursor mask
08h	1 byte	Laptop adjustment
09h	1 byte	Memory type
0Ah	1 byte	Super VGA flag
0Bh	2 bytes	Rotation angle
0Dh	1 byte	Primary button
0Eh	1 byte	Secondary button
0Fh	1 byte	Click lock enabled
10h	324 bytes	Acceleration curve tables

Function 34h, Get MOUSE.INI

Category: Mouse and driver control

Register or Flag	On Entry	On Return
AX	34h	0
DX		Buffer offset
ES		Buffer segment

Syntax:

```
MOV    AX,34h              ;Get MOUSE.INI path
INT    33h
```

Description: You can use this function to determine the location of the MOUSE.INI file. On return, ES:DX contains a pointer to a buffer containing the full path for the location of the file. This file is used to set configuration defaults for the mouse driver.

The EMS Functions

The functions listed in this appendix are introduced in Chapter 6, "Expanded and Extended Memory." All of the functions are based on the LIM EMS 4.0 specification, and can be accessed through interrupt 67h. Table C.1 lists the EMS functions by number and indicates the EMS specification version in which the function became available.

Table C.1. The EMS functions.

| EMS Specification | | | Function Number | | |
3.0	3.2	4.0	Func	Subfunc	Meaning
X	X	X	40h		Get EMM status
X	X	X	41h		Get page frame segment address
X	X	X	42h		Get number of pages
X	X	X	43h		Allocate memory
X	X	X	44h		Map expanded memory page
X	X	X	45h		Release memory
X	X	X	46h		Get EMM version
X	X	X	47h		Save page map
X	X	X	48h		Restore page map

continues

Table C.1. Continued

EMS Specification			Function Number		
3.0	3.2	4.0	Func	Subfunc	Meaning
X	X	X	4Bh		Get handle count
X	X	X	4Ch		Get pages for one handle
X	X	X	4Dh		Get pages for all handles
	X	X	4Eh	00h	Save page map registers
	X	X	4Eh	01h	Restore page map
	X	X	4Eh	02h	Save and restore page map
	X	X	4Eh	03h	Get page map array size
		X	4Fh	00h	Save partial page map
		X	4Fh	01h	Restore partial page map
		X	4Fh	02h	Get partial page map array size
		X	50h	00h	Map multiple pages (by number)
		X	50h	01h	Map multiple pages (by address)
		X	51h		Reallocate pages
		X	52h	00h	Get handle attribute
		X	52h	01h	Set handle attribute
		X	52h	02h	Get attribute capability
		X	53h	00h	Get handle name
		X	53h	01h	Set handle name
		X	54h	00h	Get all handle names
		X	54h	01h	Search for handle name
		X	54h	02h	Get total handles
		X	55h	00h	Map pages and jump (by number)
		X	55h	01h	Map pages and jump (by address)
		X	56h	00h	Map pages and call (by number)

EMS Specification			Function Number		
3.0	3.2	4.0	Func	Subfunc	Meaning
		X	56h	01h	Map pages and call (by address)
		X	56h	02h	Get stack space for map page and call
		X	57h	00h	Move memory region
		X	57h	01h	Exchange memory region
		X	58h	00h	Get addresses of mappable pages
		X	58h	01h	Get number of mappable pages
		X	59h	00h	Get hardware configuration
		X	59h	01h	Get number of raw pages
		X	5Ah	00h	Allocate standard pages
		X	5Ah	01h	Allocate raw pages
		X	5Bh	00h	Get alternate map registers
		X	5Bh	01h	Set alternate map registers
		X	5Bh	02h	Get size of alternate map register save area
		X	5Bh	03h	Allocate alternate map register set
		X	5Bh	04h	Release alternate map register set
		X	5Bh	05h	Allocate DMA register set
		X	5Bh	06h	Enable DMA on alternate map register set
		X	5Bh	07h	Disable DMA on alternate map register set
		X	5Bh	08h	Release DMA register set
		X	5Ch		Prepare EMM for warm boot
		X	5Dh	00h	Enable EMM operating system functions
		X	5Dh	01h	Disable EMM operating system functions
		X	5Dh	02h	Release access key

Function 40h, Get EMM Status

Register or Flag	On Entry	On Return If Successful	On Return If Unsuccessful
AH	40h	00h	Error code

When you have determined that an expanded memory manager is present, you can use this function to determine whether it is functional. If it is, AH is zero on return.

Function 41h, Get Page Frame Segment Address

Register or Flag	On Entry	On Return If Successful	On Return If Unsuccessful
AH	41h	00h	Error code
BX		Page frame segment address	

This function is used to determine the page frame address for accessing expanded memory. The page frame marks the beginning of a 64K segment, which is divided into four 16K memory pages. Page frames are described in further detail in Chapter 6, "Expanded and Extended Memory."

Function 42h, Get Number of Pages

Register or Flag	On Entry	On Return If Successful	On Return If Unsuccessful
AH	42h	00h	Error code
BX		Available pages	
DX		Total pages	

This function is used to determine the number of 16K memory pages controlled by the EMM, as well as how many of those pages are still available.

Function 43h, Allocate Memory

Register or Flag	On Entry	On Return If Successful	If Unsuccessful
AH	43h	00h	Error code
BX	Number of pages		
DX		Handle	

You use this function to allocate a block of memory for your program. The value in BX is the number of 16K pages you want; on successful return, DX contains a numeric handle for the block. This handle is used to refer to the block when you are doing other EMS operations such as mapping, resizing, or releasing the memory.

You should take care to release any memory you allocate with this function. To do so, you use function 45h. If you do not release the memory, it is not accessible to any other programs until your system is rebooted.

Function 44h, Map Expanded Memory Page

Register or Flag	On Entry	On Return If Successful	If Unsuccessful
AH	44h	00h	Error code
AL	Page in frame		
BX	Logical page		
DX	Handle		

After you have allocated memory using function 43h, you must map portions of it to pages within the page frame. This action makes the memory visible to your programs. DX should be loaded with the handle for the memory block, and BX will contain the logical 16K page within that block you want to map. AL will contain the 16K page number to which you want your memory mapped within the page frame. All page numbers for this function (AL and BX) are zero-based.

If you want, you can call this function with BX equal to –1. Your memory will be "unmapped" from within the page frame, thereby making it unavailable until it is mapped again later.

Function 45h, Release Memory

Register or Flag	On Entry	On Return If Successful	If Unsuccessful
AH	45h	90h	Error code
DX	Handle		

This function is used to release any memory block you previously allocated with function 43h. You just provide the handle for the memory block. Released memory is placed back in the pool of available memory pages, and then can be accessed by other functions or programs.

You should take care to release any memory you allocate with function 43h. If you do not, the memory is not accessible to any other programs until your system is rebooted.

Function 46h, Get EMM Version

Register or Flag	On Entry	On Return If Successful	If Unsuccessful
AH	46h	00h	Error code
AL		Version number	

This function returns the EMS version number supported by the memory manager. The value returned in AL is in BCD format, with an implied decimal point between the digits. Therefore, if an EMM is compliant with EMS version 4.0, AL contains 40h on successful completion of this function.

Function 47h, Save Page Map

Register or Flag	On Entry	On Return If Successful	If Unsuccessful
AH	47h	00h	Error code
DX	Handle		

If you are developing a TSR or device driver that accesses expanded memory (see the example in Chapter 9, "Device Drivers"), you use this function to save temporarily the state of the page-mapping registers on the EMS board. This action saves the condition of the EMS system, and you then can manipulate

EMS in any way you want. Later, you can use function 48h to restore the page-mapping registers to their original condition.

This function saves only the state in relation to the 64K of memory currently mapped into the page frame. The way this function operates is compliant with version 3.0 of the EMS specification. If your program will be disturbing any memory outside of that area, you should save the system state using function 4Eh.

Function 48h, Restore Page Map

Register or Flag	On Entry	On Return	
		If Successful	If Unsuccessful
AH	48h	00h	Error code
DX	Handle		

The opposite of function 47h, this function enables you to restore the state of the page-mapping registers. You must have used function 47h before calling this function. The same caveats noted for function 47h apply to this function also.

Function 4Bh, Get Handle Count

Register or Flag	On Entry	On Return	
		If Successful	If Unsuccessful
AH	4Bh	00h	Error code
BX		Active handle count	

This function returns a value ranging from 0 to 255, which represents the number of allocated memory handles. If BX is 0, no EMS memory is allocated.

Function 4Ch, Get Pages For One Handle

Register or Flag	On Entry	On Return	
		If Successful	If Unsuccessful
AH	4Ch	00h	Error code
BX		Number of pages	
DX	Handle		

You can use this function to determine the number of 16K memory pages assigned to a specific memory handle.

Function 4Dh, Get Pages For All Handles

Register or Flag	On Entry	On Return If Successful	If Unsuccessful
AH	4Dh	00h	Error code
BX		Active handle count	
DI	Buffer offset		
ES	Buffer segment		

Using this function enables you to to determine the number of 16K memory pages assigned to every active memory handle. On entry, ES:DI must point to an array to be filled in by the EMM. Each entry in the array is a doubleword (four bytes). The first word represents a handle number, and the second represents the number of pages assigned to that handle.

Because there cannot be more than 256 handles at any time, you can set up an array of 1,024 bytes, or you can dynamically set the buffer size by using function 4Bh to determine the number of active handles before using this function.

Function 4Eh, Subfunction 00h, Save Page Map Registers

Register or Flag	On Entry	On Return If Successful	If Unsuccessful
AH	4Eh	00h	Error code
AL	00h		
DI	Buffer offset		
ES	Buffer segment		

This function is related to function 47h in that it stores the state of the EMS page-mapping registers. These values are stored to the buffer you specify in ES:DI. Before using this function, you should use function 4Eh, subfunction 03h, to determine the size of buffer you need.

Function 4Eh, Subfunction 01h, Restore Page Map

Register or Flag	On Entry	On Return	
		If Successful	If Unsuccessful
AH	4Eh	00h	Error code
AL	01h		
SI	Buffer offset		
DS	Buffer segment		

This function is used to restore the EMS page-map registers previously stored in a memory buffer with function 4Eh, subfunction 00h. DS:SI points to the buffer to use.

Function 4Eh, Subfunction 02h, Save and Restore Page Map

Register or Flag	On Entry	On Return	
		If Successful	If Unsuccessful
AH	4Eh	00h	Error code
AL	02h		
SI	Restore buffer offset		
DI	Save buffer offset		
DS	Restore buffer segment		
ES	Save buffer segment		

This function combines both subfunctions 00h and 01h of function 4Eh. It first stores the EMS page-mapping registers in the buffer pointed to by ES:DI, and then sets them from the register pointed to by DS:SI. This capability enables you to exchange one memory context for another in one operation.

The size of the buffer necessary for the save operation can be determined with function 4Eh, subfunction 03h.

Function 4Eh, Subfunction 03h, Get Page Map Array Size

Register or Flag	On Entry	On Return If Successful	If Unsuccessful
AH	4Eh	00h	Error code
AL	03h	Buffer size	

If you plan to use any of the other subfunctions for function 4Eh, you should use this function first to determine the proper buffer size to use to save the EMS page-mapping registers. On successful return, AL contains the number of bytes of memory required.

Function 4Fh, Subfunction 00h, Save Partial Page Map

Register or Flag	On Entry	On Return If Successful	If Unsuccessful
AH	4Fh	00h	Error code
AL	00h		
SI	Map list offset		
DI	Buffer offset		
DS	Map list segment		
ES	Buffer segment		

This version of function 47h is more flexible. It enables you to save not only the page-mapping registers for the pages currently mapped in the page frame, but also the same information for any page controlled by the EMM.

Two parameters are required when you call this function. ES:DI should point to a buffer that will be filled in by the EMM. The size of this buffer can be determined with function 4Fh, subfunction 02h. The other parameter is a map list pointed to by DS:SI. The first word of this list is a count of the number of page identifiers in the list. Immediately following the count word is a series of words, one per entry, indicating page numbers whose page-mapping state you want saved in your buffer.

Function 4Fh, Subfunction 01h, Restore Partial Page Map

Register or Flag	On Entry	On Return If Successful	If Unsuccessful
AH	4Fh	00h	Error code
AL	01h		
SI	Buffer offset		
DS	Buffer segment		

This function enables you to restore EMS page-mapping registers saved previously with function 4Fh, subfunction 00h. No map list is required by this function; you have to provide only a pointer (DS:SI) to the buffer created by the saving function.

Function 4Fh, Subfunction 02h, Get Partial Page Map Array Size

Register or Flag	On Entry	On Return If Successful	If Unsuccessful
AH	4Fh	00h	Error code
AL	02h	Array size	
BX	Page count		

You can use this function to determine the size of the buffer required in order to save the EMS page-mapping registers for a specified number of pages. The value in BX should be the same as the first word in the map list used in function 4Fh, subfunction 00h. The buffer size, in bytes, is returned in AL.

Function 50h, Subfunction 00h, Map Multiple Pages (by Number)

| Register | | On Return | |
or Flag	On Entry	If Successful	If Unsuccessful
AH	50h	00h	Error code
AL	00h		
CX	Page count		
DX	Handle		
SI	Buffer offset		
DS	Buffer segment		

If you are using an EMM that is compliant with EMS 4.0, this function enables you to map multiple EMS memory pages in a single function. Although the pages to be mapped do not have to be contiguous, they all must be allocated to the same handle.

CX contains the number of pages to map, and DS:SI points to a buffer containing a table that details how the mapping should occur. Each entry consists of two words. The first indicates the logical EMS page to be mapped, and the second indicates the page within the page frame to which it should be mapped.

Function 50h, Subfunction 01h, Map Multiple Pages (by Address)

| Register | | On Return | |
or Flag	On Entry	If Successful	If Unsuccessful
AH	50h	00h	Error code
AL	01h		
CX	Page count		
DX	Handle		
SI	Buffer offset		
DS	Buffer segment		

You can use this function, similar to function 50h, subfunction 00h, to map multiple pages of EMS memory in a single step. Although the pages to be mapped do not have to be contiguous, they all must be allocated to the same handle.

CX contains the number of pages to map, and DS:SI points to a buffer containing a table that details how the mapping should occur. As with function 50h, subfunction 00h, each table entry consists of two words. The first indicates the logical EMS page to be mapped, and the second contains a physical page segment address where the page should be mapped. You can use function 58h, subfunction 00h, to determine valid segment addresses for mapping.

Function 51h, Reallocate Pages

Register or Flag	On Entry	On Return If Successful	If Unsuccessful
AH	51h	00h	Error code
BX	New page count	Actual page count	
DX	Handle		

This function enables you to modify the number of EMS memory pages allocated to an existing memory handle. You specify the handle in DX and in BX the new number of pages you want.

If the handle in DX originally was allocated with function 43h or function 5Ah, subfunction 00h, the pages allocated by this function are standard 16K pages. If DX was allocated with function 5Ah, subfunction 01h, the page size is determined by the EMS hardware.

Function 52h, Subfunction 00h, Get Handle Attribute

Register or Flag	On Entry	On Return If Successful	If Unsuccessful
AH	52h	00h	Error code
AL	00h	Attribute	
DX	Handle		

Depending on your EMS hardware, it is possible for the contents of EMS memory to not be lost during a warm boot. If your hardware has this capability, the EMS memory is said to be *nonvolatile*. If the memory contents are lost during a warm boot, the memory is *volatile*.

This function returns an attribute for memory assigned to a memory handle that indicates whether the memory is volatile. If the memory is volatile, AL is 0 on return; if it is not, AL is 1. Assuming that the capability is supported by your hardware, you can set the memory attribute with function 52h, subfunction 01h.

Function 52h, Subfunction 01h, Set Handle Attribute

Register or Flag	On Entry	On Return	
		If Successful	If Unsuccessful
AH	52h	00h	Error code
AL	01h		
BL	Attribute		
DX	Handle		

This function enables you to indicate whether you want the contents of memory assigned to a specific memory handle to be erased during a warm boot. See function 52h, subfunction 00h, for more information.

If this capability is not supported by your EMS hardware, an error will be generated.

Function 52h, Subfunction 02h, Get Attribute Capability

Register or Flag	On Entry	On Return	
		If Successful	If Unsuccessful
AH	52h	00h	Error code
AL	02h	Attribute flag	

If your EMM is compliant with EMS 4.0, and if your EMS hardware supports the capability, it is possible to do a warm boot without erasing the contents of EMS memory. This function enables you to determine whether this capability is supported in your system. On return, AL contains 0 if the capability is not supported, and 1 if it is.

If nonvolatile memory is supported (AL equals 1), you can use function 52h, subfunctions 00h and 01h, to manage the volatility attribute of each memory block.

Function 53h, Subfunction 00h, Get Handle Name

Register or Flag	On Entry	On Return	
		If Successful	If Unsuccessful
AH	53h	00h	Error code
AL	00h		
DX	Handle		
DI	Buffer offset		
ES	Buffer segment		

If your EMM supports EMS 4.0, you can have 8-character names assigned to memory blocks. These names can be used to identify the process or program responsible for the memory.

This function enables you to determine the name previously assigned to a memory block. The name can be as much as eight characters long, and is initially set to eight nul characters. You can assign a name to a memory block with function 53h, subfunction 01h.

Function 53h, Subfunction 01h, Set Handle Name

Register or Flag	On Entry	On Return	
		If Successful	If Unsuccessful
AH	53h	00h	Error code
AL	01h		
DX	Handle		
SI	Buffer offset		
DS	Buffer segment		

If your EMM supports EMS 4.0, you can have 8-byte names assigned to memory blocks. These names can be used to identify the process or program responsible for the memory, or to search for the memory block at a later time. This capability is particularly useful with nonvolatile memory. After a warm boot, you can search for a name, thereby identifying a memory block you set up before the boot.

Names can be as long as eight bytes, and initially are set to eight nul characters. If the name you assign contains less than eight significant characters, it should be left-justified in the field and the remaining bytes set to nul.

Function 54h, Subfunction 00h, Get All Handle Names

| Register | | On Return | |
or Flag	On Entry	If Successful	If Unsuccessful
AH	54h	00h	Error code
AL	00h	Active handle count	
DI	Buffer offset		
ES	Buffer segment		

This function constructs at ES:DI a table of all the assigned handles and their associated names. Each entry in the table is ten bytes long. The first word of the entry is the memory handle, and the remaining eight bytes are the name.

You can use a maximum buffer size determined by the maximum number of handles (function 54h, subfunction 02h) at ten bytes per handle, or you can use function 4Bh to determine the number of active handles and then set the buffer size dynamically.

Function 54h, Subfunction 01h, Search For Handle Name

| Register | | On Return | |
or Flag	On Entry	If Successful	If Unsuccessful
AH	54h	00h	Error code
AL	01h		
DX	Handle		
DS	Handle name offset		
DS	Handle name segment		

If you are using named memory blocks in your system, you can search for a block by a specific name using this function. This capability is particularly useful in conjunction with nonvolatile memory. After a warm boot, you can search for a memory block by name (assigned before the boot), and then access its contents again. In this way, it is possible to provide continuity of programs or data across a warm boot cycle.

Function 54h, Subfunction 02h, Get Total Handles

Register or Flag	On Entry	On Return If Successful	On Return If Unsuccessful
AH	54h	00h	Error code
AL	02h		
BX		Handle count	

Whereas function 4Bh returns the number of active handles in a system, this function returns a number indicating the number that the EMM is capable of assigning.

Function 55h, Subfunction 00h, Map Pages and Jump (by Number)

Register or Flag	On Entry	On Return If Successful	On Return If Unsuccessful
AH	55h	00h	Error code
AL	00h		
DX	Handle		
SI	Buffer offset		
DS	Buffer segment		

This function is closely related to function 55h, subfunction 01h, and is used to support program code in EMS. To use it, you must specify in DS:SI a 9-byte buffer with the layout shown in Table C.2.

Table C.2. Buffer layout for function 55h, subfunctions 00h and 01h.

Offset	Length	Meaning
00h	4 bytes	Far pointer for jump
04h	1 byte	Count of map array entries
05h	4 bytes	Address of map array

The address at offset 00h in this table is where control is transferred after the mapping is completed. The address at offset 05h is a pointer to a map array that contains a series of 2-word entries, the number of entries being specified by the byte at offset 04h. The first word in the map array contains the logical page number, within the memory block defined by memory handle DX, that is to be mapped. The second word contains the physical page number within the page frame where the logical page will be mapped.

Function 55h, Subfunction 01h, Map Pages and Jump (by Address)

Register or Flag	On Entry	On Return	
		If Successful	If Unsuccessful
AH	55h	00h	Error code
AL	01h		
DX	Handle		
SI	Buffer offset		
DS	Buffer segment		

This function is closely related to function 55h, subfunction 00h, and is used to support program code in EMS. To use it, you must specify in DS:SI an 8-byte buffer with the layout shown in Table C.2.

The address at offset 00h in this table is where control is transferred after the mapping is completed. The address at offset 05h is a pointer to a map array that contains a series of 2-word entries, the number of entries being specified by the byte at offset 04h. The first word in the map array contains the logical page number, within the memory block defined by memory handle DX, that will be mapped. The second word contains the segment address of the physical page where the logical page will be mapped.

You can use function 58h, subfunction 00h, to determine valid segment addresses for mapping.

Function 56h, Subfunction 00h, Map Pages and Call (by Number)

Register or Flag	On Entry	On Return If Successful	If Unsuccessful
AH	56h	00h	Error code
AL	00h		
DX	Handle		
SI	Buffer offset		
DS	Buffer segment		

This function exists to support executable code in EMS pages. With it, you can map code pages to memory, execute code contained therein, and restore the mapping that existed before the call.

To use this function, you specify in DS:SI a 22-byte buffer that has the layout shown in Table C.3.

Table C.3. Buffer layout for function 56h, subfunctions 00h and 01h.

Offset	Length	Meaning
00h	4 bytes	Address of start of subroutine
04h	1 byte	Count of new map array entries
05h	4 bytes	Address of new map array
09h	1 byte	Count of old map array entries
0Ah	4 bytes	Address of old map array
0Eh	8 bytes	Reserved; used by EMM

The address at offset 00h in this table is where control is transferred after the mapping is completed. The address at offset 05h is a pointer to a map array that contains a series of 2-word entries, the number of entries being specified by the byte at offset 04h. The first word in the map array contains the logical page number, within the memory block defined by memory handle DX, that will be mapped. The second word contains the physical page number within the page frame where the logical page will be mapped.

When a far return (RETF) is encountered in the subroutine, control is returned to the EMM. The address at offset 0Ah points to the map array as you want it to exist when the subroutine is completed. This map array has the same layout as the new map array just described.

Before using this function, you should use function 56h, subfunction 02h, to determine the number of bytes necessary to adjust the stack on return from your subroutine.

Function 56h, Subfunction 01h, Map Pages and Call (by Address)

Register or Flag	On Entry	On Return If Successful	On Return If Unsuccessful
AH	56h	00h	Error code
AL	01h		
DX	Handle		
SI	Buffer offset		
DS	Buffer segment		

This function exists to support executable code in EMS pages. With it, you can map code pages to memory, execute code contained therein, and restore the mapping that existed before the call. The function operates exactly the same as function 56h, subfunction 00h, except that the map arrays are constructed slightly differently.

For this function, the map arrays still consist of 2-word entries, and the first word of each entry is the same as described for function 56h, subfunction 00h. The second word, however, contains the segment address of the physical page where the logical page will be mapped.

You can use function 58h, subfunction 00h, to determine valid segment addresses for mapping.

Before using this function, you should use function 56h, subfunction 02h, to determine the number of bytes necessary to adjust the stack on return from your subroutine.

Function 56h, Subfunction 02h, Get Stack Space for Map Page and Call

Register or Flag	On Entry	On Return If Successful	On Return If Unsuccessful
AH	56h	00h	Error code
AL	02h		
BX		Stack space required	

This function should be called before using function 56h, subfunctions 00h or 01h. It returns a value that indicates by how much the stack must be adjusted after return from the call.

Function 57h, Subfunction 00h, Move Memory Region

Register or Flag	On Entry	On Return If Successful	On Return If Unsuccessful
AH	57h	00h	Error code
AL	00h		
SI	Buffer offset		
DS	Buffer segment		

This function enables you to copy as much as 1 megabyte of memory from any place in memory to any other place in memory, conventional or expanded. To use this function, you must specify in DS:SI an 18-byte buffer that has the layout shown in Table C.4.

Table C.4. Buffer layout for function 57, subfunctions 00h and 01h.

Offset	Length	Meaning
00h	4 bytes	Number of bytes to move
04h	1 byte	Source-memory type code
05h	2 bytes	Source handle
07h	2 bytes	Source offset
09h	2 bytes	Source page number or segment

continues

Table C.4. Continued		
Offset	**Length**	**Meaning**
0Bh	1 byte	Destination-memory type code
0Ch	2 bytes	Destination handle
0Eh	2 bytes	Destination offset
10h	2 bytes	Destination page number or segment

The memory type codes at offsets 04h and 0Bh indicate whether the source or destination is conventional or expanded memory. If it is conventional memory, the type code is 0; if it is expanded, it is 1. The values you place at offsets 09h and 10h depend on the memory type code for the block. The value can be either a logical page number (if it is type code 1, it is expanded memory) or a segment address (if it is type code 0, it is conventional memory).

Function 57h, Subfunction 01h, Exchange Memory Region

Register or Flag	On Entry	On Return	
		If Successful	**If Unsuccessful**
AH	57h	00h	Error code
AL	01h		
SI	Buffer offset		
DS	Buffer segment		

This function performs an exchange of two memory regions. The memory regions can be as much as 1 megabyte long and in either expanded or conventional memory. This function uses the same buffer layout as described in function 57h, subfunction 01h.

Function 58h, Subfunction 00h, Get Addresses of Mappable Pages

Register or Flag	On Entry	On Return If Successful	If Unsuccessful
AH	58h	00h	Error code
AL	00h		
CX		Array entry count	
DI	Buffer offset		
ES	Buffer segment		

You can use this function to determine the segment address that can be mapped by the EMM. This information is useful in other EMS functions that accept segment addresses as mapping parameters.

To use this function, you must specify a buffer in ES:DI that will be filled in by the EMM with the mapping information. Each entry in the buffer consists of two words. The first word contains the segment address of a mappable physical page—where in memory a logical page can be mapped. The second word indicates the logical page mapped to that segment address.

You can use function 58h, subfunction 01h, to determine the number of mappable pages. This information can be used to determine the size of the buffer you should allow for in this function.

Function 58h, Subfunction 01h, Get Number of Mappable Pages

Register or Flag	On Entry	On Return If Successful	If Unsuccessful
AH	58h	00h	Error code
AL	01h		
CX		Mappable page count	

Returns the number of mappable physical pages supported by the EMM. This information can be used in preparing a suitable buffer for use in function 58h, subfunction 00h.

Function 59h, Subfunction 00h, Get Hardware Configuration

Register or Flag	On Entry	On Return If Successful	On Return If Unsuccessful
AH	59h	00h	Error code
AL	00h		
DI	Buffer offset		
ES	Buffer segment		

Returns hardware-specific information about your EMS hardware. The 10-byte buffer pointed to by ES:DI is filled in with information as shown in Table C.5.

Table C.5. Hardware information returned by function 59h, subfunction 00h.

Offset	Length	Meaning
00h	2 bytes	Raw page size, in paragraphs
02h	2 bytes	Alternate page-mapping register sets available
04h	2 bytes	Bytes required to save page-mapping register set
06h	2 bytes	Number of register sets assignable to DMA channels
08h	2 bytes	DMA operation type flag

The information at offset 04h is the same information returned by function 4Eh, subfunction 03h. The DMA operation type flag at offset 08h indicates whether only one DMA register set is available (flag equals 1) or whether the DMA can be used with alternate register sets (flag equals 0).

Function 59h, Subfunction 01h, Get Number of Raw Pages

Register or Flag	On Entry	On Return If Successful	If Unsuccessful
AH	59h	00h	Error code
AL	01h		
BX		Available raw pages	
DX		Total raw pages	

This function returns the number of raw pages supported by the EMM and the EMS hardware. The size of the raw pages can be determined by function 59h, subfunction 00h. If the raw size matches the standard 16K EMS page size, this function returns the same value as function 42h.

Function 5Ah, Subfunction 00h, Allocate Standard Pages

Register or Flag	On Entry	On Return If Successful	If Unsuccessful
AH	5Ah	00h	Error code
AL	00h		
BX	Number of pages		
DX		Handle	

This function is operationally equivalent to function 43h. It enables you to allocate 16K memory pages and assign the block a unique handle used for future reference.

You should take care to release any memory you allocate with this function. To do so, you use function 45h. If you do not release the memory, it is not accessible to any other programs until your system is rebooted.

Function 5Ah, Subfunction 01h, Allocate Raw Pages

| Register | | On Return | |
or Flag	On Entry	If Successful	If Unsuccessful
AH	5Ah	00h	Error code
AL	01h		
BX	Number of pages		
DX		Handle	

This function does not limit the size of the pages assigned to a handle to only 16K. The raw page size is hardware specific, and may vary from board to board.

You should take care to release any memory you allocate with this function. To do so, you use function 45h. If you do not release the memory, it is not accessible to any other programs until your system is rebooted.

Function 5Bh, Subfunction 00h, Get Alternate Map Registers

| Register | | On Return | |
or Flag	On Entry	If Successful	If Unsuccessful
AH	5Bh	00h	Error code
AL	00h		
BL		Alternate map register set	
DI		Save area offset	
ES		Save area segment	

The availability of this function can be disabled with function 5Dh, subfunction 01h. It typically is disabled and subsequently used by only the operating system. Because this function is for operating system use only, it is beyond the scope of this book. For more information, refer to the LIM EMS 4.0 specification.

Function 5Bh, Subfunction 01h, Set Alternate Map Registers

Register or Flag	On Entry	On Return If Successful	On Return If Unsuccessful
AH	5Bh	00h	Error code
AL	01h		
BL	Map set number		
DI	Context area offset		
ES	Context area segment		

The availability of this function can be disabled with function 5Dh, subfunction 01h. It typically is disabled and subsequently used by only the operating system. Because this function is for operating system use only, it is beyond the scope of this reference. For more information, refer to the LIM EMS 4.0 specification.

Function 5Bh, Subfunction 02h, Get Size of Alternate Map Register Save Area

Register or Flag	On Entry	On Return If Successful	On Return If Unsuccessful
AH	5Bh	00h	Error code
AL	02h		
DX		Buffer size	

This function is used to indicate the buffer size necessary for successful use of function 5Bh, subfunctions 00h and 01h. The availability of this function can be disabled with function 5Dh, subfunction 01h. It typically is disabled and subsequently used by only the operating system.

Function 5Bh, Subfunction 03h, Allocate Alternate Map Register Set

Register or Flag	On Entry	On Return	
		If Successful	If Unsuccessful
AH	5Bh	00h	Error code
AL	03h		
BL		Map set number	

This function is used to allocate an alternate map register set number for use with function 5Bh, subfunctions 00h and 01h. Allocated alternate map register sets can be released with function 5Bh, subfunction 04h.

The availability of this function can be disabled with function 5Dh, subfunction 01h. It typically is disabled and subsequently used by only the operating system.

Function 5Bh, Subfunction 04h, Release Alternate Map Register Set

Register or Flag	On Entry	On Return	
		If Successful	If Unsuccessful
AH	5Bh	00h	Error code
AL	04h		
BL	Map set number		

This function is used to release an alternate map register set number previously allocated with function 5Bh, subfunction 03h. The current alternate map register cannot be released.

The availability of this function can be disabled with function 5Dh, subfunction 01h. It typically is disabled and subsequently used by only the operating system.

Function 5Bh, Subfunction 05h, Allocate DMA Register Set

Register or Flag	On Entry	On Return	
		If Successful	If Unsuccessful
AH	5Bh	00h	Error code
AL	05h		
BL		DMA set number	

This function is used to allocate a DMA register set number. Allocated alternate map register sets can be released with function 5Bh, subfunction 08h.

The value returned in BL is zero if no DMA register sets were available.

The availability of this function can be disabled with function 5Dh, subfunction 01h. It typically is disabled and subsequently used by only the operating system.

Function 5Bh, Subfunction 06h, Enable DMA On Alternate Map Register Set

Register or Flag	On Entry	On Return	
		If Successful	If Unsuccessful
AH	5Bh	00h	Error code
AL	06h		
BL	Map set number		
DL	DMA channel		

The availability of this function can be disabled with function 5Dh, subfunction 01h. It typically is disabled and subsequently used by only the operating system. Because this function is for operating system use only, it is beyond the scope of this book. For more information, refer to the LIM EMS 4.0 specification.

Function 5Bh, Subfunction 07h, Disable DMA On Alternate Map Register Set

Register or Flag	On Entry	On Return	
		If Successful	If Unsuccessful
AH	5Bh	00h	Error code
AL	07h		
BL	DMA set number		

The availability of this function can be disabled with function 5Dh, subfunction 01h. It typically is disabled and subsequently used by only the operating system. Because this function is for operating system use only, it is beyond the scope of this book. For more information, refer to the LIM EMS 4.0 specification.

Function 5Bh, Subfunction 08h, Release DMA Register Set

Register or Flag	On Entry	On Return	
		If Successful	If Unsuccessful
AH	5Bh	00h	Error code
AL	03h		
BL	DMA set number		

This function is used to release a DMA register set number previously allocated with function 5Bh, subfunction 04h. The availability of this function can be disabled with function 5Dh, subfunction 01h. It typically is disabled and subsequently used by only the operating system.

Function 5Ch, Prepare EMM For Warm Boot

Register or Flag	On Entry	On Return	
		If Successful	If Unsuccessful
AH	5Ch	00h	Error code

This function typically is used by the operating system when a warm boot (Ctrl-Alt-Del) is executed. It prepares the EMM for the warm boot so that nonvolatile memory is not lost during the process. It saves the current mapping context, alternate map register sets, and DMA register set information, along with any other information necessary to leave the EMS condition intact after the reboot.

Function 5Dh, Subfunction 00h, Enable EMM Operating System Functions

| Register | | On Return | |
or Flag	On Entry	If Successful	If Unsuccessful
AH	5Dh	00h	Error code
AL	00h		
BX	Access key, high word	Access key, high word	
CX	Access key, low word	Access key, low word	

This function is used to enable operating-system-specific functions 59h, 5Bh, and 5Dh. If this is the first time this function is called, or if function 5Dh, subfunction 02h, has been called since the last access, a 32-bit access key is returned in BX:CX. Similar to a password, this access key is required for all subsequent access to this function.

Function 5Dh, Subfunction 01h, Disable EMM Operating System Functions

| Register | | On Return | |
or Flag	On Entry	If Successful	If Unsuccessful
AH	5Dh	00h	Error code
AL	01h		
BX	Access key, high word	Access key, high word	
CX	Access key, low word	Access key, low word	

This function is used to disable operating-system-specific functions 59h, 5Bh, and 5Dh. If this is the first time this function is called, or if function 5Dh, subfunction 02h, has been called since the last access, a 32-bit access key is returned in BX:CX. Similar to a password, this access key is required for all subsequent access to this function.

Function 5Dh, Subfunction 02h, Release Access Key

Register or Flag	On Entry	On Return If Successful	On Return If Unsuccessful
AH	5Dh	00h	Error code
AL	02h		
BX	Access key, high word		
CX	Access key, low word		

Returns operating-system-specific functions 59h, 5Bh, and 5Dh to their default condition. The 32-bit access key returned by function 5Dh, subfunctions 00h or 01h, is required for access to this function.

The XMS Functions

The XMS functions are implemented through an extended memory manager (XMM). The available functions are shown in Table D.1. Note that the first two functions listed in the table, 4300h and 4310h, are accessed through interrupt 2Fh. The other functions are accessed through the entry point address returned from function 4310h.

Table D.1. The XMS functions.

Function	Purpose
4300h	Check XMS installation
4310h	Get XMS driver entry point
00h	Get XMS version number
01h	Request high memory area
02h	Release high memory area
03h	Global enable A20 line
04h	Global disable A20 line
05h	Local enable A20 line
06h	Local disable A20 line
07h	Query A20 line
08h	Query free extended memory
09h	Allocate extended memory block

continues

Table D.1. Continued

Function	Purpose
0Ah	Release extended memory block
0Bh	Move extended memory block
0Ch	Lock extended memory block
0Dh	Unlock extended memory block
0Eh	Get handle information
0Fh	Reallocate extended memory block
10h	Request upper memory block
11h	Release upper memory block

Interrupt 2Fh, Function 4300h, Check XMS Installation

Register or Flag	On Entry	On Return If Successful	If Unsuccessful
AH	43h		
AL	00h	80h	00h

This function is used to determine whether an XMM has been loaded as a device driver in your system. On return, the value in AL indicates whether the XMM is loaded. If it is available, AL contains 80h; otherwise, AL is zero.

Interrupt 2Fh, Function 4310h, Get XMS Driver Entry Point

Register or Flag	On Entry	On Return If Successful	If Unsuccessful
AX	4310h		
BX		Entry point offset	
ES		Entry point segment	

After you have successfully used interrupt 2Fh, function 4300h, you can use this function to return the entry point address of the XMM. You use this address to access all other XMS functions.

Function 00h, Get XMS Version Number

Register or Flag	On Entry	On Return
AX	0000h	Version number
BX		Driver revision
DX		HMA existence flag

You can use this function to determine the version of the XMS supported by your extended memory manager. The number returned in AH is the major version number, and AL contains the minor version number. The version number is returned in BCD format.

The driver revision number is for internal use by the XMM developer. The value returned in DX indicates whether the high memory area (HMA) exists on the computer. To determine whether HMA memory is available, you have to use XMS function 01h.

Function 01h, Request High Memory Area

Register or Flag	On Entry	On Return If Successful	If Unsuccessful
AX	0100h	01h	00h
BL			Error code
DX	Space desired, in bytes		

If you want to use the HMA (1,024K to 1,088K), you can use this function to allocate it. Because the HMA is allocated as an entire block and cannot be subdivided by the XMM, the value loaded in DX when you are calling this function should be 0FFFFh.

If you are operating under DOS 5, there is a good chance the area already has been allocated for use by DOS.

Function 02h, Release High Memory Area

| Register | | On Return | |
or Flag	On Entry	If Successful	If Unsuccessful
AX	0200h	01h	00h
BL			Error code

If you previously requested the HMA and were granted possession, this function is used to release the area for use by other programs. You should release the HMA before ending your program; DOS does not do so automatically. If you do not release the HMA, it remains unavailable to other programs until you reboot the computer.

Function 03h, Global Enable A20 Line

| Register | | On Return | |
or Flag	On Entry	If Successful	If Unsuccessful
AX	0300h	01h	00h
BL			Error code

This function is used to enable the A20 line, which enables use of the HMA. If you test the A20 line (function 07h) and find it disabled, and you want to use the HMA, you should use this function to enable it before requesting memory in the HMA.

Function 04h, Global Disable A20 Line

| Register | | On Return | |
or Flag	On Entry	If Successful	If Unsuccessful
AX	0400h	01h	00h
BL			Error code

This function is the opposite of function 03h. It is used to disable the HMA. You should make sure that you are not executing a program within the HMA when you disable the A20 line, because your program no longer will be executable.

Function 05h, Local Enable A20 Line

| Register | | On Return | |
or Flag	On Entry	If Successful	If Unsuccessful
AX	0500h	01h	00h
BL			Error code

For systems that have implemented multitasking, this function enables the A20 line for only the local process. The A20 pin setting for other applications is not affected.

Function 06h, Local Disable A20 Line

| Register | | On Return | |
or Flag	On Entry	If Successful	If Unsuccessful
AX	0600h	01h	00h
BL			Error code

The opposite of function 05h, this function enables you to turn off the A20 line, thereby disabling the HMA, for only the local process. Operating conditions for other processes are not disturbed.

Function 07h, Query A20 Line

| Register | | On Return | |
or Flag	On Entry	If Successful	If Unsuccessful
AX	0700h	01h	00h
BL			Error code

You can use this function to determine the current setting of the A20 line. This function indicates the setting in AX. If AX is 1, the A20 line is enabled. If AX is 0 *and* BL is 0, the line is disabled.

Function 08h, Query Free Extended Memory

| Register | | On Return | |
or Flag	On Entry	If Successful	If Unsuccessful
AX	0800h	Largest block size available	00h
BL			Error code
DX		Total extended memory	

This function enables you to determine the extended memory resources available on your system. On successful return, the values in AX and DX indicate the largest block size and the total extended memory, both in 1K blocks.

Function 09h, Allocate Extended Memory Block

| Register | | On Return | |
or Flag	On Entry	If Successful	If Unsuccessful
AX	0900h	01h	00h
BL			Error code
DX	Size wanted	Block handle	

With this function, you can request a memory block in extended memory. You specify in DX the amount of memory you want, in 1K increments. Therefore, if you want 4K of memory, the value in DX should be 4.

On returning successfully, DX indicates a handle that should be used for all future XMS operations affecting the block.

Function 0Ah, Release Extended Memory Block

| Register | | On Return | |
or Flag	On Entry	If Successful	If Unsuccessful
AX	0A00h	01h	00h
BL			Error code
DX	Block handle		

You can use this function to release an extended memory block previously allocated with function 09h. You supply the block handle in DX.

Function 0Bh, Move Extended Memory Block

Register or Flag	On Entry	On Return If Successful	If Unsuccessful
AX	0B00h	01h	00h
BL			Error code
SI	Buffer offset		
DS	Buffer segment		

You can use this function to move blocks of memory, regardless of the type (it doesn't have to be extended memory). The pointer in DS:SI is an address for a buffer that contains the structure shown in Table D.2, which defines the parameters of the move.

Table D.2. Parameter buffer structure for XMS function 0Bh.

Offset	Length	Meaning
00h	4 bytes	Number of bytes to move
04h	2 bytes	Source block handle
06h	4 bytes	Source offset
0Ah	2 bytes	Destination block handle
0Ch	4 bytes	Destination offset

Function 0Ch, Lock Extended Memory Block

Register or Flag	On Entry	On Return If Successful	If Unsuccessful
AX	0C00h	01h	00h
BX		Linear block address, low word	Error code
DX	Block handle	Linear block address, high word	

This function enables you to anchor an extended memory block to a specific linear address. Because the XMM cannot move a locked block, it should not remain locked for long periods of time.

Function 0Dh, Unlock Extended Memory Block

Register or Flag	On Entry	On Return	
		If Successful	If Unsuccessful
AX	0D00h	01h	00h
BL			Error code
DX	Block handle		

This function is used to unlock an extended memory block that was previously locked with function 0Ch.

Function 0Eh, Get Handle Information

Register or Flag	On Entry	On Return	
		If Successful	If Unsuccessful
AX	0E00h	01h	00h
BH		Lock count for block	
BL		Available EMB handles	Error code
DX	Block handle	Block size	

With this function, you can determine whether a block is locked (the lock count in BH will be greater than zero) and how many remaining extended memory block handles are in the system. The value returned in DX indicates, in 1K blocks, the size of the memory block.

Function 0Fh, Reallocate Extended Memory Block

Register or Flag	On Entry	On Return	
		If Successful	If Unsuccessful
AX	0F00h	01h	00h
BX	New size wanted		Error code
DX	Block handle		

This function is used to change the size of a previously allocated memory block (see function 09h). The new block size you stipulate in BX is in 1K chunks.

Function 10h, Request Upper Memory Block

Register or Flag	On Entry	On Return	
		If Successful	If Unsuccessful
AX	1000h	01h	00h
BX		Block segment address	Error code
DX	Block size	Block size	Largest block size available

This function enables you to allocate memory in the area between 640K and 1,024K. It no longer is necessary to use this function if you are using DOS 5, because it successfully allocates memory within the upper memory area.

Function 11h, Release Upper Memory Block

Register or Flag	On Entry	On Return	
		If Successful	If Unsuccessful
AX	1100h	01h	00h
BL			Error code
DX	Block segment address		

You can use this function to release a memory block in the upper memory area that was previously allocated with function 10h.

The VCPI Functions

V CPI, or virtual control program interface, is a specification that allows cooperative access to protected mode and extended memory by EMS emulators (commonly called memory managers) and DOS extenders. The VCPI specification is considered an extension to EMS 4.0 (refer to Appendix C, "The EMS Functions").

The 13 VCPI function calls all are accessed through interrupt 67h, function DEh. Table E.1 shows the VCPI function calls.

Table E.1. The VCPI functions.

Function	Purpose
00h	VCPI installation check
01h	Get protected mode interface
02h	Get maximum physical memory address
03h	Get number of free 4K pages
04h	Allocate a 4K page
05h	Release a 4K page
06h	Get physical address of 4K page in first megabyte
07h	Read CR0
08h	Read debug registers
09h	Load debug registers

continues

Table E.1. Continued

Function	Purpose
0Ah	Get 8259 interrupt vector mappings
0Bh	Set 8259 interrupt vector mappings
0Ch	Switch CPU mode

Function 00h, VCPI Installation Check

Register or Flag	On Entry	On Return If Successful	If Unsuccessful
AH	0DEh	00h	< >0
AL	00h		
BX		Version number	

This function is used to determine whether the memory manager provides a VCPI interface. It should be used only after you have tested for the presence of an EMS device driver and have allocated a page of EMS memory. This action ensures that the driver is active and has switched the processor to V86 mode.

On return from this function, the value in AH indicates the success or failure of the operation. A nonzero value indicates that VCPI is not supported.

If the function was successful, the VCPI version number supported is returned as a BCD value in BX. The major version number is in BH, and the minor version number is in BL.

This function can be called only from real mode.

Function 01h, Get Protected Mode Interface

Register or Flag	On Entry	On Return If Successful	If Unsuccessful
AH	0DEh	00h	< >0
AL	01h		
EBX		Offset of server's protected mode entry point	

Register or Flag	On Entry	On Return If Successful	If Unsuccessful
DS	GDT pointer, offset address		
DI	Page table buffer, offset address	First uninitialized page table entry in page table buffer, offset address	
DS	GDT pointer, segment address		
ES	Page table buffer, segment address	First uninitialized page table entry in page table buffer, segment address	

This function accomplishes two things: It enables the server to prepare for an impending switch to protected mode by the client, and it enables the client to determine the protected mode entry point address used to access VCPI functions 03h, 04h, 05h, and 0Ch from protected mode.

The buffer address in ES:DI is a pointer to a 4K buffer used by the server to construct a page table that maps the first 4 megabytes of address space available to the client in protected mode.

The address pointed to by DS:SI is a global descriptor table; and the first three entries are filled in by the server. The first entry is the code segment descriptor in protected mode. The protected mode entry point returned in EBX is an offset in this segment.

This function can be called only from real mode.

Function 02h, Get Maximum Physical Memory Address

Register or Flag	On Entry	On Return If Successful	If Unsuccessful
AH	0DEh	00h	< >0
AL	02h		
EDX		Physical address	

This function enables the VCPI client, from real mode, to determine the address of the highest possible memory page that can be allocated by the server.

This information is returned as a 32-bit address in EDX; it typically is used by the client to prepare memory mapping to be used when operating in protected mode.

This function can be called only from real mode.

Function 03h, Get Number Of Free 4K Pages

Register or Flag	On Entry	On Return If Successful	If Unsuccessful
AH	0DEh	00h	< >0
AL	03h		
EDX		Number of free pages	

This function returns the total number of 4K extended memory pages available for allocation by the server.

This function can be called from either real or protected mode.

Function 04h, Allocate A 4K Page

Register or Flag	On Entry	On Return If Successful	If Unsuccessful
AH	0DEh	00h	< >0
AL	04h		
EDX		Physical page address	

The VCPI client calls this function, from either real or protected mode, to allocate a 4K block of extended memory. Unlike similar EMS functions, no handle is returned by this function. Instead, the physical address of the page is returned in EDX. All memory allocated with this function should be released with VCPI function 05h.

Function 05h, Release A 4K Page

Register or Flag	On Entry	On Return If Successful	If Unsuccessful
AH	0DEh	00h	< >0
AL	05h		
EDX	Physical page address		

This function releases a 4K block of memory allocated with VCPI function 04h. This function should not be used to free any memory blocks allocated with the EMS functions, because this action may confuse the server and lead to an unstable system.

This function can be called from either real or protected mode.

Function 06h, Get Physical Address of 4K Page in First Megabyte

Register or Flag	On Entry	On Return If Successful	If Unsuccessful
AH	0DEh	00h	< >0
AL	06h		
CX	Page number		
EDX		Physical page address	

This function is used to determine the physical address of a 4K memory block allocated with an EMS function, and therefore mapped into the first megabyte of memory. The page number supplied in CX is the linear address of the page (in real memory) shifted right 12 bits. A nonzero return value in AH indicates that an invalid page number was supplied in CX.

This function can be called only from real mode.

Function 07h, Read CRO

Register or Flag	On Entry	On Return
AH	0DEh	00h
AL	07h	
EBX		CR0 register value

Using this function enables a client to determine the value of the CPU's control register 0. This value normally is not accessible from real mode.

This function can be called only from real mode.

Function 08h, Read Debug Registers

Register or Flag	On Entry	On Return If Successful	If Unsuccessful
AH	0DEh	00h	< >0
AL	08h		
DI	Register array address, offset		
ES	Register array address, segment		

This function enables a client, from real mode, to determine the contents of the CPU protected mode debug registers. The address in ES:DI points to a 32-byte array that will receive the register values. Table E.2 indicates the layout of this table.

Table E.2. The debug register array for VCPI function 08h.

Offset	Length	Meaning
00h	4 bytes	Debug register 0 (DR0)
04h	4 bytes	Debug register 1 (DR1)
08h	4 bytes	Debug register 2 (DR2)
0Ch	4 bytes	Debug register 3 (DR3)
10h	4 bytes	Unused
14h	4 bytes	Unused

Offset	Length	Meaning
18h	4 bytes	Debug register 6 (DR0)
1Ch	4 bytes	Debug register 7 (DR0)

This function can be called only from real mode.

Function 09h, Load Debug Registers

Register or Flag	On Entry	On Return If Successful	On Return If Unsuccessful
AH	0DEh	00h	< >0
AL	09h		
DI	Register array address, offset		
ES	Register array address, segment		

Using this function, a client can set the values for the CPU's protected mode debug registers. The register array pointed to by ES:DI has the layout shown in Table E.2.

This function can be called only from real mode.

Function 0Ah, Get 8259 Interrupt Vector Mappings

Register or Flag	On Entry	On Return If Successful	On Return If Unsuccessful
AH	0DEh	00h	< >0
AL	0Ah		
BX		IRQ0 vector	
CX		IRQ8 vector	

This function is used to determine the interrupt vectors used by the 8259 interrupt controller. The values returned in BX and CX are the beginning interrupt vectors for the 8259. If a cascaded 8259 is not in the system, the value in CX is undefined.

This function can be called only from real mode.

Function 0Bh, Set 8259 Interrupt Vector Mappings

Register or Flag	On Entry	On Return If Successful	On Return If Unsuccessful
AH	0DEh	00h	< >0
AL	0Bh		
BX	IRQ0 vector		
CX	IRQ8 vector		

The opposite of function 0Ah, this function enables you to inform the server that you have reset the interrupt vectors to point to your handlers. This function should be called before enabling interrupts, but after you have programmed the 8259 chips. If your client program changes the interrupt vectors, it should restore them before program termination.

This function can be called only from real mode.

Function 0Ch, Switch CPU Mode (Calling from Real Mode)

Register or Flag	On Entry	On Return
AH	0DEh	Unspecified
AL	0Ch	Unspecified
ESI	System register table address	Unspecified
DS		Unspecified
ES		Unspecified
FS		Unspecified
GS		Unspecified

This function is called from real mode to switch the CPU to protected mode. On calling this function, interrupts must be disabled, and the linear address in ESI must point to a 21-byte table with the layout shown in Table E.3.

Table E.3. The system register table used in VCPI function 0Ch when calling from real mode.

Offset	Length	Meaning
00h	4 bytes	Value for CR3
04h	4 bytes	GDTR linear address within first megabyte of memory
08h	4 bytes	IDTR linear address within first megabyte of memory
0Ch	2 bytes	LDTR value
0Eh	2 bytes	TR value
10h	6 bytes	CS:EIP of protected mode entry point

The GDTR and IDTR values pointed to by the address at offset 04h and 08h are each six bytes long. Upon switching the protected mode, control is passed to the client program entry point specified at offset 10h.

Function 0Ch, Switch CPU Mode (Calling from Protected Mode)

Register or Flag	On Entry	On Return
AH	0DEh	Unspecified
AL	0Ch	Unspecified
ESP	System register table address, offset	
DS	Segment selector	
SS	System register table address, selector	

This function is called from real mode to switch the CPU to protected mode. Upon calling this function, interrupts must be disabled. The segment selector loaded in DS is the selector returned in the table used in VCPI function 01h. The system register table pointed to by SS:ESP (on the stack) must reside within the first megabyte of memory, and has the layout shown in Table E.4.

Table E.4. System register table used in VCPI function 0Ch when calling from protected mode.

Offset	Length	Meaning
00h	8 bytes	Far return address from procedure (unused)
08h	4 bytes	Client V86 EIP value
0Ch	4 bytes	Client V86 CS value
10h	4 bytes	EFLAGS
14h	4 bytes	Client V86 ESP value
18h	4 bytes	Client V86 SS value
1Ch	4 bytes	Client V86 ES value
20h	4 bytes	Client V86 DS value
24h	4 bytes	Client V86 FS value
28h	4 bytes	Client V86 GS value

On completion of a successful mode switch, the values specified on the stack (refer to Table E.4) are loaded into the appropriate real mode registers, and the value of EAX is undefined.

The DPMI Functions

Typically, an applications programmer does not use the DPMI functions directly. They generally are used by systems programmers who are writing DOS extenders or operating systems. The developers of the DPMI standard, however, envision that it will be used by applications programmers in the long run as more environments support the standard. In either case, an understanding of the standard and the functions available is valuable.

This appendix details all the DPMI functions available as of DPMI specification 1.0. For more information about using DPMI in your programs, refer to Chapter 12, "Protected Mode Programming."

Seventy-seven DPMI functions are defined. Four are assigned to the multiplex interrupt (2Fh), with the remainder available through interrupt 31h. Table F.1 lists the DPMI functions.

Table F.1. The DPMI functions.

Interrupt	Function	Purpose
2Fh	1680h	Release time slice
2Fh	1686h	Get CPU mode
2Fh	1687h	Get mode switch entry point
2Fh	168Ah	Get API entry point
31h	0000h	Allocate LDT descriptor
31h	0001h	Release LDT descriptor

continues

Table F.1. Continued

Interrupt	Function	Purpose
31h	0002h	Map real mode segment to descriptor
31h	0003h	Get selector increment value
31h	0006h	Get segment base address
31h	0007h	Set segment base address
31h	0008h	Set segment limit
31h	0009h	Set descriptor access rights
31h	000Ah	Create alias descriptor
31h	000Bh	Get descriptor
31h	000Ch	Set descriptor
31h	000Dh	Allocate specific LDT descriptor
31h	000Eh	Get multiple descriptors
31h	000Fh	Set multiple descriptors
31h	0100h	Allocate DOS memory block
31h	0101h	Release DOS memory block
31h	0102h	Resize DOS memory block
31h	0200h	Get real mode interrupt vector
31h	0201h	Set real mode interrupt vector
31h	0202h	Get exception handler vector
31h	0203h	Set exception handler vector
31h	0204h	Get protected mode interrupt vector
31h	0205h	Set protected mode interrupt vector
31h	0210h	Get extended exception handler vector (protected mode)
31h	0211h	Get extended exception handler vector (real mode)
31h	0212h	Set extended exception handler vector (protected mode)
31h	0213h	Set extended exception handler vector (real mode)
31h	0300h	Simulate real mode interrupt
31h	0301h	Call real mode procedure as far routine

Interrupt	Function	Purpose
31h	0302h	Call real mode procedure as interrupt
31h	0303h	Allocate real mode callback address
31h	0304h	Release real mode callback address
31h	0305h	Get state save and restore address
31h	0306h	Get raw CPU mode switch address
31h	0400h	Get DPMI version
31h	0401h	Get DPMI capabilities
31h	0500h	Get free memory information
31h	0501h	Allocate memory block
31h	0502h	Release memory block
31h	0503h	Resize memory block
31h	0504h	Allocate linear memory block
31h	0505h	Resize linear memory block
31h	0506h	Get page attributes
31h	0507h	Set page attributes
31h	0508h	Map device in memory block
31h	0509h	Map conventional memory in memory block
31h	050Ah	Get memory block size and base
31h	050Bh	Get memory information
31h	0600h	Lock linear region
31h	0601h	Unlock linear region
31h	0602h	Mark real mode region as pageable
31h	0603h	Relock real mode region
31h	0604h	Get page size
31h	0702h	Mark page as demand paging candidate
31h	0703h	Discard page contents
31h	0800h	Physical address mapping
31h	0801h	Release physical address mapping
31h	0900h	Get and disable virtual interrupt state
31h	0901h	Get and enable virtual interrupt state

continues

Table F.1. Continued

Interrupt	Function	Purpose
31h	0902h	Get virtual interrupt state
31h	0A00h	Get API entry point
31h	0B00h	Set debug watchpoint
31h	0B01h	Clear debug watchpoint
31h	0B02h	Get state of debug watchpoint
31h	0B03h	Reset debug watchpoint
31h	0C00h	Install resident service provider callback
31h	0C01h	Terminate and stay resident
31h	0D00h	Allocate shared memory
31h	0D01h	Release shared memory
31h	0D02h	Serialize on shared memory
31h	0D03h	Release serialization on shared memory
31h	0E00h	Get coprocessor status
31h	0E01h	Set coprocessor emulation

Int 2Fh, function 1680h: Release time slice

Register		On Return	
or Flag	On Entry	If Successful	If Unsuccessful
AX	1680h	0	Unchanged

When a client program is idle, it calls this function to indicate to the DPMI host that time is available for use by other processes. "Idle" is defined as any time during which the program is waiting for outside input or an external event.

On return from this function, AL is set to 0 if the function was successful. If the function is not supported (the only case in which the function is not successful), the value in AL is unchanged.

Because the nature of a DPMI host/client relationship dictates that you regain control of the CPU from time to time, you should continue to call this function periodically. For instance, your idle time might be when you are awaiting keyboard input. Your keyboard polling procedures can first look to see whether a keypress is available. If not, you issue this function. On return from this function (when you are allocated CPU time again), you can loop back and check for keyboard input again.

Int 2Fh, function 1686h: Get CPU mode

Register or Flag	On Entry	On Return
AX	1686h	Operating mode indicator

You can use this function to determine in what mode the CPU currently is operating. On return, the value in AX indicates the CPU mode. If operating in protected mode, AX is zero. Any other value in AX indicates that the system is in real or virtual 86 mode.

Int 2Fh, function 1687h: Get mode switch entry point

Register or Flag	On Entry	On Return If Successful	If Unsuccessful
AX	1687h	0	< >0
BX		Support flag	
CL		Processor type	
DX		DPMI version number	
SI		Private data paragraph count	
DI		Entry point offset	
ES		Entry point segment	

A wealth of information is returned by this function, although it is designed to provide an address that is called only once: when you first enter protected mode. You also call this function to test for the presence of a DPMI host.

On return from this function, you should check first the value in AX. If it is zero, the function was successful. A nonzero value indicates that the function was unsuccessful.

Assuming that the function was successful, the value in BX indicates whether 32-bit programs are supported (indicates whether the DPMI host is a 32-bit implementation). If BX is 0, they are not supported; a value of 1 indicates that they are supported. CL is either 2, 3, or 4 (meaning an 80286, 80386, or 80486).

DX contains the DPMI version number, with the major version number in DH and the minor version number in DL. These version numbers are decimal numbers in binary representation. If the DPMI version number is 0.90, therefore, the value in DH is 0 and the value in DL is 90 (5Ah).

The value in SI indicates the number of paragraphs of data required by the DPMI host for its own data needs. This memory is what you need to reserve using the DOS functions before entering protected mode. Finally, ES:DI provides the entry point for switching to protected mode. Again, this address should be used only once—the first time you enter protected mode.

Int 2Fh, function 168Ah: Get API entry point

Register or Flag	On Entry	On Return If Successful	If Unsuccessful
AX	1686h	0	Unchanged
SI	Vendor ASCIIZ offset		
DI		Entry point offset	
DS	Vendor ASCIIZ selector		
ES		Entry point selector	

This method is the primary one used to discover which address you should use to take advantage of a vendor's extensions to the DPMI standard. You also can use Int 31h, function 0A00h, but this function requires less overhead and execution time.

The status code returned in AX indicates the success of the function. A 0 means success; any other value means failure. Assuming that the function was successful, the address returned in ES:DI indicates the entry point for the vendor's DPMI extensions. The exact makeup of those extensions is vendor-specific. For further information, refer to the vendor's documentation.

Int 31h, function 0000h: Allocate LDT descriptor

Register or Flag	On Entry	On Return If Successful	If Unsuccessful
AX	0000h	Base selector	Error code
CX	Number wanted		
Carry		Clear	Set

This function is used to allocate one or more descriptors in the local descriptor table (LDT). You specify in the CX register the number of descriptors you want.

On return, the carry flag indicates whether the function was successful. If it was successful, AX points to the first descriptor in a contiguous array of descriptors. To access other descriptors in the array, you can use the value returned by Int 31h, function 0003h.

All the descriptors allocated by this function are initialized as data descriptors with the same privilege level as the program requesting the descriptors. The present bit is set, and the base and limit values are set to 0.

To release individual descriptors allocated with this function, use Int 31h, function 0001h.

Int 31h, function 0001h: Release LDT descriptor

Regis or Flag	On Entry	On Return If Successful	If Unsuccessful
AX	0001h		Error code
BX	Selector		
Carry		Clear	Set

This function is used to release descriptors previously allocated with Int 31h, function 0000h. Although the allocation function can be used to allocate an entire group of descriptors, this function operates only on single descriptors.

Int 31h, function 0002h: Map real mode segment to descriptor

Register or Flag	On Entry	On Return	
		If Successful	**If Unsuccessful**
AX	0002h	Selector	Error code
BX	Segment address		
Carry		Clear	Set

When you use this function, a specific real mode segment address is mapped to a protected mode descriptor. This mapping is permanent; the descriptor allocated by this function cannot be released. It should be used only for universal data areas that remain constant regardless of the application rather than for transient data areas. Examples of typical uses are to map descriptors to static data areas such as the start of video memory or the beginning of the interrupt vector table.

Int 31h, function 0003h: Get selector increment value

Register or Flag	On Entry	On Return
AX	0003h	Increment value
Carry		Clear

You use this function to determine the value to add to the base selector value returned by Int 31h, function 0000h to access additional selectors for the descriptor array.

Int 31h, function 0006h: Get segment base address

Register or Flag	On Entry	On Return	
		If Successful	**If Unsuccessful**
AX	0006h		Error code
BX	Selector		
CX		Base address of segment (high-order word)	

Register or Flag	On Entry	On Return If Successful	If Unsuccessful
DX		Base address of segment (low-order word)	
Carry		Clear	Set

This function returns the base address of the segment associated with the descriptor specified by the selector in BX. This address is stored in the base address field of the descriptor and is returned in CX:DX as a 32-bit linear address.

Int 31h, function 0007h: Set segment base address

Register or Flag	On Entry	On Return If Successful	If Unsuccessful
AX	0007h		Error code
BX	Selector		
CX	Base address of segment (high-order word)		
DX	Base address of segment (low-order word)		
Carry		Clear	Set

This function is the opposite of Int 31h, function 0006h. It enables you to set in CX:DX the linear base address of a segment. This address is stored in the base address field of the descriptor specified by the selector in BX.

Int 31h, function 0008h: Set segment limit

Register or Flag	On Entry	On Return If Successful	If Unsuccessful
AX	0008h		Error code
BX	Selector		
CX	Segment limit (high-order word)		
DX	Segment limit (low-order word)		
Carry		Clear	Set

Use this function to set the limit field in the descriptor specified by the selector in BX. The value in CX:DX is the length, in bytes, of the segment referenced by the descriptor. An error is returned if any element in BX or CX:DX is invalid.

Int 31h, function 0009h: Set descriptor access rights

| Register | | On Return | |
or Flag	On Entry	If Successful	If Unsuccessful
AX	0009h		Error code
BX	Selector		
CX	Access rights		
Carry		Clear	Set

This function enables you to modify the access rights field of the descriptor specified by the selector in BX. The access rights specified in CX have the bit meanings shown in Table F.2.

Table F.2. Access rights bit meanings.

Bit settings FEDCBA98 76543210	Meaning
1	Descriptor has been accessed
0	Descriptor has not been accessed
1	Read/write data (if bit 3 is 0); if bit 3 is 1, this bit must be 1
0	Read-only data (if bit 3 is 0)
1	Expand-down segment (if bit 3 is 0)
0	Expand-up segment (if bit 3 is 0); if bit 3 is 1, this bit must be 0
1	Segment contains executable code
0	Segment contains data
1	Segment descriptor (must be set to 1)
xx	Descriptor privilege level (DPL)
1	Data is present in memory
0	Data is not present in memory
xxxx	Reserved (unused)

Bit settings FEDCBA98 76543210	Meaning
x	Operating system use (vendor specific)
0	Reserved (must be 0)
1	32-bit operands and addresses
0	16-bit operands and addresses
1	Limit field is page granular
0	Limit field is byte granular

You should note that the high-order byte of CX is not applicable on 80286 machines.

Int 31h, function 000Ah: Create alias descriptor

Register or Flag	On Entry	On Return If Successful	If Unsuccessful
AX	000Ah	Alias selector	Error code
BX	Selector		
Carry		Clear	Set

This function allocates a new LDT descriptor with the same base address field and limit field contents as the descriptor specified by the selector in BX.

Int 31h, function 000Bh: Get descriptor

Register or Flag	On Entry	On Return If Successful	If Unsuccessful
AX	000Bh		Error code
BX	Selector		
DI	Buffer offset		
ES	Buffer selector		
Carry		Clear	Set

This function is the opposite of Int 31h, function 000Ch. It copies the descriptor specified by the selector in BX into an 8-byte buffer. The buffer pointed to by ES:DI (ES:EDI for 32-bit DPMI host implementations) contains the copy on successful return from the function.

To copy more than one descriptor into a buffer, use Int 31h, function 000Eh.

Int 31h, function 000Ch: Set descriptor

Register or Flag	On Entry	On Return	
		If Successful	If Unsuccessful
AX	000Ch		Error code
BX	Selector		
DI	Buffer offset		
ES	Buffer selector		
Carry		Clear	Set

This function is the opposite of Int 31h, function 000Bh. It copies the contents of an 8-byte buffer into the descriptor specified by the selector in BX.

Int 31h, function 000Dh: Allocate specific LDT descriptor

Register or Flag	On Entry	On Return	
		If Successful	If Unsuccessful
AX	000Dh		Error code
BX	Selector		
Carry		Clear	Set

This function handles allocation of a descriptor based on a specific selector you want to have assigned to that descriptor. You can assign as many as 16 descriptors with this function; selectors can have the values 4 through 7Ch.

Int 31h, function 000Eh: Get multiple descriptors

Register or Flag	On Entry	On Return	
		If Successful	If Unsuccessful
AX	000Eh		Error code
CX	Number to copy		Number actually copied
DI	Buffer offset		

Register or Flag	On Entry	On Return If Successful	On Return If Unsuccessful
ES	Buffer selector		
Carry		Clear	Set

Similar in nature to Int 31h, function 000Bh, this function copies multiple descriptors from the LDT into a buffer. The buffer contents must be set before calling the function, because values placed there control which descriptors are copied. Each entry in the buffer pointed to by ES:DI (ES:EDI for 32-bit DPMI host implementations) occupies ten bytes, and should appear as shown in Table F.3.

Table F.3. The buffer entry layout for Int 31h, function 000Eh.

Offset	Length	Meaning
00h	2 bytes	Selector for descriptor to be copied
02h	8 bytes	Space for copied descriptor

You can include as many entries in the buffer as you want; you specify how many entries there are by the value placed in CX before calling the function.

On return from the function, the buffer is filled in with the copied descriptors. If an error occurred, CX contains the number of descriptors that were copied successfully into the buffer.

This function is the opposite of Int 31h, function 000Fh.

Int 31h, function 000Fh: Set multiple descriptors

Register or Flag	On Entry	On Return If Successful	On Return If Unsuccessful
AX	000Fh		Error code
CX	Number to copy		Number actually copied
DI	Buffer offset		
ES	Buffer selector		
Carry		Clear	Set

This function is the opposite of Int 31h, function 000Eh, and is similar to Int 31h, function 000Ch. You use this function to copy multiple descriptors into the LDT from a special buffer. Each entry in the buffer pointed to by ES:DI (ES:EDI for 32-bit DPMI host implementations) occupies ten bytes, and should appear as shown in Table F.3. You fill in the selector value and the eight bytes for each descriptor. The buffer can include as many entries as necessary; you specify how many entries there are by the value placed in CX before calling the function.

If an error occurred during the function, on return CX contains the number of descriptors that were copied successfully from the buffer.

Int 31h, function 0100h: Allocate DOS memory block

Register or Flag	On Entry	On Return	
		If Successful	If Unsuccessful
AX	0100h	Real mode segment	Error code of memory block
BX			Size of largest available block
DX	Paragraphs to allocate	Selector of descriptor for memory block	
Carry		Clear	Set

This function provides a protected mode version of DOS function 48h. It switches to real mode, issues the proper DOS function call, and then returns to protected mode with the information indicated.

Notice that this function allocates a descriptor in the LDT for the DOS memory block that was allocated. To release this descriptor, you should use Int 31h, function 0101h. Do not use Int 31h, function 0001h or any other function that modifies the descriptor.

If an error occurs during the function, BX contains the maximum number of paragraphs that were available under DOS.

Int 31h, function 0101h: Release DOS memory block

Register or Flag	On Entry	On Return	
		If Successful	If Unsuccessful
AX	0101h		Error code
DX	Selector		
Carry		Clear	Set

This function is used to release a memory block allocated with Int 31h, function 0100h, and to release the descriptor associated with the memory block.

Int 31h, function 0102h: Resize DOS memory block

Register or Flag	On Entry	On Return If Successful	On Return If Unsuccessful
AX	0102h		Error code
BX	New block size (in paragraphs)		Size of largest available block
DX	Selector		
Carry		Clear	Set

Use this function to modify the size of a block of DOS memory allocated previously using Int 31h, function 0100h. BX should contain the modified size of the block, in 16-byte paragraphs. DX contains the selector that represents the descriptor assigned to the memory block.

If an error occurs during the function, BX contains the maximum number of paragraphs that were available under DOS.

Int 31h, function 0200h: Get real mode interrupt vector

Register or Flag	On Entry	On Return
AX	0200h	
BL	Interrupt	
CX		Vector segment
DX		Vector offset
Carry		Clear

If you want to determine the address of an interrupt handler under DOS, this function retrieves the information for you. You specify in BL the interrupt number whose vector you want retrieved. On return, the real mode address is in CX:DX, where CX is the segment and DX is the offset.

Int 31h, function 0201h: Set real mode interrupt vector

Register or Flag	On Entry	On Return
AX	0201h	
BL	Interrupt	
CX	Vector segment	
DX	Vector offset	
Carry		Clear

Use this function to modify a real mode interrupt vector. The address you pass in CX:DX is assigned to the interrupt number you specify in BL.

If you are modifying the vector associated with a hardware interrupt, you must lock the memory used by the interrupt handler. See Int 31h, function 0600h for more information.

Int 31h, function 0202h: Get exception handler vector

Register or Flag	On Entry	On Return — If Successful	On Return — If Unsuccessful
AX	0202h		Error code
BL	Exception		
CX		Handler selector	
DX		Handler offset	
Carry		Clear	Set

This function enables you to determine the address of a protected mode exception handler assigned to the exception number in BL. Exception numbers must be in the range 0 through 1Fh.

If you are using a host that is compliant with DPMI version 1.0, you should avoid this function and use Int 31h, functions 0210h or 0211h instead.

Int 31h, function 0203h: Set exception handler vector

Register or Flag	On Entry	On Return If Successful	On Return If Unsuccessful
AX	0203h		Error code
BL	Exception		
CX	Handler selector		
DX	Handler offset		
Carry		Clear	Set

This function enables you to modify the address of a protected mode exception handler assigned to the exception number in BL. Exception numbers must be in the range 0 through 1Fh.

If you are using a host that is compliant with DPMI version 1.0, you should avoid this function and use Int 31h, functions 0212h or 0213h instead.

Int 31h, function 0204h: Get protected mode interrupt vector

Register or Flag	On Entry	On Return If Successful	On Return If Unsuccessful
AX	0204h		Error code
BL	Interrupt		
CX		Handler selector	
DX		Handler offset	
Carry		Clear	Set

This function is analogous to Int 31h, function 0202h. Although that function retrieves exception handler addresses, this one does the same thing for protected mode interrupt handlers.

The value passed in CX as part of the CX:DX (CX:EDX for 32-bit DPMI host implementations) address must represent a valid selector.

Int 31h, function 0205h: Set protected mode interrupt vector

Register or Flag	On Entry	On Return If Successful	On Return If Unsuccessful
AX	0205h		Error code
BL	Interrupt		
CX	Handler selector		
DX	Handler offset		
Carry		Clear	Set

This function is analogous to Int 31h, function 0203h. Although that function enables you to set vectors for exceptions, this function does the same thing for protected mode interrupts.

The value passed in CX as part of the CX:DX (CX:EDX for 32-bit DPMI host implementations) address must represent a valid selector.

Int 31h, function 0210h: Get extended exception handler vector (protected mode)

Register or Flag	On Entry	On Return If Successful	On Return If Unsuccessful
AX	0210h		Error code
BL	Exception		
CX		Handler selector	
DX		Handler offset	
Carry		Clear	Set

This function enables you to determine the address of a protected mode exception handler assigned to the exception number in BL. Exception numbers must be in the range 0 through 1Fh.

If you are using a host that is compliant with DPMI version 1.0, you should use this function rather than Int 31h, function 0202h.

Int 31h, function 0211h: Get extended exception handler vector (real mode)

Register or Flag	On Entry	On Return	
		If Successful	If Unsuccessful
AX	0211h		Error code
BL	Exception		
CX		Handler selector	
DX		Handler offset	
Carry		Clear	Set

This function enables you to determine the address of a real mode exception handler assigned to the exception number in BL. Exception numbers must be in the range 0 through 1Fh.

If you are using a host that is compliant with DPMI version 1.0, you should use this function rather than Int 31h, function 0202h.

Int 31h, function 0212h: Set extended exception handler vector (protected mode)

Register or Flag	On Entry	On Return	
		If Successful	If Unsuccessful
AX	0212h		Error code
BL	Exception		
CX	Handler selector		
DX	Handler offset		
Carry		Clear	Set

This function enables you to modify the address of a protected mode exception handler assigned to the exception number in BL. Exception numbers must be in the range 0 through 1Fh.

If you are using a host that is compliant with DPMI version 1.0, you should use this function rather than Int 31h, function 0203h.

Int 31h, function 0213h: Set extended exception handler vector (real mode)

Register or Flag	On Entry	On Return If Successful	On Return If Unsuccessful
AX	0213h		Error code
BL	Exception		
CX	Handler selector		
DX	Handler offset		
Carry		Clear	Set

This function enables you to modify the address of a real mode exception handler assigned to the exception number in BL. Exception numbers must be in the range 0 through 1Fh.

If you are using a host that is compliant with DPMI version 1.0, you should use this function rather than Int 31h, function 0203h.

Int 31h, function 0300h: Simulate real mode interrupt

Register or Flag	On Entry	On Return If Successful	On Return If Unsuccessful
AX	0300h		Error code
BH	0		
BL	Interrupt		
CX	Copy word count		
DI	Buffer offset	Buffer offset	
ES	Buffer selector	Buffer selector	
Carry		Clear	Set

This function enables you to imitate a real mode interrupt from within protected mode. You specify in BL the interrupt number you want simulated. The value in CX is the number of words to copy from the protected mode stack to the real mode stack. The buffer pointed to by ES:DI (ES:EDI for 32-bit DPMI host implementations) contains a data structure that is used to specify the register set in real mode. Table F.4 details the layout of the buffer.

Table F.4. The register set buffer layout for Int 31h, functions 0300h, 0301h, and 0302h.

Offset	Length	Register Represented
00h	4 bytes	DI or EDI
04h	4 bytes	SI or ESI
08h	4 bytes	BP or EBP
0Ch	4 bytes	Reserved (set to 0)
10h	4 bytes	BX or EBX
14h	4 bytes	DX or EDX
18h	4 bytes	CX or ECX
1Ch	4 bytes	AX or EAX
20h	2 bytes	Flags
22h	2 bytes	ES
24h	2 bytes	DS
26h	2 bytes	FS
28h	2 bytes	GS
2Ah	2 bytes	IP
2Ch	2 bytes	CS
2Eh	2 bytes	SP
30h	2 bytes	SS

The register values you store in the buffer are loaded into the CPU registers after the CPU is switched to real mode. The flag values in the buffer are pushed on the stack, and the buffer values for CS:IP are ignored. If SS:SP is set to zero, the DPMI host takes care of providing a stack for the interrupt.

After the real mode interrupt handler is completed, it must return control through the IRET instruction (because the flags are pushed on the stack). On return from the function, the buffer contains the register values that existed when the interrupt handler completed execution.

Int 31h, function 0301h: Call real mode procedure as far routine

Register or Flag	On Entry	On Return If Successful	If Unsuccessful
AX	0301h		Error code
BH	0		
CX	Copy word count		
DI	Buffer offset	Buffer offset	
ES	Buffer selector	Buffer selector	
Carry		Clear	Set

This function enables you to call a real mode subroutine from protected mode. The value in CX is the number of words to copy from the protected mode stack to the real mode stack. The buffer pointed to by ES:DI (ES:EDI for 32-bit DPMI host implementations) contains a data structure that is used to specify the register set in real mode. Table F.4 shows the layout of the buffer (see Int 31h, function 0300h).

The register values you store in the buffer are loaded into the CPU registers after the CPU is switched to real mode. The buffer values for CS:IP are used to specify the address of the real mode subroutine to call. If SS:SP is set to zero, the DPMI host provides a stack for the interrupt.

After the real mode subroutine is completed, it must return control through the RETF instruction. On return from the function, the buffer contains the register values that existed when the subroutine completed execution.

Int 31h, function 0302h: Call real mode procedure as interrupt

Register or Flag	On Entry	On Return If Successful	If Unsuccessful
AX	0302h		Error code
BH	0		
CX	Copy word count		
DI	Buffer offset	Buffer offset	

| Register | | On Return | |
or Flag	On Entry	If Successful	If Unsuccessful
ES	Buffer selector	Buffer selector	
Carry		Clear	Set

This function is a hybrid of Int 31h, functions 0300h and 0301h.

With this function, you can call a real mode subroutine from protected mode as though the subroutine were an interrupt handler. The only difference between this function and Int 31h, function 0301h is that the DPMI host pushes the contents of the flags register (as defined in the buffer area) on the real mode stack before passing control to the subroutine.

On entering the function, the value in CX is the number of words to copy from the protected mode stack to the real mode stack. The buffer pointed to by ES:DI (ES:EDI for 32-bit DPMI host implementations) contains a data structure used to specify the register set in real mode. Table F.4 shows the layout of the buffer (see Int 31h, function 0300h).

The register values you store in the buffer are loaded into the CPU registers after the CPU is switched to real mode. The flag values in the buffer are pushed on the stack, and the buffer values for CS:IP are used to specify the address of the real mode subroutine being called. If SS:SP is set to zero, the DPMI host provides a stack for the interrupt.

After the real mode subroutine is completed, it must return control through the IRET instruction (because the flags are pushed on the stack). On return from the function, the buffer contains the register values that existed when the subroutine completed execution.

Int 31h, function 0303h: Allocate real mode callback address

| Register | | On Return | |
or Flag	On Entry	If Successful	If Unsuccessful
AX	0303h		Error code
CX		Callback segment	
DX		Callback offset	
SI	Protected mode procedure offset		
DI	Buffer offset		

| Register | | On Return | |
or Flag	On Entry	If Successful	If Unsuccessful
DS	Protected mode procedure selector		
ES	Buffer selector		
Carry		Clear	Set

Sometimes you might want your real mode program to have the capability to call a protected mode subroutine. This function provides a unique callback address that can be used by your real mode program. By definition, the DPMI host must provide at least 16 callback addresses to each client.

The buffer pointed to by ES:DI (ES:EDI for 32-bit DPMI host implementations) contains a data structure used to specify the real mode register structure to be used in calling the callback routine. Table F.4 shows the layout of the buffer (see Int 31h, function 0300h).

On return from this function, the value in CX:DX represents a real mode address in the segment:offset format. To release the callback address (when it no longer is needed), use Int 31h, function 0304h.

Int 31h, function 0304h: Release real mode callback address

| Register | | On Return | |
or Flag	On Entry	If Successful	If Unsuccessful
AX	0304h		Error code
CX	Callback segment		
DX	Callback offset		
Carry		Clear	Set

This function enables you to release a callback address that had been allocated with Int 31h, function 0303h. For more information about real mode callback addresses, see the information for that function.

Int 31h, function 0305h: Get state save and restore address

Register or Flag	On Entry	On Return
AX	0305h	Buffer size required
BX		Real mode routine address segment
CX		Real mode routine address offset
SI		Protected mode routine address selector
DI		Protected mode routine address offset
Carry		Clear

You can use this routine to save and restore the condition of the CPU registers in the opposite mode from what is currently executing. This function is intended to be used in conjunction with Int 31h, function 0306h.

As an example of how this function is intended to be used, assume that you are operating in protected mode. You call the protected mode subroutine (the address at SI:DI for 16-bit programs, or SI:EDI for 32-bit DPMI host implementations) to save the real mode register values. Likewise, when you are operating in real mode, you call the real mode subroutine (address BX:CX) to save the protected mode register values.

Regardless of the CPU mode and which routine you call, the value in AL indicates the function you want to perform. If AL is 0, the registers are saved; if it is 1, they are restored. Also, the address of the buffer in which to save the registers (or from which to restore them) is contained in ES:DI for real mode or 16-bit protected mode programs (in real mode, ES contains a segment value; in protected mode, it contains a selector value). If you call the routine from a 32-bit protected mode program, ES:EDI is used for the buffer address.

The value returned in AX indicates the size (in bytes) of the buffer required to save the register state. This number is the number of bytes that are written to memory by the save and restore functions whose addresses are returned by this function.

Int 31h, function 0306h: Get raw CPU mode switch address

Register or Flag	On Entry	On Return
AX	0306h	
BX		Real-mode mode switch address segment
CX		Real-mode mode switch address offset
SI		Protected mode-mode switch address selector
DI		Protected mode-mode switch address offset
Carry		Clear

This function returns two addresses that can be used to switch from one CPU mode to another. This is a lower-level mode switch than is done with Int 31h, functions 0300h, 0301h, or 0302h.

The address returned in BX:CX is used to switch from real mode to protected mode, and the one returned in SI:DI (SI:EDI from 32-bit DPMI host implementations) is used to switch from protected mode to real mode. To switch modes, you should issue a far jump to the appropriate address, with the registers set to the values indicated in Table F.5.

Table F.5. Mode switch register settings.	
Register	**Contents**
AX	New DS
BX	New SP
CX	New ES
DX	New SS
SI	New CS
DI	New IP

As far as other registers are concerned, the value in BP is maintained, and the FS and GS registers are zeroed. All other register values are undefined.

Int 31h, function 0400h: Get DPMI version

Register or Flag	On Entry	On Return
AX	0400h	DPMI version
BX		Implementation flags
CL		Processor type
DH		Master PIC base interrupt
DL		Slave PIC base interrupt
Carry		Clear

This function returns some information similar to that returned by Int 2Fh, function 1687h. On return, AX contains the DPMI version number, with the major version number in AH and the minor version number in AL. These version numbers are decimal numbers in binary representation. Therefore, if the DPMI version number is 0.90, the value in AH is 0 and the value in AL is 90 (5Ah).

The value returned in BX indicates specific information about the implementation of DPMI in this particular system. Table F.6 indicates the bit meanings for this register.

Table F.6. Bit meanings returned in the BX register from Int 31h, function 0400h.

Bit settings FEDCAB98 76543210	Meaning
1	32-bit DPMI host implementation
0	16-bit DPMI host implementation
1	Reflected interrupts handled in real mode
0	Reflected interrupts handled in virtual 86 mode
1	Virtual memory supported
0	Virtual memory not supported
xxxxxxxx xxxxx	Reserved

The value in CL is either 2, 3, or 4, indicating whether the computer uses an 80286, 80386, or 80486 CPU.

Int 31h, function 0401h: Get DPMI capabilities

Register or Flag	On Entry	On Return If Successful	If Unsuccessful
AX	0401h	Capabilities	
CX		0	
DX		0	
DI	Buffer offset		
ES	Buffer selector		
Carry		Clear	Set

You can use this function under DPMI version 1.0 to determine the capabilities of the DPMI host. Notice that if the function fails, no error code is returned in AX. Instead, only the carry flag is set.

On return, AX contains bit flags that indicate the capabilities of the host. Table F.7 indicates the bit meanings for AX.

Table F.7. Bit meanings returned in the AX register from Int 31h, function 0401h. (If the designated bit is set, the feature is supported by the DPMI host.)

Bit settings FEDCBA98 76543210	Meaning
1	Page accessed/dirty capability
1	Exceptions restartability
1	Device mapping
1	Conventional memory mapping
1	Demand zero fill
1	Write-protect client
1	Write-protect host
xxxxxxxx x	Reserved

The value in ES:DI (ES:EDI for 32-bit DPMI host implementations) is the address of a 128-byte buffer that has the layout shown in Table F.8.

Table F.8. Buffer layout pointed to by ES:DI on return from Int 31h, function 0401h.

Offset	Length	Meaning
00h	1 byte	Host major version number (binary representation of a decimal number)
01h	1 byte	Host minor version number (binary representation of a decimal number)
02h	As much as 126 bytes	Host vendor ID string (ASCIIZ)

Int 31h, function 0500h: Get free memory information

Register or Flag	On Entry	On Return
AX	0500h	
DI	Buffer offset	
ES	Buffer selector	
Carry		Clear

This function returns information about available system memory, both in RAM and on disk. When you are calling this function, ES:DI (ES:EDI for 32-bit DPMI host implementations) should point to a 48-byte buffer. On return, this buffer is filled with information as shown in Table F.9.

Table F.9. Information returned by Int 31h, function 0500h.

Offset	Length	Meaning
00h	4 bytes	Largest free block, in bytes
04h	4 bytes	Maximum unlocked page allocation, in pages
08h	4 bytes	Maximum locked page allocation, in pages
0Ch	4 bytes	Linear address space, in pages
10h	4 bytes	Total unlocked pages

continues

Table F.9. Continued

Offset	Length	Meaning
14h	4 bytes	Total free pages
18h	4 bytes	Total physical pages
1Ch	4 bytes	Free linear address space, in pages
20h	4 bytes	Size of paging file or partition, in pages
24h	12 bytes	Reserved, each byte set to 0FFh

If any fields are set to –1, it indicates that the field is not supported by the DPMI host.

Programs that support DPMI version 1.0 should not use this function; use Int 31h, function 050Bh instead.

Int 31h, function 0501h: Allocate memory block

Register or Flag	On Entry	On Return If Successful	If Unsuccessful
AX	0501h		Error code
BX	Block size, high word	Linear address of memory block, high word	
CX	Block size, low word	Linear address of memory block, low word	
SI		Memory block handle, high word	
DI		Memory block handle, low word	
Carry		Clear	Set

You can use this function to allocate a block of linear memory space. The value in BX:CX indicates, in bytes, the amount of memory needed. On return, the value in BX:CX indicates the linear base address of the block, which should be at least page-aligned. The value in SI:DI is a handle used to modify the allocated block through Int 31h, functions 0502h or 0503h.

This function does not provide addressability by other DPMI functions. You must use other functions to provide a descriptor that can be pointed to the memory area.

Int 31h, function 0502h: Release memory block

Register or Flag	On Entry	On Return If Successful	If Unsuccessful
AX	0502h		Error code
SI	Memory block handle, high word		
DI	Memory block handle, low word		
Carry		Clear	Set

This function is used to free a linear memory block previously allocated with Int 31h, function 0501h or 0504h. If you have used descriptors to point into the memory area being released, this function does not release those descriptors—you must use the appropriate DPMI functions.

Int 31h, function 0503h: Resize memory block

Register or Flag	On Entry	On Return If Successful	If Unsuccessful
AX	0503h		Error code
BX	Block size, high word	Linear address of memory block, high word	
CX	Block size, low word	Linear address of memory block, low word	
SI	Memory block handle, high word	Memory block handle, high word	
DI	Memory block handle, low word	Memory block handle, low word	
Carry		Clear	Set

This function is used to change the size of a linear memory block previously allocated with Int 31h, function 0501h or 0504h. If you have used descriptors that point into the memory area being modified, this function does not release or change the limit fields of those descriptors—you must use the appropriate DPMI functions.

Int 31h, function 0504h: Allocate linear memory block

Register or Flag	On Entry	On Return If Successful	On Return If Unsuccessful
AX	0504h		Error code
EBX	Desired base linear address for memory block (page aligned)	Base linear address of memory block	
ECX	Block size		
EDX	Action code		
ESI		Memory block handle	
Carry		Clear	Set

This function performs much the same action as provided by Int 31h, function 0501h. It allocates a block of linear memory, but the similarity ends there. This function, which works on only 32-bit DPMI host systems, also enables you to request that the block begin at a specific address (specified in EBX). If the value you specify in EBX is zero, the host assigns an address. The action code in EDX also enables you to indicate whether the host should create uncommitted (0) or committed (1) pages. The value in ECX is the size of the requested memory block, in bytes.

Another important attribute of this function is that the memory block assigned is page aligned. The handle returned in ESI is used by functions that act on the allocated memory block, in particular, Int 31h, functions 0505h, 0506h, 0507h, 0508h, and 0509h.

Int 31h, function 0505h: Resize linear memory block

Register or Flag	On Entry	On Return If Successful	On Return If Unsuccessful
AX	0505h		Error code
EBX	Buffer offset	Base linear address of memory block	
ECX	Block size		
EDX	Action code		
ESI	Memory block handle	Memory block handle	

Register or Flag	On Entry	On Return	
		If Successful	If Unsuccessful
EDI	Selector count		
ES	Buffer selector		
Carry		Clear	Set

This function is available on only 32-bit DPMI host implementations. It enables you to resize a block of memory previously allocated with Int 31h, function 0504h. The value passed in ESI is the memory block handle returned when the memory block was first allocated.

The action code passed in EDX controls the way this function operates. Bit 0 controls whether the host should commit the allocated pages; if it is set, the pages are committed. Bit 1 controls whether the host should update an array of segment descriptors you are using for this memory block. If bit 1 is set, the address in ES:EBX is used to indicate the buffer containing the selector array, and EDI contains the number of selectors in the array. The buffer contains nothing more than a series of 16-bit selectors associated with the descriptors the host will update. If bit 1 of EDX is not set, the contents of ES:EBX and EDI are not significant.

Int 31h, function 0506h: Get page attributes

Register or Flag	On Entry	On Return	
		If Successful	If Unsuccessful
AX	0506h		Error code
EBX	Offset of page within memory block		
ECX	Page count		
EDX	Buffer offset		
ESI	Memory block handle		
ES	Buffer selector		
Carry		Clear	Set

This function is available on only 32-bit DPMI host implementations. It enables you to retrieve the attributes of one or more pages in a memory block. EBX indicates the offset of the first page within the memory block for which you want attributes, and ECX indicates the number of pages for which you want them.

The buffer pointed to by ES:EDX contains one word (2 bytes) for each page requested by the function; the number of bytes in the buffer, therefore, should be twice the value in ECX. On successful return from the function, each bit of each attribute word in the buffer has the meaning shown in Table F.10.

Table F.10. Bit meanings in page attribute words returned by Int 31h, function 0506h.

Bit settings FEDCBA98 76543210	Meaning
000	Uncommitted
001	Committed
010	Mapped
1	Read-write
0	Read-only
1	Accessed/dirty bits valid
0	Accessed/dirty bits invalid
1	Page accessed (if bit 4 is set)
0	Page unaccessed (if bit 4 is set)
1	Page modified (if bit 4 is set)
0	Page unmodified (if bit 4 is set)
xxxxxxxx x	Reserved

Int 31h, function 0507h: Set page attributes

Register or Flag	On Entry	On Return If Successful	If Unsuccessful
AX	0507h		Error code
EBX	Offset of page within memory block		
ECX	Page count modified		Number of pages
EDX	Buffer offset		

Register or Flag	On Entry	On Return If Successful	If Unsuccessful
ESI	Memory block handle		
ES	Buffer selector		
Carry		Clear	Set

This function is only available on 32-bit DPMI host implementations. It enables you to modify the attributes of one or more pages in a memory block. EBX indicates the offset of the first page within the memory block for which you want attributes, and ECX indicates the number of pages for which you want them.

The buffer pointed to by ES:EDX contains one word (2 bytes) for each page to be modified by this function. Each bit in each attribute word is set as shown in Table F.11.

Table F.11. Bit meanings in page attribute words returned by Int 31h, function 0506h.

Bit settings FEDCBA98 76543210	Meaning
000	Make page uncommitted
001	Commit page
011	Modify attributes but not page type
1	Make page read-write
0	Make page read-only
1	Modify accessed/dirty bits
0	Don't modify accessed/dirty bits
1	Mark page as accessed (if bit 4 is set)
0	Mark page as unaccessed (if bit 4 is set)
1	Mark page as modified (if bit 4 is set)
0	Mark page as unmodified (if bit 4 is set)
XXXXXXX X	Reserved

If the function is unsuccessful, the value returned in ECX indicates the number of actual pages that were modified before the error occurred.

Int 31h, function 0508h: Map device in memory block

Register or Flag	On Entry	On Return If Successful	If Unsuccessful
AX	0508h		Error code
EBX	Offset of page within memory block		
ECX	Page count		
EDX	Device address		
ESI	Memory block handle		
Carry		Clear	Set

With this function, you can map the physical address assigned to a device (loaded in EDX) to a linear address within a memory block (page aligned, offset in EBX). This function is available only with 32-bit DPMI host implementations; even then, it is optional (some hosts may not support it and still be considered DPMI compliant). The memory block must have been allocated previously with Int 31h, function 0504h. The handle specified in ESI is returned by that function.

Int 31h, function 0509h: Map conventional memory in memory block

Register or Flag	On Entry	On Return If Successful	If Unsuccessful
AX	0509h		Error code
EBX	Offset of page within memory block		
ECX	Page count		
EDX	Linear address of conventional memory		
ESI	Memory block handle		
Carry		Clear	Set

This function enables you to map a linear memory address below the 1M boundary to a memory block above the boundary. The memory block whose handle is specified in ESI must have been allocated previously with Int 31h, function 0504h. This function is available on only 32-bit DPMI host implementations; even then, it is optional (some hosts may not support it and still be considered DPMI compliant).

The conventional memory to be allocated is specified in the linear address loaded in EDX. This memory must be page aligned, and the client must have allocated the memory previously with a call to Int 31h, function 0100h, or with DOS function 48h.

Int 31h, function 050Ah: Get memory block size and base

Register or Flag	On Entry	On Return	
		If Successful	If Unsuccessful
AX	050Ah		Error code
SI	Memory block handle, high word	Memory block size, high word	
DI	Memory block handle, low word	Memory block size, low word	
Carry		Clear	Set

If you need to know the size of a memory block allocated previously with Int 31h, functions 0501h or 0504h, you can use this function. The block handle is specified in SI:DI, and the block size is returned in the same registers.

Int 31h, function 050Bh: Get memory information

Register or Flag	On Entry	On Return	
		If Successful	If Unsuccessful
AX	050Bh		Error code
DI	Offset selector		
ES	Buffer selector		
Carry		Clear	Set

This function is used to determine information about the memory in the computer system. In calling the function, you specify the address of a 128-byte buffer in ES:DI (ES:EDI for 32-bit DPMI host implementations). The function fills in the contents of the buffer as shown in Table F.12.

Table F.12. Memory information returned by Int 31h, function 050Bh.

Offset	Length	Meaning
00h	4 bytes	Allocated physical memory controlled by DPMI host, in bytes
04h	4 bytes	Allocated virtual memory controlled by DPMI host, in bytes
08h	4 bytes	Available virtual memory controlled by DPMI host, in bytes
0Ch	4 bytes	Allocated virtual memory for this virtual machine, in bytes
10h	4 bytes	Available virtual memory for this virtual machine, in bytes
14h	4 bytes	Allocated virtual memory for this client, in bytes
18h	4 bytes	Available virtual memory for this client, in bytes
1Ch	4 bytes	Locked memory for this client, in bytes
20h	4 bytes	Maximum locked memory for this client, in bytes
24h	4 bytes	Maximum linear address for this client
28h	4 bytes	Maximum free memory block size, in bytes
2Ch	4 bytes	Minimum allocation unit, in bytes
30h	4 bytes	Allocation alignment unit, in bytes
34h	76 bytes	Reserved

Programs that support DPMI version 1.0 should use this function rather than Int 31h, function 050Bh.

Int 31h, function 0600h: Lock linear region

Register or Flag	On Entry	On Return If Successful	If Unsuccessful
AX	0600h		Error code
BX	Linear address of memory to lock, high word		
CX	Linear address of memory to lock, low word		
SI	Bytes to lock, high word		
DI	Bytes to lock, low word		
Carry		Clear	Set

Use this function to lock an area of memory SI:DI bytes long beginning at BX:CX. Locking the memory inhibits swapping of that memory region to disk by the host. To unlock the memory later, use Int 31h, function 0601h.

Int 31h, function 0601h: Unlock linear region

Register or Flag	On Entry	On Return If Successful	If Unsuccessful
AX	0601h		Error code
BX	Linear address of memory to unlock, high word		
CX	Linear address of memory to unlock, low word		
SI	Bytes to unlock, high word		
DI	Bytes to unlock, low word		
Carry		Clear	Set

This function enables you to unlock an area of memory SI:DI bytes long beginning at BX:CX. This area should be a memory area that was locked previously with Int 31h, function 0600h.

Int 31h, function 0602h: Mark real mode region as pageable

Register or Flag	On Entry	On Return If Successful	If Unsuccessful
AX	0602h		Error code
BX	Linear address of memory to mark, high word		
CX	Linear address of memory to mark, low word		
SI	Bytes in region, high word		
DI	Bytes in region, low word		
Carry		Clear	Set

If you have allocated conventional memory to your program through the use of Int 31h, function 0100h, or with DOS function 48h, this function enables you to inform the DPMI host that this memory can be virtualized—that is, paged to disk. Memory that has been marked as pageable by this function should be relocked with Int 31h, function 0603h before the end of your program. If you do not do this, subsequent programs can try to use the same memory area to crash.

Int 31h, function 0603h: Relock real mode region

Register or Flag	On Entry	On Return If Successful	If Unsuccessful
AX	0603h		Error code
BX	Linear address of memory to relock, high word		
CX	Linear address of memory to relock, low word		
SI	Bytes in region, high word		
DI	Bytes in region, low word		
Carry		Clear	Set

This function is the opposite of Int 31h, function 0602h. It is used to inform the DPMI host that conventional memory marked previously as pageable to disk no longer is pageable. For compliance with DPMI version 0.9 implementations, you should use this function to relock conventional memory regions before ending your program. This precaution is not necessary in DPMI version 1.0 implementations because version 1.0 hosts relock a client's conventional memory when the program ends.

Int 31h, function 0604h: Get page size

Register or Flag	On Entry	On Return If Successful	If Unsuccessful
AX	0604h		Error code
BX		Page size, high word	
CX		Page size, low word	
Carry		Clear	Set

This function is used to determine the size of each page implemented by the DPMI host.

Int 31h, function 0702h: Mark page as demand paging candidate

Register or Flag	On Entry	On Return If Successful	If Unsuccessful
AX	0702h		Error code
BX	Linear address of memory region, high word		
CX	Linear address of memory region, low word		
SI	Bytes in region, high word		
DI	Bytes in region, low word		
Carry		Clear	Set

If a DPMI host supports paging to disk, this function enables you to specify a block of memory as available for immediate paging. The memory must be allocated to the client through other DPMI functions.

Typically, a host pages a block of memory only if it has not been accessed in a relatively long time. This function enables you to inform the host that you do not plan to access a particular memory block for a while, and therefore it can be written to disk if necessary.

The start of the block is specified by a linear address placed in BX:CX, and the length (in bytes) is contained in SI:DI.

Int 31h, function 0703h: Discard page contents

Register or Flag	On Entry	On Return If Successful	If Unsuccessful
AX	0703h		Error code
BX	Linear address of memory region, high word		
CX	Linear address of memory region, low word		

Register or Flag	On Entry	On Return If Successful	If Unsuccessful
SI	Bytes in region, high word		
DI	Bytes in region, low word		
Carry		Clear	Set

When you load the starting page address of a memory region in BX:CX and load the length of the region (in bytes) in SI:DI, and then call this function, you are notifying the DPMI host that you no longer have need for the data stored within that memory. The host will make no effort to page the memory to disk, if the memory is needed for other functions.

Only unlocked memory regions can be marked for discard. After calling this function, the contents of the memory region are undefined.

Int 31h, function 0800h: Physical address mapping

Register or Flag	On Entry	On Return If Successful	If Unsuccessful
AX	0800h		Error code
BX	Base physical address, high word	Base linear address, high word	
CX	Base physical address, low word	Base linear address, low word	
Carry		Clear	Set

This function is used to convert a physical address, typically associated with a device, to a linear address. The linear address is maintained by the DPMI host. The address returned by this function is either a newly mapped address or one that was mapped previously (if the physical address or device was mapped previously by the host).

After a linear address is known, you still must use the appropriate DPMI functions to allocate descriptors to the memory area so that it can be accessed further.

This function should be used only to determine linear addresses above the 1M boundary used with mapped devices—not to access memory below the 1M boundary. When you are finished with a device mapping created through this function, you should use Int 31h, function 0801h to release the mapping.

Int 31h, function 0801h: Release physical address mapping

Register or Flag	On Entry	On Return If Successful	On Return If Unsuccessful
AX	0801h		Error code
BX	Linear address, high word		
CX	Linear address, low word		
Carry		Clear	Set

This function enables you to release the mapping of a physical address accomplished with Int 31h, function 0800h.

Int 31h, function 0900h: Get and disable virtual interrupt state

Register or Flag	On Entry	On Return
AX	0900h	Previous condition
Carry		Clear

This function turns off virtual interrupts by disabling the client's virtual interrupt flag (not the physical one maintained in the CPU). The previous state of the flag is returned in the AL register. If AL is 0, virtual interrupts were disabled previously; if it is 1, they were enabled.

You can use Int 31h, function 0901h to enable the virtual interrupt state, or you can use Int 31h, function 0902h to discover the current state without changing it.

Int 31h, function 0901h: Get and enable virtual interrupt state

Register or Flag	On Entry	On Return
AX	0901h	Previous condition
Carry		Clear

This function is the opposite of Int 31h, function 0900h. It turns on virtual interrupts by enabling the client's virtual interrupt flag (not the physical one maintained in the CPU). The previous state of the flag is returned in the AL register. If AL is 0, virtual interrupts were disabled previously; if it is 1, they were enabled.

You can use Int 31h, function 0902h to determine the current virtual interrupt state without changing it.

Int 31h, function 0902h: Get virtual interrupt state

Register or Flag	On Entry	On Return
AX	0902h	Previous condition
Carry		Clear

This function returns, in AL, the current condition of the client's virtual interrupt flag (not the physical one maintained in the CPU). If AL is 0, virtual interrupts are disabled; if it is 1, they are enabled.

Int 31h, function 0A00h: Get API entry point

Register or Flag	On Entry	On Return If Successful	If Unsuccessful
AX	0A00h	Undefined	Error code
EBX		Undefined	
ECX		Undefined	
EDX		Undefined	
SI	Vendor ASCIIZ offset	Undefined	

Register or Flag	On Entry	On Return	
		If Successful	If Unsuccessful
DI		Entry point offset	
DS	Vendor ASCIIZ selector	Undefined	
ES		Entry point selector	
FS		Undefined	
GS		Undefined	
EBP		Undefined	
Carry		Clear	Set

This function enables you to determine the address you should use to take advantage of a vendor's extensions to the DPMI standard. This function is included in DPMI version 1.0 for compatibility with DPMI version 0.9. If your host is DPMI version 1.0 compliant, you should use Int 2Fh, function 168Ah instead.

The address returned in ES:DI (ES:EDI for 32-bit DPMI host implementations) indicates the entry point for the vendor's DPMI extensions. This entry point then is accessed by a far call. The exact makeup of any DPMI extension is vendor-specific. For further information, refer to the vendor's documentation.

Int 31h, function 0B00h: Set debug watchpoint

Register or Flag	On Entry	On Return	
		If Successful	If Unsuccessful
AX	0B00h		Error code
BX	Linear address, high word	Watchpoint handle	
CX	Linear address, low word		
DH	Watchpoint type		
DL	Watchpoint size		
Carry		Clear	Set

This function should be used in debugging programs operating in the DPMI environment. It enables you to set a watchpoint that, when accessed, causes a system exception. You can specify also the type of access that causes the watchpoint to trigger.

The value in BX:CX is the linear address to be watched. The value in DL indicates the size of the memory unit to be watched, in bytes (1, 2, or 4). The value in DH indicates the type of watchpoint. 0 indicates that the trigger should occur if the memory address is executed; 1 indicates that it should be triggered if a memory write is attempted; 2 triggers a read or write attempt.

The function returns in BX a handle that is used to modify the watchpoint later.

Int 31h, function 0B01h: Clear debug watchpoint

Register or Flag	On Entry	On Return If Successful	If Unsuccessful
AX	0B01h		Error code
BX	Watchpoint handle		
Carry		Clear	Set

This function turns off and releases a watchpoint previously set with Int 31h, function 0B00h.

Int 31h, function 0B02h: Get state of debug watchpoint

Register or Flag	On Entry	On Return If Successful	If Unsuccessful
AX	0B02h	Watchpoint status	Error code
BX	Watchpoint handle		
Carry		Clear	Set

After a watchpoint has been set (Int 31h, function 0B00h), this function can be used to determine its status. The value returned in AX indicates the status. 0 means that the watchpoint has not been encountered; 1 means that it has.

This function does not clear the condition of the watchpoint—you must use Int 31h, function 0B03h. If you want to clear and release the watchpoint, use Int 31h, function 0B01h.

Int 31h, function 0B03h: Reset debug watchpoint

Register		On Return	
or Flag	On Entry	If Successful	If Unsuccessful
AX	0B03h		Error code
BX	Watchpoint handle		
Carry		Clear	Set

You can use this function to clear a watchpoint that was set previously with Int 31h, function 0B00h.

Int 31h, function 0C00h: Install resident service provider callback

Register		On Return	
or Flag	On Entry	If Successful	If Unsuccessful
AX	0C00h	Error code	
DI	Buffer offset		
ES	Buffer selector		
Carry		Clear	Set

If you are developing a protected mode TSR program, this function enables you to notify the DPMI host of your intentions and indicate that your routine should be called whenever another DPMI program in the same virtual machine is loaded or ended.

The buffer pointed to by ES:DI (ES:EDI for 32-bit DPMI host implementations) should be 40 bytes long and constructed as shown in Table F.13.

Table F.13. Buffer layout for Int 31h, function 0C00h.

Offset	Length	Meaning
00h	8 bytes	16-bit data segment descriptor
08h	8 bytes	16-bit code segment descriptor
10h	2 bytes	16-bit callback procedure offset
12h	2 bytes	Reserved

continues

Table F.13. Continued

Offset	Length	Meaning
14h	8 bytes	32-bit data segment descriptor
1Ch	8 bytes	32-bit code segment descriptor
24h	4 bytes	32-bit callback procedure offset

The buffer layout shown in Table F.13 allows for both 16-bit and 32-bit callback addresses for the TSR. If your program does not support both types of programs, simply set to 0 the fields relating to the type you do not want to support.

Int 31h, function 0C01h: Terminate and stay resident

Register or Flag	On Entry
AX	0C01h
BL	Exit code
DX	Memory to reserve, in paragraphs

This function is analogous to the DOS TSR function (Int 21h, function 31h). It provides a way to end a program and leave intact all or a portion of the memory occupied by the program.

Before calling this function, you should have used Int 31h, function 0C00h to declare your intentions to the DPMI host. If you have not done so, this function simply terminates your program; if you have, this function leaves all allocated protected mode memory intact and exits through Int 21h, function 31h. The value in BL is the exit code for the program, and DX is the number of 16-byte paragraphs to reserve in the real mode memory area (below 1M).

You should use this function only if you want to provide protected mode TSR functions. If you want to provide real mode TSR functions, use only the DOS TSR function, thereby freeing up any protected mode resources you may have used.

Int 31h, function 0D00h: Allocate shared memory

| Register | | On Return | |
or Flag	On Entry	If Successful	If Unsuccessful
AX	0D00h		Error code
DI	Buffer offset		
ES	Buffer selector		
Carry		Clear	Set

This function is used to allocate memory intended to be shared between multiple DPMI clients. The buffer pointed to by ES:DI (ES:EDI for 32-bit DPMI host implementations) contains a data structure that defines the parameters of the memory request. The layout for this structure is shown in Table F.14.

Table F.14. Shared memory allocation data structure used by Int 31h, function 0D00h.

Offset	Length	Meaning
00h	4 bytes	Desired memory block size, in bytes
04h	4 bytes	Actual memory block size, in bytes
08h	4 bytes	Memory block handle
0Ch	4 bytes	Linear address of memory block
10h	4 bytes	Offset of ASCIIZ name string
14h	2 bytes	Selector of ASCIIZ name string
16h	2 bytes	Reserved
18h	4 bytes	Reserved (must be 0)

To use this function, you fill in the desired memory block size (offset 00h) and the address of the name string (offset 10h and 14h). The name string is an ASCIIZ string as much as 128 bytes long used to identify the shared area. The host uses this name to determine whether the memory area has been defined previously.

On return, the actual block size (offset 04h), memory block handle (offset 08h), and linear address of the block (offset 0Ch) all are provided by the host. Notice that the length you request for the memory block may not match what the DPMI host returns, because the shared block may have been requested already by a different client using a different block size. If you are the first client to request a particular shared block, however, the actual size always equals the requested size.

This function allocates only the memory; you still must set up addressability using the DPMI functions that allocate descriptors. Before ending your program, you also must release any descriptors and free the shared memory block (see Int 31h, function 0D01h).

Int 31h, function 0D01h: Release shared memory

Register or Flag	On Entry	On Return If Successful	If Unsuccessful
AX	0D01h		Error code
SI	Memory block handle, high byte		
DI	Memory block handle, low byte		
Carry		Clear	Set

This function informs the DPMI host that you no longer need access to the shared memory area belonging to the handle in SI:DI. If multiple clients have access to the memory block, this function does not release the memory block unless you are the last client to use this function.

Int 31h, function 0D02h: Serialize on shared memory

Register or Flag	On Entry	On Return If Successful	If Unsuccessful
AX	0D02h		Error code
DX	Option flags		
SI	Memory block handle, high byte		
DI	Memory block handle, low byte		
Carry		Clear	Set

Successful use of this function asserts ownership of the memory block by your client program: You have primary rights to update the information in the block. The value loaded into DX indicates how you want this function to operate. Bit meanings for DX are shown in Table F.15.

Table F.15. Bit meanings for the option flags register (DX) for Int 31h, function 0D02h.

Bit settings FEDCBA98 76543210	Meaning
1	Return with error code if serialization is not possible
0	Suspend execution until serialization is possible
1	Shared serialization requested
0	Exclusive serialization requested
00000000 000000	Reserved (must be 0)

If you set bit 1 of DX and the function is successful, you have exclusive access to the memory block. Therefore, it no longer is shared with other clients until you use Int 31h, function 0D03h to release the serialization.

Int 31h, function 0D03h: Release serialization on shared memory

Register or Flag	On Entry	On Return	
		If Successful	**If Unsuccessful**
AX	0D03h		Error code
DX	Option flags		
SI	Memory block handle, high byte		
DI	Memory block handle, low byte		
Carry		Clear	Set

This function releases any serialization done on shared memory blocks with Int 31h, function 0D02h. For more information about serialization, see the description of that function.

The value you load into DX indicates how you want this function to operate. Each bit has a meaning (see Table F.16).

Bit settings FEDCBA98 76543210	Meaning
Table F.16. Bit meanings for the option flags register (DX) for Int 31h, function 0D03h.	
1	Release shared serialization
0	Release exclusive serialization
1	Free pending serialization
0	Do not free pending serialization
00000000 000000	Reserved (must be 0)

Bit 1 of DX is used to control disposition of any serialization still pending from Int 31h, function 0D02h. That function enables you to suspend program execution until a serialization request can be completed successfully. Using this function with bit 1 of DX set cancels that previous command. Such use of this function must be done from an interrupt handler for the client.

Int 31h, function 0E00h: Get coprocessor status

Register or Flag	On Entry	On Return If Successful	If Unsuccessful
AX	0E00h	Status code	Error code
Carry		Clear	Set

This function returns information about a coprocessor that may be installed in the system. On return, AX contains a status code that contains this information. The bit meanings for AX are shown in Table F.17.

Table F.17. Bit meanings for the coprocessor status code.

Bit settings FEDCBA98 76543210	Meaning
1	NPX enabled for this client
0	NPX disabled for this client
1	Emulation active for this client
0	Emulation inactive for this client
1	NPX present
0	NPX not present
1	Emulation active for host
0	Emulation inactive for host
0000	No NPX
0010	80287 NPX present
0011	80387 NPX present
0100	80486 with NPX
00000000	Reserved

The value of bits 0 and 1 can be modified by using Int 31h, function 0E01h.

Int 31h, function 0E01h: Set coprocessor emulation

Register or Flag	On Entry	On Return If Successful	If Unsuccessful
AX	0E01h		Error code
BX	Action code		
Carry		Clear	Set

This function enables you to change the coprocessor status flags for your virtual machine. The value loaded in BX controls this action; each bit has a meaning as shown in Table F.18.

Table F.18. Bit meanings for the coprocessor status code.

Bit settings FEDCBA98 76543210	Meaning
1	Enable NPX for this client
0	Disable NPX for this client
1	Indicate that client will supply NPX emulation
0	Indicate that client will not supply NPX emulation
00000000 000000	Reserved

Numbers

A

B

Q

R

S

U

V